Fodor's 2009

WASHINGTON, D.C.

Where to Stay and Eat
for All Budgets

Must-See Sights
and Local Secrets

Ratings You Can Trust

Fodor's Travel Publications   New York, Toronto, London, Sydney, Auckland
www.fodors.com

FODOR'S WASHINGTON, D.C. 2009

Editor: Salwa Jabado

Editorial Contributors: Mary Beth Bohman, Coral Davenport, Valerie Hamilton, Beth Kanter, Kathryn McKay, Cathy Sharpe, Elana Schor, Mitchell Tropin

Editorial Production: Tom Holton

Maps & Illustrations: David Lindroth, Mark Stroud, *cartographers*; Bob Blake, Rebecca Baer, *map editors;* William Wu, *information graphics*

Design: Fabrizio La Rocca, *creative director*; Guido Caroti, Siobhan O'Hare, *art directors*; Tina Malaney, Chie Ushio, Ann McBride, Jessica Walsh, *designers*; Melanie Marin, *senior picture editor;*

Cover Photo: (U.S. Capitol dome): Joseph Sohm/Pan America/Jupiter Images

Production/Manufacturing: Angela L. McLean

COPYRIGHT

Copyright © 2009 by Fodor's Travel, a division of Random House, Inc.

Fodor's is a registered trademark of Random House, Inc.

All rights reserved. Published in the United States by Fodor's Travel, a division of Random House, Inc., and simultaneously in Canada by Random House of Canada, Limited, Toronto. Distributed by Random House, Inc., New York.

No maps, illustrations, or other portions of this book may be reproduced in any form without written permission from the publisher.

ISBN 978–1–4000–1963–2

ISSN 0743–9741

SPECIAL SALES

This book is available at special discounts for bulk purchases for sales promotions or premiums. Special editions, including personalized covers, excerpts of existing books, and corporate imprints, can be created in large quantities for special needs. For more information, write to Special Markets/Premium Sales, 1745 Broadway, MD 6-2, New York, New York 10019, or e-mail specialmarkets@randomhouse.com.

AN IMPORTANT TIP & AN INVITATION

Although all prices, opening times, and other details in this book are based on information supplied to us at press time, changes occur all the time in the travel world, and Fodor's cannot accept responsibility for facts that become outdated or for inadvertent errors or omissions. So **always confirm information when it matters,** especially if you're making a detour to visit a specific place. Your experiences—positive and negative—matter to us. If we have missed or misstated something, **please write to us.** We follow up on all suggestions. Contact the Washington, D.C. editor at editors@fodors.com or c/o Fodor's at 1745 Broadway, New York, NY 10019.

PRINTED IN THE UNITED STATES OF AMERICA

10 9 8 7 6 5 4 3 2 1

Be a Fodor's Correspondent

Your opinion matters. It matters to us. It matters to your fellow Fodor's travelers, too. And we'd like to hear it. In fact, we need to hear it.

When you share your experiences and opinions, you become an active member of the Fodor's community. That means we'll not only use your feedback to make our books better, but we'll publish your names and comments whenever possible. Throughout our guides, look for "Word of Mouth," excerpts of your unvarnished feedback.

Here's how you can help improve Fodor's for all of us.

Tell us when we're right. We rely on local writers to give you an insider's perspective. But our writers and staff editors—who are the best in the business—depend on you. Your positive feedback is a vote to renew our recommendations for the next edition.

Tell us when we're wrong. We're proud that we update most of our guides every year. But we're not perfect. Things change. Hotels cut services. Museums change hours. Charming cafés lose charm. If our writer didn't quite capture the essence of a place, tell us how you'd do it differently. If any of our descriptions are inaccurate or inadequate, we'll incorporate your changes in the next edition and will correct factual errors at fodors.com immediately.

Tell us what to include. You probably have had fantastic travel experiences that aren't yet in Fodor's. Why not share them with a community of like-minded travelers? Maybe you chanced upon a beach or bistro or B&B that you don't want to keep to yourself. Tell us why we should include it. And share your discoveries and experiences with everyone directly at fodors.com. Your input may lead us to add a new listing or highlight a place we cover with a "Highly Recommended" star or with our highest rating, "Fodor's Choice."

Give us your opinion instantly at our feedback center at www.fodors.com/feedback. You may also e-mail editors@fodors.com with the subject line "Washington, D.C. Editor." Or send your nominations, comments, and complaints by mail to Washington, D.C. Editor, Fodor's, 1745 Broadway, New York, NY 10019.

You and travelers like you are the heart of the Fodor's community. Make our community richer by sharing your experiences. Be a Fodor's correspondent.

Happy Traveling

Tim Jarrell, Publisher

CONTENTS

WASHINGTON, D.C. IN FOCUS

MAPS

ABOUT THIS BOOK

Our Ratings

Sometimes you find terrific travel experiences and sometimes they just find you. But usually the burden is on you to select the right combination of experiences. That's where our ratings come in.

As travelers we've all discovered a place so wonderful that its worthiness is obvious. And sometimes that place is so unique that superlatives don't do it justice: you just have to be there to know. These sights, properties, and experiences get our highest rating, **Fodor's Choice**, indicated by orange stars throughout this book.

Black stars highlight sights and properties we deem **Highly Recommended**, places that our writers, editors, and readers praise again and again for consistency and excellence.

By default, there's another category: any place we include in this book is by definition worth your time, unless we say otherwise. And we will.

Disagree with any of our choices? Care to nominate a place or suggest that we rate one more highly? Visit our feedback center at www.fodors.com/feedback.

Budget Well

Hotel and restaurant price categories from ¢ to $$$$ are defined in the opening pages of the respective chapters. For attractions, we always give standard adult admission fees; reductions are usually available for children, students, and senior citizens. Want to pay with plastic? **AE, D, DC, MC, V** following restaurant and hotel listings indicate whether American Express, Discover, Diners Club, MasterCard, and Visa are accepted.

Restaurants

Unless we state otherwise, restaurants are open for lunch and dinner daily. We mention dress only when there's a specific requirement and reservations only when they're essential or not accepted—it's always best to book ahead.

Hotels

Hotels have private bath, phone, TV, and air-conditioning and operate on the European Plan (aka EP, meaning without meals), unless we specify that they use the Continental Plan (CP, with a Continental breakfast), Breakfast Plan (BP, with a full breakfast), or Modified American Plan (MAP, with breakfast and dinner), or are all-inclusive (including all meals and most activities). We always list facilities but not whether you'll be charged an extra fee to use them.

Many Listings

★	Fodor's Choice
★	Highly recommended
✉	Physical address
✛	Directions
⌖	Mailing address
☎	Telephone
🖷	Fax
⊕	On the Web
✎	E-mail
💷	Admission fee
☉	Open/closed times
Ⓜ	Metro stations
▭	Credit cards

Hotels & Restaurants

🏨	Hotel
↔	Number of rooms
⌂	Facilities
⍩	Meal plans
✕	Restaurant
⌘	Reservations
↘	Smoking
⌁	BYOB
✕🏨	Hotel with restaurant that warrants a visit

Outdoors

⚑	Golf
⛺	Camping

Other

☾	Family-friendly
⇨	See also
✉	Branch address
☞	Take note

Experience
Washington, D.C.

WORD OF MOUTH

"We walked our feet off, the Disney Parks have nothing on walking city blocks in Downtown DC. Every step, every foot cramp and blister, was well worth it."

—tdmort

"[M]ake sure you leave some time to have a picnic under the [cherry] trees. You are not allowed to pick [the blossoms], but they make for beautiful pictures!"

—McAllister

WASHINGTON, D.C. TODAY

Outwardly serene and classically beautiful, the Capitol, the White House, and the Supreme Court stand at the heart of Washington, D.C. They are powerful, steadfast symbols of the stability and strength of the nation. But the city that revolves around this axis is in a constant state of change, lived on a more human scale.

Today's D.C. . . .

. . . is obsessed with politics—local politics. Residents take a different view of national elections than the rest of the country. Given the city's measly three electoral votes and general lack of representation at the Capitol, Washingtonians may be more interested in what the outcome means for their employment than in the actual candidate-to-candidate battles. What city dwellers are more passionate about is the often scandalous and always contentious world of local politics.

Mayor Adrian Fenty, who began his term in 2007, is number one on the hot topics list. D.C. mayors have always been colorful characters—remember Marion Barry and his drug-abuse scandals?—and Fenty is no exception. Within the first weeks of his term, he

had announced a plan to wrest control of the school system from the Board of Education. Some applauded his dedication to improving D.C.'s failing schools, while others argued that his hard-line solution wouldn't actually improve academic achievement. Check the *Washington Post* to see what other controversies Fenty is raising during his term.

The quest to secure the vote for D.C. continues. A bill that paired one vote in the House for the liberal-leaning district (whose license plates read "Taxation Without Representation") with an extra House seat for conservative Utah passed the House but stalled in the Senate. It was the first bill to get that far in over 30 years, and proponents see a reason to hope. It appears likely that the D.C. vote will have to be brought up again with the 2009 Congress.

. . . is certifiably sports crazy. And not all of the drama plays out on the field. Loyal Redskins fans are extremely passionate, selling out every game. The 2007 season got off to a rocky start and was brought to a standstill by the murder of safety Sean Taylor in November. Veteran head coach Joe Gibbs brought the team

---

D.C.: JUST THE FACTS

THE PEOPLE
Population, city: 581,530

Population, metro area: 5,162,029

Median age: 35

Ethnic makeup: African-American 55.4%; white 34.5%; Hispanic 8.2%; Asian 3.4%; multiracial 1.5%

Infant mortality rate: 12 per 1,000 births

Literacy: 63%

Crime rate: 77.1 offenses per 1,000 residents

Type of government: Limited representational democracy with no voting members of Congress. Elected mayor and nine-member council.

Workforce: 2,823,018

Per capita income: $37,043

Unemployment: 3.7%

together in the wake of the tragedy, ending the regular season with a winning streak. The beloved Gibbs announced his resignation in January of 2008, leaving the next chapter for the burgundy and gold wide open.

The nation's pastime has a new home in the nation's capital; the Nationals have a new sports complex on the Anacostia waterfront. The $611 million project was opposed by many residents and City Council members, who thought taxpayers would be contributing too much money for insufficient financial return. Those who have wanted a baseball team in D.C. since the dawn of time have turned a blind eye to the hard numbers.

Even soccer draws a fiercely loyal following in the District. Local team D.C. United isn't immune to stadium controversy, either. At this writing, the team, which has long played at RFK Stadium, is looking for a new home, possibly in the suburbs. D.C. Council members looking to keep the team in the District are hoping to have the city subsidize a new stadium at Poplar Point, a 110-acre park along the Anacostia River, to the tune of $150 million.

. . . is stuck in traffic. Spend an hour in gridlock on the Beltway—or wait 20 minutes for a Metro train to come—and you'll know why residents gripe so much about transportation. Metro initiated the largest fare increases in its history in early 2008; almost simultaneously, performance data revealed that on-time service had declined over the preceding 17-month period. The most major Metro extension is, of course, the most hotly contested. A project has been approved to build a new rail line linking the Orange Line to Tysons Corner, Dulles Airport, and other northern Virginia destinations. Although the entire project should be completed by 2015, arguments over whether the Tysons Corner section should be elevated or underground have held up the entire process. Given the poor public transit options from D.C. to Dulles, locals hope that someday the Metro will reach two airports—not just one.

Major industries: Government, law, tourism, high-tech, higher education

Official motto: Justitia omnibus (justice for all)

Official food: The half-smoke, a large, smoked link sausage most famously found at Ben's Chili Bowl on U Street.

THE LAND
Land area: 61 square mi

Nicknames: The District, D.C., Inside the Beltway

Latitude: 38° N

Longitude: 77° W

Elevation: From sea level to 420 feet.

Environmental issues: High levels of lead in the water supplies of some households; elevated arsenic levels near American University, where World War I ordnance was buried

Natural hazards: Lobbyists, motorcades, lack of congressional representation

WASHINGTON, D.C. PLANNER

When to Go

D.C. has two delightful seasons: spring and autumn. In spring the city's ornamental fruit trees are budding, and its many gardens are in bloom. By autumn most of the summer crowds have left and you can enjoy the sights in peace. Summers can be uncomfortably hot and humid. Winter weather is mild by East Coast standards, but a handful of modest snowstorms each year bring this southern city to a standstill.

Safety Tips

D.C. is a relatively safe city, but crimes do occur, even in typically "safe" neighborhoods. The best way to protect yourself is to stick to well-lighted and populated areas and avoid walking alone after dark. Many of the city's business and government districts become deserted at night, but the public transportation system is exceptionally safe, with only a few incidents of crime reported each year.

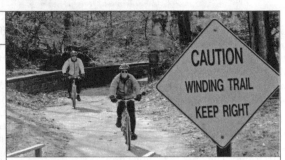

Getting Your Bearings

Four Quadrants: The address system in D.C. takes some getting used to. The city is divided into the four quadrants of a compass (NW, NE, SE, SW), with the U.S. Capitol at the center. Because the Capitol doesn't sit in the exact center of the city (the Washington Monument does), Northwest is the largest quadrant. Northwest also has most of the important landmarks, although Northeast and Southwest have their fair share. The boundaries are North Capitol Street, East Capitol Street, South Capitol Street, and the National Mall. That's where street addresses start.

Numbered Streets & Lettered Streets: Within each quadrant, numbered streets run north to south, and lettered streets run east to west (the letter J was omitted to avoid confusion with the letter I). The streets form a fairly simple grid—for instance, 900 G Street NW is the intersection of 9th and G streets in the northwest quadrant of the city. Likewise, if you count the letters of the alphabet, skipping J, you can get a good sense of the location of an address on a numbered street. For instance, 1600 16th Street NW is close to Q Street, Q being the 16th letter of the alphabet if you skip J.

Avenues on the Diagonal: As if all this weren't confusing enough, Major Pierre L'Enfant, the Frenchman who originally designed the city, threw in diagonal avenues recalling those of Paris. Most of D.C.'s avenues are named after U.S. states. You can find addresses on avenues the same way you find those on numbered streets, so 1200 Connecticut Avenue NW is close to M Street, because M is the 12th letter of the alphabet when you skip J.

D.C. by Public Transit

Driving in D.C. can be a headache. Traffic is usually congested, and the road layout is designed for frustration, with one-way streets popping up at just the wrong moment. Once you've reached your destination, the real challenge begins: D.C. may be the most difficult city in America in which to find a place to park. All of which means, if you have a car you'd be wise to leave it at your hotel and use public transit whenever possible.

Metro & Bus: The Washington Metropolitan Area Transit Authority operates a network of subway lines (known locally as the Metro) and bus routes throughout D.C. Most popular tourist attractions are near Metro stops, though certain areas are only accessible by bus, most notably Georgetown and Adams-Morgan.

Metro fares depend on the distance traveled. Fares range from $1.65 to $4.50 during morning and evening rush hours and after 2 AM, and from $1.35 to $2.35 at all other times. Bus fares are $1.35 (exact change only) for regular routes, and $3.10 for express routes. Transfers between buses are free; transfers from the Metro to the bus take 90¢ cents off your bus fare. One-day passes on the Metro are available for $7.80.

For fare information, route maps, and trip planning help, visit ⊕ *www.wmata.com* or call ☎ *202/637–7000.*

Taxi: At this writing enforcement had begun on the switch from zone to metered taxi cabs in the District. Taxis must have time and distance meters or they'll be forced to pay a $1,000 fine. There is a $3 minimum base charge with the rate increasing 25¢ for every sixth of a mile and for every minute stopped in traffic or going slower than 10 miles per hour. The old zone system, which required an intimate knowledge of District geography and the zone map to understand fares, was widely criticized. Whether the fare system will be embraced, however, remains to be seen. For the latest information on the switch, visit ⊕*www.dctaxi.dc.gov.*

The Visitor Center

1

The D.C. Visitor Information Center (⊠ *1300 Pennsylvania Ave. NW* ☎ *866/324–7386* ⊕ *www. dcvisit.com*) is in the Ronald Reagan International Trade Center Building. It's open weekdays year-round and also on Saturday in spring and summer. Visitors can pick up maps and brochures, book a hotel, purchase tickets for tours or performances, and use interactive kiosks to get more information on attractions and services in D.C.

The Smoking Ban

Smoking is no longer allowed in restaurants, bars, nightclubs, and taverns. It is allowed outside, leading to the increased popularity of establishments with rooftop bars or back decks. The flipside of the decision is that crowds now gather on the sidewalks in front of clubs, blocking pedestrian traffic and creating noise issues for residents. Then again, if you can't handle a little noise, why live above a bar?

WHAT'S WHERE

1 The Mall. This expanse of green is at the heart of D.C., stretching from the Capitol to the Washington Monument. It's lined by some of America's finest museums

2 The Monuments. D.C.'s most famous monuments are concentrated west of the Mall and along the Tidal Basin.

3 The White House Area & Foggy Bottom. There's great art at the Corcoran and Renwick galleries, as well as performances at the Kennedy Center, and a whiff of scandal at the Watergate.

4 Capitol Hill. The Capitol itself, along with the Supreme Court and Library of Congress, dominates this area. Follow Hill staffers to find restaurants, bars, and a thriving outdoor market.

5 Downtown. The Federal Triangle and Penn Quarter attract visitors to Ford's Theatre, the International Spy Museum, the National Portrait Gallery, and the American Art Museum. By night, crowds head to the Verizon Center and Chinatown's bars and restaurants.

6 Georgetown. The capital's wealthiest neighborhood is great for strolling, shopping, and partying, the scene centering around Wisconsin and M streets. The C&O Canal provides recreation in and out of the water.

7 Dupont Circle. This hub of fashionable restaurants and shops is also home to the most visible segment of the gay community. The Kalorama neighborhood is an enclave of embassies, luxurious homes, and small museums.

8 Adams-Morgan. One of D.C.'s most ethnically diverse neighborhoods has offbeat restaurants and shops and happening nightlife. Grand 19th-century apartment buildings and row houses have lured young professionals.

9 Upper Northwest. This mostly residential swath of D.C. holds two must-see attractions: the National Cathedral and the National Zoo.

10 U Street Corridor. Revitalization has brought trendy boutiques and hip eateries to the area around 14th and U, which was a hotbed of African-American culture in the early 20th century.

TOP WASHINGTON, D.C. ATTRACTIONS

Capitol

(A) Home of the Senate and the House of Representatives, the marble Capitol is an architectural marvel filled with frescoes and statues. Its grounds are equally stunning—Frederick Law Olmsted, the landscape architect famous for New York City's Central Park, designed them. A tour of the interior is impressive, but nothing beats attending a live debate on the House or Senate floor.

White House

(B) 1600 Pennsylvania Avenue may be the best-known address in the United States. Every president but George Washington has lived here, and many heads of state have passed through its hallowed halls. The self-guided tour lets you follow their footsteps through the historic rooms. Note that it takes advance planning to visit the White House. See Chapter 5, "Official Washington," for details.

Washington Monument

(C) The epitome of a landmark attraction, this 555-foot, 5-inch obelisk is visible from nearly everywhere in the city. Ride to the top to see views of the District, Maryland, and Virginia.

Jefferson, Lincoln, and FDR Memorials

(D) The key to all three of these memorials is to stop, stand, and read the writing on the walls. There's nothing quite like reading the Gettysburg Address while the massive marble statue of Lincoln broods behind you. Ponder the first lines of the Declaration of Independence at the Jefferson Memorial, and remember the line "We have nothing to fear but fear itself" as you encounter the stark monuments to poverty and war at the FDR Memorial.

World War II, Korean War Veterans, and Vietnam Veterans Memorials

(E) Touch a name on the "the Wall." See your reflection alongside the statues of veterans of the Korean War. Search for the stories of relatives who lost their lives in WWII. These memorials are highly interactive, deeply personal, and ultimately unforgettable.

Smithsonian Museums

(F) It's tough to pick a favorite Smithsonian museum because each is outstanding. Mostly flanking the National Mall, these illustrious galleries hold everything from Kermit the Frog to the *Spirit of St Louis* and the Hope Diamond to Rodin's *Burghers of Calais*.

National Zoo

(G) The pandas may be the zoo's most famous attraction, but they're not the only highlight. Monkeys, elephants, and lions never fail to delight animal lovers, and more exotic residents, such as sloth bears, red pandas, clouded leopards, and Japanese giant salamanders, can be found on the Asia Trail.

National Cathedral

(H) Like its 14th-century counterparts, this 20th-century cathedral has a nave, flying buttresses, transepts, and vaults that were built stone by stone. Unlike those historic buildings, the National Cathedral possesses a gargoyle in the shape of Darth Vader. For a unique experience, come for a tour and tea.

Arlington National Cemetery

(I) The serene hills across the Potomac from the Tidal Basin are the final resting place for some 300,000 members of the armed services, from Civil War casualties to fallen soldiers of the Iraq War. A visit here can be both sobering and deeply moving.

Dumbarton Oaks

(J) If you have an affection for formal gardens, visit the 10-acre grounds of Dumbarton Oaks, one of the loveliest spots in the city.

GREAT ITINERARIES

ONE DAY IN D.C.

If you have a day or less (and even a dollar or less!) in D.C., your sightseeing strategy is simple: take the Metro to the Smithsonian stop and explore the area around the Mall. You'll be at the undisputed heart of the city—a beautiful setting in which you'll find America's greatest collection of museums, with the city's spectacular monuments and the halls of government a stone's throw away.

As you face the Capitol, to your left are the **Museum of Natural History,** the **National Gallery of Art,** and the **National Archives.** To your right are the **Museum of African Art,** the **Hirshhorn Museum,** the **National Air and Space Museum,** and more. Head the other direction, toward the **Washington Monument,** and you're also on your way to the **World War II Memorial,** the **Lincoln Memorial,** the **Vietnam Veterans Memorial,** and more monuments to America's presidents and its past. A lover of American history and culture could spend a thoroughly happy month, much less a day, wandering the Mall and its surroundings.

If you're here first thing in the morning: You can hit monuments and memorials early. They're open 24 hours a day and staffed beginning at 8:00 AM. The outdoor sculpture garden at the **Hirshhorn** opens at 7:30 and the Smithsonian Institution Building ("the Castle") opens at 8:30. In the Castle you can grab a cup of coffee, watch an 18-minute film about D.C., and see examples of objects from many of the 18 Smithsonian museums.

If you only have a few hours in the evening: Experience the beauty of monuments at dusk and after dark. Many people think they're even more striking when the sun goes down. National Park Service rangers staff most monuments until midnight.

FIVE DAYS IN D.C.

Day 1

With more time at your disposal, you have a chance both to see the sights and to get to know the city. A guided bus tour is a good way to get yourself oriented; if you take one of the hop-on, hop-off tours we recommend under "Day Tours & Guides" in the "Travel Smart Washington, D.C." chapter at the back of this book, you'll get genuine insights without a lot of tourist hokum.

Because you can get on and off wherever you like, it's good idea to explore **Georgetown** and the **Washington National Cathedral** while on a bus tour; neither of which is easily accessible by Metro.

Day 2

Devote your next day to the Mall, where you can check out the museums and monuments that were probably a prime motivation for your coming to D.C. in the first place. There's no way you can do it all in one day, so just play favorites and save the rest for next time. Try visiting the monuments in the evening: they remain open long after the museums are closed and are dramatically lighted after dark.

Keep in mind that the **National Air and Space Museum** is the most crowded. The **National Museum of Natural History,** the **National Gallery of Art,** and the **Museum of American History** are very popular as well. If you visit the **U.S. Holocaust Memorial Museum,** plan on spending two to three hours. If you're with kids on the Mall, take a break by riding the carousel.

Cafés and cafeterias within the museums are your best option for lunch. Two excellent picks are the Cascade Café at the National Gallery of Art and the Mitsitam café at the National Museum of the American Indian, where they serve creative dishes inspired by native cultures.

If the weather is fine, consider a walk from the **Washington Monument** to the **Lincoln Memorial** and around the **Tidal Basin**, where you can see the **Jefferson Memorial** and the **FDR Memorial**. It's a healthy walk, however, so don't attempt it if you are already weary with museum fatigue.

Day 3
Make this your day on **Capitol Hill**, where you'll have the option of visiting the **Capitol**, the **U.S. Botanic Gardens**, the **Library of Congress**, the **Supreme Court**, and the **Folger Shakespeare Library**.

Call your senators or congressional representative in advance for passes to see Congress in session—a memorable experience. Likewise, check the Supreme Court's Web site (⊕ *www.supremecourtus.gov*) for dates of oral arguments. If you show up at court early enough, you might gain admission for either a short (three-minute) visit or the full morning session.

Day 4
Head to the **National Zoo** and say good morning to the pandas. If the weather is bad, you can still enjoy the numerous indoor animal houses. Then hop on the Metro to **Dupont Circle** for lunch. Walk west on P Street NW to **Georgetown**, where you can shop, admire the architecture, and people-watch through the afternoon.

If you got a good dose of Georgetown on your first day, consider hitting the **International Spy Museum** instead, which tends to be less crowded after 2 PM. From there you can walk over to the **Smithsonian American Art Museum** and **National Portrait Gallery**, which stay open until 7.

Day 5
Spend the morning at **Arlington National Cemetery**, one of the D.C. area's most moving experiences. While you're there, don't miss the changing of the guard at the Tomb of the Unknowns, which takes place every hour or half hour, depending on the time of year. A short detour north of the cemetery brings you to the **Marine Corps War Memorial**, a giant bronze rendering of one of the most famous images in U.S. military history.

After your quiet, contemplative morning, head across town to spend the afternoon in the neighborhoods of **Adams-Morgan** and **Dupont Circle**, both of which have unusual shops, restaurants, and clubs. Lunch at one of Adams-Morgan's Ethiopian, El Salvadoran, or Mexican restaurants, and take in the Dupont Circle art scene—there's an assortment of galleries, as well as the renowned **Phillips Collection**.

D.C. WITH KIDS

D.C. is filled with kid-friendly attractions. These sights are sure winners:

National Air and Space Museum
There's a good reason why this place is the most popular museum in the world: kids love it. The 23 galleries here tell the story of aviation and space from the earliest human attempts at flight. All three gift shops sell freeze-dried astronaut food—not as tasty as what we eat on Earth, but it doesn't melt or drip.

Museum of Natural History
Say hello to Henry. One of the largest elephants ever found in the world, this stuffed beast has greeted generations of kids in the rotunda of this huge museum dedicated to natural wonders. Take your kid to the O. Orkin Insect Zoo, home to live ants, bees, centipedes, tarantulas, roaches (some as large as mice), and other critters you wouldn't want in your house.

International Spy Museum
This museum takes the art of espionage to new levels for junior James Bonds. Even the most cynical preteens and teenagers are usually enthralled with all the cool gadgetry. Note that this museum is best for older tweens and teens—if you bring along a younger sibling, you could be in for a workout: there aren't many places to sit down, and strollers aren't allowed in the museum.

National Zoo
Known more for its political animals than its real animals, D.C. nevertheless has one of the world's foremost zoos. If your child is crazy about animals, this is an absolute must—it's huge!

Washington Monument
Kids say it looks like a giant pencil, and from the top some think D.C. looks like Legoland. Older kids like to find the White House and other D.C. landmarks.

Bureau of Engraving and Printing
Any youngster who gets an allowance will enjoy watching as bills roll off the presses. Despite the lack of free samples, the self-guided, 35-minute bureau tour is one of the city's most popular attractions.

Mount Vernon
Farm animals, a hands-on discovery center, an interactive museum, movies about the nation's first action hero, and more make this a place where families can stay all day.

National Museum of American History
Oh say you can see . . . the flag that inspired "The Star Spangled Banner," Oscar the Grouch, the ruby-red slippers from *The Wizard of Oz,* an impressive collection of trains, and more pieces of Americana can be found here.

D.C. Duck
What do you get when you cross a tour bus with a boat? A duck, of course—D.C. Duck, that is. Tour the city by both land and water without leaving your seats aboard these unusual amphibious vehicles: standard 2½-ton GM trucks in water-tight shells with propellers.

D.C. LIKE A LOCAL

If you want to "go native" and get a sense for D.C. as the locals know it, try these experiences.

Happy Hour on the Hill

At 6 PM on a weekday evening, bars in D.C. are hopping like it's Saturday night. The happy-hour culture here is strong, as government employees, lawyers, and other city workers unwind or network over half-price beers, well drinks, and pub grub. For the quintessential D.C. happy-hour experience, throw on something business casual and head to the Hill—no one will know you're not a Congressional staffer.

Shop at an Outdoor Market

Instead of sleeping in on a Saturday morning, grab your trusty mesh bag and a wad of cash and head to one of D.C.'s outdoor markets. The best-known venue, Eastern Market on Capitol Hill, lost its main building in a 2007 fire, but residents still come here to buy fresh produce, flowers, and handmade crafts in a temporary, indoor space across the street while the historic redbrick building is renovated. The Dupont Circle farmers' market and Georgetown flea market are also popular with residents.

Dine on Ethiopian Food

The District's many Ethiopian expats have introduced the community to their unique African cooking. The best restaurants, such as Etete, are in the U Street neighborhood. Meat and vegetarian dishes are ladled onto a large round of spongy *injera* bread, and diners eat with their hands, ripping off pieces of bread to scoop up the delectable stews. Using your hands instead of utensils adds to the sensual appeal of this cuisine.

Go for a Bike Ride

Your typical Mall-and-monuments tourist may not know that D.C. is home to several great bike trails. The Capitol Crescent Trail and Rock Creek Trail are popular routes between D.C. and Maryland. For hard-core bikers, the Custis Trail in Arlington links D.C. to the 45-mi Washington & Old Dominion (W&OD) trail in Virginia. On a warm, sunny day, expect to find the paths bustling with cyclists, rollerbladers, and strollers.

Hang Out on U Street

You won't find many tourists in the U Street neighborhood, and many locals have only recently discovered the area. During the day, browse through the unique boutiques that line 14th and U streets NW, or read the *Washington City Paper* at one of the many cafés. In the evening, select from trendy or ethnic restaurants, hang out at a local bar like the Chi Cha Lounge, or catch live music at the 9:30 Club or Bohemian Caverns.

Catch a Flick

A typical date night's dinner and a movie gets a little more exciting in D.C. In July and August locals head to the Mall for Screen on the Green, which shows classic films al fresco. The American City Diner on Connecticut Avenue shows movie classics from the '40s through '60s while customers chow down on diner fare. If you'd prefer beer and pizza, you can order both while watching second-run movies at the Arlington Cinema 'N' Drafthouse in Virginia. For classics and art films, head to the American Film Institute Silver Theatre in Silver Spring, Maryland.

FREE IN D.C.

It's actually hard to spend money on activities in D.C. All the Smithsonian museums and national memorials are free, as are many other museums, too many, in fact, to list here. Many of the top attractions are also free, like Ford's Theater and Dumbarton Oaks. Summertime is heaven for budget travelers, when free outdoor concerts and festivals occur every week.

Free Attractions

Anderson House
Dumbarton Oaks (free from November 1 to March 14)
Ford's Theatre
Franciscan Monastery
Kenilworth Aquatic Gardens
Kennedy Center tours
National Arboretum
National Shrine of the Immaculate Conception
Old Post Office Pavilion
Old Stone House
Rock Creek Park
Supreme Court of the United States
U.S. Capitol
U.S. Botanic Garden
Washington National Cathedral
White House

Free Performances

The Kennedy Center hosts performances every day at 6 PM on the Millennium Stage. Also, every September the Prelude Festival kicks off the Kennedy Center's fall performance schedule with many free events. Choral and church groups perform at the National Cathedral, often at no charge.

In the summer, folk, pop, and rock bands perform on Monday and Thursday nights atop Fort Reno Park. You can also hear jazz in the National Gallery of Art's sculpture garden Fridays in summer. The Carter Barron Amphitheatre in Rock Creek Park hosts performances by the Shakespeare Theatre Company and concerts throughout the spring and summer.

Performances of military music take place around the city. From June through August the U.S. Navy Band, U.S. Air Force Band, U.S. Marine Band, and U.S. Army Band take turns playing concerts on the grounds of the U.S. Capitol weekdays at 8 PM. You can also see the U.S. Marine Band every Friday night from May through August during the Evening Parade at the Marine Barracks.

D.C. is a city of festivals, many of which are free to the public (food and souvenirs cost extra). Check the National Mall lawn and Pennsylvania Avenue for music and dance performances, concerts, talks, cooking demonstrations, parades, and more. For a complete list of annual events, visit the Washington, D.C. Convention and Tourism Corporation at ⊕ *www.washington.org.*

TICKETPlace sells half-price tickets to D.C.'s theater and music events. If you're visiting in late October, reserve your seats early for D.C.'s Free Night of Theater.

Almost every day of the year, the Politics and Prose independent bookstore on Connecticut Avenue invites fiction and nonfiction authors to the store for book readings, talks, and Q&A sessions.

SIGHTSEE D.C.

If ever there was a "do it yourself" city, it's D.C. The Metro system is safe and easy to navigate. Most of the major sights and museums are concentrated in a single area. Many museums and monuments are free, and all the signs are in English. Armed with a Metro map, a map of the Mall, and a comfortable pair of shoes, you can do it all, all by yourself.

Nevertheless, sometimes a guided tour just makes more sense, especially when it comes to experience, insider knowledge, and a parking pass. If for no other reason, taking a guided tour can be a nice break; let someone else sweat the details for a day. Consider a guided tour if your trip matches one of the situations below; see the "Travel Smart Washington, D.C." chapter for more information.

If this is your first trip . . .

The Metro might be the most convenient way to get around, but it is notably lacking in city views. If you'd like to get the lay of the land, don't tax your patience (or that of your fellow drivers) by trying to navigate the district's one-way streets while looking for sights on your own. Take a guided tour and leave the driving, and the parking, to the pros.

Old Town Trolley Tours and the Tourmobile buses operated by the National Park Service take you to the major sites in the District and offer hop-on, hop-off convenience. It's perfect for your first day in the city.

A bike tour is also a wonderful way to take in the sights. Traversing the Mall on foot can quickly turn into a forced march; on a bike it's a gentle ride with show-stopping scenery. It's also inspirational: D.C. and its surroundings are a fantastic destination for cyclists, and you just might find yourself planning future trips with a bike in mind. See the "Sports & the Outdoors" chapter for more information.

If you want an insider's look . . .

Arranging constituent visits to the White House and to the sessions of Congress is one of the duties of your representative and senators. Don't let them shirk this important responsibility; contact their offices in advance to arrange your visit. The Web sites of the House of Representatives (www.house.gov) and the Senate (www.senate.gov) have contact information for the members of Congress, as well as general visitor information.

Several other government buildings, like the State Department, require advance reservations for a tour. See the "Official Washington" chapter for more information.

If you just can't get enough . . .

Are you mad about the movies, the political gossip, or the Civil War? Indulge your obsessions with a tour that will add fuel to your fire. Visit The Exorcist steps or the bar from St. Elmo's Fire with On Location Tours, or hear the juicy bits from Washington's rumor mill with Gross National Product's Scandal Tours. Or, take a guided walking tour with Smithsonian Associates that focuses on the Civil War history of the area, stopping at sights like Manassas National Battlefield Park at Bull Run.

D.C. TRAVEL TIPS

Travelers posting in the Travel Talk Forums at Fodors.com recommend the following D.C. travel tips.

Sights

"Order tickets for the Washington Monument on line in advance of your trip. Take advantage of the 'walk down tour' if given the opportunity—you'll get to see the insides of the granite blocks used to build the structure. They are all carved by the states and organizations that donated the blocks." —bennnie

"Panda bed-time is earlier than the rest of the zoo closing. Call your Congressman or Senator (with plenty of notice) for a free, private tour of the Capitol. The Virginia wineries make a lovely day trip. The ones in Northern Virginia are only an hour away. ⊕ www.virginiawines.org." —alyssabc

"Don't be afraid to visit DC during the winter. If the weather is bad, you can spend a lot of time in the museums and take a shuttle tour to the monuments. You'll have the place almost to yourselves. [T]ake the kids ice skating at the Sculpture Garden next to the Natl Gallery of Art. It will break up the forced march feeling." —Devonmcj

Transportation

"You shouldn't drive in DC. However, if you are driving to DC watch for traffic light locations. Not all lights are hanging in the middle of the intersection. A good number are on a pole at the corner. —ncgrrl

"Take the Old Town Trolley. You can get on/off all day and the drivers are great guides." —tovarich

Lodging

"This excellent website answers that question, 'How far is X hotel from Y Metro stop.' ⊕ www.stationmasters.com. Also helps first time visitors with orientation." —mlgb

"I don't have kids, but I'm pretty sure that Hotel Monaco will fit the bill. It's centrally located, right near the Metro, beside the Spy Museum and the Museum of American Art. It's in the old post office building, and it's really nice. They also give you a goldfish upon check-in." —kgh8m

Food & Drink

"I recommend: Eastern Market—a local farmer's market, art show and flea market combined. Since the original Eastern Market building burned last year, they've opened a temporary food hall that's filled with everything from local produce, meats and sausages, fresh fish. Get a crab cake sandwich from the stand in the hall before checking out antiques and picking up prints and handmade purses and hats from the neighboring flea/art market. Get an afternoon pick-me-up at Murky Coffee and pick up some Uncle Brutha's award-winning hot sauce." —melsollid

"Some cheap but good eats: Old Ebbitt's Express: For $4 you get a great daily pasta takeout (there are tables). New food carts downtown: Among the best are new "SmartKarts" flanking the Portrait Gallery. At 7th and H, it's Julia's Empanadas and great $2 tacos. At 7th and F, (across from the Verizon Center metro entrance), it Rocklin's BBC." —repete

Neighborhoods

Georgetown

WORD OF MOUTH

"It was perfect timing to see the White House towards the end of our 6-day visit. By then we understood that DC is about power and ideals. Even brand new interns we had met at the Capitol admitted feeling important and having ambitions to rise in power. It was a real eye-opener. We have to admit that feeling of Power is contagious in DC."

—Melissa5

Washington Neighborhoods

0   500 yards

0   500 meters

Florida Ave.

U Street-Cardozo

U St.

T St.

S St.

Dupont Circle

R St.

Q St.

Church St.

Logan Circle

Rhode Island Ave.

O St.

N St.

M St.

Thomas Circle

Massachusetts Ave.

City Museum

Mt. Vernon Square

Washington Convention Center

New York Ave.

T St.

H St.

G St.

F St.

E St.

Downtown

D St.

National Gallery Sculpture Garden

Constitution Ave.

Madison Dr.

National Gallery of Art

THE MALL

Smithsonian Institution

Jefferson Dr.

Independence Ave.

National Air and Space Museum

C St.

Capitol Hill

Union Station

Columbus Memorial Fountain

Stanton Park

US Capitol

E. Capitol St.

Maryland Ave.

Folger Park

The Mall

D St.

NW   NE

NE   SE

SW   SE

Florida Ave.

S St.

Rhode Island Ave.

R St.

Q St.

P St.

O St.

N St.

M St.

New York Ave.

North Capitol St.

New Jersey Ave.

Louisiana Ave.

Delaware Ave.

E St.

Virginia Ave.

G St.

ridge

son erial

Francis Case Memorial Bridge

Southwest Fwy.

G St.

I St.

Water St.

Maine Ave.

Washington Canal

Updated
by Valerie
Hamilton

WASHINGTON IS A CITY OF vistas—pleasant views that shift and change from block to block, a marriage of geometry and art. Unlike other large cities, it isn't dominated by skyscrapers, largely because, in 1899, Congress passed a height-restrictions act to prevent federal monuments from being overshadowed by commercial construction. The result: the world's first planned capital is also one of its most beautiful. And although the federal government dominates many of the city's activities and buildings, there are always places where you can leave politics behind.

Washington's old-fashioned neighborhoods have largely been swept away by tides of gentrification and the city's inherent transience; you'll be hard-pressed to find any kids playing kickball in the street or old folks sipping lemonade on the front stoop. But as the city has grown in sophistication, it has developed new charms. Most parts of the city have a clearly defined personality, and some, like Capitol Hill, still hold small-town appeal.

HOW D.C. CAME TO BE

The city that invented American politicking, back scratching, and delicate diplomatic maneuvering is itself the result of a compromise. Tired of its nomadic existence after having set up shop in eight locations, Congress voted in 1785 to establish a permanent federal city. Northern lawmakers wanted the capital on the Delaware River, in the North; Southerners wanted it on the Potomac, in the South. A deal was struck when Virginia's Thomas Jefferson agreed to support the proposal that the federal government assume the war debts of the colonies if New York's Alexander Hamilton and other northern legislators would agree to locate the capital on the banks of the Potomac.

George Washington himself selected the site of the capital, a diamond-shaped, 100-square-mi plot that encompassed the confluence of the Potomac and Anacostia rivers, not far from his estate at Mount Vernon. To give the young city a head start, Washington included the already thriving tobacco ports of Alexandria, Virginia, and Georgetown, Maryland, in the District of Columbia. In 1791 Pierre-Charles L'Enfant, a French engineer who had fought in the Revolution, created the classic plan for the city.

It took the Civil War—and every war thereafter—to energize the city, by attracting thousands of new residents and spurring building booms that extended the capital in all directions. Streets were paved in the 1870s, and the first streetcars ran in the 1880s. Memorials to famous Americans such as Lincoln and Jefferson were built in the first decades of the 20th century, along with the massive Federal Triangle, a monument to thousands of less-famous government workers.

THE MALL
AMERICA'S TOWN GREEN

It could be said that the Mall—the heart of almost every visitor's trip to Washington—has influenced life in the U.S. more than any other expanse of lawn. The Mall is a picnicking park, a jogging path, and an outdoor stage for festivals and fireworks. People come here from around the globe to tour the illustrious Smithsonian Institution museums, celebrate special events, or rally to make the world a better place.

The AIDS Memorial Quilt on the Mall in 1996

A BRIEF HISTORY OF THE MALL

Got a beef? The Mall is the birthplace of American political protest, where citizens have come for more than a century to air grievances and demand change.

1894: Coxey's Army, a group of unemployed workers from Ohio, stage the first-ever protest march on Washington.

1939: Contralto Marian Anderson gives an Easter Sunday concert on the grounds of the Lincoln Memorial after the Daughters of the American Revolution bar her from performing at their headquarters because she's black.

1963: The Lincoln Memorial is the site of Martin Luther King Jr.'s inspirational "I have a dream" speech during the March on Washington.

1971: The Vietnam Veterans Against the War camp out on the Mall to persuade Congress to end military actions in Southeast Asia.

1972: The first Earth Day is celebrated on April 22 on the National Mall.

1987: The AIDS Memorial Quilt is displayed for the first time in its entirety. It returns to the Mall in 1988, 1989, 1992, and 1996.

1995: Nearly 400,000 African-American men fill the Mall, from the Capitol to the Washington Monument, during the Million Man March.

WHAT ABOUT THE MONUMENTS?

Visitors often confuse the Mall with the similarly named National Mall. The Mall is the expanse of lawn between 3rd and 14th Streets, while the National Mall is the national park that spans from the Capitol to the Potomac, including the Mall, the monuments, and the Tidal Basin. To reach the monuments, head west from the Mall or south from the White House and be prepared for a long walk. To visit all the monuments in one day requires marathon-level stamina and good walking shoes; to visit the monuments and the Mall in the same day would be the Ironman of tourism. For more about D.C.'s monuments and memorials, see Chapter 4.

FROM TRASH HEAP TO TOURIST ATTRACTION

In 1791, Pierre Charles L'Enfant designed Washington, D.C., with a mile-long Grand Avenue running west from the Congress building. According to his plan, the boulevard would be lined with homes for statesmen and open green spaces, including a central garden bordered by a dense grove of trees.

L'Enfant's grandiose plan took more than 100 years to become a reality. By 1850, the area we now know as the Mall had not become a park, but was used instead as a storage area for lumber, firewood, and trash. With President Fillmore's permission, a group of businessmen hired landscape designer Andrew Jackson Downing to plan a national park featuring natural-style gardening. Sadly, Downing was killed in 1852, and his plan was never fully implemented.

Despite this setback, progress continued. The first Smithsonian museum on the Mall, the National Museum (now the Arts and Industries Building), opened to the public in 1881, and after 35 years of construction, the Washington Monument was completed in 1884.

A victory for the Mall occurred in 1901, when the Senate Park Commission, or McMillan Commission, was created to redesign the Mall as the city's ceremonial center. The McMillan plan embraced L'Enfant's vision of formal, public spaces and civic art, but replaced his Grand Avenue with a 300-foot expanse of grass bordered by American elms. It also called for cultural and educational institutions to line the Mall. Finally, a modified version of L'Enfant's great open space in the heart of Washington would become a reality.

The National Park Service assumed management of the Mall in 1933. In the latter half of the twentieth century, new museums and monuments opened on the Mall to create the public gathering place, tourist attraction, and tribute to our nation's heroes that we know today.

TOP 15 THINGS
TO DO ON THE MALL

1. Ride the old-fashioned carousel in front of the Smithsonian Castle.

2. Watch the fireworks on the Fourth of July.

3. See the original *Spirit of St. Louis,* and then learn how things fly at the National Air and Space Museum.

4. Gross out your friends at the Natural History Museum's Insect Zoo.

5. Gawk at Dorothy's ruby slippers, Kermit the Frog, Abraham Lincoln's top hat, and Lewis and Clark's compass at the American History Museum.

6. Twirl around the ice skating rink in the National Gallery of Art's sculpture garden.

7. View astonishing wooden masks at the Museum of African Art.

8. Taste North, South, and Central American dishes at the National Museum of the American Indian's Mitsitam Café.

9. Exercise your First Amendment rights by joining a rally or protest.

10. Peek at the many-armed and elephant-headed statues of Hindu gods at the Sackler Gallery.

11. Pose with sculptures by Auguste Rodin and Henry Moore at the Hirshhorn Sculpture Garden.

12. Learn how you make money—literally—at the Bureau of Engraving and Printing.

13. Follow the lives of the people who lived and died in Nazi Germany at the Holocaust Memorial Museum.

14. Eat, drink, watch, listen, and learn at an outdoor cultural festival.

15. Picnic and people-watch on the lawn after a hard day of sightseeing.

VISITING THE MUSEUMS ON THE MALL

MAKE THE MOST OF YOUR TIME

With 12 museums spread out along 11 city blocks, you just can't expect to see everything in one day. Few people have the stamina for more than half a day of museum- or gallery-hopping at a time; children definitely don't. To avoid mental and physical exhaustion, try to devote at least two days to the Mall and use these itineraries (and our listings in Chapter 3) to make the best use of your time.

Historical Appeal: For a day devoted to history and culture, start with the **Holocaust Museum,** grabbing lunch at its excellent cafeteria. After refueling, the next stop is the **American History Museum.** If the museum's still closed for renovations—it's scheduled to reopen in fall 2008—check out the "Treasures of American History" exhibit on loan at the **Air and Space Museum.** Or, cross the length of the Mall to visit the **Museum of the American Indian** instead.

Art Start: To fill a day with paintings and sculptures, begin at the twin buildings of the **National Gallery of Art.** Enjoy the museum's sculpture while you dine in the garden's outdoor café. You'll find a second sculpture garden directly across the Mall at the **Hirshhorn.** If you like the avant-garde, visit the Hirshhorn's indoor galleries; for a cosmopolitan collection

Constitution Ave.

Pennsylvania Ave.

National Gallery Art

3rd St.

U.S. Capitol

U.S. Botanic Garden

National Museum of the American Indian

1st St.

Independence Ave.

Bartholdi Park

Canal St.

S. Capitol St.

New Jersey Ave.

lth and Human vices

M FEDERAL CTR. SW

0   200 yds

0   200 meters

of Asian and African art and artifacts, head instead to the **Sackler Gallery** and **Museum of African Art**.

Taking the Kids: The most kid-friendly museum of them all, the **National Air and Space Museum** is a must-see for the young and young-at-heart. There's only fast food in the museum or a hot dog cart outside, but the **Museum of the American Indian** next door has healthier options. If your young bunch can handle two museums in a day, cross the lawn to the **Natural History Museum**. This itinerary works well for science buffs, too.

Fodor's Choice: Got one day and want to see the best of the Smithsonian? Start at the **Air and Space Museum**, then skip to the side-by-side **Natural History** and **American History Museums**. Picnic on the Mall or hit the museum cafeterias so as not to waste a moment.

NOT ANOTHER HOT DOG!
A SURVIVAL GUIDE TO EATING WELL ON THE MALL

Even locals wonder where to grab a decent bite to eat when touring the Smithsonian Museums. Hot dogs, soft pretzels, and ice cream from a cart don't make for a nutritious lunch, and the museum cafeterias mostly provide mediocre meals at sky-high prices. On a weekday, the streets north of Constitution Avenue offer easy-to-find lunch spots, but virtually all are closed on weekends.

Here are some places for better dining by the Mall, though several require a few blocks' walk.

Museum of the American Indian: The Mitsitam Café—the name means "let's eat" in the language of the Delaware and Piscataway people—is one of the best museum cafeterias on the Mall. Food stations serve native-inspired sandwiches, entrees, soups, and desserts from five regions of the western hemisphere.

Pavilion Café: Located in the National Gallery's Sculpture Garden, this eatery offers indoor and outdoor seating with views of the artwork and fountain/ice rink outside. The menu includes salads, sandwiches, and pizzas.

Pennsylvania Avenue SE: If lunchtime finds you on the east end of the Mall, head past the Capitol to Pennsylvania Avenue SE. Between Second and Fourth Streets, you'll find plenty of pubs, cafés, and sandwich shops. It's a bit of a hike, but well worth the shoe leather.

Old Post Office Pavilion: The food court here (✉ *1100 Pennsylvania Ave. NW*) is open seven days a week. The selection is predictable—sushi, pizza, deli, bagels, Chinese food—but they provide cheap fare for a variety of tastes.

Ronald Reagan Building and International Trade Center: The food court here is another option, but is closed on Sundays during the winter.

ANNUAL EVENTS

The Mall's spacious lawn is ideal for all kinds of outdoor festivals. These annual events are local favorites and definitely worth a stop if you're in town when they're on.

St. Patrick's Day Parade

WINTER

Ice Skating: Whirl and twirl at the outdoor ice rink in the National Gallery of Art's Sculpture Garden. *Mid-November through mid-March*

St. Patrick's Day Parade: Dancers, bands, and bagpipes celebrate all things Irish along Constitution Avenue. *Mid-March*

SPRING

National Cherry Blossom Festival: When the cherry trees burst into bloom, you know that spring has arrived. Fly a kite, watch a parade, and learn about Japanese culture in a setting sprinkled with pink and white flowers. *Late March through early April*

Cherry Blossom Festival

SUMMER

Smithsonian Folklife Festival: Performers, cooks, farmers, and craftsmen demonstrate cultural traditions from around the world. *Around July 4*

Independence Day: What better place to celebrate the birth of our nation than in the capital city? Enjoy concerts and parades on the Mall, then watch the fireworks explode over the Washington Monument. *July 4*

Smithsonian Folklife Festival

Screen on the Green: Film favorites are shown on a gigantic movie screen on Monday nights. Bring a blanket and picnic dinner to better enjoy the warm summer evenings. *Mid-July through mid-August*

FALL

Black Family Reunion: D.C. celebrates African-American family values. Pavilions showcase businesses owned by African-Americans and events and performances feature black entertainers, celebrities, and experts. *September*

Independence Day Reenactment

National Book Festival: Meet your favorite author in person at the Library of Congress' annual literary festival. Over 70 writers and illustrators participate in readings, live interviews, and events for kids. *September*

Marine Corps Marathon: The "Marathon of the Monuments" starts in Virginia but winds its way around the entire National Mall. It's as fun to cheer as it is to run. *Late October*

Marine Corps Marathon

PLANNING YOUR VISIT

KEEP IN MIND

■ All of the museums on the Mall are free to the public.

■ Since 9/11, security has increased, and visitors will need to go through screenings and bag checks, which create long lines during peak tourist season.

■ Two museums require timed-entry passes: the Holocaust Museum and the Bureau of Printing and Engraving. If you've got a jam-packed day planned, it's best to get your tickets early in the morning or in advance.

GETTING HERE & GETTING AROUND

By Metro: You can access the Mall from several Metro stations. On the Blue and Orange lines, the Federal Triangle stop is convenient to the Natural History and American History museums, and the Smithsonian stop is close to the Holocaust Memorial Museum and Sackler Gallery. On the Yellow and Green lines, Archives/Navy Memorial takes you to the National Gallery of Art. The L'Enfant Plaza stop, accessible from the Blue, Orange, Yellow, and Green lines, is the best exit for the Hirshhorn and Air and Space Museum.

By Bus: Walking from the Holocaust Memorial Museum to the National Gallery of Art is quite a trek. Many visitors take advantage of the hop-on, hop-off Tourmobile (☎ 800/551–SEAT, 💳 $25 per person), which stops at most major attractions on the Mall, as well as key monuments and Arlington National Cemetery.

Parking is hard to find along the Mall. You can find private parking garages north of the Mall in the Downtown area, where you'll have to pay to leave your car. If you're willing to walk, limited free parking is available on Ohio Drive SW near the Jefferson Memorial and East Potomac Park.

HELP, THERE'S A PROTEST ON THE MALL!

Since the 1890s, protesters have gathered on the Mall to make their opinions heard. If you're not in a rallying mood, you don't have to let First Amendment activities prevent you from visiting the Smithsonian museums or enjoying a visit to the Mall.

■ **Use the back door:** All of the Smithsonian museums have entrances on Constitution or Independence Avenues, which do not border the Mall's lawn. Use these doors to gain admission without crossing the Mall itself.

■ **Know you're protected:** The Mall is a national park, just like Yosemite or Yellowstone. The National Park Service has a responsibility to visitors to make sure they can safely view park attractions. To this end, demonstrators are often required to keep main streets open.

■ **Avoid the crowds:** Even the biggest rallies don't cover the entire National Mall. If the crowd is by the Capitol, head west to visit the Lincoln Memorial. If protestors are gathered around the Washington Monument, visit the Jefferson Memorial on the opposite side of the Tidal Basin. There's plenty to see.

THE WHITE HOUSE AREA & FOGGY BOTTOM

Sightseeing
★★★★☆
Dining
★★★☆☆
Lodging
★★★☆☆
Shopping
★☆☆☆☆
Nightlife
★★☆☆☆

Tops on every first-timer's D.C. to-do list should be a visit to the White House. The home of every U.S. President but George Washington, the 132-room mansion is as impressive in real life as it is on television. After taking the self-guided tour, strike out into the surrounding streets to explore the President's neighborhood, which includes massive government buildings, small museums, and some of the city's oldest houses. Follow the grassy lawn of the Tidal Basin to the city's famous monuments, or continue west to Foggy Bottom with its three main claims to fame: the Kennedy Center, George Washington University, and the infamous Watergate complex.

WHAT'S HERE

Many visitors take a tour of the White House then head straight to the Tidal Basin and the monuments. After all, the imposing gray government buildings in the President's backyard don't necessarily scream vacation-time fun. But, if you stop to take a look around, you'll discover a well-kept secret: this area is filled with small museums, special exhibitions, and historic rooms that savvy visitors can tour while the crowds are at the Smithsonians. Many sites require advance reservations and few are kid-friendly, but history and art buffs shouldn't miss these hidden gems.

Tours of this area usually start with the **White House,** the most recognizable residence in town. Plan ahead: you must make arrangements for admission months in advance with your member of Congress or embassy. For more information, stop at the **White House Visitor Center,** in the Department of Commerce building.

The White House is flanked by two imposing buildings you can view but not enter. To the west, the granite edifice that looks like a wedding cake is the Eisenhower **Executive Office Building,** styled after the Louvre. Built as a headquarters of the State, War, and Navy departments, it now houses offices for the Vice President and other members of the executive branch. It was here that Secretary of State Cordell Hull met with Japanese diplomats after the bombing of Pearl Harbor, and the building was the site of both the first presidential press conference in 1950 and the first televised press conference five years later. To the east, the **Treasury Building** is the largest Greek Revival edifice in Washington. Robert Mills, the architect responsible for the Washington Monument and the Patent Office (now the Smithsonian American Art Museum), designed the grand colonnade that stretches down 15th Street. The building's southern facade has a **statue of Alexander Hamilton,** the department's first secretary.

Directly north of the White House, the trees and flowerbeds of **Lafayette Square** make for an intimate oasis amid downtown Washington. The park was named for the Marquis de Lafayette, the young French nobleman who came to America to fight in the Revolution. His **statue** is in the southeast corner of the park. In the center, the large **statue of Andrew Jackson** is the second equestrian statue made in America.

St. John's Episcopal Church has sat across from the park since 1816. Every President since Madison has visited the church, and many have worshipped here regularly. The **Decatur House** was the first private residence on Lafayette Square, and now houses a museum that shows the living quarters as they were in the Federal period and in the Victorian era.

A green canopy marks the entrance to **Blair House,** the residence used by heads of state visiting Washington. Down the street, the **Renwick Gallery** of the Smithsonian American Art Museum exhibits American crafts and decorative arts.

The expanse of lawn south of the White House is called the Ellipse, and was once part of the president's backyard. The northern end provides excellent views of the rear of the White House and its south lawn. On the southern end stand a weather-beaten **gatehouse** that once stood on Capitol Hill and the **Boy Scouts Memorial.**

From here you can cross the street to enter the **Constitution Gardens** and **Tidal Basin** area. The scenic park houses the famous monuments that honor past presidents (Washington, Lincoln, Jefferson, and Roosevelt) and the heroes and fallen soldiers of past wars (Vietnam, Korea, World War II). Each spring the cherry trees around the Tidal Basin burst into pink-and-white blooms, and the city celebrates the beauty of this gift from Japan with a two-week Cherry Blossom Festival.

By the southeast corner of the White House lawn, the **Tecumseh Sherman Monument** depicts the Civil War general mounted on his steed,

GETTING ORIENTED

GREAT EXPERIENCES IN THE WHITE HOUSE AREA

Corcoran Gallery of Art: The great 19th-century American painters were inspired by the sublime majesty of the American West. See the most definitive works—Albert Bierstadt's *Mount Corcoran* and Frederick Church's *Niagara.*

John F. Kennedy Center for the Performing Arts: See a free performance by anyone from Norah Jones to the National Symphony Orchestra here on the Millennium Stage.

The Renwick Gallery: If the White House tour doesn't satisfy your inner decorating diva, perhaps the Tiffany objets d'art, intricately carved antique tables, and opulent Victorian Grand Salon here will do the trick.

Thompson Boat Center: Take in Washington's marble monuments, lush Roosevelt Island, and the Virginia coastline with a canoe ride down the Potomac.

The White House: You have to plan weeks, if not months, in advance, and you're only allowed into eight of the 132 rooms, but there's no denying the kick of touring 1600 Pennsylvania Avenue—especially around Christmas.

GETTING HERE

The White House can be reached by the Red Line's Farragut North stop or the Blue and Orange lines' McPherson Square and Farragut West stops. Foggy Bottom has its own Metro stop, also on the Blue and Orange lines. A free shuttle runs from the station to the Kennedy Center. Many of the other attractions are a considerable distance from the nearest subway stop. If you don't relish long walks or time is limited, check the map to see if you need to make alternate travel arrangements to visit specific sights.

PLANNING YOUR TIME

Touring the area around the White House could easily take a day or even two, depending on how long you visit each of the museums along the way. To see Foggy Bottom's more westerly sights will add still more time.

If you enjoy history, you may be most interested in the Decatur House, DAR Museum, and State Department. If it's art you crave, devote the hours to the Corcoran and Renwick galleries instead. Save the Kennedy Center and Watergate for the evening, when you can catch a performance or enjoy dinner in the area.

QUICK BITES

The Corcoran Gallery's Café des Artistes (⊠ *500 17th St. NW* ☎ *202/639–1700*) serves lunch, light fare on Thursday evenings, and brunch on Sunday. It's closed Monday and Tuesday.

Loeb's Restaurant (⊠ *832 15th St. NW* ☎ *202/371–1150*) makes deli-style salads and sandwiches to eat there or take with you—perfect for a picnic in Lafayette Park.

The Old Ebbitt Grill (⊠ *675 15th St. NW* ☎ *202/347–4800*), once the haunt of presidents Grant, Cleveland, Harding, and Theodore Roosevelt, is still a popular watering hole for journalists and off-duty Secret Servicemen.

You have a choice of eateries at the **Shops at 2000 Penn** (⊠ *2000 Pennsylvania Ave.*), both sit-down and carryout.

surrounded by four sentries. Across 15th Street, **Pershing Park** honors General John J. "Black Jack" Pershing. Ice-skaters glide on the square pool here in winter.

To the southwest, the **Corcoran Gallery of Art** displays an impressive collection of historic and contemporary American art, as well as significant works by European artists.

The headquarters of many government departments and national organizations reside along the blocks between E Street and Constitution Avenue west of the Ellipse. Several offer tours or exhibits for the public, but always check whether advance reservations are required, and bring a photo ID.

The highlights here are the tour of the **Department of State's Diplomatic Reception Rooms** and the **Daughters of the American Revolution headquarters.** You must reserve a tour at the State Department months in advance, but it's worth the effort. A docent takes you to the top floor's Diplomatic Reception Rooms—usually reserved for heads of states and special honorees, and the great halls and gathering spaces are furnished with American antiques and art.

A tour of the DAR headquarters lets you peek into a few of the 32 period rooms—each decorated in a style unique to one state and one time period—and the Beaux-Arts auditorium now used as a genealogy library. The museum on the first floor hosts changing exhibitions.

The **Department of the Interior** contains a museum with exhibits based on the work of its branches, such as the Bureau of Land Management, National Park Service, and U.S. Geological Survey. The **Federal Reserve Building** displays special art exhibitions that are only worth visiting if you're fascinated with the subject or want to see the inside of the Fed. The **National Academy of Sciences** offers two galleries of science-related art. Robert Berks's sculpture of Albert Einstein outside the building has broader appeal; the creator of the theory of relativity looks—dare we say?—cuddly.

The headquarters of the **Organization of American States,** which is made up of nations from North, South, and Central America, contains a patio adorned with a pre-Columbian–style fountain and lush tropical plants. This tiny rain forest is a good place to rest when Washington's summer heat is at its most oppressive.

Away from the White House and federal buildings, northern Foggy Bottom is the home of **George Washington University.** The university has no separate campus, but occupies many of the modern buildings and 19th-century houses between 19th and 24th streets south of Pennsylvania Avenue.

Along the Potomac River, west of the university, the **John F. Kennedy Center for the Performing Arts** is both a memorial to the late president and a bustling cultural center with six theaters for the performance of music, dance, opera, and dramatic arts.

Dining Near the White House

AT A GLANCE

For reviews, see the Where to Eat chapter.

BUDGET DINING
Bombay Club, *Indian, 815 Connecticut Ave. NW*

Teaism, *Japanese, 400 8th St. NW*

MODERATE DINING
Blue Duck Tavern, *New American, 1201 24th St. NW*

Marcel's, *Belgian, 2401 Pennsylvania Ave. NW*

Kinkead's, *Seafood, 2000 Pennsylvania Ave. NW*

TenPenh, *Asian, 10th St. and Pennsylvania Ave. NW*

Nearby along the water, the **Watergate** made history on the night of June 17, 1972, but the apartment-office complex doesn't look so scandalous in person. Famous—and infamous—residents have included Attorney General John Mitchell and presidential secretary Rose Mary Woods of Nixon White House fame, as well as such D.C. insiders as Jacob Javits, Alan Cranston, Bob and Elizabeth Dole, Monica Lewinsky, and Secretary of State Condoleezza Rice.

If looking at the Potomac makes you yearn to get closer, the **Thompson Boat Center,** at the end of Virginia Avenue, rents canoes and kayaks in the warmer months. Bike rentals are also available.

CAPITOL HILL

Sightseeing
★★★★☆

Dining
★★★☆☆

Lodging
★★★☆☆

Shopping
★★☆☆☆

Nightlife
★★☆☆☆

The people who live and work on "the Hill" do so in the shadow of the edifice that lends the neighborhood its name: the gleaming white Capitol. Not only can you tour these hallowed halls, you can also sit in on a Supreme Court hearing, marvel at the Library of Congress's Great Hall, and stop and smell the roses at the Botanic Garden. The Hill also includes charming residential blocks lined with Victorian row houses and a fine assortment of restaurants, bars, and shops.

WHAT'S HERE

Capitol Hill's exact boundaries are disputed. While most say it's bordered to the west, north, and south by the Capitol, H Street NE, and I Street SE, respectively, extending east only to 14th Street, some real-estate speculators argue that the trendy neighborhood extends east to the Anacostia River. What's clear is that Capitol Hill's historic-preservation movement is hard at work, restoring more and more 19th-century houses and fighting the urban blight that creeps in around the edges of this historic part of Washington.

The Capitol is the point from which the city is divided into quadrants: northwest, southwest, northeast, and southeast. North Capitol Street, which runs north from the Capitol, separates northeast from northwest; East Capitol Street separates northeast and southeast; South Capitol Street separates southwest and southeast; and the Mall (Independence Avenue on the south and Constitution Avenue on the north) separates northwest from southwest.

The massive **U.S. Capitol** sits majestically at the east end of the Mall, and is the foremost reason to visit Capitol Hill. Although the free tour takes you through the impressive rotunda, Statuary Hall, and Old Senate Chamber, to see your legislators at work you need to arrange in advance for (free) Gallery passes—contact your senator or representative's office. The much-anticipated and oft-delayed **Capitol Visitor Center** should open in late 2008.

In front of the Capitol three monuments flank a reflecting pool. In the center, the **Grant Memorial** is one of the largest sculpture groups in the city. To the south stands the **James Garfield Memorial,** and to the north a **Peace Monument** commemorating sailors who died in the Civil War. Across Constitution Avenue a monolithic carillon forms the **Robert A. Taft Memorial,** dedicated to the longtime Republican senator and son of the 27th president.

Across from the Garfield Memorial, the **United States Botanic Garden** is the oldest botanic garden in North America. After touring the Conservatory, be sure to wander through the rose, butterfly, and regional gardens of the **National Garden,** which opened in September 2006. Another lovely spot, the **Bartholdi Fountain** was created by Frederic-Auguste Bartholdi, sculptor of the Statue of Liberty. The aquatic monsters, sea nymphs, tritons, and lighted globes all represent the elements of water and light.

Like a king surrounded by his courtiers, the U.S. Capitol keeps some impressive company. The imposing buildings to the north and south house the offices of senators and representatives. Behind the Capitol the U.S. Supreme Court and the Jefferson Building of the Library of Congress sit side by side. You can line up to hear oral arguments inside the **Supreme Court Building** when court is in session.

The **Library of Congress** has so many books, recordings, maps, manuscripts, and photographs that it actually takes three buildings to get the job done. The Jefferson Building is the most visitor-friendly. Here you can view the Great Hall, peek into the Main Reading Room, and wander through changing exhibitions related to the library's holdings.

Behind the Library of Congress, the **Folger Shakespeare Library** holds an enormous collection of works by and about Shakespeare and his times, as well as a reproduced 16th-century theater and gallery that are open to visitors (the books are not). North of the Folger on 2nd Street, the **Sewall-Belmont House** was the headquarters of the historic National Woman's Party, and is accessible by tour.

The Beaux-Arts **Union Station,** modeled after the Roman baths, dominates the northwest corner of Capitol Hill. Thanks to a restoration project completed in 1988, the city's main train station has turned into a minimall, with shops, restaurants, and a movie theater. At the base of a column on the **Columbus Memorial Fountain,** designed by Lorado Taft, sits a steely-eyed Christopher Columbus in the station's front plaza.

GETTING ORIENTED

GREAT EXPERIENCES ON CAPITOL HILL

The Capitol: See democracy in action. Watch congressmen and -women debate, insult, and wrangle their way through the job of making laws in the Capitol's House and Senate chambers.

Eastern Market: The main building of one of D.C.'s most beloved weekend destinations was destroyed by a fire in 2007, but while rebuilding is underway you can pick up fresh produce, flowers, and locally made crafts at the market's temporary home.

The Hawk and Dove: Order a pint and listen in as Congressional staffers gripe about their famous bosses and locals debate the Redskins' Super Bowl chances at this quintessential D.C. bar and Capitol Hill institution.

The Library of Congress: Take a break from debate to contemplate the Gutenberg Bible, the lavishly sculpted Great Hall, and the splendor of the gilded Main Reading Room.

The Supreme Court: Round out your firsthand look at the three branches of government by watching the Supreme Court justices hear precedent-setting arguments at the highest court in the land.

United States Botanic Garden: Wrinkle your nose at the corpse flower, explore the jungle, gawk at the orchids, or stroll the paths of the new National Garden.

GETTING HERE

From the Red Line's Union Station stop, you can easily walk to most destinations on Capitol Hill. From the Blue and Orange Line, the Capitol South stop is close to the Capitol and Library of Congress, and the Eastern Market stop leads to the market and the Marine Corps Barracks. The Numbers 30, 32, 34, 35, and 36 buses run from Friendship Heights through Georgetown and Downtown to Independence Avenue, the Capitol, and Eastern Market. Street parking is available.

PLANNING YOUR TIME

Touring Capitol Hill should take you about four hours, allowing for about an hour each at the Capitol, the Botanic Garden, and the Library of Congress. If you want to see Congress in action, contact your legislator in advance, and bear in mind that the House and Senate are usually not in session during August. Supreme Court cases are usually heard October through April, Monday through Wednesday, two weeks out of each month. Build in extra time if you want to head out to the Navy and Marine sites.

QUICK BITES

At the **Library of Congress** there's a cafeteria (with a great view) serving breakfast and lunch on the sixth floor of the **Madison Building** (✉ *Independence Ave. SE, between 1st and 2nd Sts.* ☎ *202/707–5000*).

Pennsylvania Avenue SE between 2nd and 4th streets has a large selection of restaurants. Just off the main drag, **Le Bon Café** (✉ *210 2nd St. SE* ☎ *202/547–7200*) is a cozy bistro with excellent pastries and light lunches.

Bullfeathers (✉ *410 1st St. SE* ☎ *202/543–5005*) has been grilling burgers for members of the House since 1980.

The food court at Union Station offers everything from pizza to sushi. There are several restaurants in the station; the largest, **America** (☎ *202/682–9555*), serves regional food from all over the country.

Next door, the **National Postal Museum** will delight kids and philatelists alike. The Smithsonian takes a playful approach to stamp collecting and the history of the U.S. Postal Service with its interactive exhibits. On the other side of Union Station, the **Thurgood Marshall Federal Judiciary Building** is worth a quick peek. The atrium, designed by architect Edward Larabee Barnes, encloses a garden of bamboo five stories tall.

From 2nd Street on east, the neighborhood changes dramatically from large-scale government buildings to 19th-century town houses. Among them is the first Washington home of the abolitionist and writer **Frederick Douglass** on A Street NE. The south side of Pennsylvania Avenue SE, between 2nd and 4th streets, is the main commercial thoroughfare. Restaurants, bars, and coffee shops frequented by those who live and work on the Hill line these blocks.

On 7th Street between C and North Carolina Avenue, **Eastern Market** houses farmers, flower vendors, and other merchants who sell their fresh produce and crafts to locals and tourists alike. Although the main building was gutted in a fire in April 2007, food vendors are operating out of a temporary structure across the street while the main hall is rebuilt, and the outdoor flea market continues to bustle on weekends.

The **Marine Corps Barracks and Commandant's House,** the nation's oldest continuously active marine installation, is the home of the U.S. Marine Band. On Friday evenings from May to August you can attend the hour-long ceremony given on the parade deck by the Marine Band (the "President's Own") and the Drum and Bugle Corps (the "Commandant's Own").

On the outskirts of Capitol Hill you'll find gritty neighborhoods improving at varying rates. While there are sights worth exploring here, they're a long walk from the Capitol—drive or take public transportation instead.

On the banks of the Anacostia River, the 115-acre **Washington Navy Yard** is the Navy's oldest outpost on shore. On its premises are the Navy Museum, which chronicles the history of the U.S. Navy; the Navy Art Gallery, which exhibits navy-related paintings, sketches, and drawings; and the decommissioned U.S. Navy destroyer *Barry*, which is open for touring.

Established in 1807 "for all denomination of people," the **Congressional Cemetery** was the first national cemetery created by the government. You can take a self-guided walking tour of the premises. Farther

Dining on Capitol Hill

For reviews, see the
Where to Eat chapter.

BUDGET DINING
Belga Café, Belgian,
514 8th St. SE

**Granville Moore's
Brickyard,** Belgian,
1238 H St. NE

Jimmy T's Place,
American, 501 E. Capitol
St. SE

Johnny's Half Shell,
Seafood, 400 N. Capitol
St. NW

Locanda, Italian, 633
Pennsylvania Ave. SE

The Market Lunch,
American, 306 7th St. SE

Montmartre, French,
327 7th St.

Tortilla Café, Latin
American, 210 7th St. SE

MODERATE DINING
Bistro Bis, French, Hotel
George, 15 E St. NW

Sonoma, Contemporary,
223 Pennsylvania Ave. SE

EXPENSIVE DINING
Charlie Palmer Steak,
Steak, 101 Constitution
Ave.

upriver, and due east from the Capitol out East Capitol Street, **RFK Stadium** is the current home of the Washington Nationals baseball team and the D.C. United soccer team. A new baseball stadium is under construction just to the east of the Navy Yard along the Anacostia River. It's expected to open in spring 2008.

DOWNTOWN

Sightseeing
★★★★☆

Dining
★★★★☆

Lodging
★★★★☆

Shopping
★★★☆☆

Nightlife
★★★★☆

Downtown D.C. encompasses so many sights and small neighborhoods that the designation is practically meaningless. Government buildings line the south side of Pennsylvania Avenue in the Federal Triangle. Trendy clubs, lounges, and restaurants pepper the area around the Verizon Center in the Penn Quarter. The neighborhood attracts still more people for its culture—a burgeoning theater district and the venerable National Portrait Gallery and Smithsonian American Art Museum. There's a lot of life—but few actually live here.

WHAT'S HERE?

The downtown area can be divided into several sections, each with its own personality. The Federal Triangle is the wedge-shaped area south of Pennsylvania Avenue, north of Constitution Avenue, and east of 15th Street. It's the neighborhood's serious side, with its imposing gray buildings and all-business mentality. The Penn Quarter makes up the area directly to the north of Pennsylvania Avenue. This is Downtown's party side, where restaurants and bars mix with popular museums. Chinatown gives the neighborhood an international flair, and Judiciary Square, immediately to the east, is like a stern older uncle frowning about the goings-on.

The mass of government buildings that comprise the **Federal Triangle** was constructed between 1929 and 1938 in order to consolidate government workers in one place. The neighborhood was formerly known as Murder Bay for its notorious collection of rooming houses, taverns, tattoo parlors, and brothels. When city planners moved in, they chose a uniform classical architectural style for the new buildings. As you pass by, give a nod to the John A. Wilson Building, Internal Revenue Service Building, Department of Justice, and Apex Building, which houses the Federal Trade Commission. These buildings aren't open to the public.

The Department of Commerce houses the **National Aquarium** in its basement, a location as underwhelming as the aquarium itself. Diagonally across the street, the **Freedom Plaza** is inlaid with a map from L'Enfant's original 1791 plan for the Federal City. To compare L'Enfant's vision with today's reality, stand in the middle of the map's Pennsylvania Avenue and look west. L'Enfant had planned an unbroken vista from the Capitol to the White House, but the Treasury Building, begun in 1836, ruined the view. Turning to the east, you can see the U.S. Capitol sitting on the former Jenkins Hill. The plaza is named in honor of Martin Luther King Jr.

The **Ronald Reagan Building and International Trade Center** houses the most secure tourist office and food court you'll ever see. You need to show a photo ID and go through a security checkpoint in order to collect brochures and subway schedules. It's also home to the Capitol Steps, who perform political comedy sketches on Friday and Saturday nights. Another food court and shops take up the lower levels of the **Old Post Office.** The observation deck in the clock tower may be one of Washington's best-kept secrets. Although not as tall as the Washington Monument, it offers nearly as impressive a view. Even better, it's usually not as crowded, the windows are bigger, and—unlike the monument's windows—they're open, allowing cool breezes to waft through.

On the opposite side of the street, the **J. Edgar Hoover Federal Bureau of Investigation Building** has been a favorite attraction for visitors interested in espionage and the persecution of bad guys. Sadly, tours have been suspended indefinitely for security reasons. The **National Archives** display the original Declaration of Independence, Constitution, and Bill of Rights.

Washington's newest museum, the **Newseum,** opened its doors on April 11, 2008. The seven-level building with 14 main galleries showcases 500 years of journalism history with multimedia displays. The spectacular stone-and-glass edifice next door is the **Canadian Embassy.**

A few steps beyond Pennsylvania Avenue the **Penn Quarter** begins. This neighborhood has blossomed into one of the hottest addresses in town for nightlife and culture. Washington's theater scene revolves around this area, which is home to the venerable **Ford's Theatre** and **National Theater,** the progressive **Woolly Mammoth Theater Company,** and the **Shakespeare Theater's** new performing arts center. The **Warner Theatre** even has its own walk of fame on the sidewalk out front.

New galleries, restaurants, and other cultural hot spots have taken over much of the real estate here. Tony eateries frequented by high-powered lawyers and government bigwigs line Pennsylvania Avenue, while the area surrounding the **Verizon Center** sports arena and Chinatown is chockablock with chain restaurants, hip bars and eateries, and Chinese holes-in-the-wall. Expect crowds on weekend evenings.

GETTING ORIENTED

GETTING HERE

Take the Metro to Federal Triangle or Archives-Navy Memorial to visit the government buildings along Pennsylvania Avenue. The Gallery Place–Chinatown stop gives direct access to the Verizon Center, Chinatown, and the American Art and Spy museums. Judiciary Square has its own stop, and Metro Center is the best choice for the National Theater. Bus routes crisscross the area as well. Street parking is available; it's easier to find on nights and weekends away from the main Chinatown and Verizon Center area. Several parking garages in the neighborhood offer convenience, at a price.

GREAT EXPERIENCES DOWNTOWN

Chinatown: Dress to the nines to mingle with the *it* crowd at swanky bars and restaurants. Or wear jeans and sneakers to a Wizards game, an Irish pub, or a Chinese eatery.

International Spy Museum: Indulge your inner James Bond with a look at 007's Aston Martin from *Goldfinger*—along with more serious toys used by the CIA, FBI, and KGB.

The National Archives: After seeing the Declaration of Independence, Constitution, and Bill of Rights, lose yourself in the Public Vault, where you can find everything from the Emancipation Proclamation to *Mad* magazine.

National Portrait Gallery and Smithsonian American Art Museum: These sister museums have something for everyone, from presidential portraits to old-timey "crazy quilts."

Theater District: Catch performances ranging from Shakespeare to the avant-garde, in Penn Quarter's answer to Broadway.

2

PLANNING YOUR TIME

Downtown is densely packed with major attractions—far too many to see in one day. You'll need at least an hour inside each attraction, so pick the two that appeal most and stroll past the rest. Art lovers might focus on the National Portrait Gallery and Smithsonian American Art Museum; history buffs might limit themselves to touring the National Archives and the National Building Museum; families with kids may prefer the International Spy Museum and the National Aquarium; and media junkies will want to visit the Newseum and the Marian Koshland Science Museum, which looks at the science behind media headlines.

SAFETY

Downtown's blocks of government and office buildings become something of a ghost town when the working day is done. You may prefer not to walk alone in this area after dark. The recently revitalized Penn Quarter still carries some vestiges of its grittier past, so stick to the main commercial areas at night.

QUICK BITES

Cheap eats abound in Chinatown. Watch the chef stretching noodles by the window before you head into **Chinatown Express** (⊠ 746 6th St. NW ☎ 202/638–0424) to try some. **Full Kee** (⊠ 509 H St. NW ☎ 202/371–2233) offers a large selection of Cantonese specialties.

At **Marvelous Market** (⊠ 730 7th St. NW ☎ 202/628–0824) you can get fresh sandwiches, soups, chips, and other bakery fare, including the best brownies in Washington.

There are back-to-back food courts in the Federal Triangle, at the **Old Post Office Pavilion** (⊠ 1100 Pennsylvania Ave. NW ☎ 202/289–4224) and the **Ronald Reagan Building** (⊠ 1300 Pennsylvania Ave. NW ☎ 202/312–1300).

The historic **Willard Intercontinental Hotel** (⊠ 1401 Pennsylvania Ave. NW ☎ 202/628–9100) serves breakfast and lunch at **Café du Parc,** tea in **Peacock Alley,** and drinks in the **Round Robin Bar**.

The **National Portrait Gallery** and the **Smithsonian American Art Museum** are the newest cultural draw, having reopened in the Old Patent Office Building in 2006. The fun and interactive **International Spy Museum** across the street displays the largest collection of spy artifacts in the world. To the west, on New York Avenue, the **National Museum of Women in the Arts** showcases works by female artists from the Renaissance to the present (it has the only Frida Kahlo in the city).

Tours of **Ford's Theatre** and the **Petersen House** take you back to the night of Lincoln's assassination. John Wilkes Booth and his co-conspirators plotted out the dirty deed at **Suratt Boarding House** a few blocks away in Chinatown. This compact neighborhood is marked by the ornate, 75-foot Friendship Arch and Chinese characters on storefronts such as Ann Taylor and Starbucks. Nearly every Cantonese, Szechuan, Hunan, and Mongolian restaurant has a roast duck hanging in the window, and the shops here sell Chinese food, arts and crafts, and newspapers. Nearby, **Martin Luther King Jr. Memorial Library** is the only D.C. building designed by the illustrious modernist architect Ludwig Mies van der Rohe.

To the east, the small **Marian Koshland Science Museum** explores and explains the science behind current news headlines. City and federal courthouses, as well as the **National Law Enforcement Officers Memorial,** are in Judiciary Square. Across the street, the **National Building Museum** is known as much for its impressive interior hall as for its exhibits on architecture and the building arts. The **Old Adas Israel Synagogue** on 3rd Street is the oldest synagogue in D.C.

Dining Downtown

For reviews, see the Where to Eat chapter.

BUDGET DINING

Café Atlántico, *Latin American, 405 8th St. NW*

Full Kee, *Chinese, 509 H St. NW*

Georgia Brown's, *Southern, 950 15th St. NW*

Kaz Sushi Bistro, *Japanese, 1915 I St. NW*

Matchbox, *American, 713 H St. NW*

Poste, *New American, Hotel Monaco, 555 8th St. NW*

Zaytinya, *Middle Eastern, 701 9th St. NW*

Zola, *American, 800 F St. NW*

MODERATE DINING

Ceiba, *Latin American, 701 14th St. NW*

Central Michel Richard, *French, 1001 Pennsylvania Ave. NW*

DC Coast, *Seafood, 1401 K St. NW*

Jaleo, *Spanish, 480 7th St. NW*

Occidental Grill, *American, Willard Inter-Continental, 1475 Pennsylvania Ave. NW*

Oceanaire Seafood Room, *Seafood, 1201 F St. NW*

Old Ebbitt Grill, *American, 675 15th St. NW*

Olives, *Mediterranean, 1600 K St. NW*

Palette, *American, Madison Hotel, 1177 15th St. NW*

PS 7's, *New American, 777 I St. NW*

Rasika, *Indian, 633 D St. NW*

Taberna del Alabardero, *Spanish, 1776 I St. NW, at 18th St*

Teatro Goldoni, *Italian, 1909 K St. NW*

Tosca, *Italian, 1112 F St. NW*

EXPENSIVE DINING

Café MoZU, *Asian, Mandarin Oriental, 1330 Maryland Ave. SW*

Capital Grille, *Steak, 601 Pennsylvania Ave. NW*

Caucus Room, *Continental, 401 9th St. NW*

CityZen, *American, Mandarin Oriental, 1330 Maryland Ave. SW*

Equinox, *American, 818 Connecticut Ave. NW*

Indebleu, *Eclectic, 707 G St. NW*

Morton's of Chicago, *Steak, 1050 Connecticut Ave. NW*

2

GEORGETOWN

Sightseeing
★★★☆☆

Dining
★★★★★

Lodging
★★★★☆

Shopping
★★★★★

Nightlife
★★★★★

At first glance, Washington's oldest and wealthiest neighborhood may look genteel and staid, but don't be fooled, this is a lively part of town. The narrow streets and Federal-era town houses are for visitors but a picturesque backdrop for the restaurants, bars, nightclubs, and boutiques that line M Street and Wisconsin Avenue. By day, shoppers indulge in antiques, shoes, upscale jeans, and eclectic housewares; by night, revelers eat, drink, and make merry. To drift back in time to the Georgetown of old, leave the main drag behind and head to the tree-shaded enclaves of privilege north of M Street. Although the coveted brick homes are the province of Washington's high society, the rest of the neighborhood offers ample entertainment for everyone.

WHAT'S HERE

Georgetown can be thought of in four sections: the shopping and nightlife area, the university, the historical residential neighborhoods, and the waterfront. The most popular area is the first, located mainly on M Street and Wisconsin Avenue. Georgetown's students claim the university as their turf; the streets of town houses belong to well-to-do homeowners, museum-goers, and strollers. The C&O Canal is a sylvan spot for a bike ride, morning jog, or pleasant paddle, while the riverfront restaurants at Washington Harbour let visitors enjoy sedentary water views as well.

The hub of Georgetown is the intersection of M Street and Wisconsin Avenue. By day, the lengths of these thoroughfares are crowded with shoppers. The area is known for its high-end clothing boutiques, antiques stores, and fancy furniture shops, now squeezing cheek-to-jowl with chain stores such as J. Crew and Banana Republic or cheap and chic H&M and Zara.

By night, the hungry, the thirsty, and the ready-to-party pound the pavement on this side of D.C. You'll find Vietnamese, Thai, Middle Eastern, and Ethiopian restaurants here, as well as burgers and fries at a variety of grubby pubs. After hours, college students and recent graduates overrun the bars, but a few lounges do cater to a more mature, upscale crowd.

Slightly out-of-place amid the modern shops and cafés, the 18th-century **Old Stone House** on M Street is thought to be the oldest in the city. The former **Masonic Lodge** on Thomas Jefferson Street harks back to the area's past as a working-class city populated by tradesmen, laborers, and merchants. Many 19th-century residents prayed at **Grace Episcopal Church** on Wisconsin Avenue. An unlikely combination, the small **Museum of Contemporary Art** is in **Canal Square,** a converted 1850s warehouse.

Toward the western end of M Street, at the foot of the Key Bridge, the small **Francis Scott Key Memorial Park** honors the Washington attorney who penned the national anthem during the War of 1812. Past the old brick streetcar barn at No. 3600 (now offices), turn right to find the 75 steps that figured prominently in the horror movie *The Exorcist.*

Founded in 1789, **Georgetown** is the oldest Jesuit school in the country. About 12,000 students attend the university, known now as much for its perennially successful basketball team as for its fine programs in law, medicine, foreign service, and the liberal arts. Pleasant walks across redbrick sidewalks and past Federal and Victorian houses can be found in upper Georgetown, north of M Street and on either side of Wisconsin. Close to the university, the 3300 block of N Street is a fine example of early architecture. The group of five Federal houses between 3339 and 3327 N Street is known collectively as Cox's Row, after Colonel John Cox, a former mayor of Georgetown who built them in 1817. On O Street, **St. John's Church** is one of the oldest churches in the city.

For a more in-depth look into Georgetown's moneyed past, head east of Wisconsin on Q Street. **Tudor Place** was once the home of Thomas Peter, son of Georgetown's first mayor, and his wife, Martha Custis, Martha Washington's granddaughter. A house tour reveals many of Martha Washington's Mount Vernon possessions, as well as a 1919 Pierce Arrow roadster. Down the road, the **Dumbarton House** is a distinctive example of Federal-era architecture and furnishings.

Dumbarton Oaks (no relation to Dumbarton House) can rightfully claim to be one of the loveliest spots in Washington, D.C. The 10 acres of formal gardens and English parkland may inspire a romantic proposal or a game of hide-and-seek, and the well-placed benches offer quiet nooks to rest weary feet or have a tête-à-tête.

GETTING ORIENTED

Wisconsin Avenue NW

S Street NW

S Street NW

BURLEITH/HILLANDALE

Dumbarton Oaks

Montrose Park

Oak Hill Cemetery

35th Street NW

34th Street NW

32nd Street NW

31st Street NW

Avon Place

30th Street NW

29th Street NW

R Street NW

Reservoir Road NW

Dent Place NW

Wisconsin Avenue NW

Convent of the Visitation

Tudor Place

Q Street NW

Q Street NW

Volta Place NW

Georgetown Visitation Preparatory School

P Street NW

GEORGETOWN

P Street NW

O Street NW

36th Street NW

35th Street NW

34th Street NW

33rd Street NW

31st Street NW

O Street NW

O Street NW

Dumbarton St. NW

St. John's Church

N Street NW

N Street NW

Georgetown University

Cox's Row

Olive Avenue N

Old Stone House

Embassy of Mongolia

Prospect Street NW

Canal Square/ Museum of Contemporary Art

M Street NW

M Street NW

Francis Scott Key Memorial Park

Masonic Lodge

Vigilant Firehouse

Wisconsin Avenue NW

Grace Episcopal Church

Thomas Jefferson Street NW

The Foundry Building

Francis Dodge Warehouses

29th Street NW

Whitehurst Fwy.

Francis Scott Key Bridge

Potomac

NW

SW

TO WASHINGTON HARBOUR

0   500 ft

0   150 M

GREAT EXPERIENCES IN GEORGETOWN

C&O Canal: Walk or bike along the path here, which offers bucolic scenery from Georgetown all the way to Maryland.

Dumbarton Oaks: Stroll through the 10 acres of formal gardens—Washington's lovellest oasis.

M Street: Indulge in some serious designer retail therapy (or just window-shopping). Reward your willpower or great find with a great meal afterward—all on the same street.

Tudor Place: Step into Georgetown's past with a visit to the grand home of the Custis-Peter family. On view are antiques from George and Martha Washington's home at Mount Vernon and a 1919 Pierce Arrow roadster.

Washington Harbour: Come on a warm evening to enjoy sunset drinks while overlooking the Watergate, Kennedy Center, and Potomac River.

GETTING HERE

There's no Metro stop in Georgetown, so you have to take a bus or taxi or walk to this part of Washington. It's about a 15-minute walk from Dupont Circle or the Foggy Bottom Metro station. Perhaps the best transportation deal in Georgetown is the Circulator. For a buck you can ride from Union Station along Massachusetts Avenue and K Street to the heart of Georgetown. Or try the Georgetown Metro Connection. These little blue buses have two routes, one along Wisconsin Avenue and K Street to the Foggy Bottom Metro and the second along M Street to the Dupont Circle and Rosslyn Metros.

Other options include the G2 Georgetown University Bus, which goes west from Dupont Circle along P Street, and the 34 and 36 Friendship Heights buses, which go south down Wisconsin Avenue and west down Pennsylvania Avenue toward Georgetown.

PLANNING YOUR TIME

You can easily spend a pleasant day in Georgetown, partly because some sights (Tudor Place, Dumbarton Oaks, Oak Hill Cemetery, and Dumbarton House) are somewhat removed from the others and partly because the street scene, with its shops and people-watching, invites you to linger.

Georgetown is almost always crowded. It's not very car-friendly either, especially at night; driving and parking are usually difficult. The wise take the Metro to Foggy Bottom or Dupont Circle and then walk 15 minutes from there, or take a bus or taxi.

QUICK BITES

If the crowds of Georgetown become overwhelming, step into **Ching Ching Cha** (✉1063 Wisconsin Ave. NW ☎202/333-8288), a Chinese teahouse where tranquillity reigns supreme. In addition to tea, lunch and dinner may be ordered from a simple menu with light, healthful meals presented in lacquered bento boxes.

Wisey's (✉1440 Wisconsin Ave. NW ☎202/333-4122) is the more central outpost of university favorite **Wisemiller's Delicatessen.** Although the original is carryout only, the Wisconsin Avenue Wisey's fits a few tables into its small storefront. Healthy choices include paninis, wraps, and salads, and smoothies and specialty teas are also available.

CLOSE UP

A History of Georgetown

The area that would come to be known as George (after George II), then George Towne, and finally Georgetown was part of Maryland when it was settled in the early 1700s by Scottish immigrants, many of whom were attracted by the region's tolerant religious climate.

Georgetown's position—at the farthest point up the Potomac that's accessible by ship—made it an ideal transit and inspection point for farmers who grew tobacco in Maryland's interior. In 1789 the state granted the town a charter, but two years later Georgetown—along with Alexandria, its counterpart in Virginia—was included by George Washington in the Territory of Columbia, site of the new capital.

While Washington struggled, Georgetown thrived. Wealthy traders built their mansions on the hills overlooking the river; merchants and the working class lived in modest homes closer to the water's edge. In 1810 a third of Georgetown's population was African-American—both free people and slaves. The Mt. Zion United Methodist Church on 29th Street is the oldest organized black congregation in the city. When the church stood at 27th and P streets, it was a stop on the Underground Railroad (the original building burned down in the mid-1800s).

Georgetown's rich history and success instilled in all its residents a feeling of pride that persists today. (When Georgetowners thought the dismal capital was dragging them down, they asked to be given back to Maryland, the way Alexandria was given back to Virginia in 1845.)

Tobacco's star eventually fell, and Georgetown became a milling center, using water power from the Potomac. When the Chesapeake & Ohio (C&O) Canal was completed in 1850, the city intensified its milling operations and became the eastern end of a waterway that stretched 184 mi to the west. The canal took up some of the slack when Georgetown's harbor began to fill with silt and the port lost business to Alexandria and Baltimore, but the canal never became the success it was meant to be.

In the years that followed, Georgetown was a malodorous industrial district, a far cry from the fashionable spot it is today. Clustered near the water were a foundry, a fish market, paper and cotton mills, and a power station for the city's streetcar system

It still had its Georgian, Federal, and Victorian homes, though, and when the New Deal and World War II brought a flood of newcomers to Washington, Georgetown's tree-shaded streets and handsome brick houses were rediscovered. Pushed out in the process were many of Georgetown's renters, including many of its black residents.

Today some of Washington's most famous residents call Georgetown home, including former *Washington Post* executive editor Ben Bradlee, political pundit George Stephanopoulos, Senator (and 2004 presidential nominee) John Kerry, and *New York Times* op-ed doyenne Maureen Dowd.

Dining in Georgetown

For reviews, see the
Where to Eat chapter.

BUDGET DINING

Cafe Divan, *Turkish,*
1834 Wisconsin Ave. NW

Five Guys, *American,*
1335 Wisconsin Ave. NW

Miss Saigon, *Vietnamese, 3057 M St. NW*

MODERATE DINING

Bistro Français, *French,*
3128 M St. NW

Black Salt, *Seafood,*
4883 MacArthur Blvd

Leopold's Kafe & Konditorei, *Austrian, 3318 M St. NW*

Sushi-Ko, *Japanese,*
2309 Wisconsin Ave. NW

EXPENSIVE DINING

Cafe Milano, *Italian,*
3251 Prospect St. NW

Citronelle, *Contemporary, Latham Hotel, 3000 M St. NW*

Morton's of Chicago,
Steak, 3251 Prospect St.

1789 Restaurant,
American, 1226 36th St. NW

2

Between these two estates, **Montrose Park** entertains kids, dogs, and picnickers with wide lawns, tennis courts, and a playground. Hardy walkers should take note of the park's benches and public restrooms. The funerary obelisks, crosses, and gravestones of **Oak Hill Cemetery** mark the final resting place for actor, playwright, and diplomat John H. Payne and William Corcoran, founder of the Corcoran Gallery of Art.

Down the hill by the Potomac, **Washington Harbour** is a riverfront development specializing in pricey restaurants and bars and scenic views of the river, the Watergate complex, and the Kennedy Center. Georgetown's **C&O Canal** links the Potomac with the Ohio River. A sandy red path along the banks makes for a scenic walk or bike ride, while canoeists enjoy the waters themselves—look out for great blue herons and turtles lounging in the sun. Every summer the National Park Service offers rides on mule-drawn canal boats. Two miles north of the Key Bridge, **Fletcher's Boat House** rents kayaks, canoes, and bikes.

DUPONT CIRCLE

Sightseeing
★★★★☆

Dining
★★★★★

Lodging
★★★★☆

Shopping
★★★★☆

Nightlife
★★★☆☆

Dupont Circle is the grand hub of D.C., literally. This traffic circle is essentially the intersection of the main thoroughfares of Connecticut, New Hampshire, and Massachusetts avenues. More importantly though, the area around the circle is a vibrant center for urban and cultural life in the District. Along with wealthy tenants and basement-dwelling twentysomethings, museums, art galleries, and embassies call this upscale neighborhood home. Offbeat shops, specialty bookstores, coffeehouses, and restaurants of all ethnicities and price ranges lend the area a funkier, more urban feel. Add to the mix stores and clubs catering to the neighborhood's large gay community, and Dupont Circle becomes a big draw for nearly everyone. Perhaps that's why the fountain at the center of the traffic island is such a great spot for people-watching.

WHAT'S HERE

A visit to Dupont Circle is not complete without a visit to the actual traffic circle. The large island in the middle is a lively urban park, vibrant with rollerbladers, chess players, and a marble fountain created by Daniel Chester French. On sunny days the surrounding benches are pleasant places for people-watching, newspaper-reading, or relaxing with a cup of coffee or a snack.

The main north-south artery of Connecticut Avenue cuts through the heart of Dupont Circle. For blocks on either side of the circle, restaurants, cafés, and shops keep the area busy night and day. The one-of-a-kind bookstore **Kramerbooks** has a broad and eclectic selection of reading material, as well as a popular café.

Washington's gay scene isn't as large as in other cities, but is concentrated mostly on 17th and R streets in Dupont Circle. Gay bars and stores are scattered throughout the neighborhood; the whole area is gay-friendly.

Most of Dupont's museums here are small and located in former residences. The **Phillips Collection,** west of the Circle on P Street, was founded as the first permanent museum of modern art in the country, with a collection including works by Renoir, Degas, Van Gogh, Goya, and el Greco.

Nearby on Massachusetts Avenue, the **Anderson House** was bequeathed by Larz and Isabel Anderson to the Society of the Cincinnati, an exclusive club of the descendents of Revolutionary war officers. Next door, the **Walsh-McLean House** was once home to Evalyn Walsh-McLean, the last private owner of the Hope Diamond (now in the National Museum of Natural History).

North of Massachusetts Avenue and mainly along R Street lie a variety of art galleries. On the first Friday of each month they stay open late for a neighborhood open house, often with canapés and drinks for the public. Nestled among the galleries, the nonprofit **Fondo Del Sol Visual Arts Center** is devoted to the cultural heritage of Latin America and the Caribbean. On S Street, the **Textile Museum** is a niche museum for those interested in the fabric arts. Next door, the **Woodrow Wilson House** shows the former president's home pretty much as he left it. On display are many gifts from foreign dignitaries.

Who said all the architecture here was restrained? The **Cameroon Embassy** on Massachusetts Avenue is housed in a fanciful castle with a conical tower, bronze weather vane, and intricate detailing around the windows and balconies. And on the other side of Sheridan Circle the **Bison Bridge** is guarded by four bronze statues of the shaggy mammals and decorated with busts of Native Americans.

East of Dupont Circle, **Scott Circle** is decorated with statues of General Winfield Scott, Daniel Webster, and S. C. F. Hahnemann. If you walk to the south side of the circle and look down 16th Street, you'll get a familiar view of the columns of the White House, six blocks away.

A few sights lie clustered on or near M Street south of Scott Circle, including two noteworthy religious institutions. The **Metropolitan African Methodist Episcopal Church** is one of the most influential African-American churches in the city. The Renaissance-style **St. Matthew's Cathedral** is the seat of Washington's Roman Catholic diocese, and the historic site of President Kennedy's funeral Mass.

Nearby, the **National Geographic Society** brings its magazines to life with interactive exhibits, photo galleries, and live shows. By appointment, you can tour the newsroom that broke the Watergate scandal at the

GETTING ORIENTED

QUICK BITES

At the independent bookstore and café **Kramerbooks & Afterwords** (✉ *1517 Connecticut Ave. NW* ☎ *202/387–1400*) you can relax over dinner or a drink after browsing.

For lunch or a light dinner (or just a cup of tea and an oatmeal cookie), visit **Teaism** (✉ *2009 R St. NW* ☎ *202/667–3827*). In addition to several dozen varieties of tea, there's a selection of seafood and vegetarian entrées, many available in bento boxes and seasoned with tea.

GREAT EXPERIENCES AROUND DUPONT CIRCLE

Anderson House: Glimpse into the life of a fabulously wealthy turn-of-the-19th-century U.S. diplomat, Larz Anderson, and his glamorous, art-loving wife Isabel at their magnificent mansion.

Dupont Circle: Grab a cup of coffee and a *CityPaper* and take in the scene—artists, alt-groovers, power-lunchers, chess players, Olympic-caliber bike messengers—around the always-buzzing fountain.

Gallery Hop: On the first Friday of every month, D.C.'s best art scene is on display when most of Dupont Circle's art spaces are open late, free, and often with complimentary drinks.

National Geographic Society: See *National Geographic* magazine come to life in rotating exhibits at the society's Explorers Hall.

Phillips Collection: Admire masterpieces such as Renoir's *Luncheon of the Boating Party* and Degas's *Dancers at the Barre* at the country's first museum of modern art.

CARDOZO/SHAW

S Street NW

R Street NW

Corcoran Street NW

National Museum of American
Jewish Military History

Q Street NW

Church Street NW

P Street NW

16th Street NW
15th Street NW
13th Street NW
Vermont Avenue NW

LOGAN
CIRCLE

Q Street NW

Rhode Island Avenue NW

Mary McLeod Bethune
Council House

O Street

N Street NW

Embassy
Australia

Embassy
of Tunisia

Massachusetts Avenue NW

SCOTT
CIRCLE

Charles E. Sumner
School Museum and
Archives

THOMAS
CIRCLE

Metropolitan African
Methodist Episcopal
Church

M Street NW

Washington
Post Building

0   500 ft

0   150 M

A GOOD WALK: KALORAMA

To see the embassies and luxurious homes that make up the
Kalorama neighborhood, begin
your walk at the corner of S and
23rd streets.

■Head north up 23rd, keeping an
eye out for the emergency call
boxes now turned into public art.

■At the corner of Kalorama Road
head west, but don't miss the
Tudor mansion at 2221 Kalorama
Road, now home to the French
ambassador.

■Turn right on Kalorama Circle,
where you can look down over
Rock Creek Park and into Adams-
Morgan. Kalorama means "beautiful view" in Greek, and this is the
sight that inspired the name.

■From here, you can retrace your
steps, or take Kalorama Circle
back to Kalorama Road, turn right
and make a left on Wyoming to
bring you back to 23rd.

PLANNING YOUR TIME

Visiting the Dupont Circle area takes at least half a day,
although you can find things to keep you busy all day. You'll
likely spend the most time at the Phillips Collection, Anderson House, and Woodrow Wilson House. The hours will also
fly if you linger over lunch or indulge in serious browsing
in area shops.

GETTING HERE

Dupont Circle has its own stop on the Metro's Red Line. Exit
on Q Street for the Phillips Collection, Anderson House, and
Kalorama attractions. Take the Connecticut Avenue exit for the
National Geographic Society, Christian Heurich House museum,
or shopping between Dupont Circle and Farragut North. On-
street parking is available on the residential streets away from
the circle, but gets harder to find on weekend evenings.

Dining in Dupont Circle

For reviews, see the Where to Eat chapter.

BUDGET DINING
Bistrot du Coin, *French, 1738 Connecticut Ave. NW*

Firefly, *American, Hotel Madera, 1310 New Hampshire Ave. NW*

Hank's Oyster Bar, *Seafood, 1624 Q St. NW*

Kramerbooks & Afterwords, *Café, 1517 Connecticut Ave. NW*

Malaysia Kopitiam, *Malaysian, 1827 M St. NW*

Nooshi, *Asian, 1120 19th St. NW*

Pizzeria Paradiso, *Italian, 2029 P St. NW*

Sala Thai, *Thai, 2016 P St. NW*

Skewers–Café Luna, *Middle Eastern, 1633 P St. NW*

MODERATE DINING
Nora, *Contemporary, 2132 Florida Ave. NW*

Palm, *Steak, 1225 19th St. NW*

Tabard Inn, *New American, Hotel Tabard Inn, 1739 N St. NW*

Vidalia, *Southern, 1990 M St. NW*

EXPENSIVE DINING
Komi, *Contemporary, 1509 17th St*

Obelisk, *Italian, 2029 P St. NW*

Sam and Harry's, *Steak, 1200 19th St. NW*

Washington Post Building. Farther east out Vermont Avenue, the **Mary McLeod Bethune Council House** features exhibits on the achievements of African-American women.

Two other small Dupont Circle museums may be worth a stop. The **Christian Heurich House Museum,** once known as the Brewmaster's Castle, was the home of a German-born beer magnate. The **National Museum of American Jewish Military History** displays weapons, uniforms, medals, recruitment posters, and other military memorabilia related to American Jews serving in the U.S. military.

2

ADAMS-MORGAN

Sightseeing
★☆☆☆☆

Dining
★★★★☆

Lodging
★★☆☆☆

Shopping
★★★★☆

Nightlife
★★★★☆

To the urban and hip, Adams-Morgan is a beacon of light in an otherwise stuffy landscape. D.C. may have a reputation for being staid and traditional, but drab suits, classical tastes, and bland food make no appearance here. This ethnically diverse neighborhood is a United Nations of cuisines, offbeat shops, and funky bars and clubs. It's also the city's Latin Quarter. The area wakes up as the sun goes down, and twentysomethings in their weekend best congregate along the sidewalks, crowding the doors of this week's hot bar or nightclub. Typical tourist attractions are sparse, but the scene on a Saturday night has its own appeal.

WHAT'S HERE?

The rough outlines of Adams-Morgan are Florida Avenue on the south, Connecticut Avenue on the west, and 16th Street NW on the east. The heart of the neighborhood lies at the intersection of Columbia Road and 18th Street, and the area's dining and nightlife scene spreads out along these roads for several blocks. Outside of this central area, Adams-Morgan starts to feel gritty, and most visitors never venture farther.

The neighborhood's restaurant corridor lies on 18th Street south of Columbia and the parts of Columbia and Calvert directly adjacent. The city's most diverse eats are served along these few blocks, a succession of Salvadoran pupusas (stuffed tortillas), Ethiopian injera (pancake-like sourdough bread), French ratatouille (savory vegetable stew), and West African moi moi (black-eyed pea cakes) unrivaled in the city.

GETTING ORIENTED

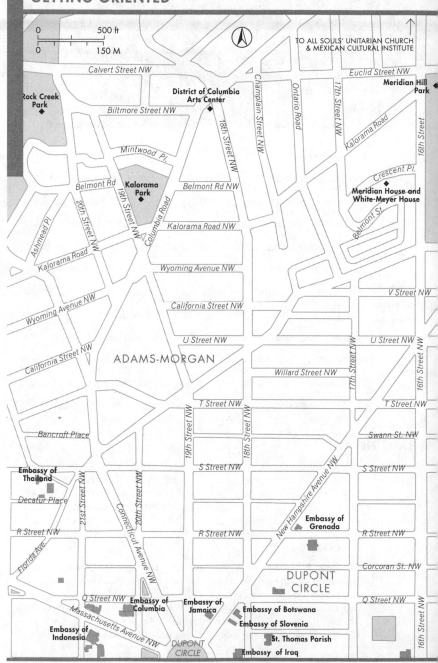

0 — 500 ft
0 — 150 M

TO ALL SOULS' UNITARIAN CHURCH
& MEXICAN CULTURAL INSTITUTE

Calvert Street NW

Euclid Street NW

District of Columbia Arts Center ◆

Meridian Hill Park

Rock Creek Park ◆

Biltmore Street NW

Champlain Street NW

Ontario Road

17th Street NW

Euclid Street NW

Kalorama Road

16th Street

Mintwood Pl.

18th Street NW

Crescent Pl.

Belmont Rd

Kalorama Park ◆

Belmont Rd NW

Meridian House and White-Meyer House ◆

Belmont St.

19th Street NW

Columbia Road

Kalorama Road NW

20th Street NW

Wyoming Avenue NW

V Street NW

Ashmead Pl

Kalorama Road

California Street NW

Wyoming Avenue NW

U Street NW

U Street NW

California Street NW

ADAMS-MORGAN

Willard Street NW

17th Street NW

16th Street NW

T Street NW

T Street NW

Bancroft Place

19th Street NW

18th Street NW

Swann St. NW

21st Street NW

S Street NW

S Street NW

Embassy of Thailand

Connecticut Avenue NW

20th Street NW

New Hampshire Avenue NW

Embassy of Grenada

Decatur Place

R Street NW

R Street NW

R Street NW

Florida Ave.

Corcoran St. NW

DUPONT CIRCLE

Q Street NW

Embassy of Columbia

Embassy of Jamaica

Embassy of Botswana

Q Street NW

16th Street NW

Massachusetts Avenue NW

Embassy of Slovenia

Embassy of Indonesia

DUPONT CIRCLE

St. Thomas Parish

Embassy of Iraq

2

GREAT EXPERIENCES IN ADAMS-MORGAN

Eat ethnic food: Adams-Morgan rivals U Street with its plentiful and delicious Ethiopian restaurants. If you'd rather dine using utensils, you can choose from Japanese, Brazilian, Mexican, Indian, and other ethnic cuisines.

Hang out like a local: The residents of Adams-Morgan make an art of relaxing. Follow their lead and settle into one of Tryst's overstuffed armchairs with a laptop or a copy of the *New Republic* and a coffee, or kill hours browsing the "rare and medium-rare" selections at Idle Time Books.

Stay out all night: If you want to party on until the break of dawn, this is the place to do it. Don't miss the live music at Madam's Organ, the salsa dancing at Habana Village, and the cool kids making the scene at the Leftbank.

GETTING HERE

Like Georgetown, Adams-Morgan has no Metro stop. It's a pleasant 15-minute walk from the Woodley Park/Zoo Metro station: walk south on Connecticut, then turn left on Calvert Street, and cross over Rock Creek Park on the Duke Ellington Bridge. Or you can get off at the Dupont Circle Metro stop and walk east to (and turn left onto) 18th Street.

The heart of Adams-Morgan is at the intersection of Adams Mill Road, Columbia Road, and 18th Street. Don't even dream about finding parking here on weekend evenings.

If you take the Metro, remember that stations close at 3 AM on Friday and Saturday nights and midnight other nights. If you're not ready to turn in by then, you'll need to hail a cab.

SAFETY

Part of Adams-Morgan's appeal is its real, rough-and-tumble ambience. Be aware of your surroundings, especially at night, if you venture past the well-trafficked blocks into less crowded locales.

PLANNING YOUR TIME

A window-shopping wander around Adams-Morgan can occupy the better part of an afternoon. And if you take advantage of the restaurants and nightlife here, there's no telling when your head will hit the pillow.

The few tourist attractions in this area aren't time-intensive, but they can be a long walk from restaurants.

QUICK BITES

Julia's Empanadas (✉ *2542 18th St. NW* ☎ *202 328 6232*) serves spicy Salvadoran snacks until 3 AM. The empanadas go well with tangy salads; all in portions you can comfortably eat standing up—a good thing, because this is mostly a to-go joint.

Everyone feels at home relaxing on the old couches and comfy chairs at **Tryst** (✉ *2459 18th St. NW* ☎ *202/232–5500*). Stop in for breakfast, sandwiches, or dessert, or sip hot chocolate or something stronger after hours.

Whether it's 1 PM or 1 AM, the **Amsterdam Falafelshop** (✉ *2425 18th St. NW* ☎ *202/234–1969*) is happy to feed you. The bargain-priced menu consists entirely of top-it-yourself falafels in pita, Dutch-style french fries, and brownies. It's open until 4 AM on weekends.

Dining in Adams-Morgan

AT A GLANCE

For reviews, see the Where to Eat chapter.

BUDGET DINING

Bardia's New Orleans Café, *Southern, 2412 18th St. NW*

Pasta Mia, *Italian, 1790 Columbia Rd. NW*

MODERATE DINING

Cashion's Eat Place, *American, 1819 Columbia Rd. NW*

La Fourchette, *French, 2429 18th St. NW*

Adams-Morgan's bar and club scene caters mostly to a young crowd in their twenties. The popular clubs often have lines out the door, and walking down 18th Street around midnight is a little like trying to drive on the Beltway at rush hour, but on your feet. If you're game for a drink, try the Leftbank for a trendy vibe amid retro furnishings or the Reef with its unpretentious atmosphere, colorful fish tanks, and large beer selection. The multistory Madam's Organ is a neighborhood institution with live music every night, and Habana Village is one of the best places in the city for salsa dancing and Latin music.

The shops on 18th Street feed an appetite for the offbeat. Here you can find collectibles such as Mission furniture, Russel Wright crockery and Fiesta ware, aerodynamic art deco armchairs, Bakelite telephones, massive chromium toasters, kidney-shaped coffee tables, skinny neckties, and oddball salt-and-pepper shakers. On the west side of 18th Street are antiques shops as well as secondhand shops set up in alleys or warehouses. Nearby is the **District of Columbia Arts Center,** a combination art gallery and performance space.

The stretch of Columbia Road between 16th and 18th is the area's Latin Quarter, as bilingual as it gets in Washington. At tables stretched along the street, vendors hawk watches, leather goods, knockoff perfumes, CDs, sneakers, clothes, and handmade jewelry. On Saturday morning a market springs up on the plaza at the southwest corner of 18th and Columbia, with stands selling fruits, vegetables, flowers, and fresh bread.

At the corner of 16th and Columbia, **All Souls' Unitarian Church** was a cornerstone of the civil rights movement and community activism during the 20th century. Heading south on 16th, the **Mexican Cultural Institute** promotes Mexican art, culture, and science. Farther down the street, the public can explore two mansions owned by the Meridian International Center, a nonprofit promoting international understanding. The **Meridian and White-Meyer Houses** hold periodic art exhibits with an international flavor.

2

U STREET CORRIDOR

Sightseeing
★☆☆☆☆

Dining
★★★★☆

Lodging
★☆☆☆☆

Shopping
★★★★☆

Nightlife
★★★★☆

Home-style Ethiopian food, offbeat boutiques, and live music are fueling the revival of the U Street area. Just a few years back this neighborhood was running on fumes, surviving on memories of its heyday of black culture and jazz music in the first half of the 20th century. Now the crowds are back, and this diverse neighborhood faces the threat of yuppification. A longtime center for African-American life in the District, U Street is now home to many of the city's East African immigrants, who've brought their culinary traditions to the neighborhood restaurants. Clubs have expanded beyond jazz to include all kinds of rock music, and new shops have popped up to bring in even more business.

WHAT'S HERE

U Street's past often speaks louder than its present. The neighborhood was especially vibrant from the 1920s to the 1950s, when it was home to jazz genius Duke Ellington, social activist Mary McLeod Bethune, and poets Langston Hughes and Georgia Douglas Johnson. The area's nightclubs hosted Louis Armstrong, Cab Calloway, and Sarah Vaughn. In the 1950s, Supreme Court Justice Thurgood Marshall, then still a lawyer, organized the landmark *Brown v. Board of Education* case at the 12th Street YMCA.

To find historic U Street, start at 10th and U streets at the **African-American Civil War Memorial,** honoring the black soldiers who fought in the Union Army. For more on that story, walk two blocks to the **African-American Civil War Museum,** which tells the tale of Africans in America from the slave trade through the Civil Rights movement with numer-

GETTING ORIENTED

W Street NW

V Street NW

New Hampshire Avenue NW

Vermont Avenue NW

Bohemian Caverns ♦

Lincoln Theater ♦

U Street NW

Ben's Chili Bowl ♦   African-American ♦ Civil War Museum

African-American ♦ Civil War Memorial

15th Street NW

14th Street NW

12th Street

11th Street NW

9th Street NW

16th Street NW

T Street NW

Thurgood Marshall Center

Swann Street NW

Westminster St. NW

CARDOZO
♦ Black Cat

S Street NW

13th Street NW

10th Street NW

9th Street NW

R Street NW

TO HOWARD → UNIVERSITY

Corcoran Street NW

Vermont Avenue NW

11th Street NW

Q Street NW

Church Street NW

Rhode Island Avenue NW

P Street NW

LOGAN CIRCLE

O Street NW

16th Street NW

LOGAN CIRCLE/SHAW

Rhode Island Avenue NW

14th Street NW

13th Street NW

P Street NW

O Street NW

Barrel House ♦

SCOTT CIRCLE

N Street NW

Massachusetts Avenue NW

Embassy of Tunisia

Vermont Avenue NW

THOMAS CIRCLE

16th Street NW

15th Street NW

M Street NW

Massachusetts Ave.

12th Street NW

11th Street NW

10th Street NW

9th Street NW

0		500 ft
0		150 M

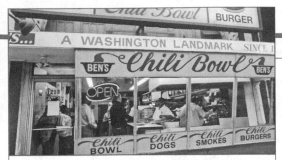

GREAT EXPERIENCES ON THE U STREET CORRIDOR

African-American Civil War Memorial and Museum:
Learn about the lives of slaves and freedmen, and discover
whether your ancestors fought in black regiments during
the Civil War.

Ben's Chili Bowl: If you can top it with chili, it's on the menu.
This D.C. institution has perfected its recipe over the last 50
years and satisfies meat-eaters and vegetarians alike.

Boutiques: Whether you're after funky footwear or flashy
housewares, hit the shops on U and 14th streets for trendy
finds.

Ethopian food: Nothing brings you closer to your meal than
eating with your hands. Use the spongy Injera bread to scoop
up delectable dishes from East Africa.

Jazz and live music: Music greats like Duke Ellington made
this neighborhood famous back in the 1920s. Relive the glory
years at a jazz performance at Bohemian Caverns or HR 57,
or rock out to today's music at the 9:30 Club or Black Cat.

GETTING HERE

The Green Line Metro stops at 13th and U, in the middle of
the main business district. To get to the African-American
Civil War Memorial, get out at the 10th Street exit. Parking
can be found on the residential streets north and south of U
Street, but as the area gets more popular, spots are getting
harder to find on weekend nights.

The area is within walking distance from Dupont Circle and
Adams-Morgan, but at night you're better off on the bus,
especially if you're alone. The 90, 92, and 98 buses travel
from Woodley Park through Adams-Morgan to 14th and U,
while the 52 and 54 buses travel north from several Downtown metro stops up 14th Street.

PLANNING YOUR TIME

You'll need half a day at most
to see U Street's attractions and
visit its boutiques. You can also
fill an evening with dinner on U
Street, a show at the 9:30 Club
or Bohemian Caverns, and drinks
afterward. If you're not driving,
allow plenty of time for public
transportation.

QUICK BITES

Ben's Chili Bowl (✉ *1213 U
St. NW* ☎ *202/667–0909*) has
been a U Street institution since
1958. It serves cheap and filling
chili (both meat and vegetarian)
any which way imaginable. The
quintessential meal here is the
chili half-smoke, a spicy grilled
hot dog covered with mustard,
onions, and, of course, chili.

For a more intellectual snack, stop
into **Busboys and Poets** (✉ *1390
V St. NW* ☎ *202/387–7638*). This
bookstore cum restaurant cum
coffee lounge serves up a com-
fort-food menu of sandwiches,
pizzas, and burgers. Events to
liven up your meal include literary
readings, open-mike nights, and
musical performances.

SAFETY

The commercial district here
borders a much less gentrified
area. The blocks between 10th
and 16th streets are well lighted
and busy, but the neighborhood
gets grittier to the north and east.
Use your street sense, especially
at night. It's wise to splurge on a
cab rather than waiting for a bus
late at night.

ous photos and documents. The museum is housed in the former **True Reformers Building,** now the Public Welfare Foundation. Back in the day, Duke Ellington and others performed in the upstairs ballroom. Don't miss the **Duke Ellington mural** on the western side of the building.

Once the hub of black cultural life with first-run movies and live performances, the **Lincoln Theater** now functions as a theater and event venue. The 12th Street YMCA has been made over to the **Thurgood Marshall Center,** which houses a museum on the history of African-Americans in the U Street/Shaw neighborhood. Duke Ellington fans can find his former homes at 1806 and 1813 13th Street.

Although the neighborhood was nearly destroyed in the rioting that followed the 1968 assassination of Martin Luther King Jr., U Street has recently reclaimed some of its former pulse. **Bohemian Caverns** combines an elegant restaurant with an underground music venue and upstairs club. It's been hosting jazz greats since 1926. On V Street, the **9:30 Club** attracts big-name rock bands and lesser-known indie artists alike to one of the East Coast's coolest concert halls. South on 14th Street, the **Black Cat** rocks out with independent and alternative bands from the city and around the world.

Known unofficially as D.C.'s Little Ethiopia, this is a great place to try East African cuisine. Standout restaurants such as **Etete** tempt diners with spongy injera bread and hearty meat and vegetarian dishes. Multiculti dining is in abundance here, but the city's humble roots are not yet forgotten; the granddaddy of Washington diners, **Ben's Chili Bowl,** has been serving chili, chili dogs, chili burgers, and half-smokes, spicy sausages served in a hot dog bun, since 1958.

U Street's shopping scene has garnered attention in recent years as well. Most of the boutiques are clustered on U Street between 14th and 16th streets and on 14th Street itself. Pop in and out of the little shops to find cutting-edge footwear, Asian furnishings, playful housewares, and eclectic or vintage clothing.

East of the commercial district, the historically Black Howard University has been educating African-American men and women since 1867. Notable graduates include authors Zora Neale Hurston and Toni Morrison, opera singer Jessye Norman, and Nobel Peace Prize–winner Ralph Bunche.

Dining in U Street Corridor

AT A GLANCE

2

*For reviews, see the
Where to Eat chapter.*

BUDGET DINING
Ben's Chili Bowl, *American, 1213 U St. NW*

Café Nema, *African,
1334 U St. NW*

Coppi's Organic Restaurant, *Italian, 1414 U
St. NW*

Etete, *African, 1942 9th
St. NW*

Oohhs & Aahhs, *Southern, 1005 U St. NW*

Polly's Café, *American,
1342 U St. NW*

MODERATE DINING
Marvin, *Belgian, 2007
14th St. NW*

UPPER NORTHWEST

Sightseeing
★★★★☆

Dining
★★☆☆☆

Lodging
★★★☆☆

Shopping
★★★★☆

Nightlife
★☆☆☆☆

The upper northwest corner of D.C. is predominantly residential and in many places practically suburban. However, there are several good reasons to visit the leafy streets, including the National Zoo and National Cathedral. If the weather is fine, spend an afternoon strolling through Hillwood Gardens or tromping through Rock Creek Park's many acres. You'll have to travel some distance to see multiple attractions in one day, but many sights are accessible on foot.

WHAT'S HERE

Upper Northwest isn't a neighborhood, rather a geographic grouping of several neighborhoods, including Cleveland Park, Woodley Park, Tenleytown, and Foxhall. The majority of attractions lie on or near Connecticut Avenue north of Woodley Park or on Massachusetts Avenue north of Georgetown. The Kreeger Museum is the exception, with its location in Foxhall, northwest of Georgetown.

The **National Zoo** is a reason in itself to head uptown. While recent attention has focused on giant pandas Tian Tian and Mei Xiang and their baby—now a toddler—Tai Shan, the Smithsonian's free zoological park is full of red pandas, clouded leopards, and Japanese giant salamanders, as well as the traditional lions, tigers, and bears. The zoo makes for a picturesque stroll on warm days, but be prepared for crowds on sunny weekends.

South of the zoo lies **Woodley Park,** a residential neighborhood filled with stately apartment buildings. The stretch of Connecticut Avenue between Calvert and Woodley Road is notable for its popular array of restaurants, such as Mr. Chen's Organic Chinese Cuisine and the Lebanese Taverna, and the **Wardman Tower,** a cross-shaped tower built in 1928 as a luxury apartment building. Once known for its famous residents, it's now part of the Marriott Wardman Park Hotel. **Woodley,** a Georgian mansion that served as the summer home of four presidents, lies on Cathedral Avenue between 29th and 31st streets.

North of the zoo, **Cleveland Park** is another residential address. Art deco enthusiasts should take note of the **Kennedy-Warren** apartment building at 3133 Connecticut and the **Cineplex Odeon Uptown,** a remodeled movie theater with an old-fashioned balcony. From the Uptown to the Cleveland Park Metro station, restaurants and bars line Connecticut Avenue. For a good walk, start at the Woodley Park Metro, head north up Connecticut stopping at the zoo, and continue to Cleveland Park for a bite to eat or a Metro ride home. You can also do the walk in reverse.

A long uphill walk from the Van Ness Red Line stop or an easy drive or cab ride away, the **Hillwood Estate, Museum and Gardens** displays cereal heiress Marjorie Merriweather Post's collection of 18th- and 19th-century French and Russian decorative art. The grounds and gardens equal the art collection in beauty and size.

Although the 1,800 acres of **Rock Creek Park** span much of Washington and into Maryland, two of the main driving entrances are in Upper Northwest. Take Tilden Road to get to the Peirce Mill and Military Road to reach the Nature Center and Planetarium. The park is accessible to pedestrians throughout the city. On sunny weekends bikers, walkers, horseback riders, tennis players, and picnickers make use of Rock Creek's trails and facilities.

Across town on Massachusetts Avenue, the **Islamic Mosque and Cultural Center,** with its 162-foot-high minaret, is the oldest Islamic house of worship in D.C. The **Khalil Gibran Memorial Garden** combines Western and Arab symbols in remembrance of the Lebanese-born poet.

Continuing north, the Greek Orthodox **St. Sophia Cathedral** is noted for the handsome mosaic work on the interior of its dome. Dominating the skyline, the **Washington National Cathedral** is the sixth-largest cathedral in the world. Its Gothic decor features fanciful gargoyles, including one shaped like Darth Vader. Come inside for a tour or tea in the Pilgrim Gallery.

Between all these houses of worship, the **U.S. Naval Observatory** makes a stand for science. The infrequent tours won't take you through the Vice President's house, but do show the master clock and refracting telescope. Also in this area, **Howard University Law School** is famed for its African-American graduates, such as Oliver Hill, Thurgood Marshall, and Charles Hamilton Houston.

When the weather is clear, two parks in this area are worth a visit. The 183-acre **Glover-Archbold Park** features a 3.5-mi nature trail. The highest point in the District, **Fort Reno Park** hosts free outdoor concerts in summer. View seekers, soccer players, and picnickers enjoy its facilities, as well.

GETTING ORIENTED

TO FRIENDSHIP
HEIGHTS
Garrison St. NW
42nd St. NW
Belt Rd. NW
39th St. NW
38th St. NW
Fessenden St. NW
Wisconsin Ave. NW
44th Pl. NW
43rd Pl. NW
Fort Reno
Park
Everett
St. NW
Ellicott St. NW
Linnean Ave. NW
Reno
Reservoir
River Rd. NW
45th St. NW
Davenport St. NW
Davenport St. NW
30th St.
Chesapeake St. NW
Brandywine St. NW
Murdock
Mill Rd. NW
emarle St. NW
Nebraska Ave. NW
Appleton St. NW
36th St. NW
Albemarle St. NW
Alton Pl. NW
Alton Pl. NW
Audubon Ter. NW
Soapstone Valley
Park
Yuma St. NW
43rd St. NW
Tenley
Circle
39th St. NW
Yuma St. NW
Windom Pl. NW
Reno Rd. NW
University
of the
District of Columbia
Howard
University Law
School
Warren St. NW
Van Ness St. NW
38th St. NW
37th St. NW
35th St. NW
Hillwood Estate,
Museum & Gardens
Nebraska Ave. NW
Van Ness St. NW
Upton St. NW
Tindall St.
Wisconsin Ave. NW
Tilden St. NW
Ward
Circle
Naval
Security
Station
Melvin Hazen
Park
Rodman St. NW
CLEVELAND
PARK
American
University
Glover-
Archbold
Park
Porter St. NW
Porter St.
Ordway St. NW
Idaho Ave. NW
38th St. NW
Newark St. NW
Cineplex Odeon
Uptown
TO
NATIONAL
ZOO
Newark St. NW
Macomb St. NW
Massachusetts Ave. NW
Macomb St. NW
Lowell St. NW
33rd St.
34th St.
Lowell St. NW
Klingle St. NW
Woodley Rd.
WOODLEY
PARK
Connecticut Ave.
Cathedral Ave. NW
Washington National
Cathedral
WESLEY HEIGHTS
Hawthorne St. NW
32nd St.
Cathedral Ave. NW
39th St. NW
St. Sophia
Cathedral
Garfield St. NW
Woodley
44th St. NW
Fulton St. NW
Wisconsin Ave. NW
36th Pl. NW
35th Pl. NW
34th St. NW
Cleveland Ave. NW
Woodland Dr.
29th St. NW
28th St. NW
27th St. NW
Foxhall Rd.
Glover-
Archbold
Park
41st St. NW
Davis Pl.
36th St. NW
Circle
◆ Kreeger Museum
Calvert St. NW
40th Pl. NW
40th St. NW
39th Pl. NW
39th St. NW
Observatory
U.S. Naval
Observatory
◆ Kahil Gibran
Memorial Garden
Massachusetts Ave. NW
0   400 yards
0   400 meters
Dumbarton
Oaks Park
Rock Creek
Islamic Mosque
and Cultural Center

GREAT EXPERIENCES IN UPPER NORTHWEST

House museums: The Hillwood Estate, Museum and Gardens showcases cereal heiress Marjorie Merriweather Post's collection of Imperial Russian art and Fabergé eggs, and 12 gorgeous acres of formal French and Japanese gardens. Chagalls, Picassos, and Monets inside contrast with the architecture at the modernist Kreeger Museum.

National Zoo: Visit the giant pandas, elephants, lions, and other members of the animal kingdom while you enjoy a stroll outdoors.

Shopping in Friendship Heights: The city's most glamorous shopping lines Wisconsin Avenue at the Maryland border. Want to actually buy something? Plenty of stores cater to shoppers on a budget, too.

U.S. Naval Observatory: View the heavens through one of the world's most powerful telescopes.

Washington National Cathedral: Look for the Darth Vader gargoyle on the soaring towers of this cathedral, then relax among the rose bushes in the Bishop's Garden.

GETTING HERE

Connecticut Avenue attractions, such as the Zoo, are accessible from the Red Line Metro stops between Woodley Park/Zoo and Van Ness. The Friendship Heights Bus travels north from Georgetown along Wisconsin Avenue and takes you to the National Cathedral.

Parking can be tricky along Massachusetts Avenue; to see these sights, it's often more practical for good walkers to hoof it up the street or take the N2, N4, or N6 bus between Dupont Circle and Friendship Heights. For more outlying sights, driving or cabbing it may be the best way to visit.

PLANNING YOUR TIME

The amount of time you spend at the Zoo is up to you; animal enthusiasts could easily spend a full day here. You may want to plan your trip around daily programs, such as the elephant-training session or the eagle feeding.

For other itineraries, be sure to leave room in your schedule for travel between sights and, if you have a car, for parking. To maximize your time, call ahead to inquire whether on-site parking is available and when the next tour will begin.

QUICK BITES

The blocks immediately surrounding the Woodley Park and Cleveland Park Metro stations are chockablock with restaurants. If you've got the time, skip lunch at the Zoo's eateries and head north or south on Connecticut to find a wealth of dining options, then head back.

FINDING A RESTROOM AT THE ZOO

At the National Zoo, unlike most everywhere else in D.C., public restrooms can be found in four convenient locations: in the Panda Plaza, next to the Zoo Police Station, inside the visitor center, and inside Amazonia.

2

AT A GLANCE

Dining in Upper Northwest

For reviews, see the
Where to Eat chapter.

BUDGET DINING

Ardeo, *New American,*
3311 Connecticut Ave.
NW

Bistrot Lepic, *French,*
1736 Wisconsin Ave. NW

Heritage India, *Indian,*
2400 Wisconsin Ave. NW

Lebanese Taverna,
Middle Eastern, 2641
Connecticut Ave. NW

2 Amys, *Pizza, 3715*
Macomb St. NW

MODERATE DINING

New Heights, *New*
American, 2317 Calvert
St. NW

Palena, *New American,*
3529 Connecticut Ave.
NW

Tucked away in the Foxhall neighborhood to the west, the **Kreeger Museum** showcases the small but impressive collections of paintings, sculpture, and African art collected by wealthy businessman David Kreeger. Tour the hall where he entertained famous musicians and the dining room decorated entirely with Monets.

At the Maryland border, the intersection of Wisconsin Avenue and Western Avenue forms **Friendship Heights.** This shopping-mall district is particularly friendly to well-heeled shoppers, as it's the place to pick up the latest finds at Tiffany, Louis Vuitton, and Neiman Marcus. Filene's Basement and Loehmann's provide designer deals.

Museums

Tourists visiting inside the National Gallery of Art, East Building

WORD OF MOUTH

"Holocaust Museum—for a small fee I ordered tickets online and that was a big help. Heavy duty security check. . . . WOW this museum is hard to put into words but don't miss it—very powerful. Lots of reading, but also many artifacts, videos, recordings, etc. DH and I were moved to tears as were many other visitors. We spent about 3 hours here and probably could have spent more."

—BBEAR

MUSEUMS PLANNER

Special Events

The Smithsonian museums regularly host an incredible spectrum of special events, from evenings of jazz to DJ'd dance nights to food and wine tastings, films, lectures, and events for families and kids. A full schedule is available at ⊕ *www.si.edu/ events/evening.asp.* Among the most popular events are live jazz on Friday evenings in summer at the National Gallery of Art sculpture garden and in winter in the National Museum of Natural History. Both include a cash bar. Every three months the Hirshhorn Museum throws a wildly popular after-hours party with DJs, sound-and-light art installations, a cash bar, and a dance floor.

On Thursday the Phillips Collection stays open late for live jazz, gallery talks, and a cash bar. From September to May there's a Sunday afternoon concert series at 4 PM.

Late Hours

Corcoran Gallery of Art, Thursday until 9 PM.

Phillips Collection, Thursday until 8:30 PM.

International Spy Museum, April–October, daily until 8 PM.

The Smithsonian

Most of the 18 Smithsonian Institution museums are open between 10 and 5:30 over 360 days a year, and all are free (though there may be charges for some special exhibits). To get oriented, start with a visit to the Smithsonian Institution building—aka "The Castle" for its swooping towers-and-turrets architecture—which has information on all the museums.

With Kids

They'll need to meet a giant T-rex, see live tarantulas, and take in an IMAX movie at the Museum of Natural History. They can see history's most famous spaceships and fighter planes at the National Air and Space Museum's Steven F. Udvar-Hazy Center. At the Corcoran Gallery of Art, exhibitions are set up with an interactive "Exploration Gallery" for younger visitors and "conversation starter" brochures for parents. The Freer Gallery of Art and Hirshhorn Museum offer free art workshops for kids. The National Building Museum has interactive exhibits and workshops, and at the DAR Museum kids can play games and try on costumes from the time of the American Revolution.

Best Gift Shops

National Gallery of Art. Here you can find one of the country's largest selections of books on art and art history, along with beautiful posters, prints, reproductions, stationery, and gifts.

National Building Museum. With shelves filled with Philippe Starck–designed kitchenware, jewelry made out of nails and cement, and slickly photographed tomes on architecture, design lovers and modernists will be in heaven here.

National Air and Space Museum. The three-story museum store is the largest of all the Smithsonian musuem stores, and is packed with books, toys, and kits on space and aviation.

3

By Coral
Davenport

The internationally renowned collections of the Smithsonian—137 million objects, specimens, and artworks displayed in the world's largest museum complex—make Washington one of the great museum cities. The holdings of the 18 Smithsonian museums span the depth and breadth of history, art, and science, ranging from a 65-million-year-old Tyrannosaurus Rex skeleton to masterpieces by DaVinci and Picasso, the Hope Diamond, the original Star-Spangled Banner, and the space shuttle *Enterprise*—and all are on view for free. The city also has plenty of fascinating specialty museums, like the high-tech International Spy Museum, the design-centric National Building Museum, and the media-saturated Newseum.

JUST THE HIGHLIGHTS, PLEASE

Nowhere else can you see the Declaration of Independence and the Constitution, both displayed at the National Archives. Touch a moon rock beneath the *Spirit of St. Louis* at the National Air and Space Museum. The masterpieces of Monet and Matisse at the National Gallery of Art are must-sees, as are Thomas Jefferson's desk and Dorothy's ruby slippers at the newly renovated National Museum of American History.

For modern art, it's tough to beat the constantly changing Hirshhorn Museum, where an Alexander Calder mobile might hover over a multimedia installation by today's hottest talent. For intimately grouped masterpieces in a mansion, head to the Phillips Collection. Lovers of architecture and design shouldn't miss a pilgrimage to the National Building Museum.

CORCORAN GALLERY OF ART

✉ 500 17th St. NW, White House area

☎ 202/639–1700

🌐 www.corcoran.org

🎫 $6; admission for special exhibitions, around $12

🕐 Sun., Mon., and Wed. 10–5, Thurs. 10–9, Fri. and Sat. 10–5.

Ⓜ Farragut W or Farragut N

TIPS

■ There's free live jazz every first and third Wednesday of the month, 12:30–1:30. The museum hosts concerts most Friday nights, and frequent lectures and special events too.

■ There are free docent-led tours Wednesday through Saturday at noon, 7:30 Thursday evenings, and 2:30 on weekends.

■ Purchase advance tickets for special exhibitions, as they tend to be popular.

■ If you're visiting with children, pick up the "Conversation Starters" pamphlets at the entrance.

■ Kids may also enjoy the Exploration Galleries—a room of hands-on, educational activities created to accompany different exhibitions.

■ The museum's café, set in the marble-columned atrium, is a great place for a sophisticated lunch, brunch, or drinks.

The Corcoran looks like a museum and acts like a gallery, blending classic elegance and experimental edge. Washington's first art museum is housed in a Beaux-Arts marble mansion, and home to an important collection of 18th-, 19th-, and 20th-century European and American art. As the parent of the Corcoran School of Art, the museum is also devoted to showcasing cutting-edge contemporary art, from established superstars to undiscovered talents.

HIGHLIGHTS

A prize collection of masterworks by the great early American artists, including John Copley, Gilbert Stuart, Rembrandt Peale, Mary Cassatt, and John Singer Sargent, is in constant rotation, but you're always guaranteed to see a selection of the most important pieces, displayed in gilded frames in high-ceilinged marble rooms

You're also sure to see something contemporary and fun: mixed-media, sound, and video art transforming a room, or even live performance art.

Photography is one of the museum's great strengths: recent exhibits of works by Ansel Adams, Annie Leibovitz, and Richard Avedon drew sold-out crowds.

The exhibition space Gallery 31 shows work by students, faculty, and alumni of the highly reputed Corcoran School of Art.

FREER GALLERY OF ART

✉ 12th St. and Jefferson Dr. SW, The Mall

☎ 202/633–1000, 202/357–1729 TDD

🌐 www.asia.si.edu

🎫 Free

🕙 Daily 10–5:30

Ⓜ Smithsonian

3

TIPS

■ A lower-level exhibition gallery connects the building to the Arthur M. Sackler Gallery.

■ The Freer and Sackler galleries are home to the largest Asian art research library in the U.S., open to the public five days a week without appointment.

■ Free highlight tours meet at 12:15 every day, except Wednesday and Federal holidays, at the information desks.

■ The museum regularly hosts films, concerts, readings and other events; check the Web site to see what's on.

■ Take advantage of the Freer's wide menu of excellent brochures on everything from Islamic art and Japanese painting to South Asian sculpture and Near Eastern ceramics.

■ At the Imaginasia workshops, held most weekends at the adjacent Arthur M. Sackler Gallery, children ages 6 to 14 work on projects such as origami and Asian board games.

Home to one of the world's finest collections of Asian art, the Smithsonian's Freer Gallery of Art was made possible by an endowment from Detroit industrialist Charles Lang Freer, who retired in 1900 and devoted the rest of his life to collecting art. Opened in 1923, the collection includes more than 27,000 works of art from the Far and Near East. The Japanese screens, Chinese porcelains, Korean stoneware, Islamic manuscripts, Indian sculptures, and other items date from Neolithic times to the 20th century.

HIGHLIGHTS

Pick a china pattern, or a favorite jade carving, or a painted silk scroll, from the rich collections of exquisite Imperial Chinese luxury decorative arts.

Behold the bodhisattva: A 12th-century Japanese sculpture of a Buddhist approaching Nirvana, seated on a giant lotus-blossom throne, is among the many masterpieces of Buddhist art.

Ogle the undulating curves of the 10th-century Indian and Himalayan sculptures, especially the bronze of the dancing god Shiva and his voluptuous, bare-breasted wife, the goddess Parvati.

Don't miss the Americans! Freer was introduced to Asian art by his friend James McNeill Whistler, and the museum is home to the world's largest collection of paintings by the famed American artist. Be sure not to bypass the Peacock Room, a jewel box of a space that Whistler designed for a British shipping magnate, with gold peacock murals on deep peacock-blue walls, and a lush peacock-feather pattern on the gold leaf ceiling. Freer paid $30,000 for the entire room and moved it from London to the United States in 1904.

HIRSHHORN MUSEUM AND SCULPTURE GARDEN

✉ Independence Ave. and 7th St. SW, , The Mall

☎ 202/633–1000, 202/633–8043 TDD

🌐 www.hirshhorn.si.edu

💳 Free

🕙 Museum daily 10–5:30, sculpture garden 7:30–dusk

Ⓜ Smithsonian or L'Enfant Plaza (Maryland Ave. exit)

TIPS

■ The sculpture garden makes an inspiring spot for a picnic.

■ Free docent-led tours run daily at noon, weekdays at 3, and weekends at 2. In summer, sculpture garden tours head out Monday to Saturday at 10:30 AM.

■ There are free activities and projects for children ages 5 to 11 and their parents at the museum's drop-in Improv Art Room on the lower level.

■ Check out Hirshhorn After Hours—late-night events centered around exhibitions.

■ The museum screens weekly free films, focusing on independent, experimental cinema, documentaries, and films by and about artists.

■ Exhibitions change regularly. If you're looking for a specific work or artist, browse the museum Web site's "Collection Search" feature.

Sculpture on the National Mall runs mostly to marble columns and dead presidents, but in 2003 the Hirshhorn made a bold addition: a 32-foot-tall yellow cartoon brush-stroke sculpture by pop-art iconographer Roy Lichtenstein. It became a beloved local landmark, and an apt symbol of the Hirshhorn itself. Conceived as the nation's museum of modern and contemporary art, the Hirshhorn is home to more than 11,500 works by masters like Pablo Picasso, Joan Miró, Piet Mondrian, Willem de Kooning, and Andy Warhol. These are displayed in a round 1974 poured-concrete building designed by Gordon Bunshaft. Dubbed the "Doughnut on the Mall" when it was built, it's now seen as a fitting home for contemporary art. Most of the collection was bequeathed by the museum's founder, Joseph H. Hirshhorn, a Latvian immigrant who made his fortune in uranium mines.

HIGHLIGHTS

The internationally renowned sculpture collection has masterpieces by Henry Moore, Alberto Giacometti, and Constantin Brancusi. Outside, sculptures dot a grass-and-granite garden, which, in addition to the Lichtenstein, boasts Henri Matisse's *Backs I–IV* and Auguste Rodin's *Burghers of Calais.*

Don't miss the giant Alexander Calder mobiles.

The collection is constantly updated with the best of contemporary art, which often includes fun, interactive installations, such as Danish artist Olafur Eliasson's *Round Rainbow,* a room in which a rotating prism transforms a beam of light into undulating colors bathing visitors' faces.

Video and multimedia installations are viewed in the Black Box Theater.

INTERNATIONAL SPY MUSEUM

✉ 800 F St. NW, East End

☎ 202/393–7798

🌐 www.spymuseum.org

🎫 Permanent exhibition only, $18; children, $15; Operation Spy only, $14; combination admission, $25

🕙 Apr.–Oct., daily 9–8; Nov.–Mar., daily 10–6; hrs subject to change; check Web site before visiting

Ⓜ Gallery Pl./Chinatown

TIPS

■ Advance tickets (purchased at the museum or on its Web site) are highly recommended. All tickets are date and time specific. Tickets are most likely available (and your visit less crowded) on Tuesday, Wednesday, and Thursday, or daily after 2 PM.

■ This is a great museum for kids age 12 and up; younger ones might not get it.

■ At the popular monthly KidSpy workshops for kids ages 10–14, participants can assume a cover identity and disguise, make a portable lie detector, crack a cipher, check out surveillance electronics, and more.

■ The museum regularly hosts films, events, and lectures by espionage experts, and more elaborate programs like a "Spy Scavenger Hunt" and a "Spy City Tour" of Washington.

■ A large gift shop, a café, and the restaurant Zola are here as well.

It's believed that there are more spies in Washington than in any other city in the world, making it a fitting home for this museum, which displays the world's largest collection of spy artifacts. Museum advisors include top cryptologists, masters of disguise, and former CIA, FBI, and KGB operatives. Exhibits range from the coded letters of Revolutionary War über-spy Benedict Arnold to the KGB's lipstick pistol, to high-tech 21st-century espionage toys, showcased with theatrical panache in a five-building complex (one, the Warder-Atlas Building, held Washington's Communist party in the 1940s).

HIGHLIGHTS

"Operation Spy," a one-hour "immersive experience" works like a live-action game, dropping you in the middle of a high-stakes foreign intelligence mission. Each step of the operation—which includes decrypting secret audio files, a car chase, and interrogating a suspect agent—is taken from actual intelligence operations.

"The Secret History of History" exhibit takes you through the espionage behind the headlines, from Moses' use of spies in Canaan to Abraham Lincoln's employment of the Pinkerton National Detective Agency as a full-scale secret service in the Civil War, to the birth of Lenin's state-run espionage ring—later known as the KGB.

There's a heavy mix of flash and fun, with toys used by actual operatives as well as James Bond's Aston Martin and tales of celebrity spies like singer Josephine Baker, chef Julia Child, and actress Marlene Dietrich.

The story of Cold War espionage is displayed in a maze of mirrors, a flashy but apt visual metaphor for the deadly game of spying and counter-spying that gripped the U.S. and Soviet Union.

3

NATIONAL AIR AND SPACE MUSEUM

✉ Independence Ave. and 6th St. SW, The Mall

☎ 202/357–1729, 202/357–1686 movie information, 202/357–1729 TDD

⊕ www.nasm.si.edu

🎫 Free, IMAX $10, planetarium $8.50

🕑 Daily 10–5:30

Ⓜ Smithsonian

TIPS

■ Buy IMAX theater and planetarium tickets up to two weeks in advance or as soon as you arrive (times and prices vary); then tour the museum.

■ Free docent-led tours leave daily at 11 and 1 from the museum's Welcome Center.

■ The three-story museum store is the largest in all the Smithsonian museums, and one of the best. Along with souvenirs, books, and collectors' items, it also displays a model of the USS *Enterprise*, used in the filming of the first "Star Trek" television series.

■ A huge food court offers fast food, from pizza to McDonald's.

This is the world's most-visited museum, attracting 9 million people annually to the world's largest collection of historic aircraft and spacecraft. Its 23 galleries tell the story of aviation from the earliest human attempts at flight to supersonic jets and spacecraft.

HIGHLIGHTS

Look up to see the world's most famous aircraft: Hovering above are the *Wright 1903 Flyer,* which Wilbur Wright piloted over the sands of Kitty Hawk, North Carolina; Charles Lindbergh's *Spirit of St. Louis*; the X-1 rocket plane in which Chuck Yeager broke the sound barrier; an X-15, the first aircraft to exceed Mach 6; and the Lockheed Vega that Amelia Earhart piloted in 1932: it was the first solo transatlantic flight by a woman.

You can touch the displayed 4-billion-year-old slice of moon rock collected by *Apollo 17* astronauts.

Strap into a flight simulator, walk through a model of the Skylab orbital workshop, and learn about the history of flight and the scientific study of the universe from the permanent exhibits.

Immerse yourself in space by taking in an IMAX film or a planetarium presentation. The movies—some in 3D—employ swooping aerial scenes that make you feel as if you've left the ground and fascinating high-definition footage taken in deep space.

For more giant jets and spaceships, visit the **National Air and Space Museum Steven F. Udvar-Hazy Center,** at Washington Dulles International Airport in northern Virginia. A shuttle bus runs from the museum entrance on the Mall to the outdoor center.

NATIONAL ARCHIVES

3

✉ Constitution Ave. between 7th and 9th Sts. NW, The Mall

☎ 202/501–5000, 202/501–5205 tours

🌐 www.nara.gov

🎟 Free

🕐 Mar. 15–Labor Day, daily 10 -7; Labor Day–Mar. 14, daily 10–5:30; tours weekdays at 10:15 and 1:15

Ⓜ Archives/Navy Memorial

TIPS

■ The Archives are a research resource open to anyone. Family genealogists can find birth, death, military, and census records, immigrant ships' passenger lists, letters, and maps since the beginning of the nation's history. Assistants in the Archives can help you track down ancestors' records, or anything else you might be looking for.

■ Reservations to visit the Archives are recommended: without one, you could wait up to an hour to get in. Reservations for guided tours, or for a self-guided visit, must be made at least six weeks in advance.

■ Expect to spend about 90 minutes here, viewing the charter documents and touring the permanent exhibit.

■ Before your tour, check out the informative introductory film in the McGowan Theater.

■ The Archives regularly host films and lectures; check the Web site to see what's on.

The National Archives are at once monument, museum, and the nation's memory. Headquartered in a grand marble edifice on Constitution Avenue, the National Archives and Records Administration is charged with preserving and archiving the most historically important U.S. government records. Its 8 billion paper records and 4 billion electronic records date back to 1775.

HIGHLIGHTS

The star attractions, which draw millions of reverential viewers every year, are the Declaration of Independence, Constitution, and Bill of Rights. These are housed in the Archives' cathedral-like rotunda, each on a marble platform, encased in bulletproof glass, and floating in pressurized helium, which protects the irreplaceable documents. To the right of the rotunda, displayed with great majesty, is the 1297 Magna Carta, the document of English common law whose language inspired the Constitution: it's one of four remaining originals.

The permanent exhibit showcases the breadth of the Archives' holdings. You can find anything from the Emancipation Proclamation to the first issue of *Mad* magazine (used as evidence in Congressional hearings on juvenile delinquency), or the rifle believed to have assassinated John F. Kennedy.

Watch films of flying saucers, used as evidence in Congressional UFO hearings, listen to the Nuremberg trials, or Congress debating Prohibition—selections from the Archives 500,000 film and audio recordings.

Many exhibits are interactive and kid-friendly. One room of letters from children to U.S. presidents includes a letter from seventh-grader Andy Smith, asking Ronald Regan for Federal funds to clean up a disaster area—his room.

NATIONAL GALLERY OF ART, WEST BUILDING

✉ 4th St. and Constitution Ave. NW, The Mall

☎ 202/737–4215, 202/842–6176 TDD

🌐 www.nga.gov

🎟 Free

🕐 Mon.–Sat. 10–5, Sun. 11–6

Ⓜ Archives/Navy Memorial

TIPS

■ There are many free docent-led tours every day and a recorded tour of highlights is available for a $5 rental fee on the main floor adjacent to the rotunda. For a cheat-sheet tour, pick up the laminated "What to See in One Hour" (the same guide is available for the East Building collections and on the Web); it pinpoints 12 must-see masterworks.

■ The Micro Gallery near the rotunda maintains computerized information on more than 1,700 works of art from the permanent collection. Touch-screen monitors provide access to color images, text, animation, and sounds to help you better understand—and appreciate—the works on display.

■ The Gallery has a full calendar of concerts, films, lectures, and other events, many free to the public. Among the most popular is the free "Jazz in the Garden" series, held Friday evenings in the sculpture garden throughout the summer.

■ Check out the outstanding museum store's books on art and art history.

The two buildings of the National Gallery hold one of the world's foremost collections of paintings, sculptures, and graphics, from the 13th to the 21st centuries. If you want to view the museum's holdings in (more or less) chronological order, it's best to start your exploration in the West Building. Opened in 1941, the domed West Building was a gift to the nation from industrialist and Treasury Secretary Andrew Mellon. The rotunda, with 24 marble columns surrounding a fountain topped with a statue of Mercury, sets the stage for the masterpieces on display in more than 100 galleries.

HIGHLIGHTS

The only painting by Leonardo da Vinci on display in the western hemisphere, Ginevra *de'Benci* is the centerpiece of the collection's comprehensive survey of Italian Renaissance paintings and sculpture; it also includes Raphael's *Alba Madonna* and Sandro Botticelli's *Adoration of the Magi*.

The masters of painting light, Rembrandt van Rijn and Johannes Vermeer, anchor the magnificent collection of Dutch and Flemish works.

The gallery of gorgeous French Impressionist masterworks by such superstars as Claude Monet, Auguste Renoir, and Edgar Degas, is unmissable.

Walk beneath flowering trees in the sculpture garden, on the Mall between 7th and 9th streets. Granite walkways take you through a shaded landscape and sculptures from the museum's permanent collection, including Roy Lichtenstein's playful *House I*; Miró's *Personnage Gothique, Oiseau-Eclair*; and Isamu Noguchi's *Great Rock of Inner Seeking*. The huge central fountain becomes a skating rink in winter.

NATIONAL GALLERY OF ART, EAST BUILDING

✉ Constitution Ave. between 3rd and 4th Sts. NW, The Mall

☎ 202/737–4215, 202/842–6176 TDD

🌐 www.nga.gov

🎟 Free

🕐 Mon.–Sat. 10–5, Sun. 11–6

Ⓜ Archives/Navy Memorial

3

TIPS

■ To reach the East Building from the West Building, you can take the underground concourse, lined with gift shops, a café, and a cafeteria, but to best appreciate the building's sleek and celebrated angular architecture, enter from outside rather than underground: exit the West Building through its eastern doors, and cross 4th Street.

■ To protect the pigments and paper of the Matisse cutouts, the works are on view only between 10 and 2 Monday through Saturday, and 11 to 3 on Sunday.

■ Free docent-led tours leave from the information desk weekdays at 11:30 and 1:30, and weekends at 11:30 and 3:30.

■ Pick up the cheat sheet "What to See in An Hour": it pinpoints 15 highlights of the East Building.

The East Building opened in 1978 in response to the changing needs of the National Gallery, especially its growing collection of modern art. The trapezoidal shape of the site prompted architect I.M. Pei's dramatic approach: two interlocking spaces shaped like triangles provide room for galleries, auditoriums, and administrative offices. Despite its severe angularity, Pei's building is inviting. The ax-blade-like southwest corner has been darkened and polished smooth by thousands of hands irresistibly drawn to it. Inside, the sunlit atrium is dominated by a colorful 76-foot long Alexander Calder mobile, the perfect introduction to galleries filled with masterworks of modern and contemporary art.

HIGHLIGHTS

Masterpieces from every famous name in 20th-century art—Pablo Picasso, Jackson Pollock, Piet Mondrian, Roy Lichtenstein, Joan Miró, Georgia O'Keeffe, and dozens of others—fill the galleries.

The bold shapes and brilliant teals and fuschias of Henri Matisse's giant paper cutouts make them among the most innovative, important, and purely enjoyable works of modern art. The National Gallery's collection of these is considered the world's greatest; entering the "Matisse Room" full of colorful floor-to-ceiling works is a delight.

Huge, color-drenched Mark Rothko works are a perennial favorite—the gallery owns over 1,000 paintings by the iconic American modernist.

World-class temporary exhibitions are a big draw. Recent years have seen the collected works of Paul Cézanne, Edward Hopper, Cy Twombly, Jasper Johns, Pablo Picasso, Willem de Kooning, and Henri de Toulouse-Lautrec.

NATIONAL MUSEUM OF AMERICAN HISTORY

- ✉ Constitution Ave. and 14th St. NW, The Mall
- ☎ 202/633–1000, 202/633–5285 TDD
- 🌐 www.americanhistory.si.edu
- 🎫 Free
- 🕐 Daily 10–5:30
- Ⓜ Smithsonian or Federal Triangle

TIPS

■ Renovations are frequently subject to delay. Check the Web site to confirm that the museum has reopened.

■ A cafeteria is planned for the museum's lower level.

■ This is the only museum in the world with an active program of using its historic musical instruments (which range from an 18th-century Stradivarius cello to a 19th-century Steinway grand piano) for live performances. The Smithsonian Chamber Music Society holds regular concerts using the instruments, with compositions that accurately represent the music they once would have played.

■ For a more interactive visit, check out the "Hands on Science" center, where visitors of all ages can use lasers to learn about light spectrums, create chemical reactions, and even sequence DNA strands in the laboratory.

The 3 million artifacts in the country's largest history museum explore America's cultural, political, technical, and scientific past, with holdings as diverse and iconic as the desk on which Thomas Jefferson wrote the Declaration of Independence, the top hat Abraham Lincoln was wearing the night he was assassinated, and Judy Garland's ruby slippers from *The Wizard of Oz.* At this writing, the museum was scheduled to reopen in fall 2008 after a two-year $85 million architectural renovation, aimed in part at reconfiguring the museum's infamously labyrinthine layout.

HIGHLIGHTS

The original Star-Spangled Banner that flew over Fort McHenry in 1814 and inspired Francis Scott Key to write the national anthem is the centerpiece of the museum's vast collections. The 2008 re-opening will unveil a new gallery showcasing the banner, with accompanying displays on its history and significance.

Horatio Greenough's statue of the first president was commissioned by Congress in 1832 and intended to grace the Capitol Rotunda. It was there for only a short while, however, because the toga-clad likeness proved distasteful to some legislators, who grumbled that it looked as if the father of our country had just emerged from a bath.

Iconic objects of entertainment housed here go beyond Dorothy's slippers: you can see everything from Dizzy Gillespie's trumpet to the Bunkers' living-room furniture from *All in the Family,* to Julia Child's kitchen.

Explore the intersection of science and society with the "Science in American Life" exhibit, ranging from Thomas Edison's first light bulbs to the development of the atomic bomb.

NATIONAL MUSEUM OF THE AMERICAN INDIAN

✉ 4th St. and Independence Ave. SW

☎ 202/633-1000

🌐 www.americanindian.si.edu

🎫 Free

🕐 Daily 10–5:30

Ⓜ L'Enfant Plaza

3

TIPS

■ Visit between 10 and 2 on a sunny day to see the central atrium awash in rainbows created by light refracted through prisms in the ceiling aligned with the earth's cardinal points.

■ The Mitsitam Native Foods Café serves a Native American–inspired menu, ranging from pulled buffalo sandwiches and black beans to maple-roasted turkey.

■ Free timed-entrance passes, required for entry, are distributed beginning at 10 AM from the museum's east entrance, but by midday, especially during winter months, you may find that you don't actually need one. You can also buy the passes in advance online.

■ Free tours leave from the entrance atrium weekdays at 1:30 and 3. On weekends and in summer there are also tours at 11, except on Monday.

■ The Chesapeake Museum Store is the place to buy hand-crafted jewelry, textiles, and one-of-a-kind works by Native American artisans.

The Smithsonian's newest museum stands apart visually and conceptually from the other cultural institutions on the Mall. Opened in 2004, it is the first national museum devoted to Native American artifacts, presented from a Native American perspective. The undulating exterior, clad in pinkish-gold limestone from Minnesota, evokes natural rock formations shaped by wind and water. Inside, four floors of galleries cover 10,000 years of history of the thousands of native tribes of the western hemisphere. However, only five percent of the museum's holdings are on display at any one time, and they are arranged to showcase specific tribes and themes, rather than a chronological history. Some visitors find this approach confusing, but touring with one of the Native guides can help bring the history and legends to life.

HIGHLIGHTS

Live music, dance, theater, and storytelling are central to experiencing this museum. Tribal groups stage performances in the two theaters and sunlit ceremonial atrium.

The "Our Universe" exhibit tells the unique creation legends of eight different tribes, with carvings, costumes, and videos of tribal storytellers. The stories rotate to give exposure to the different tribes of the Americas.

Central to the Native story is the transformation that convulsed the tribes of America in 1492, the year of first contact with Europeans. The exhibits focusing on the Native world before and after "first contact" are among the most compelling.

The museum's signature film, *A Thousand Roads*, about four contemporary Native people is shown daily.

NATIONAL MUSEUM OF NATURAL HISTORY

✉ Constitution Ave. and 10th
St. NW, The Mall

☎ 202/633–1000, 202/357–
1729 TDD

⊕ www.mnh.si.edu

🎟 Free, IMAX $8.50, Butterfly
Pavilion $6, but free on
Tuesdays

🕐 Museum daily 10–5:30;
Discovery Room Tues.–Fri.
noon–2:30, weekends
10:30–3:30; free passes
for Discovery Room near
Discovery Room door

Ⓜ Smithsonian or Federal
Triangle

This is one of the world's great natural history muse-ums. The giant dinosaur fossils, glittering gems, creepy-crawly insects, and other natural delights—over 126 million specimens in all—attract more than 7 million visitors annually.

TIPS

■ The IMAX theater shows 2-
and 3-dimensional natural-his-
tory films throughout the day.
Buy advance tickets at the box
office when you arrive, then
tour the museum.

■ Visit Friday evenings from
6:30–10 for the "Smithsonian Jazz Café": live entertainment, food and wine,
museum store shopping, and
special IMAX films.

■ Watch paleontologists at
work in the glassed-in fossil
labs throughout Dinosaur Hall
and the Life in the Ancient
Seas gallery.

■ There are two main gift
shops on the ground floor, a
stuffed-animal-centric shop in
Mammal Hall on the first floor,
and a jewel-and-gem-themed
shop on the second floor.

■ If you visit in spring, don't
miss the quirky orchid and
train show.

HIGHLIGHTS

Get between Tyrannosaurus Rex and his dinner, a feisty Triceratops. The two giant fossils are poised for action, as are the other occupants of the popular Dinosaur Hall, which range from a 72-foot-long Diplodocus lon-gus to a tiny *Thescelosaurus neglectus* (a small dinosaur so named because its disconnected bones sat for years in a college drawer before being reassembled).

Watch out for the cheetah above you on the tree branch in Mammal Hall, which explains mammals' evolution, diversity, and role in the food chain with 238 taxidermy mounts.

See the vivid ecosystem of a living coral reef in Ocean Hall, the museum's largest exhibit, scheduled to open in September 2008. The "Ocean Explorer" theater simu-lates a dive into the depths of the sea.

Drool over the jewels in the Janet Annenberg Hooker Hall of Geology, Gems, and Minerals: Marie Antoi-nette's earrings, the Rosser Reeves ruby, and the Hope Diamond, a rare 45.52-carat blue gem donated by Harry Winston in 1958.

Walk among hundreds of brilliantly colored butterflies in the new Butterfly Pavilion, which requires a sepa-rate admission. For a different kind of entomological experience, check out the O. Orkin Insect Zoo, named for the pest-control magnate who donated money to modernize the exhibits. Tarantula feedings are Tuesday through Friday at 10:30, 11:30, and 1:30.

NATIONAL PORTRAIT GALLERY

✉ 8th and F Sts. NW, East End

☎ 202/633–8300, 202/357–1729 TDD

🌐 www.npg.si.edu

🎟 Free

🕐 Daily 11:30–7

Ⓜ Gallery Pl./Chinatown

3

TIPS

■ The Portrait Gallery and American Art Museum are two different entities within the same building—the art complements the portraits, setting up a rich dialogue between the two.

■ The elegant covered courtyard has a café, free Wi-Fi, and is frequently the site of performances and special events.

■ At the "Portrait Connection" computer kiosks you can search a database of the gallery's collections. Look up the portrait's subject, and the database can tell you where in the gallery it is and show you an image, even if it's not currently on exhibit.

■ There are free docent-led tours most weekdays at 11:45, 1, and 2:15, and most Saturdays and Sundays at 11:45, 1:30 and 3:15. Check the Web site to confirm times.

■ At the Lunder Conservation Center on the third and fourth floors you can watch conservators preserving and restoring works.

Devoted to the intersection of art, biography, and history, this collection houses nearly 20,000 images of men and women who have shaped U.S. history. There are prints, paintings, photos, and multimedia sculptures of subjects from George Washington to Madonna. This museum shares the landmark Old Patent Office Building with the Smithsonian American Art Museum.

HIGHLIGHTS

The building itself: Built between 1836 and 1863, this gracious marble edifice is considered one of the country's finest examples of Greek Revival architecture.

The gallery has the only complete collection of presidential portraits outside the White House, starting with Gilbert Stuart's iconic "Lansdowne" portrait of George Washington. Interesting perspectives include the plaster cast of Abraham Lincoln's head and hands, and political cartoonist Pat Oliphant's sculpture of George H.W. Bush bowling.

The "American Origins" exhibit chronicles the first contact between Europeans and Native Americans, the Founding Fathers, and historic figures through the Industrial Age. Subjects include Benjamin Franklin (the painting, by Joseph Duplessis, is the basis for Franklin's likeness on the $100 bill); Native American diplomat Pocohantas; Thomas Edison in his workshop; and a full-length likeness of bushy-browed, cigarillo-smoking humorist Samuel Clemens, aka Mark Twain.

From a moving bronze sculpture of Martin Luther King Jr. to Andy Warhol's Marilyn Monroe prints, to Madonna's 1985 Time magazine cover, the third-floor gallery of 20th-century Americans offers a vibrant and colorful tour of the people who shaped the country and culture of today.

NEWSEUM

✉ 555 Pennsylvania Ave. NW, East End

☎ 888/639–7386

⊕ www.newseum.org

🎟 $20

🕘 Daily 9 - 5

Ⓜ Archives/Navy Memorial

TIPS

■ ABC's *This Week* with George Stephanopoulos is filmed live here every Sunday morning; museum visitors are welcome to watch.

■ Celebrity chef Wolfgang Puck designed the menu for the food court, as well as for the well-reviewed restaurant The Source, adjoining the museum.

■ The best way to tour the museum is by viewing the orientation films on the ground floor, then taking the elevator up to the top floor and working your way down.

■ Tickets for the Newseum are date specific and subject to availability; purchasing them in advance on the Web site is recommended.

■ The top-floor terrace offers one of best public views of the Capitol, and looks directly down onto Pennsylvania Avenue.

■ The museum is best for children over 12.

The brand-new Newseum opened to great fanfare in 2008, in a landmark $450 million glass-and-silver structure on Pennsylvania Avenue, set smack between the White House and the Capitol: a fitting location for a museum devoted to the First Amendment and the essential role of a free press in maintaining democracy. The museum has a serious purpose, but the space and exhibits are high-tech, interactive, multimedia, and sometimes shamelessly fun. Visitors enter into a 90-foot-high media-saturated atrium, overlooked by a giant breaking news screen and a news helicopter suspended overhead. From there, 14 galleries display 500 years of the history of news, including exhibits on the First Amendment, global news, the rise of multimedia, and the way radio, television, and especially the Internet, have transformed how we find out about the world.

HIGHLIGHTS

Live news programs—from presidential debates to town hall meetings—are regularly filmed in the museum's central live news studio, and audiences are often welcome to watch.

The largest piece of the Berlin wall outside Germany, including a guard tower, is permanently installed in an exhibit explaining how a free press was a key contributor to the fall of the Wall.

Five state-of-the art theaters, including an eye-popping "4-D" theater and another with a 90-foot-long screen, show features, news, sports, and documentaries throughout the day.

In the interactive games gallery you can create your own standup newscast, be a photographer in an action news event, and win or lose at making ethics decisions on deadline.

PHILLIPS COLLECTION

✉ 1600 21st St. NW, Dupont Circle

☎ 202/387–2151

🌐 www.phillipscollection.org

🎟 Free for permanent collection on weekdays; admission varies on weekends and for special exhibitions

🕙 Tues., Wed., Fri., and Sat. 10–5, Thurs. 10–8:30, Sun. 11–6

Ⓜ Dupont Circle

3

TIPS

■ The Phillips employs students of art history, many of whom are artists themselves, to sit by the paintings and answer questions.

■ On Thursday the museum stays open late for live jazz, gallery talks, and a cash bar.

■ The museum holds a Sunday afternoon concert in its oak-paneled music room nearly every week. Seats are unreserved and included with museum admission, but showing up early is recommended.

■ Take a break in the Firehook Café, overlooking the museum courtyard.

■ There are tours of the museum and permanent collection on Saturday at 11; special exhibitions tours are on Friday at 11. Tours are unreserved and included in the price of admission.

The first museum of modern art in the country, the masterpiece-filled Phillips Collection is unique in origin and content. It opened in 1921 in the Georgian Revival mansion of collector Duncan Phillips, who wanted to showcase his art in a museum that would stand as a memorial to his father and brother. Having no interest in a painting's market value or its faddishness, Phillips searched for pieces that impressed him as outstanding products of a particular artist's unique vision. At the heart of the collections are Impressionist and modern masterpieces by Pierre-Auguste Renoir, Vincent van Gogh, Paul Cézanne, Edgar Degas, Pablo Picasso, Paul Klee, and Henri Matisse. These are grouped by theme and artist throughout the Phillips mansion, making for a museum-going experience that is as intimate as it is inspiring.

HIGHLIGHTS

The collection's most famous piece is Renoir's magnificent work of Impressionism, *Luncheon of the Boating Party*. Other celebrity works include Degas's *Dancers at the Barre*, Vincent van Gogh's *Entrance to the Public Garden at Arles*, and *A Bowl of Plums* by 18th-century artist Jean-Baptiste Siméon Chardin, whom Phillips called "the first modern painter."

The glowing, chapel-like Rothko Room emerged from a bond between Phillips and modern master Mark Rothko. Rothko said he preferred to exhibit his paintings in smaller, more intimately scaled rooms, and Phillips designed the gallery specifically to the artist's preferences.

Cézanne's intense, piercing self-portrait was the painting Phillips said he would save first if the gallery caught fire.

PRESIDENT LINCOLN'S COTTAGE

✉ Armed Forces Retirement Home at Rock Creek Church Rd. and Upshur St. NW., Upper Northwest

☎ 202/829-0436

🌐 www.lincolncottage.org

💲 $12

🕐 April 1–Oct. 31, Mon.–Sat. 9:30–5:30, Sun. 11:30–5:30; Nov. 1–March 31, Mon.–Sat. 9:30–4:30, Sun. 11:30–4:30

Ⓜ Georgia Ave./Petworth

TIPS

■ There are 20 spots available per tour and only scheduled tours are given; advance reservations are available on the Web site and are highly recommended. April 1–Oct. 31, Mon.–Sat., tours every hour 10–4, Sun., every hour 12–4. Nov. 1–March 31, Mon.–Sat., tours every hour 10–3, Sun., every hour 12–3.

■ Although the museum is reachable by Metro and bus, it's much easier to drive or take a cab. There is on-site parking. If arriving by Metro, take the H8 bus from the station; it will drop you at the Eagle Gate entrance.

■ There is a café in the Visitors Center, and a diner, The Hitching Post, across the street from the main entrance gate.

■ Visitors may also picnic on the cottage grounds, which have been landscaped to look as they did when Lincoln lived there.

In June of 1862, President Lincoln moved from the White House to this Gothic Revival cottage on the grounds of the Soldiers' Home to escape the oppressive heat of wartime Washington and to grieve the loss of his son Willie. Lincoln and his wife lived in the cottage from June to November of 1862, 1863, and 1864—a quarter of his presidency—and it was here that he became consumed with the idea of emancipation and wrote the Emancipation Proclamation. Considered the most significant historic site of Lincoln's presidency outside the White House, Lincoln's Cottage opened for public tours in 2008. The tours attempt to re-create a visit to the cottage similar to what Lincoln's many visitors in the 1860s experienced, and to take visitors inside Lincoln's mind as he anguished over the Civil War and emancipation.

HIGHLIGHTS

Audio recordings read from Lincoln's writings, and from visitors' accounts of meeting with the President at his cottage.

Browse through period editions of the books that most influenced Lincoln, including the works of Shakespeare and Alexander Pope, in the accurate re-creation of his library.

Tours start and end at the Visitors Center, which has exhibitions and multimedia displays on Lincoln and the Civil War.

SMITHSONIAN AMERICAN ART MUSEUM

✉ 8th and G Sts. NW, East End

☎ 202/633–7970, 202/633–5285 TDD

🌐 www.americanart.si.edu

🎟 Free

🕐 11:30–7:30

Ⓜ Gallery Pl./Chinatown

3

TIPS

■ At any given time, more than 3,000 of the museum's holdings are in storage, but you can view them all at Luce Foundation Center's glassed-in archives on the third and fourth floors. At computer kiosks set among the archives, you can look up any work and find out exactly where it is in the exhibits or archives.

■ The third-floor Upper West Side café offers a good rest stop, with drinks, snacks, and a view into the Luce Foundation Center's glassed-in archives.

■ There are free docent-led tours every day at noon and 2.

■ The museum regularly holds lectures, films, and evenings of live jazz among the exhibits. Check the Web site for what's on during your visit.

Home to the United States' first federal art collection, the Smithsonian American Art Museum is considered the world's biggest and most diverse collection of American art. Its more than 41,000 works span three centuries, from colonial portraits to 21st-century abstractionists. Among the thousands of American artists represented are John Singleton Copley, Winslow Homer, Mary Cassatt, Georgia O'Keeffe, Edward Hopper, David Hockney, and Robert Rauschenberg. This museum is in the Old Patent Office Building along with the National Portrait Gallery.

HIGHLIGHTS

The American folk-art exhibit is fabulous, from the ceramic Elvis Presley–shaped jug and the enormous intricately crafted tinfoil altarpiece, to the Coke-bottle quilt sewn by a grandmother from Yakoo County, Mississippi.

American art came into its own by the late 19th and early 20th century. The museum's collections of works from this period are among the world's biggest and best, from the light-filled neo-Impressionist canvasses of Mary Cassatt and Childe Hassam to the sophisticated Gilded Age portraits of turn-of-the-century high society by Winslow Homer, John Singer Sargent, and James McNeill Whistler.

An explosion of American innovation shifted the center of the 20th-century art world from Paris to New York. The museum's top floor celebrates these achievements: a hallway lined with Andy Warhol's prints, Jackson Pollock's splatter canvases, and Robert Indiana's seminal The Figure Five leads to rooms of quintessentially American installations, like Alexander Calder mobiles, and Nam June Paik's billboard-size neon-and-television-screen U.S. map.

UNITED STATES HOLOCAUST MEMORIAL MUSEUM

⊠ 100 Raoul Wallenberg Pl.
SW, enter from Raoul Wal-
lenberg Pl. or 14th St. SW,
The Mall

☎ 202/488–0400, 800/400–
9373 tickets.com

🌐 www.ushmm.org

💲 Free

🕙 Daily 10–5:30

Ⓜ Smithsonian

TIPS

■ Like the history it covers,
the museum can be pro-
foundly disturbing; it's not recommended for children under
11, although Daniel's Story,
in a ground-floor exhibit not
requiring tickets, is designed
for children ages 8 and up.

■ Plan to spend two to three
hours here.

■ In addition to the permanent exhibition, the museum
also has a multimedia learning
center, a resource center for
students and teachers, a registry of Holocaust survivors, and
occasional special exhibitions.

■ Timed-entry passes
(distributed on a first-come,
first-served basis at the 14th
Street entrance starting at
10 or available in advance
through 🌐 tickets.com) are
necessary for the permanent
exhibition. Allow extra time to
enter the building in spring
and summer, when long lines
can form.

Museums usually celebrate the best that humanity can
achieve, but this museum instead documents the worst.
A permanent exhibition tells the stories of the millions
of Jews, Gypsies, Jehovah's Witnesses, homosexuals,
political prisoners, the mentally ill, and others killed
by the Nazis between 1933 and 1945. The exhibitions
are detailed and graphic; the experiences memorable
and powerful.

HIGHLIGHTS

Striving to give a you-are-there experience, the presentation is as extraordinary as the subject matter: upon
arrival, you are issued an "identity card" containing
biographical information on a real person from the
Holocaust. As you move through the museum, you read
sequential updates on your card.

Hitler's rise to power and the spread of European anti-
semitism are thoroughly documented in the musuem's
early exhibits, with films of Nazi rallies, posters, newspaper articles, and recordings of Hitler's speeches
immersing you in the world that led to the Holocaust.

You are confronted with the gruesome, appalling truths
of the Holocaust in the deeply disturbing exhibit "The
Final Solution," which details the Nazis' execution of 6
million Jews. Exhibits include film footage of scientific
experiments done on Jews, artifacts such as a freight
car like those used to transport Jews from Warsaw to
the Treblinka death camp, and crematoria implements.
There are films and audio recordings of Holocaust survivors telling their harrowing stories.

After this powerful experience, the adjacent Hall of
Remembrance, filled with candles and hand-painted
tiles dedicated to children who died in the Holocaust,
provides a much-needed space for quiet reflection.

OTHER MUSEUMS

Anacostia Community Museum. The richness of African-American culture is on display in this Smithsonian museum and research facility in southeast Washington's Anacostia neighborhood. The museum's facade uses traditional African design elements: brickwork patterns evoke West African kente cloth, and the concrete cylinders reference the stone towers of Zimbabwe and are ornamented with diamond patterns like those found on the adobe houses of Mali. Special exhibitions showcase fine art—photography, painting, sculpture—as well as crafts, social history, and popular culture. ⊠*1901 Fort Pl. SE, Anacostia* ☎*202/633–4820* ⊕*anacostia. si.edu* ⊠*Free* ⊙*Daily 10–5* Ⓜ*Anacostia, then W2/W3 bus.*

Anderson House. A palatial home that's a mystery even to many longtime Washingtonians, Anderson House isn't an embassy, though it does have a link to that world. Larz Anderson was a diplomat from 1891 to 1913 whose career included postings to Japan and Belgium. Anderson and his heiress wife Isabel toured the world, picking up objects that struck their fancy. They filled their residence, which was constructed for them in 1905, with the booty of their travels. Visitors to Anderson House will receive a guided tour of the first and second floors, gorgeously furnished with the Andersons' eclectic collection of furniture, tapestries, paintings, sculpture, historic artifacts, and Asian art, and learn about entertaining in Gilded Age Washington. Among the highlights of the house are several floor-to-ceiling murals that reveal the splendor of the era as well as the Andersons' patriotism and pastimes. Today the house is often used by the federal government to entertain visiting dignitaries. ⊠*2118 Massachusetts Ave. NW, Dupont Circle* ☎*202/785-2040* ⊕*www.societyofthe cincinnati.org* ⊠*Free* ⊙*Tues.–Sat. 1–4* Ⓜ*Dupont Circle.*

Art Museum of the Americas. Changing exhibits highlight 20th-century Latin American artists in this small gallery, part of the Organization of American States. There are also documentaries on South and Central American art. A public garden connects the Art Museum and the OAS building. ⊠*201 18th St. NW, White House area* ☎*202/458–6016* ⊕*www.museum.oas.org* ⊠*Free* ⊙*Tues.–Sun. 10–5* Ⓜ*Farragut W.*

★ **Arthur M. Sackler Gallery.** When Charles Freer endowed the gallery that bears his name, he insisted on a few conditions: objects in the collection could not be lent out, nor could objects from outside the collections be put on display. Because of the restrictions, it was necessary to build a second, complementary museum to house the Asian art collection of Arthur M. Sackler, a wealthy medical researcher and publisher who began collecting Asian art as a student in the 1940s. Sackler allowed Smithsonian curators to select 1,000 items from his ample collection and pledged $4 million toward the construction of the museum. The collection includes works from China, Southeast Asia, Korea, Tibet, and Japan. Objects in the permanent collection include Chinese ritual bronzes, jade ornaments from the third millennium BC, Persian manuscripts, and Indian paintings in gold, silver, lapis lazuli, and malachite. The lower level connects to the Freer Gallery of Art. ⊠*1050 Independence Ave. SW, The Mall* ☎*202/633–1000, 202/357–1729 TDD*

⊕*www.asia.si.edu* ✉*Free* ⊙*Daily 10–5:30* Ⓜ*Smithsonian.*

Christian Heurich House Museum. This opulent Romanesque Revival mansion, once known as the Brewmaster's Castle, was the home of Christian Heurich, a German orphan who made his fortune in the beer business. Heurich's brewery was in Foggy Bottom, where the Kennedy Center stands today.

Most of the furnishings in the house were owned and used by the Heurichs. The Victorian interior is an eclectic gathering of plaster detailing, carved wooden doors, and painted ceilings. The downstairs breakfast room, in which Heurich, his wife, and their three children ate most of their meals, is decorated like a Rathskeller and adorned with German sayings such as "A good drink makes old people young."

Heurich must have taken proverbs seriously. He drank beer daily, had three wives (in succession), and lived to be 102. (In 1986 Heurich's grandson Gary started brewing the family beer again, now renamed Foggy Bottom Lager. Though the beer is currently from Utica, New York, Gary vows to someday build another brewery near Washington.) The current owners, descendants of Christian Heurich, offer guided tours and rent the house for special events. ✉*1307 New Hampshire Ave. NW, Dupont Circle* ☎*202/429–1894* ✉*$5* ⊙*Tours Wed.–Fri. at 11:30 and 1, Sat. at 11:30, 1, and 2:30.* Ⓜ*Dupont Circle.*

� **DAR Museum.** The headquarters of the Daughters of the American Revolution, the Beaux-Arts Memorial Continental Hall was the site of the DAR's annual congress until the larger Constitution Hall was built around the corner. An entrance on D Street leads to the museum. Its 30,000-item collection includes fine examples of colonial and Federal furniture, textiles, quilts, silver, china, porcelain, stoneware, earthenware, and glass. Thirty-one period rooms are decorated in styles representative of various U.S. states, ranging from an 1850 California adobe parlor to a New Hampshire attic filled with 18th- and 19th-century toys. Two galleries—one of them permanent—hold decorative arts. Docent tours are available weekdays 10–2:30 and Saturday 9–5. In the "Touch of Independence" education center for children, families can explore early American life through period games and costumes. During the "Colonial Adventure" tours, held the first and third Sunday of the month at 1:30 and 3 from September through May, costumed docents use the objects on display to teach children ages five to seven about day-to-day life in colonial America. Reservations are required two weeks in advance. ✉*1776 D St. NW, White House area* ☎*202/879-3241* ⊕*www.dar.org* ✉*Free* ⊙*Weekdays 9:30–4, Sat. 9–5* Ⓜ*Farragut W.*

Decatur House. Designed by a celebrity architect and located across from the White House, this may have been the nation's hottest piece of real estate when it was built in 1818. The distinguished neoclassical design is the work of Benjamin Henry Latrobe, the country's first professional architect and engineer most famous for his construction of the Capitol and design of many of that icon's most beautiful interior spaces. Today this is one of the oldest surviving homes in Washington, and one of only three remaining residential buildings designed by Latrobe. ⊠*748 Jackson Pl. NW, White House area* ☎*202/842–0920* ⊕*www.decatur house.org* ▣*Free* ☉*Tues.–Sat. 10–5, Sun. noon–4; tours every hr at quarter past the hr* Ⓜ*Farragut W.*

Drug Enforcement Administration Museum. Just across the street from the Fashion Centre at Pentagon City—a destination in itself for shoppers—is the DEA Museum, within the U.S. Drug Enforcement Administration's headquarters. It explores the effect of drugs on American society, starting with quaint 19th-century ads for opium-laced patent medicines and "cocaine tooth drops" (opiates, cannabis, and cocaine were unregulated then). But documentation of these addictive substances' medical dangers, as well as the corrosive political effect of the opium trade, which China detested, is hard-hitting. A similar contrast is found between the period feel of artifacts from a 1970s head shop and displays on the realities of present-day drug trafficking. ⊠*700 Army Navy Dr., at Hayes St.,* ☎*202/307–3463* ⊕*www.deamuseum. org* ▣*Free* ☉*Tues.–Fri. 10–4* Ⓜ*Pentagon City.*

Folger Shakespeare Library. The Folger Library's collection of works by and about Shakespeare and his times is second to none. Unfortunately, the library itself is open only by appointment to academic researchers. But the white-marble art deco building, decorated with sculpted scenes from the Bard's plays, is well worth a look. Inside is a reproduction of a 16th-century inn-yard theater—the site for performances of chamber music, baroque opera, and Shakespearean plays—and a gallery, designed in the manner of an Elizabethan Great Hall, which holds rotating exhibits from the library's collection. A manicured Elizabethan garden on the grounds is open to the public. The building was designed by architect Paul Philippe Cret and dedicated in 1932. Henry Clay Folger, the library's founder, was Standard Oil's president and chairman of the board. ⊠*201 E. Capitol St. SE, Capitol Hill* ☎*202/544–4600* ⊕*www.folger.edu* ▣*Free* ☉*Mon.–Sat. 10–4* Ⓜ*Capitol S.*

Ford's Theatre. In 1859 Baltimore theater impresario John T. Ford leased the First Baptist Church building that stood on this site and turned it into a successful music hall. The building burned down late in 1863, but Ford built a new structure on the same spot. The events that occurred less than two years later would shock the nation. On the night of April 14, 1865, during a performance of *Our American Cousin,* John Wilkes Booth entered the state box and shot Abraham Lincoln in the back of the head. The stricken president was carried across the street to the house of tai-

CAPITAL FACTS

The federal government bought Ford's Theatre in 1866 for $100,000 and converted it into office space. It was remodeled as a Lincoln museum in 1932 and was restored to its 1865 appearance in 1968.

lor William Petersen. Charles Augustus Leale, a 23-year-old surgeon, was the first man to attend the president. To let Lincoln know that someone was nearby, Leale held his hand throughout the night. Lincoln died the next morning. In 2007 the Ford's Theater Society launched a two-year, $40-million campaign to transform the theater and its basement museum of Lincoln artifacts into a block-long, Lincoln-centered cultural campus commemorating the president. Scheduled to open in early 2009, it will include a renovated Ford's theater, which will run a full schedule of plays; a new Lincoln museum; the historically restored home of William Peterson; and a new Center for Education and Leadership focused on Lincoln's life and presidency. ✉ *511 10th St. NW, East End* ☎*202/426–6924* ⊕*www.fords.org* ✍*Free* ⊙*Daily 9–5; theater closed to visitors during rehearsals and matinees, generally Thurs. and weekends; Lincoln museum in basement remains open at these times* Ⓜ*Metro Center or Gallery Pl.*

Frederick Douglass National Historic Site. Cedar Hill, the Anacostia home of abolitionist Frederick Douglass, was the first Black National Historic Site that Congress designated. Douglass, a former slave who delivered rousing abolitionist speeches at home and abroad, resided here from 1877 until his death in 1895. The house has a wonderful view of Washington across the Anacostia River and contains many of Douglass's personal belongings. The home has been meticulously restored to its original grandeur; you can view Douglass's hundreds of books displayed on his custom-built bookshelves, and Limoges china on the Douglass family dining table. A short film on Douglass's life is shown at a nearby visitor center. Reservations are required for tours. To get here, take the B2 bus from the Anacostia Metro stop. ✉*1411 W St. SE, Anacostia* ☎*202/426–5961, 800/967–2283 tour reservations* ⊕*www. nps.gov/frdo* ✍*Free* ⊙*Mid-Oct.–mid-Apr., daily 9–4; mid-Apr.–mid-Oct., daily 9–5; call ahead for tour times* Ⓜ*Anacostia.*

★ **Hillwood Estate, Museum and Gardens.** Long before the age of Paris Hilton, cereal heiress Marjorie Merriweather Post was the most celebrated socialite of the twentieth century, famous for her fabulous wealth and beauty, as well as her passion for collecting art and creating some of the world's most lavish homes. Of these, the twenty-five acre Hillwood Estate, which Merriweather Post bought in 1955, is the only one now open to the public. The 40-room Georgian mansion, where she regularly hosted presidents, diplomats, and royalty, is sumptuously appointed, with a formal Louis XVI drawing room, private movie theater and ballroom, and magnificent libraries filled with portraits of the glamorous hostess and her four husbands, as well as works from her rich art collection. She was especially fascinated with Russian art, and her collection of Russian icons, tapestries, gold and silver work, and Fabergé eggs is museum-quality. She devoted equal attention to her gardens: you can wander through thirteen acres of them. For more information about the gardens, *see* the Gardens section in the "Sports & the Outdoors" chapter. You should allow two to three hours to take in the estate and gardens. Reservations are recommended on spring weekends for tours and lunch or tea in the café. The estate is best reached by taxi or car (parking is available on the grounds). It's a 20 to 30-minute walk from the Metro. ✉*4155 Linnean Ave. NW, Northwest* ☎*202/686–5807 or 202/686–8500* 🌐*www.hillwoodmuseum.org* 🏠*House and grounds $12* 🕐 *Feb.–Dec., Tues.–Sat. 10–5* Ⓜ *Van Ness/UDC.*

Kreeger Museum. The cool white domes and elegant lines of this post-modern landmark stand in stark contrast to the traditional feel of the rest of the Foxhall Road neighborhood. Designed in 1963 by iconic architect Philip Johnson, the building was once the home of GEICO insurance executive David Lloyd Kreeger and his wife Carmen. Music is a central theme of the art and the space: the Kreegers wanted a show-piece residence that would also function as a gallery and recital hall. The art collection includes works by Renoir, Degas, Cézanne, and Munch, African artifacts, and pieces with musical themes. The domed rooms also have wonderful acoustics, and serve as an excellent performance venue for the classical concerts that are regularly performed here. Infor-mation about upcoming performances is available on the museum's Web site. The museum is not reachable by Metro; you need to take a car or taxi to get here. ✉*2401 Foxhall Rd. NW, Foxhall* ☎*202/337–3050* 🌐*www.kreegermuseum.org* 🎟*$8* 🕐*Sat. 10–4, tours, reservations required, Tues.–Fri. at 10:30 and 1:30, Sat. at 10:30.*

Madame Tussauds. The D.C. branch of this famous London-based wax-works franchise opened in late 2007, with a focus on local history: you can see (and pose for pictures with) uncanny likenesses of the founding fathers and political heavyweights like Bill and Hilary Clinton, and even sit in an Oval Office painstakingly recreated in wax. If you want a taste of the celebrity, you can enter a "nightclub" room populated with waxen recre-ations of Julia Roberts, J.Lo, and Brad Pitt, among many others. ✉*1025 F Street, NW, East End* ☎ *202/942–7300* 🌐*www.madametussaudsdc.com* 🎟*$20* 🕐 *Daily 10–6.* Ⓜ*Metro Center and Gallery Pl./Chinatown.*

Marian Koshland Science Museum. Sponsored by the National Academy of Sciences, this small but engaging museum explores and explains the science behind current news headlines. A permanent exhibit includes animations of groundbreaking science with interactive displays show-ing how these discoveries make their way into the public realm. The other exhibits illustrate the research of the Academy on subjects that intersect with public policy, such as global warming and the spread of infectious diseases like SARS. You can look through microscopes at live bacteria, or play a game determining the fate of the planet based on how governments regulate human activities. Exhibits are changed and updated to reflect new discoveries and fields of research. Though the interactive exhibits are fun and educational, they are aimed at ages 13 and up. ✉*At 6th and E Sts. NW, East End* ☎*202/334–1201* 🌐*www. koshland-science-museum.org* 🎟*$5* 🕐*Sun., Mon., and Wed.–Sat. 10–6* Ⓜ *Gallery Pl./Chinatown and Judiciary Sq.*

National Aquarium. Established in 1873, this is the country's oldest pub-lic aquarium, with more than 1,200 fish and other creatures—such as eels, sharks, and alligators—representing 270 species of fresh- and saltwater life. Seekers of a transcendent aquarium experience will probably be happier visiting the Balti-more National Aquarium, which is routinely ranked among the nation's best. But the easy-to-view tanks, accessible touching pool (with crabs and sea urchins), low admission fee, and lack of crowds make this a good outing with children. There are also animal keeper talks and feedings every day at 2. ⊠ *14th St. and Constitution Ave. NW, East End* ☎ *202/482–2825* ⊕ *www.nationalaquarium.com*

🖃 *$5* ⊗ *Daily 9–5, last admission at 4:30; sharks fed Mon., Wed., and Sat. at 2; piranhas fed Tues., Thurs., and Sun. at 2; alligators fed Fri. at 2* Ⓜ *Federal Triangle.*

★ **National Building Museum.** Devoted to architecture, design, landscaping,
Ⓒ and urban planning, the National Building Museum is the nation's premier cultural organization devoted to the built environment. The open interior of the mammoth redbrick edifice is one of the city's great spaces, and has been the site of many Presidential inaugural balls. The eight central Corinthian columns are among the largest in the world, rising to a height of 75 feet. Although they resemble Siena marble, each is made of 70,000 bricks that have been covered with plaster and painted. For years, the annual *Christmas in Washington* TV special has been filmed in this breathtaking hall.

The permanent exhibit "Washington: Symbol and City" tells the story of the birth and evolution of the backwater that eventually became the nation's capital (beginning by debunking the myth that Washington was built on a swamp!). You can touch the perfectly scaled, intricately detailed models of the White House, the Capitol, the Washington Monument, and the Lincoln and Jefferson memorials, and look at original drawings, building plans, maps, videos, and photographs that trace the city's architectural history.

Among the most popular permanent exhibits is the "Building Zone," where kids ages two to six can get a hands-on introduction to building by constructing a tower, exploring a kid-sized playhouse, or playing with bulldozers and construction trucks.

There is also a constant series of temporary exhibits: recent ones have covered environmentally sustainable architecture, Shakespeare's Globe Theatre, and the influential work of modernist designer Marcel Breuer.

Tours are offered at 12:30 Monday through Wednesday; 11:30, 12:30, and 1:30 Thursday through Saturday; and 12:30 and 1:30 on Sunday. Family programs are available at 2:30 on weekends. ⊠ *401 F St. NW, between 4th and 5th Sts., East End* ☎ *202/272–2448* ⊕ *www.nbm.org* 🖃 *Free* ⊗ *Mon.–Sat. 10–5, Sun. 11–5* Ⓜ *Judiciary Sq.*

☉ **National Geographic Society.** Founded in 1888, the society is best known for its magazine. It has sponsored numerous expeditions throughout its 100-year history, including those of admirals Robert Peary and Richard Byrd and underwater explorer Jacques Cousteau. Explorers Hall, entered from 17th Street, invites you to learn about the world in a decidedly interactive way: you can experience a mini-tornado, or use video touch screens that explain geographic concepts and then quiz you. The most dramatic events take place in Earth Station One Interactive Theatre, a 72-seat amphitheater that sends the audience on a journey around the world. The centerpiece is a hand-painted globe, 11 feet in diameter, that floats and spins on a cushion of air, showing off different features of the planet. ✉*17th and M Sts. NW, Dupont Circle* ☎*202/857–7588, 202/857–7689 group tours* ⊕*www.national geographic.com* ✇*Free* ☉*Mon.–Sat. 9–5, Sun. 10–5* Ⓜ*Farragut N.*

☉ **National Museum of African Art.** This unique underground building houses galleries, a library, photographic archives, and educational facilities. Its rotating exhibits present African visual arts, including sculpture, textiles, photography, archaeology, and modern art. Long-term installations explore the sculpture of sub-Saharan Africa, the art of Benin, the pottery of Central Africa, the archaeology of the ancient Nubian city of Kerma, and the artistry of everyday objects. The museum's educational programs include films with contemporary perspectives on African life, storytelling programs, festivals, and hands-on workshops for families, all of which bring Africa's oral traditions, literature, and art to life. Workshops and demonstrations by African and African-American artists offer a chance to meet and talk to practicing artists. ∎**TIP➜If you're traveling with children, look for the museum's free guide to the permanent Images of Power and Identity exhibition.** ✉*950 Independence Ave. SW, The Mall* ☎*202/633–1000, 202/357–1729 TDD* ⊕*www.nmafa.si.edu* ✇*Free* ☉*Daily 10–5:30* Ⓜ*Smithsonian.*

National Museum of Crime and Punishment. Set to open in May 2008, this museum will explore the history of crime and punishment in America, from pirates and Wild West outlaws to white-collar criminals and computer hackers. The museum was created in partnership with "America's Most Wanted" host John Walsh, and includes a behind-the-scenes look at the program. Exhibits will range from a medieval torture chamber to the actual getaway car used by bank robbers Bonnie and Clyde. There will be plenty of opportunity for interactive displays: you can put your hands in pillory stocks, take a lie-detector test, and experience a simulated crime scene investigation. The museum recommends purchasing advance tickets on the Web site: tickets are hourly with a specific date and time. ✉*575 7th St. NW, East End* ☎*202/393–1099 TDD* ⊕*w www.crimemuseum.org* ✇*$17.95* ☉*Sept.–Feb., daily 10–6; Mar.–Aug., daily 9–7* Ⓜ*Gallery Pl./Chinatown.*

National Museum of Health and Medicine. Open since the 1860s, this medical museum illustrates medicine's fight against injury and disease. It has one of the world's largest collections of microscopes. Because some exhibits are fairly graphic (the wax surgical models and the preserved organs come to mind), the museum may not be suitable for young children or the squeamish, but may be perfect for teenagers. In the presidential display you'll see one of the most famous artifacts: the bullet that killed Abraham Lincoln, as well as pieces of his skull and plaster molds of his head and hands. ■ TIP→The museum is on the campus of Walter Reed Army Medical Center, so you may be asked for identification going in. To get here from Adams-Morgan, catch Bus S2 or S4 to Silver Spring on 16th Street. ⊠ *Walter Reed Army Medical Center, 6900 Georgia Ave. and Elder St., NW, Upper Northwest* ☎*202/782–2200* ⊕*nmhm.washingtondc.museum* ⊠*Free* ⊙*Daily 10–5:30; tours 2nd and 4th Sat. of month at 1.*

National Museum of Women in the Arts. Works by female artists from the Renaissance to the present are showcased at this museum. The beautifully restored 1907 Renaissance Revival building was designed by Waddy B. Wood; it was once a Masonic temple, for men only. In addition to displaying traveling shows, the museum has a permanent collection that includes paintings, drawings, sculpture, prints, and photographs by Georgia O'Keeffe, Mary Cassatt, Élisabeth Vigée-Lebrun, Frida Kahlo, and Camille Claudel. ⊠*1250 New York Ave. NW, East End* ☎*202/783–5000* ⊕*www. nmwa.org* ⊠*$10* ⊙*Mon.–Sat. 10–5, Sun. noon–5* Ⓜ*Metro Center.*

☯ **National Postal Museum.** The Smithsonian's stamp collection, housed here, consists of a whopping 11 million stamps. Exhibits, underscoring the important part the mail has played in America's development, include horse-drawn mail coaches, railway mail cars, airmail planes, and a collection of philatelic rarities. The National Museum of Natural History has the Hope Diamond, but the National Postal Museum has the container used to mail the gem to the Smithsonian. The family-oriented museum has more than 40 interactive and touch-screen exhibits. The museum takes up only a portion of what is the old Washington City Post Office, designed by Daniel Burnham and completed in 1914. Nostalgic odes to the noble mail carrier are inscribed on the exterior of the marble building; one of them, "The Letter," eulogizes the "Messenger of sympathy and love / Servant of parted friends / Consoler of the lonely / Bond of the scattered family / Enlarger of the common life." ⊠*2 Massachusetts Ave. NE, Capitol Hill* ☎*202/633–5555, 202/633–9849 TDD* ⊕*www.postalmuseum.si.edu* ⊠*Free* ⊙*Daily 10–5:30* Ⓜ*Union Station.*

Old Stone House. What was early American life like? Here's the capital's oldest window into the past. Work on this fieldstone house, thought to be Washington's oldest surviving building, was begun in 1764 by a cabinetmaker named Christopher Layman. Now a museum, it was used as both a residence and a place of business by a succession of occupants. Five of the house's rooms are furnished with the simple, sturdy artifacts—plain tables, spinning wheels, and so forth—of 18th-century middle-class life. The National Park Service maintains the house and its lovely gardens, which are planted with

> ### WORD OF MOUTH
>
> "Georgetown is more a place to see and be seen and browse fancy boutiques than sightsee, but the Old Stone House in the heart of it has a lovely small garden to sit in and enjoy the day."
>
> —nicegirl512

fruit trees and perennials. ✉*3051 M St. NW, Georgetown* ☎*202/426–6851* ⊕*www.nps.gov/olst/* ✆*Free* ⊘ *Wed.–Sun. 10–5.*

Pope John Paul II Cultural Center. Part museum, part place of pilgrimage, the Pope John Paul II Cultural Center is a spectacular architectural embodiment of the Roman Catholic church's desire to celebrate its charismatic leader and its rich artistic tradition. Themes covered include church and papal history, representations of the Virgin Mary, Polish heritage, and the Catholic tradition of community activism. These are explored through traditional displays of art and artifacts as well as with audiovisual presentations and interactive computer stations. The center is about a mile from the Metro and can easily be combined with a visit to the National Shrine of the Immaculate Conception. ✉*3900 Harewood Rd. NE, Catholic University* ☎*202/635–5400* ⊕*www.jp2cc.org* ✆*Free* ⊘ *Tues.–Sat. 10–5, Sun. noon–5* Ⓜ*Brookland/Catholic University.*

Renwick Gallery. The Renwick Gallery is a luscious French Second Empire–style mansion across the street from the White House and the Eisenhower Executive Office Building. But even with such lofty neighbors, this fancy-gingerbread house, which has the words DEDICATED TO ART engraved above the entrance, is still the most appealing architecture on the block. Designed by James Renwick in 1859 to hold the art collection of Washington merchant and banker William Wilson Corcoran, the building today is a branch of Smithsonian American Art Museum, housing the museum's collection of decorative art and crafts. The building's interior matches the architecture—much red velvet and gold trim—but the exquisitely crafted works on display have a modern and witty edge. Larry Fuente's 1988 sculpture Game Fish is a marlin fashioned entirely out of vintage toys—Superman, Gumby, and the Virgin Mary are all represented, as well as dice, yo-yos, and dominos. Best of all is Kim Schahman's 1955 Bureau of Bureaucracy: a beautifully crafted wooden cabinet full of cupboards to nowhere, bottomless drawers, drawers within drawers, hidden compartments, and more. This wonderful metaphor for the labyrinthine workings of government is appropriately set in a room with a view to the Executive Office Building, providing the perfect tongue-in-cheek commentary to the activities within. ✉*Pennsylvania Ave. at 17th St. NW, White House area* ☎*202/633–2850, 202/633–5285 TDD* ⊕*www.americanart.si.edu* ✆*Free* ⊘ *Daily 10–5:30* Ⓜ*Farragut W.*

Sewall-Belmont House. Built in 1800 by Robert Sewall, this is one of the oldest homes on Capitol Hill. Today it's the headquarters of the National Woman's Party. A museum inside chronicles the early days of the women's movement and the history of the house; the museum is open for guided 30-minute tours only. There's also a library open to researchers by appointment. From 1801 to 1813 Secretary of the Treasury Albert Gallatin lived here; he finalized the details of the Louisiana Purchase in his front-parlor office. This building was the only private house in Washington that the British set on fire during their invasion of 1814. They did so after a resident fired on advancing British troops from an upper-story window (a fact later documented by the offending British general's sworn testimony, 30 years later, on behalf of the Sewalls in their attempt to secure war reparations from the U.S. government). This shot was, in fact, the only armed resistance the British met that day. The house is filled with period furniture and portraits and busts of suffragists such as Lucretia Mott, Elizabeth Cady Stanton, and longtime resident Alice Paul, who drafted the first version of the Equal Rights Amendment in 1923. ⊠*144 Constitution Ave. NE, Capitol Hill* ☎*202/546–1210* ⊕*www.sewallbelmont.org* ✉*Suggested donation $5* ☉*Tours on the hr Tues.–Fri. 11–3, Sat. noon–4* Ⓜ*Union Station.*

Smithsonian Institution Building. The first Smithsonian museum constructed, this red sandstone, Norman-style building is better known as the Castle. It was designed by James Renwick, the architect of St. Patrick's Cathedral in New York City. Although British scientist and founder James Smithson had never visited America, his will stipulated that should his nephew, Henry James Hungerford, die without an heir, Smithson's entire fortune would go to the United States, "to found at Washington, under the name of the Smithsonian Institution, an establishment for the increase and diffusion of knowledge." The museums on the Mall are the Smithsonian's most visible example of this ideal, but the organization also sponsors traveling exhibitions and maintains research posts in outside-the-Beltway locales such as the Chesapeake Bay and the tropics of Panama.

Smithson died in 1829, Hungerford in 1835, and in 1838 the United States received gold sovereigns worth $515,169. After eight years of congressional debate over the propriety of accepting a foreign citizen's funds, the Smithsonian Institution was finally established on August 10, 1846. The Castle building was completed in 1855 and originally housed all the Smithsonian's operations, including the science and art collections, research laboratories, and living quarters for the institution's secretary and his family. The statue in front of the Castle's entrance is not of Smithson but of Joseph Henry, the scientist who served as the institution's first secretary. Smithson's body was brought to America in 1904 and is entombed in a small room to the left of the Castle's Mall entrance.

■ **TIP→** Today the Castle houses the Smithsonian Information Center, which can help you get your bearings and decide which attractions to visit. A 24-minute video gives an overview of the Smithsonian museums and the National Zoo, and monitors display information on the day's events. Interactive touch-screens provide more detailed information on the museums as well as other attractions in the capital. The center opens at 9 AM, an hour before the other museums, so you can plan your day without wasting sightseeing time. It also has a good café, offering one of the better options for lunch on the Mall, and a gift shop. ⊠*1000 Jefferson Dr. SW, The Mall* ☎*202/633–1000, 202/357–1729 TDD* ⊕*www.si.edu* ✉*Free* ☉*Daily 9–5:30* Ⓜ*Smithsonian.*

Textile Museum. The museum showcases weavings, carpets, and tapestries from the more than 17,000 works in the collection. Rotating exhibits are taken from a permanent collection of historic and ethnographic items that include Coptic and pre-Columbian textiles, Kashmir embroidery, and Turkman tribal rugs. There's at least one show of modern textiles—such as quilts or fiber art—yearly. ✉ *2320 S Street, Kalorama* ☎ *202/667–0441* ⊕ *www.textilemuseum.org* ✍ *Suggested donation $5* ⊙ *Mon.–Sat. 10–5, Sun. 1–5; highlight tours Sept.–May, Wed. and weekends at 1:30* Ⓜ *Dupont Circle.*

Tudor Place. Stop at Q Street between 31st and 32nd streets; look through the trees to the north, at the top of a sloping lawn, and you can see the neoclassical Tudor Place, designed by Capitol architect Dr. William Thornton and completed in 1816. On a house tour you can see Francis Scott Key's desk, items that belonged to George Washington, and spurs belonging to soldiers who were killed in the Civil War. The house was built for Thomas Peter, son of Georgetown's first mayor, and his wife, Martha Custis, Martha Washington's granddaughter. It was because of this connection to the president's family that Tudor Place came to house many items from Mount Vernon. The gold-colored stucco house is interesting for its architecture—especially the dramatic, two-story domed portico on the south side—but its familial heritage is even more remarkable: Tudor Place stayed in the same family for 178 years, until 1983, when Armistead Peter III died. Before his death, Peter established a foundation to restore the house and open it to the public. You can only visit the house by guided tour (reservations are advised), but afterward you can wander freely, or picnic in the formal garden, full of roses and boxwoods, many planted in the early 19th century. ✉ *1644 31st St. NW, Georgetown* ☎ *202/965–0400* ⊕ *www. tudorplace.org* ✍ *House tour, $6, includes admission to garden; garden only, $2* ⊙ *Feb.–Dec. house tours Tues.–Fri. at 10, 11:30, 1, and 2:30, Sat. hourly 10–4, last tour at 3, Sun. at noon, 1, 2, and 3. Garden Nov.–Mar. and June–Aug., Mon.–Sat. 10–4; Apr., May, Sept., and Oct., Mon.–Sat. 10–4, Sun. noon–4.*

⟳ **Washington Navy Yard.** A 115-acre historic district with its own street system, the Washington Navy Yard is the Navy's oldest outpost on shore. Established in 1799 as a shipbuilding facility, it was burned during the War of 1812. Rebuilt and converted to weapons production by the mid-19th century, it gradually fell into disuse until the 1960s, when it was revived as an administrative center.

The **Navy Museum** (☎ *202/433–4882 Navy Museum, 202/433–4882 USS Barry* ⊕ *www.history.navy.mil*), in Building 76, chronicles the history of the U.S. Navy from the Revolution to the present. Exhibits range from the fully rigged foremast of the USS *Constitution* (better known as Old Ironsides) to a U.S. Navy Corsair fighter plane dangling from the ceiling. All around are models of fighting ships, working periscopes, displays on battles, and portraits of the sailors who fought them. The decommissioned U.S. Navy destroyer *Barry,* open weekdays 10–4, floats a few hundred yards away in the Anacostia River. In front of the museum is a collection of guns, cannons, and missiles. Call ahead to schedule a free weekday highlights tour—and to double-check visiting hours and access policy, especially during periods of heightened security. Hours for the Navy Museum are generally weekdays 9–4, and appointments are necessary for those without U.S. military ID. On weekdays, civilian visitors should enter at 9th Street and M Street.

Visitors can enter at 6th Street and M Street on weekends. Note that weekend visitors should make reservations a week in advance.

The **Navy Art Gallery** (☎202/433–3815 ⊕ *www.history.navy.mil*), in Building 67, exhibits Navy-related paintings, sketches, and drawings, many created during combat by Navy artists. The bulk of the collection illustrates World War II. Hours for the Navy Art Gallery are Wednesday through Friday 9–4, Saturday 10–4, and Sunday noon–4. ✉*O and 11th Sts. SE, Capitol Hill* ☞*Free; park free with advance reservation* Ⓜ*Eastern Market.*

Woodrow Wilson House. President Wilson and his second wife, Edith Bolling Wilson, retired in 1920 to this Georgian Revival designed by Washington architect Waddy B. Wood. (Wood also designed the Department of the Interior and the National Museum of Women in the Arts.) The house was built in 1915 for a carpet merchant.

President Wilson suffered a stroke toward the end of his second term, in 1919, and he lived out the last few years of his life on this quiet street. Edith made sure he was comfortable; she had a bed constructed that had the same dimensions as the large Lincoln bed Wilson had slept in while in the White House. She also had the house's trunk lift (a sort of dumbwaiter for trunks) converted to an Otis elevator so the partially paralyzed president could move from floor to floor. When the streetcars stopped running in 1962, the elevator stopped working; it had received its electricity directly from the streetcar line.

Wilson died in 1924. Edith survived him by 37 years. After she died in 1961, the house and its contents were bequeathed to the National Trust for Historic Preservation. On view inside are such items as a Gobelin tapestry, a baseball signed by King George V, and the shell casing from the first shot fired by U.S. forces in World War I. The house also contains memorabilia related to the history of the short-lived but influential League of Nations, including the colorful flag Wilson hoped would be adopted by that organization. ✉*2340 S St. NW, Kalorama* ☎*202/387–4062* ⊕*www.woodrowwilsonhouse.org* ☞*$7.50* ⊙*Tues.–Sun. 10–4* Ⓜ*Dupont Circle.*

Monuments & Memorials

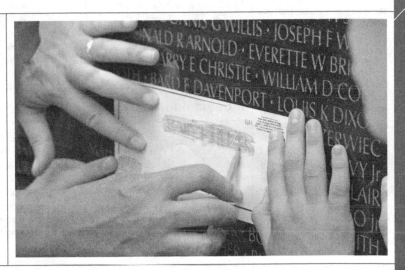

Vietnam War Memorial

WORD OF MOUTH

"I think the most amazing part of DC is the memorials—with the best one being the FDR memorial. If y'all are walkers you can do all the memorials in one day. If the weather is nice, it's a really great way to spend a day (FDR, Jefferson, Lincoln, Vietnam, Korean War, WW II)."

—Debi

MONUMENTS & MEMORIALS PLANNER

Making the Most of Your Time

It takes four or five hours to tour the monuments west of the Mall, with time to relax on a park bench and grab a snack from a vendor or one of the snack bars east of the Washington Monument, near the Lincoln Memorial.

If you're visiting during the first two weeks in April, take extra time around the Tidal Basin and the Washington Monument to marvel at the cherry blossoms. From mid-April through November, you might want to spend an hour on a paddleboat in the Tidal Basin. In summer, consider taking a Tourmobile bus and travel between the monuments in air-conditioned comfort.

Across the Potomac, Arlington National Cemetery merits a few hours on its own.

In the Works: the King Memorial

The Martin Luther King Jr. Memorial was scheduled to open in 2009, but as of this writing construction hadn't begun. When the Memorial does open, it will be the first major monument in the National Mall and Tidal Basin area devoted to a man who wasn't a president.

Ask a Ranger

You may think of park rangers as denizens of the woods, but they're a conspicuous presence at Washington's memorials—look for the olive-green and gray uniforms. Rangers lead talks about each monument and memorial run by the Park Service, with the exception of the Washington Monument, at 11, 1, 3, and 5 every day. They are an invaluable source of information; don't hesitate to ask questions of them. Kids can get Junior Park Ranger activity booklets from the ranger desks at the Lincoln, Jefferson, and World War II memorials.

Monumental Souvenirs

At Arlington National Cemetery there are gift shops at the visitor center, the Women in Military Service for America Memorial, and Arlington House. The National Park Service contracts with a private company that operates gift shops and bookstores at or near the FDR Memorial, Jefferson Memorial, Lincoln Memorial, and Washington Monument. Gift items tend to be the same at each shop. For a more eclectic selection, check out the AMERICA!'s Spirit and Making History shops in Union Station.

Walking & Biking Tours

Washington Walks (www.washingtonwalks.com) has tours with witty commentary that cover most of the major monuments and memorials. They operate from April through October, and prices range from $10 to $15. DC by Foot (www.dcbyfoot) offers free (work for tips) walking tours of the monuments. Tours meet near the Washington Monument every day at 2 and 6 from mid-February to mid-November. Bike and Roll (www.bikethesites.com) conducts tours on wheels from late March through November. The cost is $40 adults, $30 children 12 and under; price includes bike rental, helmet, bottled water, and snack.

4

Washington Circle

FOGGY BOTTOM

K St.

29

I St. NW

Pennsylvania Ave. NW

FARRAGUT NORTH

FARRAGUT WEST

16th St.

H St. NW

McPHERSON SQUARE

New York Ave.

14th St. NW

24th St. NW

23rd St. NW

22nd St. NW

Virginia Ave. NW

H St. NW

G St. NW

F St. NW

E St. NW

20th St. NW

19th St. NW

18th St. NW

17th St. NW

New York Ave.

The White House

15th St. NW

21st St. NW

23rd St. NW

D St. NW

C St. NW

C St. NW

E St. NW

The Ellipse

50

50 1

Vietnam Veterans Memorial

50

Henry Bacon Dr.

Constitution Gardens

Constitution Ave. NW

National World War II Memorial

Madison Dr.

THE MALL

U.S. Navy Memorial

Lincoln Memorial

Reflecting Pool

WEST POTOMAC PARK

Washington Monument

ington tional etery

Korean War Veterans Memorial

John Paul Jones Statue

14th St. SW

Basil Wartenberg Pl.

Daniel French Dr.

Independence Ave. SW

Kutz Bridge

toh rial idge

John Ericsson Memorial

Franklin Delano Roosevelt Memorial Park

Martin Luther King Jr. Memorial (under construction)

Maine Ave.

Boat House

Outlet Bridge

W. Basin Dr.

Tidal Basin

W. Basin Dr.

Ohio Dr. SW

Franklin Delano Roosevelt Monument

Jefferson Memorial

Francis Case Memorial Bridge

Potomac River

Inlet Bridge

EAST POTOMAC PARK

1

395

George Washington Memorial Pkwy

Columbia Island

George Mason Memorial Br.

Rochambeau Memorial Br.

Arland D. Williams Jr. Memorial Br.

Ohio Dr. SW

Lady Bird Johnson Park

IRGINIA

NITED STATES R FORCE MEMORIAL

0   200 yards

0   200 meters

By Kathryn
McKay

Washington is a monumental city. In the middle of traffic circles, on tiny slivers of park, and at street corners and intersections, you find statues, plaques, and simple blocks of marble honoring the generals, artists, and statesmen who helped shape the nation. Of these tributes, the greatest and grandest are clustered west of the Mall on ground reclaimed from the marshy flats of the Potomac—which also happens to be the location of Washington's most striking display of cherry trees.

These monuments now look like they're part of the landscape, but their beginnings were often controversial. From the Lincoln Memorial to the Vietnam Veterans Memorial, they sparked sometimes fierce debate over how and why America should enshrine its history. Over time, though, they've become icons of unquestionable significance.

Visit the memorials on the Mall and Tidal Basin at night for fewer crowds and cooler air. Although you won't get the views, the lighting is particularly beautiful on the Lincoln and Jefferson memorials. Inside the Lincoln, lights and shadows play across his face, making him look even more thoughtful.

Across the Potomac, Arlington National Cemetery memorial has a power all its own. Though it pays tribute to great Americans, including Robert and John F. Kennedy, what's most striking about the cemetery is its "sea of stones"—the thousands upon thousands of graves holding men and women who served in the U.S. military.

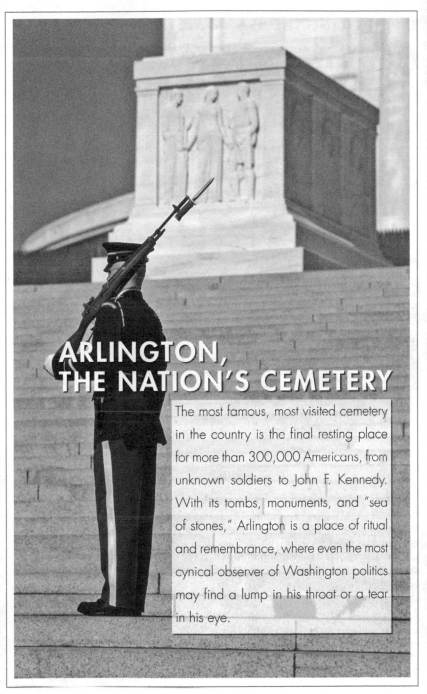

ARLINGTON, THE NATION'S CEMETERY

The most famous, most visited cemetery in the country is the final resting place for more than 300,000 Americans, from unknown soldiers to John F. Kennedy. With its tombs, monuments, and "sea of stones," Arlington is a place of ritual and remembrance, where even the most cynical observer of Washington politics may find a lump in his throat or a tear in his eye.

EXPERIENCING THE SEA OF STONES

In 1864, a 612-acre plot directly across the Potomac from Washington, part of the former plantation home of Robert E. Lee, was established as America's national cemetery.

Today, Arlington's major monuments and memorials are impressive, but the most striking experience is simply looking out over the thousands upon thousands of headstones aligned across the cemetery's hills.

Most of those buried here served in the military—from reinterred Revolutionary War soldiers to troops killed in Iraq and Afghanistan. As you walk through the cemetery, you're likely to hear a trumpet playing taps or the report of a gun salute. An average of 27 funerals a day are held here, Monday through Friday. There currently are some 300,000 graves in Arlington; it's projected that the cemetery will be filled by 2020.

FINDING A GRAVE
At the visitor center, staff members and computers can help you find the location of a specific grave. You need to provide the deceased's full name and, if possible, the branch of service and year of death.

CHARLES
ORBIE
FARRIS
RM1
US COAST GUARD
WORLD WAR II
SEP 10 1920
OCT 2 1988

WHO GETS BURIED WHERE

With few exceptions, interment at Arlington is limited to active-duty members of the armed forces, veterans, and their spouses and minor children. In Arlington's early years as a cemetery, burial location was determined by rank (as well as, initially, by race), with separate sections for enlisted soldiers and officers. Beginning in 1947, this distinction was abandoned. Gravesites are assigned on the day before burial; when possible, requests are honored to be buried near the graves of family members.

ABOUT THE HEADSTONES

Following the Civil War, Arlington's first graves were marked by simple whitewashed boards. When these decayed, they were replaced by cast iron markers covered with zinc to prevent rusting. Only one iron marker remains, for the grave of Captain Daniel Keys (Section 13, Lot 13615, Grid G-29/30).

In 1873, Congress voted in the use of marble headstones, which continues to be the practice today. The government provides the standard-issue stones free of charge. Next of kin may supply their own headstones, though they can only be used if space is available in one of the sections where individualized stones already exist.

THE SAME, BUT DIFFERENT

Regulation headstones can be engraved with one of 26 symbols indicating religious affiliation. In section 60, the headstones of soldiers killed in Afghanistan and Iraq reflect the multicultural makeup of 21st-century America. Along with a variety of crosses and the Star of David, you see the nine-pointed star of the Baha'i; a tepee and three feathers representing the Native American faiths; the Muslim crescent and star; and other signs of faith. (Or lack of it—atheism is represented by a stylized atom.)

PLANNING YOUR VISIT TO ARLINGTON

ARLINGTON BASICS

Getting There: You can reach Arlington on the Metro, by foot over Arlington Memorial Bridge (southwest of the Lincoln Memorial), or by car—there's a large parking lot by the visitor center on Memorial Drive. Also, the Tourmobile bus (⊕ *www.tourmobile.com* ☎ *202/554–7950*) and Old Town Trolley (⊕ *www.oldtowntrolley.com,* ☎ *202/832–9800*) both have Arlington National Cemetery stops in their loops.

🕑 Apr.–Sept., daily 8–7; Oct.–Mar., daily 8–5.

💳 Cemetery free, parking $1.25 per hr. Tourmobile Arlington Tour $7.50, Old Town Trolley $32.

☎ 703/607–8000 for general information and to locate a grave.

⊕ *www.arlingtoncemetery.org*

✗ No food or drink are allowed at the cemetery. There are water fountains in the Visitor Center, and from fall through spring a water fountain operates near the amphitheater at the Tomb of the Unknowns. You can also purchase bottled water at the Women's Memorial.

TOURING OPTIONS

Your first stop at the cemetery should be the visitor center, where you can pick up a free brochure with a detailed map. Once there you have a choice: tour by bus or walk.

Arlington by Bus. Tourmobile tour buses leave every 15 to 25 minutes from just outside the visitor center April through September, daily 8:30–6:30, and October through March, daily 8:30–4:30. The 45-minute tour includes stops at the Kennedy gravesites, the Tomb of the Unknowns, and Arlington House. Your bus driver will provide basic facts about the cemetery.

Arlington by Foot. Walking the cemetery requires some stamina, but it allows you to take in the thousands of graves at your own pace. On the facing page is a walking tour that includes the major points of interest.

Top left: USS Maine mast memorial listing names of crew. Top left: 3rd Infantry Honor Guard

A WALKING TOUR

■ Head west from the visitor center on Roosevelt Drive and turn right on Weeks Drive to reach the **Kennedy graves**; just to the west is **Arlington House**. (¼ mile)

■ Take Crook Walk south, following the signs, to the **Tomb of the Unknowns**; a few steps from the tomb is **Section 7A**, where many distinguished veterans are buried. (³/10 mile)

■ To visit the graves of soldiers killed in Afghanistan and Iraq, take Roosevelt Drive past section 7 and turn right on McClellan Drive, turn right when you get to Eisenhower Drive, then go left onto York Drive. The graves will be on your right. (⁶/10 mile)

■ Walk north along Eisenhower Drive, which becomes Schley Drive; turn right onto Custis Walk, which brings you to **Section 27,** where 3,800 former slaves are buried. (¾ mile)

■ Leave the cemetery through the Ord and Weitzel Gate, cross Marshall Drive carefully, and walk to the 50-bell **Netherlands Carillon**, where there's a good vista of Washington. To the north is the **United States Marine Corps War Memorial**, better known as the **Iwo Jima Memorial**. (¼ mile)

ARLINGTON'S MAIN ATTRACTIONS

The Kennedy Graves

Once while taking in the view of Washington from Arlington National Cemetery, President John F. Kennedy commented, "I could stay here forever." Seeing Kennedy's grave is a top priority for most visitors. He's buried beneath an eternal flame, next to graves of two of his children who died in infancy, and of his wife, Jacqueline Kennedy Onassis. Across from them is a low wall engraved with quotations from Kennedy's inaugural address. Nearby, marked by a simple white cross, is Robert Kennedy's grave.

The gas-fueled flame at the head of John F. Kennedy's grave was lit by Jacqueline Kennedy during his funeral. A continuously flashing electric spark reignites the gas if the flame is extinguished by rain, wind, or any other cause.

Many visitors ask where Kennedy's son John F. Kennedy Jr. is buried. His ashes were scattered in the Atlantic Ocean, near the location where his plane went down in 1999.

Arlington House

Long before Arlington was a cemetery, it was part of the 1,100-acre estate of George Washington Parke Custis, a grandchild of Martha and (by marriage) George Washington. Custis built Arlington House between 1802 and 1817. After his death, the property went to his daughter, Mary Anna Randolph Custis, who wed Robert E. Lee in 1831. The couple made Arlington House their home for the next 30 years.

In 1861 Lee turned down the position of commander of the Union forces and left Arlington House, never to return. Union troops turned the house into the Army of the Potomac's headquarters, and 200 acres were set aside as a national cemetery. By the end of the Civil War more than 16,000 headstones dotted the estate's hills.

Today the house looks much as it did in the 19th century. Most furnishings have been removed temporarily as the house undergoes renovation (scheduled to last until 2010), but you can still take a guided tour (every 20 min.) or walk through. ☎ 703/235–1530 ⊕ www.nps.gov/arho ✉ Free ☉ Daily 9:30–4:30.

Robert E. Lee

Tomb of the Unknowns

The first burial at the Tomb of the Unknowns, one of the cemetery's most imposing monuments, took place on November 11, 1921. In what was part of a world-wide trend to honor the dead after the unparalleled devastation of World War I, an unidentified soldier was interred under the large white-marble sarcophagus. Unknown servicemen killed in World War II and Korea joined him in 1958.

The Memorial Amphitheater west of the tomb is used for ceremonies on Veterans Day, Memorial Day, and Easter. Decorations awarded to the unknowns are displayed in an indoor trophy room.

One of the most striking activities at Arlington is the precision and pageantry of the changing of the guard at the Tomb of the Unknowns. From April through September, soldiers from the Army's U.S. Third Infantry (known as the Old Guard) change guard every half hour during the day. For the rest of the year, and at night all year long, the guard changes every hour.

The Iwo Jima Memorial

Ask the Tourmobile driver at Arlington where the Iwo Jima is, and you might get back the quip "very far away." The memorial commonly called the Iwo Jima is officially named the United States Marine Corps War Memorial, and it's actually located just north of the cemetery. Its bronze sculpture is based on one of the most famous photos in American military history, Joe Rosenthal's February 19, 1945, shot of five marines and a navy corpsman raising a flag atop Mt. Suribachi on the Japanese island of Iwo Jima. By executive order, a real flag flies 24 hours a day from the 78-foot-high memorial. ☎ *703/289–2500*

On Tuesday evening at 7 p.m. from late May to late August there's a Marine Corps sunset parade on the grounds of the Iwo Jima Memorial. On parade nights a free shuttle bus runs from the Arlington Cemetery visitors' parking lot.

The Old Guard are not making a fashion statement in their sunglasses—they're protecting their eyes from the sun's glare off the white marble of the tomb.

FRANKLIN DELANO ROOSEVELT MEMORIAL

- ⊠ West side of Tidal Basin
- ☎ 202/426–6841
- ⊕ www.nps.gov/fdrm
- 🎫 Free
- ⊘ Open 24 hrs; staffed daily 8 AM–midnight
- Ⓜ Smithsonian

TIPS

■ If you come with a toddler, head straight to the third room. Though youngsters can't sit on Roosevelt's lap, they can pet Fala, Roosevelt's Scottish terrier. The tips of Fala's ears and his nose shine from all the attention.

■ Allow about 30 minutes at this memorial. Take your time walking through the most expansive presidential memorial in Washington and read the lines from FDR's speeches.

■ This was the first memorial designed to be wheelchair accessible. Several pillars with Braille lettering and tactile images help the visually impaired.

■ This memorial presents good opportunities for family photographs. You can strike a pose while petting Fala, joining the men in the breadline, or listening to Roosevelt's fireside chat.

■ At night the lighting over the waterfalls creates interesting shadows, and there's not as much noise from airplanes overhead.

Unveiled in 1997, this 7½-acre memorial to the 32nd president includes waterfalls and reflecting pools, four outdoor gallery rooms—one for each of Roosevelt's presidential terms—and 10 bronze sculptures. The granite megaliths connecting the galleries are engraved with some of Roosevelt's famous statements, including, "The only thing we have to fear is fear itself."

HIGHLIGHTS

Congress established the Franklin Delano Roosevelt Memorial Commission in 1955, and invited prospective designers to look to "the character and work of Roosevelt to give us the theme of a memorial." Several decades passed before Lawrence Halprin's design for a "walking environmental experience" was selected. It incorporates work by artists Leonard Baskin, Neil Estern, Robert Graham, Thomas Hardy, and George Segal, and master stone carver John Benson.

The statue of a wheelchair-bound Roosevelt near the entrance of the memorial was added in 2001. Originally, the memorial showed little evidence of Roosevelt's polio, which he contracted at age 39. He used a wheelchair for the last 24 years of his life, but kept his disability largely hidden from public view. The statue was added after years of debate about whether to portray Roosevelt realistically, or to honor his desire not to display his disability.

A bronze statue of First Lady Eleanor Roosevelt stands in front of the United Nations symbol in the fourth room. She was a vocal spokesperson for human rights and one of the most influential women of her time.

You're encouraged to touch the handprints along the columns in the second room, which represent the working hands of the American people.

KOREAN WAR VETERANS MEMORIAL

✉ West end of Mall at Daniel French Dr. and Independence Ave.

☎ 202/426–6841

⊕ www.nps.gov/kwvm

🎟 Free

⏱ Open 24 hrs; staffed daily 8 AM–midnight

Ⓜ Foggy Bottom

4

TIPS

■ Allow about 10 or 15 minutes at this memorial.

■ A sign at the entrance to the memorial indicates the time of the next park ranger-led interpretive talk.

■ You can get service information on the soldiers who died in the Korean War from the touch-screen computer at the memorial information booth. Further information about veterans and casualties is available at ⊕ *www. koreanwar.org.*

■ For Parents: It's tempting for kids to trek through the field with the statues, but they're not allowed to. They can strike a pose next to the wall and see their reflection added to those of the 19 soldiers.

■ Visit the shop in the nearby Lincoln Memorial for books and souvenirs relating to the Korean War.

This memorial to the 1.5 million United States men and women who served in the Korean War (1950–53) highlights the high cost of freedom. Nearly 37,000 Americans were killed on the Korean peninsula, 8,000 were missing in action, and more than 103,000 were wounded. The privately funded memorial was dedicated on July 27, 1995, on the 42nd anniversary of the Korean War Armistice. Compare this memorial to the more intimate Vietnam Veterans Memorial and the grandiose World War II Memorial.

HIGHLIGHTS

In the "Field of Service," 19 oversize stainless-steel soldiers toil through a rugged triangular terrain toward an American flag; look beneath the helmets to see their weary faces. The reflection in the polished black granite wall to their right doubles their number to 38, symbolic of the 38th parallel, the latitude established as the border between North and South Korea in 1953, as well as the 38 months of the war.

Unlike many memorials, this one contains few words, but what's there is poignant. The 164-foot-long granite wall etched with the faces of 2,400 unnamed servicemen and servicewomen says simply, "Freedom is not free." The plaque at the base of the flagpole reads, "Our nation honors her sons and daughters who answered the call to defend a country they never knew and a people they never met." The only other words are the names of 22 countries that volunteered forces or medical support, including Great Britain, France, Greece, and Turkey.

The adjacent circular Pool of Remembrance honors all who were killed, captured, wounded, or missing in action; it's a quiet spot for contemplation.

LINCOLN MEMORIAL

✉ West end of Mall

☎ 202/426–6841

🌐 www.nps.gov/linc

🎫 Free

🕐 Open 24 hrs; staffed daily
   8 AM–midnight

Ⓜ Foggy Bottom

TIPS

■ On the lower level of the memorial is a small museum financed with pennies collected by schoolchildren.

■ At night the memorial is illuminated, creating a striking play of light and shadow across Lincoln's face.

■ Lincoln's face and hands look especially lifelike because they're based on castings done while he was president. Those who know sign language might recognize that the left hand is shaped like an A and the right like an L. It's unlikely this was intentional, but the sculptor, Daniel Chester French, did have a deaf son.

■ The events of April 14, 1865, which shocked the nation, continue to fascinate. See where Lincoln was shot at Ford's Theatre (✉ *511 10th St., NW*) and the bullet that killed him at the National Museum of Health and Medicine (✉ *6900 Georgia Avenue and Elder St., NW* 🌐 *nmhm. washingtondc.museum*).

Many consider the Lincoln Memorial the most inspiring monument in Washington, but that hasn't always been the case: early detractors thought it inappropriate that a president known for his humility should be honored with what amounts to a grandiose Greek temple. The memorial was intended to be a symbol of national unity, but over time it has come to represent social justice and civil rights.

HIGHLIGHTS

Daniel Chester French's statue of the seated president gazes out over the Reflecting Pool. The 19-foot-high sculpture is made of 28 pieces of Georgia marble.

The surrounding white Colorado-marble memorial was designed by Henry Bacon and completed in 1922. The 36 Doric columns represent the 36 states in the Union at the time of Lincoln's death; their names appear on the frieze above the columns. Over the frieze are the names of the 48 states in existence when the memorial was dedicated. Alaska and Hawaii are represented with an inscription on the terrace leading up to the memorial.

Two of Lincoln's great speeches—the Second Inaugural Address and the Gettysburg Address—are carved on the north and south walls. Above each is a Jules Guerin mural: the south wall has an angel of truth freeing a slave; the unity of North and South is opposite.

The memorial's powerful symbolism makes it a popular gathering place: In its shadow, Americans marched for integrated schools in 1958, rallied for an end to the Vietnam War in 1967, and laid wreaths in a ceremony honoring the Iranian hostages in 1979. It may be best known, though, as the site of Martin Luther King Jr.'s "I Have a Dream" speech.

MARTIN LUTHER KING JR. MEMORIAL

✉ 401 F St., NW

☎ 202/737-5420 or 1-888-484-3373

⊕ www.buildthedream.org

🎟 Free

⊙ Open 24 hours. Staffed daily 8 AM–midnight

Ⓜ Smithsonian

TIPS

■ Allow about 20 to 30 minutes at this memorial, which is being designed as a place for reflection. For a look at local African American history, visit the Frederick Douglass National Historic Site (✉ *1411 W St., SE* ☎ *202/426-5961 or 202/619-7222* ⊕ *www. nps.gov/frdo*). Tours focus on Douglass's life in D.C. and his mansion.

■ If the memorial isn't in place yet (or even if it is), walk over to the Lincoln Memorial, where you can stand on the same step where King delivered his "I Have a Dream" speech. There's a plaque that marks the exact spot.

■ Contrary to popular belief, King won't be the first African American with a memorial in D.C. That honor goes to Mary McLeod Bethune, founder of the National Council of Negro Women and an informal advisor to FDR. Bethune is depicted in a 17-foot tall bronze statue (✉ *Lincoln Park, East Capitol and 12th Sts, NE*). King is, however, the first African-American to be placed in Area 1 of the National Mall.

There will soon be a "King" among the presidents on the National Mall. Although the Martin Luther King Jr. memorial is expected to be dedicated sometime in 2009, thirteen years after Congress approved it in 1996 and 80 years after the famed Civil Rights leader was born in 1929, don't be surprised if there are delays. At this writing, construction had not yet begun on the memorial.

HIGHLIGHTS

Located strategically between the Lincoln and Jefferson memorials and adjacent to the FDR Memorial, the crescent shaped King Memorial will sit on a four-acre site on the curved bank of the Tidal Basin.

Visitors will enter through a center walkway cut out of a huge boulder, the Mountain of Despair. From the Mountain, the Stone of Hope will be visible. The symbolism of the mountain and stone are explained by King's words: "With this faith, we will be able to hew out of the mountain of despair a stone of hope." The centerpiece Stone will be carved by Chinese sculptor Lei Yixin; his design was chosen from more than 900 entries in an international competition. Fittingly, Yixin first read about King's "I Have a Dream" speech at age 10 while visiting the Lincoln Memorial. The 28-foot tall granite boulder will include Lei's rendering of King, whose eyes will meet Jefferson's gaze.

The themes of democracy, justice, hope, and love will be reflected through more than a dozen quotes on the south and north walls and on the Stone of Hope. The quotes reflect speeches, sermons, and writings penned by King from 1955 through 1968. Waterfalls in the memorial will reflect King's use of the biblical quote: "Let justice roll down like waters and righteousness like a mighty stream."

4

NATIONAL WORLD WAR II MEMORIAL

✉ 17th St., at east side of Washington Monument

☎ 202/426–6841

⊕ www.wwiimemorial.com

🎫 Free

🕙 Open 24 hrs

Ⓜ Smithsonian

TIPS

■ Look for veterans. Perhaps the best part of visiting this memorial might be the last opportunities to see men and women who fought in World War II and are part of what former NBC news anchor Tom Brokaw called "The Greatest Generation."

■ Computers at the National Park Service kiosk behind the Pacific side of the memorial contain information about soldiers who lost their lives in the war.

■ Kids might be bored here. You can engage their attention by asking them to look carefully at the bas-reliefs for a dog and a radio as large as today's big-screen televisions. Then try to find Kilroy, the cartoonlike character who appears to be looking over a ledge. The image and the phrase "Kilroy was here" were popular graffiti left by U.S. soldiers during the war.

Dedicated just before Memorial Day in 2004, this symmetrically designed monument honors the 16 million Americans who served in the armed forces, the more than 400,000 who died, and all who supported the war effort at home.

HIGHLIGHTS

An imposing circle of 56 granite pillars, each bearing a bronze wreath, represents the U.S. states and territories of 1941–45. Four bronze eagles, a bronze garland, and two 43-foot-tall arches inscribed with "Atlantic" and "Pacific" surround the large circular plaza. The roar of the water comes from the Rainbow Pool, here since the 1920s but newly renovated as the centerpiece of the memorial. There are also two fountains and two waterfalls.

The Field of Stars, a wall of 4,000 gold stars, commemorates the more than 400,000 Americans who lost their lives in the war.

Although the parklike setting and the place of honor between the Washington Monument and the Lincoln Memorial may seem appropriate, some people were critical when the site for the memorial was announced, because they felt it would interrupt the landscape between the two landmarks and because it uses some of the open space that had been the site of demonstrations and protests.

Bas-relief panels tell the story of how World War II affected Americans by depicting women in the military, V-J Day, medics, the bond drive, and more activities of the time. The 24 panels are divided evenly between the Atlantic front and the Pacific front.

THOMAS JEFFERSON MEMORIAL

✉ Tidal Basin, south bank
☎ 202/426–6841
⊕ www.nps.gov/thje
🎫 Free
⊙ Daily 8 AM–midnight
Ⓜ Smithsonian

TIPS

■ Check out the view of the White House from the memorial's steps—it's one of the best. Jefferson was the second president to live in the White House, but the first full-term occupant.

■ Park ranger programs are offered throughout the day, and you can ask questions of the ranger on duty.

■ Learn more about Jefferson by visiting the exhibit called Light and Liberty on the memorial's lower level. It chronicles highlights of Jefferson's life and has a timeline of world history during his lifetime.

■ Allow 15 minutes to walk here from the Metro. The memorial is the southernmost of Washington's major monuments and memorials, and it's a full four blocks and a trip around the Tidal Basin from the nearest Metro stop, Smithsonian.

■ Limited parking is available under the 14th Street Bridge, off Ohio Drive near where it intersects with East Basin Drive.

4

In the 1930s Congress decided that Thomas Jefferson deserved a monument positioned as prominently as those honoring Washington and Lincoln. Workers scooped and moved tons of the river bottom to create dry land for the spot directly south of the White House where the monument was built. Jefferson had always admired the Pantheon in Rome, so the memorial's architect, John Russell Pope, drew on it for inspiration. His finished work was dedicated on the bicentennial of Jefferson's birth, April 13, 1943.

HIGHLIGHTS

Early critics weren't kind to the memorial—rumor has it that it was nicknamed "Jefferson's muffin" for its domed shape. The design was called outdated and too similar to that of the Lincoln Memorial. Indeed, both statues of Jefferson and Lincoln are 19 feet, just six inches shorter than the statue of Freedom atop the Capitol.

The bronze statue of Jefferson, standing on a 6-foot granite pedestal, looms larger than life. It wasn't always made of bronze. The first version was made of plaster, because bronze was too expensive and was needed for the war. The statue you see today was erected in 1947.

You can get a taste of Jefferson's keen intellect from his writings about freedom and government inscribed on the marble walls surrounding his statue.

Many people may be surprised to learn that Jefferson didn't list being president as one of his greatest accomplishments. When he appraised his own life, Jefferson wanted to be remembered as the "Author of the Declaration of American Independence, of the Statute of Virginia for religious freedom, and Father of the University of Virginia."

VIETNAM VETERANS MEMORIAL

✉ Constitution Gardens, 23rd St. and Constitution Ave. NW

☎ 202/426–6841

⊕ www.nps.gov/vive

💲 Free

🕑 24 hrs; staffed daily 8 AM–midnight

Ⓜ Foggy Bottom

TIPS

■ Names on the wall are ordered by date of death. To find a name, consult the alphabetical lists found at either end of the wall. You can get assistance locating a name at the white kiosk with the brown roof near the entrance. At the wall, rangers and volunteers wearing yellow caps can look up the names and supply you with paper and pencils for making rubbings.

■ Every name on the memorial is preceded (on the west wall) or followed (on the east wall) by a symbol designating status. A diamond indicates "killed, body recovered." A plus sign (found by a small percentage of names) indicates "killed: body not recovered."

■ If you're visiting with older children or teens, be prepared for questions about war and death. Sometimes children think all 58,259 soldiers are buried at the monument. They aren't, of course, but the wall is as evocative as any cemetery.

"The Wall," as it's commonly called, is one of the most-visited sites in Washington. The names of more than 58,000 Americans who died in the Vietnam War are etched in its black granite panels, creating a somber, dignified, and powerful memorial. It was conceived by Jan Scruggs, a former infantry corporal who served in Vietnam, and designed by Maya Lin, a 21-year-old architecture student at Yale.

HIGHLIGHTS

Thousands of offerings are left at the wall each year: many people leave flowers, others leave personal objects such as the clothing of soldiers or letters of thanks from schoolchildren. The National Park Service collects and stores the items. In 2007 Congress approved the establishment of a memorial center to display many of the items left near the Wall. A small assortment, including wedding rings, a baseball, and photographs, is displayed at the National Museum of American History.

The statues near the wall came about in response to controversies surrounding the memorial. In 1984 Frederick Hart's statue of three soldiers and a flagpole was erected to the south of the wall, with the goal of winning over veterans who considered the memorial a "black gash of shame." A memorial plaque was added in 2004 at the statue of three servicemen to honor veterans who died after the war as a direct result of injuries suffered in Vietnam, but who fall outside Department of Defense guidelines for remembrance at the wall.

The Vietnam Women's Memorial was dedicated on Veterans Day 1993. Glenna Goodacre's bronze sculpture depicts two women caring for a wounded soldier while a third woman kneels nearby; eight trees around the plaza commemorate the eight women in the military who died in Vietnam.

WASHINGTON MONUMENT

✉ Constitution Ave. and 15th St. NW

☎ 202/426–6841, 877/444–6777 for advance tickets

⊕ www.nps.gov/wamo; www.recreation.gov for advance tickets

🎫 Free; $2 service fee per advance ticket

🕙 Daily 9–5

Ⓜ Smithsonian

4

TIPS

■ The monument uses a free timed-ticket system for the elevator ride. A limited number of tickets are available each day beginning a half hour before the monument opens at the marble lodge on 15th Street. In spring and summer lines are likely to start much earlier. Tickets are also available online for a $2 service charge. Each ticket is good for a designated half-hour period.

■ Maps below viewing station windows point out some of Washington's major buildings.

■ From the elevator you can see some of the monument's 192 inscribed memorial stones. Twice a day, at 10:30 and 12:30, an hour-long walking tour descends the memorial's 800 steps; on it, you learn the stories behind the stones. For your best chance of getting on the tour, snag elevator tickets for 10 or noon.

At the western end of the Mall, the 555-foot, 5-inch Washington Monument punctuates the capital like a huge exclamation point. Inside, an elevator takes you to the top for a bird's-eye view of the city.

The monument was part of Pierre L'Enfant's plan for Washington, but his intended location proved to be marshy, so it was moved 100 yards southeast to firmer ground. (A stone marker now indicates L'Enfant's original site.) Construction began in 1848 and continued, with interruptions, until 1884. The design called for an obelisk rising from a circular colonnaded building, which was to be adorned with statues of national heroes, including Washington riding in a chariot. When the Army Corps of Engineers took over construction in 1876, the building around the obelisk was abandoned. Upon its completion, the monument was the world's tallest structure. It's still the tallest in Washington.

HIGHLIGHTS

An elevator whizzes to the top of the monument in 70 seconds—a trip that in 1888 took 12 minutes via steam-powered elevator. From the viewing stations at the top you can take in most of the District of Columbia, as well as parts of Maryland and Virginia.

There's a story behind the change in color of the stone about a third of the way up the monument. In 1854, six years into construction, members of the anti-Catholic Know-Nothing Party stole and smashed a block of marble donated by Pope Pius IX. This action, combined with funding shortages and the onset of the Civil War, brought construction to a halt. After the war, building finally resumed, and though the new marble came from the same Maryland quarry as the old, it was taken from a different stratum with a slightly different shade.

OTHER MEMORIALS

National Law Enforcement Officers Memorial. This 3-foot-high wall bears the names of more than 15,000 American police officers killed in the line of duty since 1792. On the third line of panel 13W are the names of six officers killed by William Bonney, better known as Billy the Kid. J.D. Tippit, the Dallas policeman killed by Lee Harvey Oswald, is honored on the ninth line of panel 63E. Some of the most recent additions include the names of the 71 officers who died due to 9/11. Computers there allow you to look up officers by name, date of death, state, and department. Call to arrange for a free tour. A National Law Enforcement Museum is in the works, scheduled for completion in 2011. ⊠605 E St. NW, East End ☎202/737–3400 ⊕www.nleomf. com ⊠Free ⊙ Weekdays 9–5, Sat. 10–5, Sun. noon–5 Ⓜ Gallery Pl./ Chinatown or Judiciary Sq.

United States Air Force Memorial. Adjacent to the southern portion of Arlington National Cemetery and visible from the Tidal Basin and I–395 near Washington, three stainless-steel, asymmetrical spires slice through the skyline up to 270 feet, representing flight, the precision of the "bomb burst" maneuver performed by the Air Force Thunderbirds, and the three core values of the Air Force: integrity, service, and excellence. At the base of the spires is an eight-foot statue of the honor guard, a glass wall engraved with the missing man formation, and granite walls inscribed with Air Force values and accomplishments. ⊠One Air Force Memorial Drive, Arlington, VA, ☎703/979–0674 ⊕www. airforcememorial.org ⊠Free ⊙ Apr. 1–Sept. 30, daily 8–11 PM; Oct. 1–Mar. 31, daily 8–9 PM Ⓜ Pentagon.

United States Navy Memorial. Although Pierre L'Enfant included a Navy Memorial in his plans for Washington, D.C., it wasn't until 1987 that one was built. The main attraction here is an 860-ton, 100-foot-in-diameter granite map of the world, known as the Granite Sea. It's surrounded by fountains, benches, and six ship masts. The Lone Sailor, a 7-foot tall statue, stands on the map in the Pacific Ocean between the United States and Japan. The Naval Heritage Center, next to the memorial in the Market Square East Building, displays videos and exhibits of uniforms, medals, and other aspects of Navy life. If you've served in the Navy, you can enter your record of service into the Navy Log here. The theater shows a rotating series of Navy-related movies throughout the day. Bronze relief panels on the Pennsylvania Avenue side of the memorial depict 26 scenes commemorating events in the nation's naval history and honoring naval communities. ■TIP→The panels are at a perfect height for children to look at and touch; challenge your child to find these items: a helicopter, a seagull, a U.S. flag, a sailor with binoculars, a dog, penguins, and seals. If you look carefully at the flagpole nearest the entrance to the Heritage Center, you'll see a time capsule, scheduled to be opened in 2093. ⊠701 Pennsylvania Ave. NW, ☎202/737–2300 ⊕www.navymemorial.org ⊠Free ⊙24 hrs; Naval Heritage Center Mar.–Oct., Mon.–Sat. 9:30–5; Nov.–Feb., Tues.–Sat. 9:30–5 Ⓜ Archives/Navy Memorial.

Official
Washington

Supreme Court Building

WORD OF MOUTH

"Do rethink and request the Capitol tour, you will be so glad you did. Standing in the rotunda you don't get the politics vibe at all, just a terrific sense of patriotism. If you love history, it's a must. We loved the White House tour also, but you gotta go to the Capitol!"

—texasjo

OFFICIAL WASHINGTON PLANNER

Tips for Visiting with Kids

Before visiting the Capitol, talk to kids about Congress's role in the government and the Capitol's place in history. Then during the tour, encourage them to move up front to see and hear better.

Many children hope to see the President or at least a presidential pet when touring the White House; the chances of glimpsing either are nil. Kids may take some consolation in knowing they can send an e-mail to the President at ✍ *president@ whitehouse.gov* or send a letter. The First Family even has its own zip code: 20500.

For something that interests every member of the family, you can't beat money. Kids get a kick out of seeing currency printed at the Bureau of Engraving and Printing. At the gift shop they can buy bags of shredded bills and get a postcard-size rendering of a dollar with their face in the place of George Washington's.

December at the White House

The White House is decorated for Christmas during December every year. Even before you enter the State Dining Room, you can smell the gingerbread. The White House gingerbread house tradition began during the Nixon Administration, and has been continued by the White House pastry chefs ever since. In 2006 more than 300 pounds of chocolate and gingerbread were used to create a replica of the White House, complete with presidential pets.

Since 1961 the Christmas tree in the Blue Room has reflected themes. In 1974 the Fords' Christmas-tree ornaments emphasized thrift and recycling. In 1977 the Carters' tree had ornaments made by members of the National Association of Retarded Citizens. In 1991 the Bushs' tree featured needlepoint figurines.

Note: December is far and away the most difficult time of year to secure a tour. The White House is able to accommodate fewer than 10% of the tour requests it receives.

Eggs on a Roll

Kids have been rolling Easter eggs at the White House since at least 1878. Over the years, the Egg Rolls have evolved into elaborate affairs with bands and bunnies. The event is held the Monday after Easter, from 8 AM to 2 PM on the South Lawn of the White House.

The National Park Service distributes free tickets on the Saturday before Easter at 7:30 AM and at 7:30 AM the day after Easter on a first-come, first-served basis at the Ellipse Visitor Pavilion (southwest corner of 15th and E streets). Each group has to include at least one child seven years old or under and no more than two adults. Tickets are required for every attendee, including small children, to enter the White House South Lawn. No tickets are necessary for access to activities on the Ellipse.

For the most up-to-date information on the Easter Egg Roll, call the White House 24-hour information line at ☎ *202/456–7041.*

Plan Ahead

You can visit many of Washington's government offices, but you have to do some advance planning in many cases—not just for the White House and Congress, but for less high-profile places as well. Here's a rundown of how far in advance you need to make arrangements. For contact information and further details, see listings within this chapter.

Site	Time in Advance
Capitol tour	Morning of visit
Congressional session	2 weeks–2 months
White House (spring, summer, December)	6 months
White House (other times)	1–2 months
Supreme Court	Morning of visit
American Red Cross	3 business days for Saturday tours
Department of Interior	2–4 weeks
Department of State	3 months
Federal Reserve	24 hours
Pentagon	2 weeks–3 months
Treasury Building	1–2 months

No Advance Planning Required

Two of the most impressive places in Washington don't require advance reservations. The Library of Congress and the Washington National Cathedral are architectural and artistic treasures.

The cathedral was dubbed at its creation a "House of Prayer for All People," and does indeed draw people from all over the world seeking comfort and reflection. Inside, a stained-glass window with an encapsulated moon rock celebrates the *Apollo 11* space flight, and statues of George Washington and Abraham Lincoln make it clear that this is a place where church and state are welcome to coexist. The library—the largest in the world—is adorned with mosaics, paintings, and statues, not to mention millions of books and manuscripts.

Contact Your Member of Congress

To visit the White House or the houses of Congress, you have to make arrangements through your representative or senator. You can find their contact information on the Web at ⊕ *www.house.gov* and ⊕ *www.senate.gov.* (You can also find them in your local phone book.)

Don't be reluctant to contact them—it's part of their job, and they have lots of experience handling such requests. Some will even invite you to meet with them and talk about your interests and concerns (or whatever else you want to talk about).

In the Works: The Capitol Visitor Center

After decades of planning and numerous delays, the Capitol Visitor Center announced its official public opening date: December 2, 2008. It was on the same date in 1863 that the Capitol Building dome was completed. The football-field-size underground complex will be a destination in itself, with numerous museum-like features, and it will also be the starting point for tours of the Capitol, running Monday through Saturday from 9:30 to 4:30, the last tour beginning at 3:30.

5

By Kathryn
McKay

Given the heightened security concerns of present-day Washington, it might come as a surprise to learn that most government institutions continue to welcome the general public. The Founding Fathers' mandate of a free and open government lives on—just with metal detectors and bag searches. Though security checks are no one's idea of fun, most people find them a small price to pay for the opportunity to get a first-hand look at the government in action. Being in the famous halls of the Capitol, the White House, or the Supreme Court is a heady experience. It's one part celebrity sighting and one part the world's best civics lesson.

While the Capitol, White House, and Supreme Court get the lion's share of the attention, other government institutions hold their own, sometimes quirky appeal. The Library of Congress is the most visitor-friendly, and it's truly impressive, even if you're not a bookworm; the free tour gives you a sense of its scope and grandeur.

If you're fascinated by finance, you'll want to plan ahead for visits to the Bureau of Engraving and Printing, the Federal Reserve, and the Department of Treasury. You need to sign up three months in advance for a tour of the Department of State, but your advance work will be rewarded with a visit to the plush Diplomatic Reception Rooms, where few sightseers tread.

ON THE HILL, UNDER THE DOME: EXPERIENCING THE CAPITOL

In Washington, the Capitol literally stands above it all: by law, no other building in the city can reach the height of the dome's peak.

Beneath its magnificent dome, the day-to-day business of American democracy takes place: senators and representatives debate, coax, and cajole, and ultimately determine the law of the land.

For many visitors, the Capitol is the most exhilarating experience Washington has to offer. It wins them over with a three-pronged appeal:

It's the city's most impressive work of architecture.

It has on display documents, art, and artifacts from 400 years of American history.

Its legislative chambers are open to the public. You can actually see your lawmakers at work, shaping the history of tomorrow.

TWO CENTURIES AND STILL GROWING

(Clockwise from top left) Moving into the new Capitol circa 1800; 19th century print by R. Brandard; Thornton sketch circa 1797; the Capitol before the dome.

1792 William Thornton, a physician and amateur architect from the West Indies, wins the competition to design the Capitol. His plan, with its central rotunda and dome, draws inspiration from Rome's Pantheon.

1793 On September 18, 1793, George Washington lays the Capitol's cornerstone.

1800 In November, Congress moves from Philadelphia to take up residence in the first completed section, the boxlike area between the central rotunda and today's north wing.

1807 The House wing is completed, just to the south of the rotunda; a covered wooden walkway joins the two wings.

1814 British troops march on Washington and set fire to the Capitol, the White House, and other government buildings. The wooden walkway is destroyed and the two wings gutted, but the walls remain standing after a violent rainstorm douses the flames. Fearful that Congress might leave Washington, residents fund a temporary "Brick Capitol" on the spot where the Supreme Court is today.

1826 Reconstruction is completed under the guidance of architects Benjamin Henry Latrobe and Charles Bulfinch; a low dome is made of wood sheathed in copper.

1850s North and south wings are added through the 1850s and 60s to accommodate the growing government of a growing country.

1855 To maintain scale with the enlarged building, work begins on a taller, cast-iron dome. President Lincoln would be criticized for continuing the expensive project during the Civil War, but he calls the construction "a sign we intend the Union shall go on."

(Clockwise from top left)
The east front circa 1861;
rendering of the visitor center;
the dome.

1962 The east front is extended 33½ feet, creating 100 additional offices.

1983 Preservationists fight to keep the west front, the last remaining section of the Capitol's original facade, from being extended; in a compromise the facade's crumbling sandstone blocks are replaced with stronger limestone.

2000 Ground is broken on the subterranean Capitol Visitor Center, to be located beneath the grounds to the building's east side; the extensive facility, three-fourths the size of the Capitol itself, is scheduled to open in fall 2008.

UP TOP

The twin-shelled Capitol dome, a marvel of 19th-century engineering, rises 285 feet above the ground and weighs 4,500 tons. It can expand and contract as much as four inches in a day, depending on the outside temperature.

The allegorical figure on top of the dome is Freedom. Sculptor Thomas Crawford had first planned for the 19½-foot-tall bronze statue to wear the cloth liberty cap of a freed Roman slave, but southern lawmakers, led by Jefferson Davis, objected. An "American" headdress composed of a star-encircled helmet surmounted with an eagle's head and feathers was substituted. A light just below the statue burns whenever Congress is in session.

TOURING THE CAPITOL

The dome

To see the Capitol you're required to go on a 30-to-40-minute tour conducted by the Capitol Guide Service. The first stop is the Rotunda, followed by the National Statuary Hall, the Hall of Columns, the old Supreme Court Chamber, the crypt (where there are exhibits on the history of the Capitol), and the gift shop. Note that you *don't* see the Senate or House chambers on the tour. (Turn the page to learn about visiting the chambers.) The highlights of the tour are the first two stops....

THE ROTUNDA

You start off here, under the Capitol's dome. Look up and you'll see *Apotheosis of Washington,* a fresco painted in 1865 by Constantino Brumidi. The figures in the inner circle represent the 13 original states; those in the outer ring symbolize arts, sciences, and industry. Further down, around the Rotunda's rim, a frieze depicts 400 years of American history. The work was started by Brumidi in 1877 and continued by another Italian, Filippo Costaggini. American Allyn Cox added the final touches in 1953.

NATIONAL STATUARY HALL

South of the Rotunda is Statuary Hall, which was once the chamber of the House of Representatives. When the House moved out, Congress invited each state to send statues of two great deceased residents for placement in the hall. Because the weight of the statues threatened to make the floor cave in, and to keep the room from being cluttered, more than half of the sculptures have ended up in other spots in the Capitol. Ask your guide for help finding your state's statues.

ARTIST OF THE CAPITOL

Constantino Brumidi (1805-80) devoted his last 25 years to frescoing the Capitol; his work dominates the Rotunda and the Western Corridor. While painting Penn's treaty for the Rotunda's frieze, a 74-year-old Brumidi slipped from the 58-foot scaffold, hanging on until help arrived. He would continue work for another four months, before succumbing to kidney failure.

TRY THIS

Because of Statuary Hall's perfectly elliptical ceiling, a whisper uttered along the wall can be heard at the point directly opposite on the other side of the room. Try it when you're there—if it's not noisy, the trick should work.

ONE BIG HAWAIIAN

With a solid granite base weighing six tons, Hawaii's Kamehameha I in Statuary Hall is among the heaviest objects in the collection. On Kamehameha Day (June 11, a state holiday in Hawai'i), the statue is draped with leis.

Kamehameha I

United States Capitol:
Second-Floor Plan

Marble Room
(Senators' Retiring
Room)

Ceremonial Office
of the Vice President

President's
Room

Senators'
Reception
Room

Senate
Chamber

Democratic
Cloakrooms

Republican
Cloakrooms

Senators'
Conference
Room

Old Senate
Chamber

West Front

Rotunda

Prayer
Room

Congresswomen's
Suite

House Document
Room

Statuary
Hall

House
Reception
Room

Republican
Cloakrooms

Democratic
Cloakrooms

House
Chamber

Representatives'
Retiring Room

0   30 yards

0   30 meters

GOING TO THE FLOOR

In session

ONE IF BY LAND . . . ?
When flags fly over their respective wings of the Capitol, you'll know the House and Senate are in session. The House is on the south side, the Senate on the north.

A tour of the Capitol is impressive, but the best part of a visit for many people is witnessing the legislators in action. Free gallery passes into the House and Senate chambers have to be obtained from your representative's or senator's office. They aren't hard to come by, but getting them takes some planning ahead. Once you have a pass, it's good for any time the chambers are open to public, for as long as the current Congress is sitting. Senate chambers are closed when the Senate is not in session, but the House is open.

SENATE CHAMBER
With 100 members elected to six-year terms, the Senate is the smaller and ostensibly more dignified of Congress's two houses. Desks of the senators are arranged in an arc, with Republicans and Democrats divided by the center aisle. The vice president of the United States is officially the "president of the Senate," charged with presiding over the Senate's procedures. Usually, though, the senior member of the majority party oversees day-to-day operations, and is addressed as "Mr. President" or "Madam President."

HOUSE CHAMBER
The larger of two chambers may look familiar: it's here that the president delivers the annual State of the Union. When you visit, you sit in the same balcony from which the First Family and guests watch the address.

Look carefully at the panels above the platform where the Speaker of the House sits. They're blue (rather than green like the rest of the panels in the room), and when the House conducts a vote, they light up with the names of the representatives and their votes in green and red.

Judiciary Committee

House session

SWEET SPOT IN THE SENATE
In the sixth desk from the right in the back row of the Senate chamber, a drawer has been filled with candy since 1968. Whoever occupies the desk maintains the stash.

PLANNING YOUR CAPITOL DAY

THE CAPITOL VISITOR CENTER

The Capitol Visitor Center (CVC) is a $600-million subterranean complex located beneath the east lawn of the Capitol. It has been plagued by delays, but is scheduled to open in fall 2008. When it does open, it will play a central role in the experience of visiting the Capitol. It will have a great hall, complete with ticket and information booths, an expansive dining area, two gift shops, two informational movie theaters, a live video feed from Congress, and an interactive museum. See ⊕ www.aoc.gov/cvc for more information on construction updates.

LOGISTICS

To tour the Capitol, once the new CVC opens, you can register for tickets online or get them at the center where tours will start. Until then, you wait in line to get a same-day, timed-entry ticket. Tickets are distributed, one per person, on a first-come, first-served basis, at the Capitol Guide Service kiosk along the sidewalk southwest of the Capitol (near the intersection of 1st Street SW and Independence Avenue). Distribution starts at 9 AM. During the winter, the wait might only be a few minutes. In the spring and summer, lines form by 7.

To get passes to the chambers of the House and Senate, contact your representative's or senator's office. Many will also arrange for a staff member to give you a tour of the Capitol or set you up with a time for a Capitol Guide Service tour. When they're in session, some members even have time set aside to meet with constituents. You can link to the e-mail of your representative at ⊕ www.house.gov and of your senators at ⊕ www.senate.gov.

SECURITY

Expect at least a 30-minute wait going through security when you enter the Capitol. Bags can be no larger than 14" wide, 13" tall, and 4" deep, and other possessions you can bring into the building are strictly limited. (The full list of prohibited items is posted on the Capitol Web site, ⊕ www.aoc.gov; click on "Visiting the Capitol.") There are no facilities for checking belongings.

BEAN SOUP AND MORE

A favorite with legislators, the Senate bean soup has been served every day since 1901 (no one is sure exactly why, though the menu, which you can take with you, outlines a few theories) in the exclusive Senate Dining Room, but it's available for the general public in the Longworth Cafeteria (☎ 202/225-0878), on the House side. Open weekdays 7:30–2:30, the cafeteria also sells sandwiches, pizza, deli food, and hot meals. It will also be available in the dining area of the new CVC.

FURTHER INFORMATION

For the latest updates on procedures for obtaining tickets, security, and information about the new visitor center, call: ☎ 202/224-4048; 202/225-6827 (recorded updates); 202/224-4049 (TTY). Web sites for the architect of the Capitol (⊕ www.aoc.gov), the Senate (⊕ www.senate.gov), and the House (⊕ www.house.gov) all have visitor information.

THE WHITE HOUSE

✉ 1600 Pennsylvania Ave. NW

☎ 202/208–1631, 202/456–7041 24-hr info line

🌐 www.whitehouse.gov

🎫 Free; reservations required

🕑 Tours Tues.–Sat. 7:30–12:30

Ⓜ Federal Triangle, Metro Center, or McPherson Sq.

TIPS

■ To see the White House, you need to contact your representative or senator. To visit in spring or summer, you should make your request about six months in advance.

■ You need a group of 10 or more in order to visit, or the office of your representative or senator may be able to place you with another group.

■ You'll be asked for the names, birthdates, and social security numbers of everyone in your group, and you'll be told where to meet and what you can bring.

■ On the morning of your tour, call the White House Visitors Office information line, ☎202/456–7041. Tours are subject to last-minute cancellation.

■ Arrive 15 minutes early. Your group will be asked to line up in alphabetical order. Everyone 15 years or older must present photo ID. Going through security will probably take as long as the tour itself: 20 to 25 minutes.

America's most famous house is open to visitors, but getting in requires planning. (*See "Tips."*) The building was designed in 1792 by Irishman James Hoban, who took inspiration from Dublin's Georgian-style Leinster House. It was known officially as the Executive Mansion until 1902, when President Theodore Roosevelt rechristened it the White House, long its informal name. The house has undergone many structural changes: Andrew Jackson installed running water, James Garfield put in the first elevator, and Harry Truman had the entire structure gutted and restored, adding a second-story porch to the south portico.

HIGHLIGHTS

The self-guided tour includes rooms on the ground floor, but the State Floor has the highlights. The **East Room** is the largest room in the White House. It's the site of ceremonies and press conferences; it's also where Theodore Roosevelt's children roller-skated and one of Abraham Lincoln's sons harnessed a pet goat to a chair and went for a ride. The portrait of George Washington that Dolley Madison saved from torch-carrying British soldiers in 1814 hangs here. The **Green Room** is named for the moss-green watered silk covering its walls: the place where President Monroe played cards is now known to news junkies as the site of presidential photo ops with foreign heads of state. The only president to get married in the White House, Grover Cleveland, was wed in the **Blue Room.** The White House Christmas tree stands in here every winter. The **Red Room,** decorated in early-19th-century American Empire style, has been a favorite of First Ladies. Mary Todd Lincoln had her coffee and read the morning paper here. Bill Clinton's daughter, Chelsea, hosted pizza parties in the **State Dining Room,** which can seat 140.

The White House

Private Quarters of the Presidential Family

Queen's Room (Rose)

Yellow Oval Room

Treaty Room

Lincoln Suite

SECOND FLOOR

Truman Balcony

5

Family Dining Room

Entrance

Cross Hall

East Room

State Dining Room

Red Room

Blue Room

Green Room

MAIN FLOOR

Kitchen

Curator

Library

←
TO THE
WEST WING

Vaulted-arch Corridor

→
TO THE
EAST WING

White House Staff Offices

Diplomatic Reception Room

China Room

Vermeil Room

GROUND FLOOR

South Portico

THE SUPREME COURT

✉ One 1st St. NE, Capitol Hill

☎ 202/479–3000

🌐 www.supremecourtus.gov

🎫 Free

🕐 Weekdays 9–4:30; court in session Oct.–June

Ⓜ Union Station or Capitol S

TIPS

■ The *Washington Post* carries a daily listing of what cases the court will hear.

■ You can't bring your overcoat or electronics such as cameras and cell phones into the courtroom, but you can store them in a coin-operated locker.

■ When court isn't in session, you can hear lectures about the court, typically given every hour on the half hour from 9:30 to 3:30. On the ground floor you can also find revolving exhibits, a video about the court, a gift shop, an information desk, and a larger-than-life statue of John Marshall, the longest-serving chief justice in Supreme Court history.

■ The Supreme Court has a cafeteria, open to the public from 7:30 to 4, located on the ground floor.

It wasn't until 1935 that the Supreme Court got its own building: a white-marble temple with twin rows of Corinthian columns designed by Cass Gilbert. Before then, the justices had been moved around to various rooms in the Capitol; for a while they even met in a tavern. William Howard Taft, the only man to serve as both president and chief justice, was instrumental in getting the court a home of its own, though he died before it was completed. Today you can sit in the gallery and see the court in action. Even when court isn't in session, there are still things to see.

HIGHLIGHTS

The court convenes on the first Monday in October and hears cases until April. There are usually two arguments a day at 10 and 11 in the morning, Monday through Wednesday, in two-week intervals.

On mornings when court is in session, two lines form for people wanting to attend. The "three-to-five-minute" line shuttles you through, giving you a quick impression of the court at work. The full-session line gets you in for the whole show. If you want to see a full session, it's best to be in line by at least 8:30. For the most contentious cases, viewers have been known to queue up the night before.

In May and June the court takes to the bench Monday morning at 10 to release orders and opinions. Sessions usually last 15 to 30 minutes and are open to the public.

How does a hard-working Supreme Court justice unwind? Maybe on the building's basketball court, known as "the highest court in the land." It's not open to the public, but try to imagine Antonin Scalia and Ruth Bader Ginsburg trading elbows in the lane.

OTHER GOVERNMENT OFFICES & INSTITUTIONS

American Red Cross. The national headquarters for the American Red Cross is composed of three buildings. Guided tours of the oldest, a neoclassical structure of blinding-white marble built in 1917 to commemorate women who cared for the wounded on both sides during the Civil War, is known for its three stained-glass windows designed by Louis Comfort Tiffany. Other highlights of the 45-minute tour include an original Norman Rockwell painting, sculptures, and two signature quilts. One quilt was signed in 1918 by celebrities including Charlie Chaplin and Helen Keller; the other was signed in 1998 by all the living U.S. presidents and their wives. Weather permitting, the tour includes a visit to the courtyard. ⊠ *430 17th St. NW, White House area* ☎ *202/303–7066* ⊕ *www.redcross.org/museumA Free* ☉ *Tours only, Wed. and Fri. 10 and 2, Sat. noon and 2. Must make reservations on Web site or by phone 3 business days in advance for a Saturday tour* Ⓜ *Farragut W.*

Bureau of Engraving and Printing. Paper money has been printed here since 1914, when the bureau relocated from the redbrick-towered Auditors Building at the corner of 14th Street and Independence Avenue. In addition to the paper currency in the United States, military

> **CAPITAL FACTS**
>
> The Bureau of Engraving and Printing turns out some $38 million worth of currency a day.

certificates and presidential invitations are printed here, too. You can only enter the bureau on the tours, which last about 35 minutes. From March through August, same-day timed-entry tour passes are issued starting at 8 AM at the Raoul Wallenberg Place SW ticket booth. For the rest of the year, tickets aren't used. ⊠ *14th and C Sts. SW, The Mall* ☎ *202/874–8888, 877/874–4114 tour information* ⊕ *www.money factory.gov* ✉ *Free* ☉ *Sept.–Apr., weekdays 9–10:45 and 12:30–2; May–Aug., weekdays 9–10:45, 12:30–2, and 5–7* Ⓜ *Smithsonian.*

Department of Agriculture. Although there's not a lot to see inside, this gargantuan complex does have a one-room visitor center with displays and audio stations that highlight the nation's agricultural, food safety, and nutrition policies. ⊠ *Independence Ave. between 12th and 14th Sts. SW, The Mall* ☎ *202/720–4197* ⊕ *www.usda.gov* ✉ *Free* ☉ *Weekdays 9–3* Ⓜ *Smithsonian.*

Congressional Cemetery. Established in 1807 "for all denomination of people," this cemetery is the final resting place for such notables as U.S. Capitol architect William Thornton, Marine Corps march composer John Philip Sousa, Civil War photographer Mathew Brady, FBI director J. Edgar Hoover, and many members of Congress. Air Force Veteran and gay rights activist Leonard Matlovich is also buried here under a tombstone that reads "When I was in the military, they gave me a medal for killing two men and a discharge for loving one." The cemetery is about a 20-minute walk from the Capitol. A brochure with

a self-guided walking tour is avail-
able at the office and in a mailbox
near the main gate. ✉ *1801 E St.
SE, Capitol Hill* ☎ *202/543–0539*
⊕ *www.congressionalcemetery.org*
🕐 *Daily dawn–dusk; office Mon.,
Wed., and Fri. 10–2, Sat. 9–1* Ⓜ
Stadium Armory or Potomac Ave.

> ### CAPITAL FACTS
>
> The largest room in the State
> Department has a specially
> loomed carpet so heavy and
> large it had to be airlifted in
> by helicopter.

Department of State. U.S. foreign pol-
icy is administered by battalions of brainy analysts in the huge Department of State building (often referred to as the State Department). All
is presided over by the Secretary of State, who is fourth in line for
the presidency (after the Vice President, Speaker of the House, and
President *Pro Tempore* of the Senate) should the President be unable to
serve. On the top floor are the opulent Diplomatic Reception Rooms,
decorated like the great halls of Europe and the rooms of wealthy colonial American plantations. Furnishings include a Philadelphia highboy,
a Paul Revere bowl, and the desk on which the Treaty of Paris, which
ended the Revolutionary War, was signed in 1783. ■**TIP➔To visit the
reception rooms, register online for a tour three months in advance.** The
tours are recommended for those 13 and over. ✉ *2201 C St. NW,
Foggy Bottom* ☎ *202/647–3241, 202/736–4474 TDD* ⊕ *www.state.
gov* 🎫 *Free* 🕐 *Tours weekdays at 9:30, 10:30, and 2:45* Ⓜ *Foggy
Bottom.*

Department of the Interior. The outside of the building is somewhat plain,
but inside there's art that reflects the department's work. Along the
hallways are heroic oil paintings of dam construction, gold panning,
and cattle drives. A guided tour takes you past many of the 50 murals
throughout the building. ■**TIP➔Reservations for the tour are required at
least two weeks in advance.** The **Department of the Interior Museum** documents the history of the department. Exhibits in the museum outline
the work of the Bureau of Land Management, the U.S. Geological Survey, the Bureau of Indian Affairs, the National Park Service, and other
department branches. Don't expect interactive exhibits; this museum
retains a New Deal–era flavor that carries through to its dioramas of
historic events and American locales. The Indian Craft Shop across the
hall from the museum sells Native American pottery, dolls, carvings,
jewelry, baskets, and books. ✉ *C and E Sts. between 18th and 19th
Sts. NW, White House area* ☎ *202/208–4743* ⊕ *www.doi.gov* 🎫
Free 🕐 *Weekdays 8:30–4:30, third Sat. 1—4, closed* Ⓜ *Farragut W.*

Federal Reserve Building. This imposing marble edifice, its bronze entryway topped by a massive eagle, was designed by Folger Library architect
Paul Cret. Its appearance seems to say, "Your money's safe with us."
Even so, there's no money here (the Fed sets interest rates and thereby
seeks to keep the economy on track). The building's stately facade belies
a friendlier interior, with a varied collection of art and four special art
exhibitions every year. *Enter on* ✉ *20th St. and Constitution Ave. NW,
Foggy Bottom* ☎ *202/452–3000* ✉ *secy-visitorservices@frb.gov
for building tours-, 202/452–3778 art tours* ⊕ *www.federalreserve.*

Continued on page 151

SEX! POWER! MONEY!
★ ★ ★
SCANDALOUS
WASHINGTON

Every "gotcha!" headline since President Nixon's burglars at the Watergate has been affixed with a "-gate," but Washington's memory of kickbacks, sleaze, and dirty deeds goes back centuries further. Before there was Monica, there was Marilyn; before Marilyn, there was Carrie and Peggy and Nan. Most people are familiar with Whitewater, but what of the Star Route and Teapot Dome? The history of the United States is thick with plots, scams, and bad behavior. If walls could speak, then the White House, the Capitol, and even the IRS might tell us some very different stories than the ones we learned in school. Herewith, selections from Washington's long and democratic history of scandal.

SEX!

Fanne Fox

Petticoat Tales

Margaret "Peggy" Eaton

Ooh la la, whispered Washington's society matrons, when President Andrew Jackson's War Secretary John Henry Eaton fell for Margaret "Peggy" Timberlake, a young widow he had known for years. Pretty, charming Peggy had a fast reputation for 1829, and soon rumors flew about the circumstances of her husband's death, the paternity of her two children, and Eaton. It was all idle gossip—until Eaton married her, after which the other Cabinet wives shunned her, and the social stir of insult and offense all but shut down business at the White House for *two years.* In 1831, the Cabinet resigned en masse and Jackson was finally able to get some work done. As for Peggy? After Eaton's death, she sparked another scandal, by marrying her granddaughter's 19-year-old dance instructor. *(Location: Peggy Eaton is buried in Oak Hill Cemetery, 3001 R St. NW)*

Naked Ambition

In 1974, Wilbur Mills spent his days chairing the House Ways and Means Committee—and his nights with a stripper known as "Fanne Fox, the Argentine Firecracker." A typical Capitol romance, until his car was stopped one night by police, and his lady friend leapt from the car and into the Tidal Basin, leaving a drunken Mills to his fate. Surprisingly, Mills' political career survived—until he appeared later that year, drunk, onstage with Fox at a Boston burlesque. *(Location: Tidal Basin)*

Hail to the Cheat

Warren Harding

President Bill Clinton was hardly the first and likely not the worst of the White House philanderers. That dubious honor may go to President Warren Harding, a legendary Lothario who is purported to have carried on with paramours Carrie Phillips and Nan Britton (among others) in some unlikely places, including a White House closet. (When his wife Florence came by, a Secret Service agent warned him with a discreet knock on the door.) Relative propriety in the 1920's press meant that any blue dresses remained unreported, but Harding may have left behind a more incriminating piece of evidence—an illegitimate daughter, Elizabeth Ann. *(Location: White House)*

POWER SCANDALS

Reporters Bob Woodward, left, and Carl Bernstein, whose reporting of the Watergate scandal won them a Pulitzer Prize, sit in the newsroom of the *Washington Post* on May 7, 1973.

He Really Bugs Me

The Big Kahuna of Washington scandals had humble beginnings, in the discovery of a taped-open door at the Watergate Hotel one night in June of 1972. The door led to burglars, on a mission to bug the Democratic National Committee, and the burglars led through the Republican party machine straight to the White House and President Richard "Tricky Dick" Nixon. Two young reporters, Bob Woodward and Carl Bernstein, uncovered the most impossible-seeming story of the century, and their secret meetings with anonymous leaker "Deep Throat" (W. Mark Felt) are the stuff of legend. One of many fond memories of the moment when Washington lost America's trust: Nixon's immortal, and untruthful, declaration, "I am not a crook." *(Location: Watergate Hotel, Virginia Ave., near 27th St. NW)*

Former CIA officer Valerie Plame

I Spy . . .

When Valerie Plame had her CIA cover blown in 2003—in print, by a syndicated columnist—Washington's shady nexus of journalists, politicians, and sneaky leaks was, too. Who let the cat out of the bag, to whom, and most importantly, why? Vice President Dick Cheney's chief aide, Lewis "Scooter" Libby, was convicted, but only of lying to investigators. If Plame was targeted because of her husband's slapdown to the Bush Administration over the Iraq war, whoever targeted her got away with it.

From Ronald with Love

Two wrongs *can* make a right: a right-wing guerilla organization, that is. President Ronald Reagan likened Nicaragua's Contras to the Founding Fathers. Too bad funding the insurgent group was illegal. So was a secret deal the White House had made to sell arms to Iran. When it was discovered in 1986 that the cash from Iran had been funneled to the Contras, the Gipper had some explaining to do. Luckily for him, National Security Council aide Oliver North had a shredder, and he wasn't afraid to use it. North's secretary, Fawn Hall, took care of the rest by smuggling out remaining suspect documents in her boots and skirt. *(Location: Old Executive Office Building, 17th & F Streets NW)*

MONEY SCANDALS

William Adams Richardson

Taxman to Axman

When Treasury Secretary William Richardson hired contractor-cum-bounty hunter John Sanborn in 1872 to help the IRS collect taxes, the idea was simple. Sanborn chased down tax cheats, and was allowed to keep half of the take for his trouble. But when he ran out of tax evaders and went after honest companies, Richardson turned a blind eye—in exchange for his own cut.

A Cozy Deal

It may seem old hat today—access to public resources awarded in a no-bid contract to cronies of someone in the president's inner circle—but in 1922 it was front-page news. Interior Secretary Albert Fall had authority over the Teapot Dome strategic oil reserve transferred from the Department of the Navy to Interior, and once he was in charge, he leased the land to Mammoth Oil. The deal was technically legal—what *wasn't* was the $404,000 kickback he got for arranging it. Fall nearly succeeded in keeping his stake quiet, until he raised suspicions by having the office of the lead Senate investigator ransacked. (*Location: Department of Interior, 1849 C St. NW*)

The Sheik of Bribery

If Middle Eastern "businessmen" looking suspiciously like FBI agents offered *you* cash for favors, you might smell a rat—particularly if their business cards read "Abdul Enterprises." But in 1978, seven legislators gave just such men the benefit of the doubt, and had their trusting natures (and brazen avarice) rewarded with bribery convictions. Hint: Next time, guys, check the shiny shoes.

Secretary of Shame

In 1872, the House of Representatives was so determined to remove War Secretary William Belknap that it voted to impeach him, even after he had already resigned. The high-living general was caught having awarded a lucrative military trading post appointment in exchange for kickbacks; the quarterly bribes he took came to ten times his official salary. The House's venom waxed poetic: legislators voted unanimously that the Secretary was "basely prostituting his high office to his lust for private gain." Belknap resigned in disgrace—and tears—and committed suicide in 1890. (*Location: House of Representatives*) *gov* ✉ *Free* ⊘ *Weekdays 9–5 during art exhibitions, self-guided tours of permanent art collection by appointment only 24 hours in advance* Ⓜ *Foggy Bottom.*

★ **Library of Congress.** The largest library in the world has more than 134 million items on approximately 530 mi of bookshelves.

> **CAPITAL FACTS**
>
> Designed by Waddy B. Wood and built in 1937, the Department of the Interior was the first large federal building with escalators and central air-conditioning.

Only 32 million of its holdings are books—the library also has 2.8 million recordings, 12 million photographs, 5.3 million maps, and 59 million manuscripts. Also here is the Congressional Research Service, which, as the name implies, works on special projects for senators and representatives.

Built in 1897, the copper-domed Thomas Jefferson Building is the oldest of the three buildings that make up the library. Like many other structures in Washington, the library was criticized when it was completed. Detractors thought its design, based on the Paris Opera House, was too florid. Congressmen were even heard to grumble that its dome—topped with the gilt "Flame of Knowledge"—competed with that of their Capitol. It's certainly decorative, with busts of Dante, Goethe, Nathaniel Hawthorne, and other great writers perched above its entryway. The *Court of Neptune*, Roland Hinton Perry's fountain at the base of the front steps, rivals some of Rome's best fountains.

Provisions for a library to serve members of Congress were originally made in 1800, when the government set aside $5,000 to purchase books that legislators might need to consult. This small collection was housed in the Capitol, but was destroyed in 1814, when the British burned the city. Thomas Jefferson, then in retirement at Monticello, offered his personal library as a replacement, noting that "there is, in fact, no subject to which a Member of Congress may not have occasion to refer." Jefferson's collection of 6,487 books, for which Congress eventually paid him $23,950, laid the foundation for the great national library. (Sadly, another fire in 1851 destroyed two-thirds of Jefferson's books.) By the late 1800s it was clear that the Capitol could no longer contain the growing library, and the Jefferson Building was constructed. The **Adams Building,** on 2nd Street behind the Jefferson, was added in 1939. A third structure, the **James Madison Building,** opened in 1980; it's just south of the Jefferson Building, between Independence Avenue and C Street. Less architecturally interesting than the Jefferson Building, the Adams does attract visitors for evening literary readings and small exhibitions, which are open from 8:30 AM to 6 PM.

The Jefferson Building opens into the Great Hall, richly adorned with mosaics, paintings, and curving marble stairways. The grand, octagonal Main Reading Room, its central desk surrounded by mahogany readers' tables under a 160-foot-high domed ceiling, inspires researchers and readers alike. Computer terminals have replaced card catalogs, but books are still retrieved and dispersed the same way: readers (18 years or older) hand request slips to librarians and wait patiently for their materials to be delivered. Researchers aren't allowed in the stacks, and only members of Congress and other special borrowers can check books out. Items from the library's collection—which includes one of only three perfect Gutenberg Bibles in the world—are on display in the Jefferson Building's second-floor Southwest Gallery and Pavilion. Information about current and upcoming exhibitions, which can include oral-history projects, presidential papers, photographs, and the like, is available by phone or Web. ■TIP➔To even begin to come to grips with the scope and grandeur of the library, taking one of the free hourly tours is highly recommended. Well-informed docents are fonts of fascinating information about the library's history and holdings; they can decode the dozens of quirky allegorical sculptures and paintings throughout the building, and can bring you into spaces—such as the glassed-in observation deck over the Main Reading Room—that are closed to solo visitors. ☒ *Jefferson Bldg., 1st St. and Independence Ave. SE, Capitol Hill* ☎ *202/707–4604, 202/707–5000, or 202/707–6400* ⊕ *www.loc.gov* ☒ *Free* ⊙ *Mon.–Sat. 10–5:30; reading room hrs may extend later. Free tours Mon.–Sat. at 10:30, 11:30, 1:30, and 2:30, and weekdays at 3:30* Ⓜ *Capitol S.*

> **DID YOU KNOW?**
>
> In the blockbuster 2007 movie *National Treasure: Book of Secrets*, the main character played by Nicholas Cage walks through stacks of books in a public area at the Library of Congress. In reality, you can't just take books off the shelves, but you can read books at the Library. Go to Room LM140 of the Madison Building with a driver's license or passport and complete a form to get registered to use the library.

Pentagon. This office building, the headquarters of the United States Department of Defense, is the largest low-rise office building in the world. Approximately 23,000 military and civilian workers arrive daily. Astonishingly, this mammoth office building, completed in 1943, took less than two years to construct.

Following the September 2001 crash of hijacked American Airlines Flight 77 into the northwest side of the building, the damaged area was removed in just over a month, and rebuilding proceeded rapidly. Tours of the building are given on a limited basis to educational groups by advance reservation. Tours for the general public may be booked through your congressperson's office at least two weeks, but no more than three months, in advance. ☒ *I–395 at Columbia Pike and Rte. 27* ☎ *703/697–1776* ⊕ *pentagon.afis.osd.mil.*

Ronald Reagan Building and International Trade Center. This $818 million, 3.1-million-square-foot colossus is the largest federal building to be constructed in the Washington area since the Pentagon, and the first to be designed for use by both the government and the private sector. A blend of classical and modern architecture, the Indiana-limestone structure replaced what for 50 years had been an enormous parking lot. The Reagan Building houses the Environmental Protection Agency, the U.S. Customs Service, and the U.S. Agency for International Development. The **D.C. Visitor Information Center** (☎202/289–8317, 866/324–7386 ⊕*www.dchamber. org*), located here, is a convenient place to pick up brochures and see a free historical video. There's also a touch-screen computer kiosk with information about the city. Hours for the visitor center are 8:30–5:30 weekdays (March 15–Labor Day) and 9–4 Saturday; Labor Day–March 14, weekdays 9–4:30. The building has a food court on the lower level, and a theatrical group, the Capitol Steps, performs works of political satire here on Friday and Saturday nights at 7:30. ⊠ *1300 Pennsylvania Ave. NW, East End* ⊠ *Free* Ⓜ*Federal Triangle.*

WHAT'S NEW AT THE WHITE HOUSE?

The Green Room remains true to its color, but when First Lady Laura Bush oversaw the room's renovation in 2007, she added a few modern elements, including *The Builders*, a painting by Jacob Lawrence, and a green rug accented with coral, blue, red, and ecru. Mrs. Bush told the *Washington Post* "I like this room to have sort of a clubby feeling. . . . I think this is one of the more masculine rooms. The Red Room has always been considered the First Lady's favorite room, and it is my favorite room, I'll admit."

Treasury Building. Once used to store currency, this is the largest Greek Revival edifice in Washington. Robert Mills, the architect responsible for the Washington Monument and the Patent Office (now the Smithsonian American Art Museum), designed the grand colonnade that stretches down 15th Street. After the death of President Lincoln, the Andrew Johnson Suite was used as the executive office by the new president while Mrs. Lincoln moved out of the White House. Other vestiges of its earlier days are the two-story marble Cash Room and the gilded west dome. One-hour tours arranged through Congress are available most Saturdays at 9, 9:45, 10:30, and 11:15 for US citizens and legal residents only. ⊠ *15th St. and Pennsylvania Ave. NW, White House area* ☎ *202/622–0146 TDD* Ⓜ *McPherson Sq. or Metro Center.*

Fodor'sChoice **Washington National Cathedral.** Construction of Washington National
★ Cathedral—the sixth-largest cathedral in the world—started in 1907; it was finished and consecrated in 1990. Like its 14th-century Gothic counterparts, the stunning National Cathedral (officially the Cathedral Church of St. Peter and St. Paul) has a nave, flying buttresses, transepts, and vaults that were built stone by stone. State funerals for presidents Eisenhower, Reagan, and Ford were held here, and the tomb of Woodrow Wilson, the only president buried in Washington, is on the nave's south side. ■TIP→The expansive view of the city from the Pilgrim Gallery is exceptional. The cathedral is Episcopalian, but it's the site of frequent ecumenical and interfaith services, as well as state events such as the funerals of presidents.

On the grounds of the cathedral is the compact, English-style **Bishop's Garden.** Boxwoods, ivy, tea roses, yew trees, and an assortment of arches, bas-reliefs, and stonework from European ruins provide a counterpoint to the cathedral's towers. ⊠ *Wisconsin and Massachu-*

setts Aves. NW, Upper Northwest ☎ *202/537–6200, 202/537–6207 tour information* ⊕ *www.cathedral.org/cathedral* 🎟 *Suggested tour donation $3* ☾ *Weekdays 10–5, Sat. 10–4, Sun. 8–6:30 (8–2:45 for worship only). Tours Mon.–Sat. 10–4, every 30 min. Gardens open dawn–dusk* Ⓜ *Cleveland Park or Tenleytown. Take any 30 series bus.*

CAPITAL FACTS

Skilled stone carvers have adorned the Washington National Cathedral with fanciful gargoyles and grotesques, including one of Darth Vader.

Washington Post Building. Although the newspaper is no longer printed here, you can see the newsroom that broke the Watergate story on a 45-minute guided tour of the building, which is otherwise not open to the public. In addition to the newsroom, there's a small museum dedicated to the history of the newspaper and old and new printing processes. ■TIP→Tours are given only for groups of 10 to 30 people, by reservation, and children must be at least 11 years old. You can reserve up to four weeks in advance; call for further information. ✉ *1150 15th St. NW, Downtown* ☎ *202/334–7969* ⊕ *www.washingtonpost.com* 🎟 *Free* ☾ *Tours every third Mon. at 10, 11, and noon.*

Where to Eat

Dinner at Jaleo

WORD OF MOUTH

"I'm a big fan of Blue Duck Tavern—you can keep it casual and reasonable there. I sometimes just order a host of sides, because they almost outshine the entrees!"

—DoctorCarrie

"Eric Ripert's new restaurant Westend Bistro, has been getting a lot of buzz. It's casual, not too expensive, bistro fare. We had oysters and fish burgers (divine) when we ate there last Saturday."

—petitepois

THE SCENE

Updated by
Elana Schor

As host to visitors and transplants from around the world, Washington benefits from the constant infusion of different cultures. Despite D.C.'s lack of true ethnic neighborhoods and the kinds of restaurant districts found in many other cities, you *can* find almost any cuisine here, from Burmese to Ethiopian. Just follow your nose.

Although most neighborhoods lack a unified culinary flavor, make no mistake: D.C. is a city of distinctive neighborhoods, each with its own style. Adams-Morgan, for example, is known for its small family-run eateries. You'll find Ethiopian restaurants next to Italian trattorias and Asian bistros. These small ethnic spots open and close frequently; it's worth taking a stroll down the street to see what's new.

Downtown, you'll find many of the city's blue-chip law firms and deluxe, expense-account restaurants, as well as stylish lounges, microbrew pubs, and upscale eateries that have sprung up to serve the crowds that attend games at the Verizon Center.

Wherever you venture forth in the city, there are a few trends worth noting: Spanish tapas eateries and other restaurants serving small tasting portions are bigger than ever. You'll find this style of eating pervasive, whether you're at a modern Greek, Asian, or American restaurant. High-end restaurants in town also have begun to add bar menus with smaller plates that are much less expensive than their entrées, but created with the same finesse.

Though Italian, French, and New American spots continue to open at a ferocious pace, Washingtonians are always hungry to try something new, whether it's Chinese smoked lobster, fiery Indian curry, or crunchily addictive Vietnamese spring rolls.

WOODLEY PARK
casual neighborhood joints

ADAMS-MORGAN AND U STREET CORRIDOR
ethnic eats and quirky bars

SHAW
trendy restaurants and hip lounges

GEORGETOWN
mix of white-tablecloth and no-tablecloth eateries

DUPONT CIRCLE
upscale, stylish restaurants with lively bar scene

CHINATOWN
Asian cuisines galore

FOGGY BOTTOM
cheap cafés popular with students

DOWNTOWN
revitalized arts district with upscale eateries

CAPITOL HILL
pub grub and cafés aplenty for harried staffers

Florida Ave.

Columbia Rd.

16th St.

Vermont Ave.

Florida Ave.

New Hampshire Ave.

Sheridan Circle

Massachusetts Ave.

Rock Creek

Dupont Circle

Logan Circle

Rhode Island Ave.

Scott Circle

Thomas Circle

M St.

M St.

M St.

Connecticut Ave.

Whitehurst Fwy.

Washington Circle

K St.

13th St.

15th St.

New York Ave.

Pennsylvania Ave.

23rd St.

Theodore Roosevelt Island

Virginia Ave.

Constitution Ave.

THE MALL

Reflecting Pool

THE MONUMENTS

Independence Ave.

Arlington Memorial Br.

Columbia Island

Tidal Basin

Francis Case Memorial Br.

Washington Canal

Potomac River

VIRGINIA

0   500 yards

0   500 meters

D.C. DINING PLANNER

Eating Out Strategy

Where should we eat? With hundreds of D.C. eateries competing for your attention, it may seem like a daunting question. But fret not—our expert writers and editors have done most of the legwork. The 100-plus selections here represent the best this city has to offer—from hot dogs to *haute* cuisine. Search "Best Bets" for top recommendations by price, cuisine, and experience. Sample local flavor in the neighborhood features. Or find a review quickly in the alphabetical listings. Delve in, and enjoy!

Children

Though it's unusual to see children in the dining rooms of D.C.'s most elite restaurants, dining with youngsters in the nation's capital does not have to mean culinary exile. Many of the restaurants reviewed in this chapter are excellent choices for families and are marked with a ♺ symbol.

Smoking

Smoking is banned in all restaurants and bars.

Reservations

Plan ahead if you're determined to snag a sought-after reservation. Some renowned restaurants are booked weeks in advance. But you can get lucky at the last minute if you're flexible—and friendly. Most restaurants keep a few tables open for walk-ins and VIPs. Show up for dinner early (5:30 PM) or late (after 10 PM) and politely inquire about any last-minute vacancies or cancellations. If you're calling a few days ahead of time, ask if you can be put on a waiting list. Occasionally, an eatery may ask you to call the day before your scheduled meal to reconfirm: don't forget, or you could lose out.

What to Wear

As unfair as it seems, the way you look can influence how you're treated—and where you're seated. Generally speaking, jeans and a button-down shirt will suffice at most table-service restaurants in the $–$$ range. Moving up from there, some pricier restaurants require jackets, and some insist on ties. In reviews, we mention dress only when men are required to wear a jacket or a jacket and tie. But even when there's no formal dress code, we recommend wearing jackets and ties in $$$ and $$$$ restaurants. If you have doubts, call the restaurant and ask.

Hours

Washington has less of an around-the-clock mentality than other big cities, with many big-name restaurants shutting down between lunch and dinner and closing their kitchens by 11 PM. Weekend evenings spent downtown can also be a hassle for those seeking quick bites, since many popular chain eateries cater to office workers and shut down after 6 PM. For a midnight supper, the best bets are Dupont Circle and the U Street corridor, while families looking for late lunches should head north from the Mall to find kitchens that stay open between meals.

Tipping & Taxes

In most restaurants, tip the waiter 16%–20%. (To figure the amount quickly, just double the sales tax noted on the check—it's 10% of your bill.) Tip at least $1 per drink at the bar, and $1 for each coat checked. Never tip the maître d' unless you're out to impress your guests or expect to pay another visit soon.

If you're dining with a group, make sure not to over-tip: review your check to see if a gratuity has been added, as many restaurants automatically tack on an 18% tip for groups of six, eight, or more.

Prices

If you're watching your budget, be sure to ask the price of daily specials recited by the waiter or captain. The charge for specials at some restaurants is noticeably out of line with the other prices on the menu. Beware of the $10 bottle of water; ask for tap water instead. And always review your bill.

If you eat early or late you may be able to take advantage of a prix-fixe deal not offered at peak hours. Most upscale restaurants offer great lunch deals with special menus at cut-rate prices designed to give customers a true taste of the place.

Credit cards are widely accepted, but many restaurants (particularly smaller ones downtown) accept only cash. If you plan to use a credit card, it's a good idea to double-check its acceptability when making reservations or before sitting down to eat.

Some restaurants are marked with a price range ($$–$$$, for example). This indicates one of two things: either the average cost straddles two categories, or if you order strategically, you can get out for less than most diners spend.

In This Chapter

6

WHAT IT COSTS

AT DINNER

¢	$	$$	$$$	$$$$
under $10	$10–$17	$18–$25	$26–$35	over $35

Price per person for an average main course or equivalent combination of smaller dishes. Note: if a restaurant offers only prix-fixe (set-price) meals, it has been given the price category that reflects the full prix-fixe price

BEST BETS FOR D.C. DINING

With thousands of restaurants to choose from, how will you decide where to eat? Fodor's writers and editors have selected their favorite restaurants by price, cuisine, and experience in the lists below. You can also search by neighborhood for excellent eating experiences—just peruse the following pages. Or find specific details about a restaurant in the full reviews, which are listed alphabetically later in the chapter.

Fodor's Choice ★

2 Amys $
2941 Restaurant $$$
Blue Duck Tavern $$–$$$
Citronelle $$$$
Equinox $$$$
Hank's Oyster Bar $–$$
Hook $$$
Inn at Little Washington $$$$
Komi $$$$
Palena $$–$$$
Rasika $$–$$$
Restaurant Eve $$$
Teaism ¢
Zaytinya $$

Best By Price

¢

Ben's Chili Bowl
Rocklands
Teaism
Oyamel

$

Etete
Granville Moore's Brickyard
Locanda

$$

Central Michel Richard
Jaleo
Nora
Palena
Zaytinya

$$$

2491 Restaurant
Hook
Restaurant Eve

$$$$

Citronelle
CityZen
Equinox
Inn at Little Washington
Komi

Best By Cuisine

AFRICAN

Café Nema ¢–$
Etete $

AMERICAN

Cashion's Eat Place $$–$$$
Inn at Little Washington $$$$
Restaurant Eve $$$

ASIAN (VARIOUS)

Full Kee $–$$
Teaism ¢
TenPenh $$–$$$

BELGIAN

Belga Café $–$$
Granville Moore's Brickyard $
Marcel's $$$
Marvin $$

FRENCH

Bistro Bis $$–$$$
Bistro Français $$–$$$
Brasserie Beck $$–$$$
Central Michel Richard $$–$$$
Citronelle $$$$
Montmartre $–$$

GREEK/TURKISH

Cafe Divan $
Zaytinya $$

INDIAN

Heritage India $-$$
Rasika $$-$$$

ITALIAN

Café Milano $$$
Obelisk $$$$
Palena $$-$$$

JAPANESE

Kaz Sushi Bistro $$
Sushi-Ko $-$$

LATIN AMERICAN

Café Atlántico $-$$
Ceiba $$-$$$

NEW AMERICAN

2941 Restaurant $$$
Ardeo $-$$
Blue Duck Tavern $$-$$$
Komi $$$$
Palena $$-$$$

PIZZA

2 Amys $
Matchbox $-$$

SEAFOOD

Black Salt $$-$$$
Hook $$$
Johnny's Half Shell $$
Oceanaire Seafood Room $$-$$$

SOUTHERN

Georgia Brown's $-$$
Oohhs & Aahhs ¢
Zola $-$$

SPANISH

Jaleo $$-$$$
Taberna del Alabardero $$-$$$

STEAKHOUSE

Capital Grille $$$
Charlie Palmer Steak $$$$
The Palm $$$

Best By Experience

BEST BRUNCH

Belga Café $-$$
Black Salt $$-$$$
Georgia Brown's $-$$
Hook $$$

BEST FOR BUSINESS

Capital Grille $$$
Charlie Palmer Steak $$$$
The Palm $$$

BEST HOTEL DINING

Blue Duck Tavern $$-$$$
Citronelle $$$$
CityZen $$$$
Poste $$

BEST POLITICO-WATCHING

Cafe Milano $$$
Charlie Palmer Steak $$$$

BEST WITH KIDS

Kramerbooks & Afterwords $
The Market Lunch ¢
Rocklands ¢-$$

CAPITOL CLASSICS

1789 Restaurant $$$
Ben's Chili Bowl ¢-$
Occidental Grill $$-$$$

GOOD FOR GROUPS

Heritage India $-$$
Malaysia Kopitiam $
Zaytinya $$

GREAT VIEWS

2941 Restaurant $$$
Charlie Palmer Steak $$$$

PRE-THEATER

Café Atlántico $-$$
Jaleo $$-$$$
Rasika $$-$$$

QUIET MEAL

Equinox $$$$
Obelisk $$$$
Palena $$-$$$
Taberna del Alabardero $$-$$$

SPECIAL OCCASION

2941 Restaurant $$$
Citronelle $$$$
CityZen $$$$
Minibar at Café Atlántico $$$$

TRENDY

Café Atlántico $-$$
Marvin $$
Rasika $$-$$$
Weekend Bistro by Eric Ripert $$
Zaytinya $$

WINE BARS

Bistrot Lepic $-$$
Sonoma $$-$$$
Vidalia $$-$$$

6

CAPITOL HILL

Once an enclave of Congressional boarding houses in the shadow of the Capitol building, Capitol Hill is now D.C.'s largest historic district, with an eclectic mix of restaurants.

The neighborhood's central location has kept it an integral and thriving part of D.C. from the beginning. With the House, Senate, Supreme Court, Library of Congress, and other offices nearby, government is a constant presence. Dining on the Hill, you'll likely overhear political staffers complaining about their bosses, lobbyists wooing clients, and locals discussing D.C. news.

Around the Capitol South Metro station, government offices end and neighborhood dining begins. Here, along tree-lined streets, you'll find neighborhood bars and restaurants that cater to lunch and happy-hour crowds during the week, and local residents on weekends.

Near the Washington Navy Yard, Historic Barracks Row (⊠ *8th St. SE*) was originally developed in the early 1800s. Recently, new upscale restaurants have opened alongside neighborhood establishments, giving the Row a fresh, hip vibe. –*Samantha Cleaver*

WORLD FLAVOR

Travel to one of Barracks Row's best-known restaurants with international flair: **Belga Café** (⊠ *514 8th St. SE*), pictured below right, with 84 Belgian beer varieties is "the godfather of beer," says executive chef Bart Vandaele. Pair yours with grilled mussels, smoked foie gras, or shrimp-stuffed tomatoes. At **Trattoria Alberto** (⊠ *506 8th St. SE*) the pasta is made fresh daily, as is their Italian ice-cream pie. Upstairs, **Banana Café** (⊠ *500 8th St. SE*) is a rousing piano bar; downstairs it's a Cuban restaurant. The **Starfish Café** (⊠ *539 8th St. SE*) combines Creole and Caribbean cuisines, with selections like seviche and crab cakes.

CAPITOL HILL HOT SPOTS

NON-PARTISAN PUBS

Escape politics as usual at these bars and eateries favored by lobbyists, senators, and congressional representatives.

Tune Inn (✉ *331 Pennsylvania Ave. SE*) is Capitol Hill's last remaining dive bar. Here "you can plop down on a bar stool and be next to absolutely anybody," according to owner Lysa Nardelli. That "anybody" could be a senator or a congressional intern. The bar has a taxidermy theme, with stuffed deer heads decorating the walls. Stuffed deer backsides mark the location of restrooms.

Next door, **Hawk and Dove** (✉ *329 Pennsylvania Ave. SE*) is the city's oldest Irish bar and a political hot spot. The atmosphere may be old Irish pub, but the daily specials venture into American cuisine. Daily after-work specials include a $3.25 "pint of the night," and sandwiches and burgers are available until 11 PM on weeknights.

The Monocle (✉ *107 D St. NE*) has been serving up "table-cloth" dining to senators and staff since 1960. The restaurant's location, a quick dash from the Senate office at the Capitol, gives it an insider-y feel. Head to the bar for jumbo salads, roasted oysters, and fried calamari.

H IS FOR HIPSTER

Follow H Street away from the Capitol and you'll find the new Atlas District, where eclectic bars bring out politicos in heels and kids in sneakers. Live music complements the Creole bordello vibe at **The Red & the Black** (✉ *1212 H St. NE*), where happy-hour deals last from 6 PM to 8 PM every night, while **The Pug** (✉ *1234 H St. NE*) offers $3 beers all day long and hipster-cool games like Rock-'em Sock-'em Robots. Elsewhere, the **Palace of Wonders** (✉ *1210 H St. NE*) boasts rotating drink specials daily—but the traveling sideshows and circus marvels on the walls are the biggest draw.

RESTAURANTS IN THIS AREA

DINING BY CUISINE

American
Jimmy T's Place ¢
The Market Lunch ¢–$
Sonoma $$–$$$
Belgian
Belga Café $–$$
Granville Moore's Brickyard $
French
Bistro Bis $$–$$$
Montmartre $–$$
Italian
Locanda $–$$
Latin American
Tortilla Café ¢–$
Seafood
Johnny's Half Shell $$
Steakhouse
Charlie Palmer Steak $$$$

6

DOWNTOWN, CHINATOWN & WHITE HOUSE AREA

Don't let the staid steak houses and saloons fool you—the capital power brokers who dine downtown also have a taste for the quirky and fun. The area is experiencing a boom of high-concept openings.

At the popular Latin restaurant Ceiba, above, fans rave about the seviche and caipirinhas.

Until recently, tourists who trekked north from the Mall hungry for something more than Smithsonian cafeteria food were stranded downtown with little but high-end options. Now young Washingtonians are taking advantage of residential development and moving off Capitol Hill to Downtown (also called Penn Quarter), pulling trendy and affordable dining choices up north.

Chinatown is the nerve center of the area, thanks to the Verizon Center and a row of popular clothing stores, but the crowds mean an inevitable wait for tables.

If you're in the mood to splurge without feeling like a stuffed shirt, perennials like **Oceanaire Seafood Room** (⊠ *1201 F St. NW*) and **Ceiba** (⊠ *701 14th St. NW*) have a more relaxed vibe on weekends. –*Elana Schor*

MARKET SHARE

The nation's capital may be an urban jungle, but its farmers' markets are rightly revered for offering an oasis of fresh food from nearby pastures in northern Virginia. Penn Quarter's outdoor bazaar takes over 8th St. NW between D and E Sts. every Thursday afternoon from 3 PM to 7 PM, transporting tourists and working stiffs alike into the countryside with grape tomatoes from Endless Summer Harvest, goat cheese from Blue Ridge Dairy, and the indulgent fruit blends of Dolcezza gelato.

D.C. FOODIES ARE BUZZING ABOUT....

FRESH, NEW FOOD FINDS

1. **Proof** (⊠ *775 G St. NW*) is one of our favorite new wine-centric restaurants. Its Modern American menu spotlights local ingredients while focusing on 30-plus choices of wines by the glass.

2. If you spot a strange, shockingly green pushcart while museum-hopping, stop and enjoy **On the Fly** (⊠ *H St. and 8th St. NW*), the city's newest way to grab a gourmet lunch.

3. For a quick bite on the go, visit the Californian cheese whizzes at **Cowgirl Creamery** (⊠ *919 F St. NW*), where free cheese samples abound.

STARS OF THE KITCHEN

Downtown Washington has become a gourmet destination thanks to the intensely personal cooking of the city's new elite chefs. Meet three of the best, and their most special dishes.

Jose Andres. Since he began serving up tapas from **Jaleo's** (⊠ *480 7th St. NW*) kitchen in 1993, Andres has become a capital legend. The biggest of his many talents: enticing skeptical Americans to embrace the octopus, a favorite of his native Spain. It never misses.

Spike Mendelsohn. Brought into the limelight by Food Network's "Top Chef" competition, this brash young hipster is luring fans to **Good Stuff Eatery** (E *303 Pennsylvania Ave. SE*), where he turns out mouth-watering burgers made from farm-raised ingredients. You don't need to be a reality-show devotee to fall for his smokehouse sandwich, smothered in Vermont cheddar, and toasted marshmallow milkshakes.

Laurent Tourondel. This wizard of the grill charged south from Manhattan for his latest outpost of the lavish **BLT Steak** (⊠ *1625 I St. NW*), where the free baskets of warm Gruyère-cheese popovers are so wildly in demand that you can now take a copy of the recipe home.

RESTAURANTS IN THIS AREA

American
CityZen $$$$
Equinox $$$$
Georgia Brown's $–$$
Matchbox $–$$
Occidental Grill $$–$$$
Old Ebbitt Grill $$–$$$
Palette $$–$$$
Poste $–$$
PS 7's $$
Wolfgang Puck's The Source $$$–$$$$
Zola $–$$
Asian
Café MoZU $$$–$$$$
Full Kee $–$$
Kaz Sushi Bistro $–$$
Teaism ¢
TenPenh $$–$$$
Continental
Caucus Room $$$–$$$$
Eclectic
Indebleu $$$
French
Brasserie Beck $$–$$$
Central Michel Richard $$–$$$
Indian
Bombay Club $–$$
Rasika $$–$$$
Italian
Teatro Goldoni $$–$$$
Tosca $$–$$$
Latin American
Cafe Atlántico $–$$
Ceiba $$–$$$
Oyamel ¢–$
Mediterranean
Olives $$
Middle Eastern
Zaytinya $$
Seafood
DC Coast $$–$$$
Oceanaire Seafood Room $$–$$$
Spanish
Jaleo $$–$$$
Taberna del Alabardero $$–$$$
Steak
Capital Grille $$$

6

GEORGETOWN

Georgetown's picturesque Victorian streetscapes make it D.C.'s most famous neighborhood, with five-star restaurants in historic row houses and casual cafés sandwiched between large national chain stores.

At its beginnings in the mid-1700s, Georgetown was a Maryland tobacco port. Today the neighborhood is D.C.'s premiere shopping district, as well as a tourist and architectural attraction, with its grand row houses, narrow cobblestone streets, and European architectural accents. The neighborhood's restaurants range from upscale Italian to down-home barbecue. Still, since its incorporation into D.C. in 1790, Georgetown has retained much of its distinct charm and flair.

Georgetown's main thoroughfares, M Street NW and Wisconsin Avenue NW, are always bustling with university students, professionals, and tourists. On a given day you may encounter political activists on the sidewalks, wedding parties posing for photos, and gossiping teens laden with shopping bags. –*Samantha Cleaver*

SWEET SPOT

Chocoholics go ga-ga for **Leonidas Fresh Belgian Chocolates** (⊠ *1531 Wisconsin Ave. NW*), pictured below right, which imports 80 varieties of chocolates from Belgium, including its popular champagne truffle. For a cool treat, stop at **Thomas Sweet Ice Cream** (⊠ *3214 P St. NW*). Before committing to a flavor, sample our favorites: bittersweet chocolate, tiramisu, and coconut. If cakes are your poison, don't pass up **Filomena Ristorante** (⊠ *1063 Wisconsin Ave. NW*), where 15 towering cheesecake and mousse cake varieties are available daily.

NEIGHBORHOOD FAVORITES

After a day of sightseeing and shopping, it's time to unwind. Here are our favorite Georgetown haunts for taking a load off.

Elegant, country inn: The **1789 Restaurant** (✉ *1226 36th St. NW,* jacket required) is housed in a Federal building off M Street, serving American classics. Each of the restaurant's five dining rooms offers a different historical experience, from the John Carroll Room, displaying early maps of the city, to the Civil War–inspired Manassas Room.

RESTAURANTS IN THIS AREA

Asian teahouse: Ching Ching Cha (✉ *1063 Wisconsin Ave. NW*) offers 70 types of Chinese and Japanese teas, using traditional tea ware and serving techniques. Recline on thick pillows with a pot of orchid-scented Snow Dragon tea, nibbling on steamed dumplings and traditional Chinese desserts.

Bustling trattoria: Papa Razzi (✉ *1066 Wisconsin Ave. NW*), a perennial crowd-pleaser, is located in the oldest standing firehouse in D.C. Fans rave about the thin-crust, wood-fired pizzas and the award-winning "Cesare" salad.

American
1789 Restaurant **$$$**
Five Guys **¢**
Asian
Mie n Yu **$$$**
Austrian
Leopold's Kafe & Konditorei **$$**
French
Bistro Français **$$–$$$**
Citronelle **$$$$**
Italian
Cafe Milano **$$$**
Japanese
Sushi-Ko **$–$$**
Seafood
Black Salt **$$–$$$**
Hook **$$$**
Steak
Morton's of Chicago **$$$$**
Turkish
Cafe Divan **$**
Vietnamese
Miss Saigon **¢–$**

6

BY THE RIVER

Dining along the Potomac River offers fresh seafood and a stunning view of D.C. From any restaurant along the riverfront boardwalk you can see the Kennedy Center, Roosevelt Island, and the Key Bridge. **Nick's Riverside Grille** (✉ *3050 K St. NW*) makes a mean oyster po'boy sandwich for lunch, and specializes in grilled seafood at dinner. Farther down the boardwalk at **Tony and Joe's Seafood Place** (✉ *3000 K St. NW, Suite 10*), don't miss the Sunday Champagne Brunch with a live jazz band. Watch the sunset while enjoying a glass of wine at **Sequoia** (✉ *3000 K St. NW, Suite 100*), an upscale restaurant favored by high-ranking politicians. The Asian-accented American menu features standouts like duck-and-pine nut dumplings.

DUPONT CIRCLE & FOGGY BOTTOM

A mix of funky and formal, Dupont Circle and Foggy Bottom represent the progressive and the historic sides of Washington. But in the true sense of bipartisanship, dining options are as diverse as this town's political leanings.

Stop into Teaism, a café and retail shrine to tea, located in a converted town house, for more than 50 varieties of loose-leaf teas. Tea-friendly sweets and snacks are also available.

In a stark contrast to the staid, conservative reputation of Washington, Dupont Circle is like D.C. in Technicolor. The high-rent, liberal-minded neighborhood has hip art galleries, bookstores, and yoga studios that draw a mix of yuppies and activists. There's no shortage of flamboyant characters and political rallies in this always-bustling enclave. If possible, make reservations for sit-down meals, and expect crowds, especially on weekends.

The history-steeped Foggy Bottom area boasts architectural landmarks like the Watergate Hotel. Around George Washington University there's cheaper, college-friendly fare like burrito joints and coffee shops. Nearby, the Kennedy Center draws a more mature crowd with tastes that have evolved past ramen noodles and nachos. Restaurants here offer a selection of higher-end gastronomic delights. –*Colleen Egan*

TASTY TIDBITS

The capital's reigning carbohydrate kings hold court at **Bread Line** (⊠ *1751 Pennsylvania Ave. NW*), where the fresh sourdough baguettes are irresistibly fluffy and the baked goods fit for Marie Antoinette.

The indoor eating area is large but no-frills, so most locals prefer to order take-out and make a picnic with their couscous salads, spicy lamb flatbreads and chocolate-mascarpone Oreos.

LUNCH LIKE A LOCAL

Take a break from the memorials and take in another kind of sightseeing: people-watching. See Washingtonians cavorting in their natural habitats at these popular spots.

Located near The Phillips Collection, **Firefly** (✉ *1310 New Hampshire Ave. NW*) puts forth a hip, cozy atmosphere, and a menu of comforting fare like Waldorf salad with poached shrimp, seared-tuna club sandwich with avocado, and for dessert, caramelized banana split. The check, presented in a glass jar with holes poked into the lid, makes getting the bill almost endearing.

The Mediterranean-accented **Rosemary's Thyme Bistro** (✉ *1801 18th St. NW*) has a fiercely loyal following that comes for sidewalk dining and stellar happy-hour specials. Grab a spot on the patio and sample fresh favorites like the spinach ravioli or the feta-meta salad.

Eschew the neighborhood's ubiquitous coffee chains and get your caffeine or herbal tea fix at **Teaism** (✉ *2009 R St. NW*), pictured at left. In addition to a robust variety of teas, locals come for Asian-accented fare like tea-cured salmon and smoked-turkey sandwiches with wasabi mayo. Come on weekends for cilantro-scrambled tofu and sourdough waffles. Note: Don't miss the chocolate salty oat cookie that has foodies raving.

PRE-THEATER DINNER DEALS

The intimate **Notti Bianche** (✉ *824 New Hampshire Ave. NW*) in the G.W. University Inn serves indulgent Italian cuisine. The $32 three-course prix-fixe theater menu is available from 5 PM to 7 PM every day.

The French restaurant **Marcel's** (✉ *2401 Pennsylvania Ave. NW*) serves a $48 three-course pre-theater dinner menu that includes round-trip executive car service to and from the Kennedy Center. The deal is available nightly from 5:30 PM to 7 PM, and you can have dessert after the show.

RESTAURANTS IN THIS AREA

American
Firefly $–$$
Nora $$–$$$
Asian
Teaism ¢
Nooshi ¢–$
Belgian
Marcel's $$$
Café
Kramerbooks & Afterwords $
French
Bistrot du Coin $–$$
Italian
Obelisk $$$$
Pizzeria Paradiso $
Malaysian
Malaysia Kopitiam $
Middle Eastern
Skewers Café Luna $–$$
Seafood
Kinkead's $$–$$$
Hank's Oyster Bar $–$$
New American
Blue Duck Tavern $$–$$$
Komi $$$$
Tabard Inn $$–$$$
Westend Bistro by Eric Ripert $$
Southern
Vidalia $$–$$$
Steakhouse
Palm $$$
Sam and Harry's $$$–$$$$
Thai
Sala Thai ¢–$

6

ADAMS-MORGAN, U STREET CORRIDOR

Libations trump legislation in the nightlife-centric U Street/Adams-Morgan area. This irreverent side of the District is characterized by bumping bars and an up-all-night attitude.

The stylish Vegetate, pictured above and below right, serves up music and art shows along with a vegetarian menu.

The Shaw neighborhood, focused at U Street NW between 7th and 16th streets, is D.C.'s heart of African-American history and culture. Decades after the race riots nearly destroyed the area, jazz clubs and restaurants are once again flourishing here. The U Street corridor, which links Shaw to Adams-Morgan, is known for its indie rock clubs, edgy bars, and trendy restaurants. Although the urban hipster vibe is being threatened by skyrocketing rents and the intrusion of chain stores, you'll still find more tattoos and sneakers than pinstripes and pearls here.

In Adams-Morgan, legions of college kids descend on 18th Street for abundant drink specials and dance clubs. Quaint ethnic cafés (Ethiopian, French, Italian) are bustling during evening hours. But as the night wears on, the crowds gravitate to greasy spoons and "jumbo slice" pizza joints. –*Colleen Egan*

BAKED BLISS

D.C.—District of Cupcakes? Lawyer-turned-baker Warren Brown, who also hosts the Food Network show "Sugar Rush," serves up the city's most popular frosted mini-cakes at **CakeLove** (✉ *1506 U St. NW*) and neighboring **Love Café** on U Street. Customized confections are available at the cupcake bar, which offers a choice of cakes, frostings, and toppings.

A NIGHT ON THE TOWN

In this town you can get drinks, eat dinner, go dancing, and listen to live music all in one venue. Paint the town red (or blue) at one of our favorite U Street or Adams-Morgan spots.

Start out the night at **Café Saint-Ex** (⊠ *1847 14th St. NW*) by dining on farm-friendly American dishes, then head downstairs to dance off dinner with the help of a rotating cast of DJs in the often crowded but always rollicking downstairs bar.

Local 16 (⊠ *1602 U St. NW*) may have experimented with its menu (currently American with international influences), but its status as a neighborhood hot spot has never wavered. After dinner, the intimate restaurant becomes a jumping nightclub as DJs start spinning and the crowd spills out onto a balcony patio crowned by palm trees.

The multitasking **Busboys and Poets** (⊠ *2021 14th St. NW*)—a coffee shop, restaurant, bar, performance space, and progressive bookstore—wears many hats without scrimping on taste. Try the simple yet divine peanut-butter-and-honey-on-challah sandwich for a low-key lunch, or stay for the homemade meatloaf (most entrées are in the $10 to $15 range) and a live jazz show.

The walls rattle with the echo of bumping bodies at the **Wonderland Ballroom** (⊠ *1101 Kenyon St. NW*) during its über-popular weekend DJ sessions, while the beat slows down on Sundays with live music. The all-American menu features burgers and fries as good as Coney Island's and savory brunch salads.

Organic vegetarian fare isn't the only thing on the menu at **Vegetate** (⊠ *1414 9th St. NW*), where DJs spin jazz and fusion on some evenings as diners feast on small plates like crispy risotto croquettes with sun-dried tomato tapenade, or jerk-spiced veggie burgers with citrus aïoli and truffle-scented fries. Rotating art exhibits, featuring local artists, complete the total sensory experience.

RESTAURANTS IN THIS AREA

African
Café Nema ¢–$
Etete $
American
Ben's Chili Bowl ¢–$
Cashion's Eat Place $$–$$$
Firefly $–$$
Polly's Café ¢–$
Belgian
Marvin $$
French
La Fourchette $–$$
Italian
Coppi's Organic Restaurant $–$$
Pasta Mia ¢–$
Southern
Bardia's New Orleans Café ¢–$
Oohhs & Aahhs ¢

6

UPPER NORTHWEST

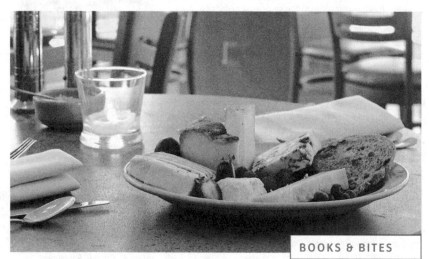

Lions, tigers, and lobbyists . . . oh my! After the requisite cooing over the pandas and other cuddly creatures at the National Zoo, consider wandering around this popular neighborhood to observe locals eat, drink, and play.

Many Hill staffers, journalists, and other inside-the-Beltway types live along this hilly stretch of Connecticut Ave. Eateries and shops line the few blocks near each of the Red Line Metro stops. Restaurants in Cleveland Park range from tiny take-out spots like Vace Italian Delicatessen, one of the few places in town to get a great slice of pizza, to nearby Ardeo, pictured at right, an upscale Modern American restaurant where you stand a good chance of spying your favorite Sunday-morning talk-show guests at a nearby table.

Ethnic dining is also abundant here, especially in Woodley Park. Tucked into the facades of row houses from the early 20th century are diverse dining options ranging from Afghan to Thai. –*Beth Kanter*

BOOKS & BITES

Hungry bibliophiles will want to make a lunchtime pilgrimage to **Politics & Prose** (✉ *5015 Connecticut Ave. NW*), one of the country's best independent bookstores. P&P boasts a full calendar of author readings, a refreshingly well-read staff, and a cozy basement café with free Internet access, dozens of tea selections, and tasty sandwiches. The café, **Modern Times**, also serves pastries and vegetarian sushi made on-site. Our favorite sandwiches are the English Roast, made with marinated roast beef, cheddar cheese, arugula, mango chutney, and plum tomatoes, and the salami and Gorgonzola panini on ciabatta, with a sun-dried tomato relish.

DINNER & A MOVIE

In a town teeming with monuments and memorials, Cleveland Park's **AMC Loews Uptown 1** (✉ *3426 Connecticut Ave. NW*)—known to locals simply as "The Uptown"—is a shrine to the glamour of days gone by. From the red-velvet curtain to the massive balcony to the 70-foot-long and 40-foot-high screen, this art-deco movie palace is a throwback to a time when the experience of seeing a movie could be as romantic as the picture you came to see.

Note: Shows sell out quickly, and coveted balcony seats fill up fast. Avoid the dreaded sold-out sign by heading to the box office early. Then, with tickets in hand, enjoy dinner at one of the many nearby restaurants.

Just a block away, **Indique** (✉ *3512-14 Connecticut Ave. NW*) offers a $20 three-course pre-theater menu from 5:30 to 7 PM. Choices at the attractive, upscale Indian spot might include tandoori chicken tikka, Tamilnad fish curry, and mango ice cream.

Across the avenue, the rustic Italian enoteca **Dino** (✉ *3435 Connecticut Ave. NW*), pictured at left, is known both for its ambience and its award-winning wine list. The daily changing menu always includes a wide selection of cured meats, cheeses, and *fritti*, or fried items.

Spices Asian Restaurant & Sushi Bar (✉ *3333-A Connecticut Ave. NW*) is a popular neighborhood pan-Asian spot offering everything from Peking duck to pad thai noodles in a bustling, bistro-esque space.

For a one-dish meal that's quick and refreshing, stop into **Nam-Viet** (✉ *3419 Connecticut Ave. NW*). The atmosphere is minimal, but you probably won't care after tucking into juicy, salty-sweet caramelized pork chops or spicy rice-noodle soup filled with seared fish or beef.

RESTAURANTS IN THIS AREA

French
Bistrot Lepic $–$$
Indian
Heritage India $–$$
Middle Eastern
Lebanese Taverna $
New American
Ardeo $–$$
New Heights $$–$$$
Palena $$–$$$
Pizza
2 Amys ¢–$

6

RESTAURANTS (IN ALPHABETICAL ORDER)

$$$
AMERICAN
Georgetown

1789 Restaurant. This dining room with Early American paintings and a fireplace could easily be a room in the White House. But all the gentility of this 19th-century town-house restaurant is offset by the down-to-earth food on the menu, which changes daily. The soups, including the seafood stew, are flavorful. Rack of lamb and fillet of beef are specialties, and the seafood dishes are excellent. Service is fluid and attentive. Try the bread pudding and crème brûlée for a sweet finish. ⊠*1226 36th St. NW, Georgetown* ☎*202/965–1789* ⚠*Reservations essential. Jacket required* ⊟*AE, D, DC, MC, V*☺*No lunch* ✛ *1:A5.*

$
PIZZA
Glover Park
Fodor's Choice
★
☾

2 Amys. Judging from the long lines here, the best pizza in D.C. is uptown. Simple recipes allow the ingredients to shine through at this Neapolitan pizzeria. You may be tempted to go for the D.O.C. pizza (it has *Denominazione di Origine Controllata* approval for Neapolitan authenticity), but don't hesitate to try the daily specials. Roasted peppers with anchovies and deviled eggs with parsley-caper sauce have by now become classics. At busy times, the wait for a table can exceed an hour, and the noisy din of a packed house may discourage some diners. ⊠*3715 Macomb St. NW, Glover Park* ☎*202/885–5700* ⚠*Reservations not accepted* ⊟*MC, V*☺*No lunch Mon.* ✛ *1:A2.*

$$$
NEW
AMERICAN
Falls Church, VA
Fodor's Choice
★

2941 Restaurant. Soaring ceilings, a woodsy lakeside location, and a koi pond make this one of the most striking dining rooms in the area. The playful cooking continually surprises, with plates like roasted veal tenderloin and sweetbreads with eggplant puree, truffled free-range chicken, a deconstructed "creamsicle" of orange sorbet and Tahitian vanilla ice cream, and little gifts from the kitchen like rainbow-hued housemade cotton candy. It's a family affair, too. The chef's father makes the artisanal breads that run from rosemary-olive to cherry-almond. You can order à la carte, go for the bargain pre-theater menu (three courses for $45), or splurge on one of the tasting menus ranging from $75 to $110. ⊠*2941 Fairview Park Dr., Falls Church, VA* ☎*703/270–1500* ⚠*Reservations essential* ⊟*AE, D, DC, MC, V*☺*No lunch Sat.* ✛ *1:A6*

$–$$
NEW AMERICAN
Cleveland Park

Ardeo. The trendy new American Ardeo and its lounge-like counterpart, the wine bar Bardeo, sit side by side in the ever-popular culinary strip of Cleveland Park. Ardeo is known for its clean design, professional and knowledgeable staff, and creative menu. Everything is skillfully prepared, from pan-roasted New Zealand rack of lamb to seared sea scallops and a loin of grilled venison. Bardeo has similar options in smaller portions, and great wine offerings, including more than 20 wines by the glass. ⊠*3311 Connecticut Ave. NW, Cleveland Park* ☎*202/244–6750* ⊟*AE, D, MC, V*Ⓜ*Cleveland Park.* ✛ *1:D1*

$$
AMERICAN
Paris, VA

Ashby Inn. If there's a recipe for a perfect country inn, Jackie and Charles Leopold have it. Head an hour west from D.C., and your reward is extraordinary comfort food. Dishes are made with the freshest local ingredients and presented in an intimate setting. Try the arugula salad with just-picked greens from the inn's garden. The roasted chicken, the first item the Ashby ever offered, remains sublime. Sunday brunch is from noon to 2:30. ⊠*692 Federal St., Paris, VA* ☎*540/592–3900* ⊟*AE, MC, V*☺*No lunch. No dinner Sun.–Tues.* ✛ *1:B1*

¢–$ **Bardia's New Orleans Café.** Locals swarm to this cozy café, where great
SOUTHERN   food is accompanied by jazz. Seafood, whether batter-fried, blackened,
Adams-Morgan   or sautéed, is always a winner. The house favorite is the blackened catfish. Po'boy sandwiches (subs on French bread) are reasonably priced,
fresh, and huge. Breakfast items, served all day, include traditional
eggs Benedict or eggs New Orleans, with fried oysters, crabmeat, and
hollandaise: they're both delicious. Don't leave without trying the
outstanding beignets (fried puffs of dough sprinkled with powdered
sugar). ⊠*2412 18th St. NW, Adams-Morgan* ☎*202/234–0420*🗖*AE,
MC, V*Ⓜ*Woodley Park/Zoo.* ✛ *1:F1*

$–$$ **Belga Cafe.** You can go traditional with mussels and the crispiest of
BELGIAN   french fries or dabble in what the chef calls Euro-fusion at this sleek
Capitol Hill   café done up with dark wood, exposed brick, and creamy chairs and
linens. Classic dishes such as *waterzooi*, the Belgian chicken stew, and a
leg of rabbit made with beer, are expertly turned out, along with newer
takes such as seared scallops with young carrots, red beets, and orange
sauce. The three-page beer list is a testament to Belgium's love of well-
made beer. Crowds at lunch and dinner sometimes mean a short wait
even with a reservation. ⊠*514 8th St. SE, Capitol Hill* ☎*202/544–
0100*🗖*AE, D, MC, V.* ✛ *2:H6*

¢–$ **Ben's Chili Bowl.** Long before U Street became hip, Ben's was serving
AMERICAN   chili. Chili on hot dogs, chili on Polish-style sausages, chili on burgers,
U Street   and just plain chili. Add cheese fries if you dare. The faux-marble bar
Ⓒ   and shiny red-vinyl stools give the impression that little has changed
since the 1950s, but turkey and vegetarian burgers and meatless chili
are a nod to modern times. Ben's closes at 2 AM Monday through
Thursday, at 4 AM on Friday and Saturday, and at 8 PM Sunday. South-
ern-style breakfast is served from 6 AM weekdays and from 7 AM on
Saturday. ⊠*1213 U St. NW, U Street corridor* ☎*202/667–0909*🗖*No
credit cards* ◷*Opens at noon Sun.* Ⓜ*U Street/Cardozo.* ✛ *1:H2*

$$$ **Bethesda Crab House.** This modest, noisy, ultracasual restaurant is the
SEAFOOD   best place to enjoy one of the Chesapeake Bay area's great delicacies—
Bethesda, MD   blue crabs steamed with Old Bay seasoning. Order as many crabs as
you want; when they're ready, they'll be dumped on your paper-cov-
ered table. That's your cue to pick up a mallet and knife and attack the
crustaceans. (The waiters gladly give instructions.) Then settle back
with a beer for some serious crab pickin'. The price varies with the time
of year. It's a good idea to call in advance to reserve your crabs—the
restaurant sometimes runs out. ⊠*4958 Bethesda Ave., Bethesda, MD*
☎*301/652–3382*🗖*MC, V*Ⓜ*Bethesda.* ✛ *1:A1*

$$–$$$ **Bistro Bis.** A zinc bar, spacious brown-leather booths, and a glass-front
FRENCH   display kitchen create great expectations at Bistro Bis, the second res-
Capitol Hill   taurant from Jeffrey Buben, the owner of the much-acclaimed Vidalia.
The seasonal menu seamlessly merges Modern American standards
with French bistro classics. For a first course, be sure to try the steak
tartare. Main-course hits on the ever-changing menu include duck
confit and grilled salmon with porcini mushrooms, braised oxtail, cel-
ery-root puree, and bordelaise sauce. ⊠*Hotel George, 15 E St. NW,
Capitol Hill* ☎*202/661–2700*⟰*Reservations essential*🗖*AE, D, DC,
MC, V*Ⓜ*Union Station.* ✛ *2:F3*

6

$$–$$$
FRENCH
Georgetown

Bistro Français. Washington's chefs head to Bistro Français for minute steak, sirloin with black-pepper or red-wine sauce, and rotisserie chicken. Daily specials may include *suprême* of salmon with broccoli mousse and beurre blanc. In the less formal café, sandwiches and omelets are available in addition to entrées. The Bistro also has fixed-price lunches ($14.95), early and late-night dinner specials ($19.95), and a champagne brunch on weekends ($21.95). ■TIP➔It stays open until 3 AM on weekdays and 4 AM on weekends. ⊠*3128 M St. NW, Georgetown* ☎*202/338–3830*⊟*AE, DC, MC, V* ✛ *1:B5.*

$–$$
FRENCH
Dupont Circle

Bistrot du Coin. An instant hit in its Dupont Circle neighborhood, this moderately priced French bistro with a monumental zinc bar is noisy, crowded, and fun. The comforting, traditional bistro fare includes starter portions of mussels in several different preparations. Steaks, garnished with a pile of crisp fries, are the main attraction, but you might also try the duck-leg confit or tripe *à la mode de Caen* (a beef tripe stew with white wine, herbs, celery, and carrots). Wash it down with house Beaujolais, Côtes du Rhône, or an Alsatian white. ⊠*1738 Connecticut Ave. NW, Dupont Circle* ☎*202/234–6969*⊟*AE, D, DC, MC, V*Ⓜ*Dupont Circle.* ✛ *1:E3*

$–$$
FRENCH
Glover Park

Bistrot Lepic. Relaxed and upbeat, with bright yellow walls and colorful paintings, this small, crowded neighborhood bistro is French in every regard—starting with the flirty servers. Traditional bistro fare has been replaced with potato-crusted salmon served with French grapes and ouzo-grape sauce. Some standards, like veal cheeks, remain. The wine is all French, with many wines available by the glass. The wine bar on the second floor has a menu of small plates such as terrine of foie gras, smoked-trout salad, and onion-bacon tart. On this level, seating is first-come, first-served, but if you reserve your spot in advance, you can order from the full menu. ⊠*1736 Wisconsin Ave. NW, Glover Park* ☎*202/333–0111* ⌕*Reservations essential*⊟*AE, D, MC, V* ✛ *1:A3.*

$$–$$$
SEAFOOD
Palisades

Black Salt. Just beyond Georgetown in the residential neighborhood of Palisades, Black Salt is part fish market, part gossipy neighborhood hangout, part swanky restaurant. Fish offerings dominate—there's only one poultry item on the dinner menu—and are varied and pristine, balancing classics like oyster stew and fried Ipswich clams with more offbeat fixings like fluke with cider vinegar, lobster with kaffir lime, and a tiramisu martini for dessert. The place can get crowded and loud, and advance reservations are a must for weekends. Regulars consider a meal at the bar a good fallback—it's one of the friendliest spots around. ⊠*4883 MacArthur Blvd., Palisades* ☎*202/342–9101* ⌕*Reservations essential*⊟*AE, D, DC, MC, V*⊘*Closed Mon.* ✛ *1:A2*

$$–$$$
NEW
AMERICAN
Foggy Bottom
Fodor'sChoice
★

Blue Duck Tavern. Many chefs are fond of artisanal and local ingredients. Chef Brian McBride is so committed to the cause that fixings are often strewn across marble counters in the restaurant's show kitchen. By now diners have gotten used to watching pastry chefs churn ice cream to be served minutes later in glass ice buckets, but sweets—and watching for the town's biggest political names to claim their favorite tables—aren't the only pleasures. The kitchen wows with Modern American riffs like a double-cut pork chop with bourbon-glazed peaches, a marrowbone with creamy insides, and a meaty hanger steak. The dining room is stylish, done up with Shaker furniture and quilts. ✉ *1201 24th St. NW, Foggy Bottom* ☎ *202/419–6755* ☜ *Reservations essential* ⊟ *AE, D, DC, MC, V* Ⓜ *Foggy Bottom/GWU.* ✛ *1:D5*

$–$$ **Bombay Club.** One block from the
INDIAN White House, the beautiful Bombay
Downtown Club tries to re-create the refined aura of British private clubs in colonial India. Potted palms and a bright blue ceiling above white plaster moldings adorn the dining room. On the menu are unusual seafood specialties and a large number of vegetarian dishes, but the real standouts are the aromatic curries. The bar, furnished with rattan chairs and dark-wood paneling, serves hot hors d'oeuvres at cocktail hour. The attire tends toward upscale business-casual. ✉ *815 Connecticut Ave. NW, Downtown* ☎ *202/659–3727* ☜ *Reservations essential* ⊟ *AE, D, DC, MC, V* ◔ *No lunch weekends* Ⓜ *Farragut W.* ✛ *1:G6*

$$–$$$ **Brasserie Beck.** Give in to sensory overload at this homage to the railway
FRENCH dining rooms that catered to the pre-war European elite. Every detail
Downtown of Beck's decor exudes luxury, from the vintage-accented clocks that stand above mahogany booths to the exposed stainless-steel kitchen (now rechristened the "epicurean solarium"). The food is just as rich as you'd expect: entrée-size salads with bacon and egg, *fruits de mer* platters laden with enough shellfish for a small army, and a dizzying lineup of artisanal beers. The production is impressive, and you'll remember the food fondly after returning home—but you might long for a simple sandwich afterwards. ✉ *1101 K St. NW, Downtown* ☎ *202/408-1717* ⊟ *AE, MC, V* ◔ *Brunch Sat. only* Ⓜ *McPherson Square.* ✛ *2:C1*

$–$$ **Café Atlántico.** The menu is always exciting at this *nuevo Latino* res-
LATIN taurant with friendly service. Conch fritters come with tiny avocado
AMERICAN ravioli, and scallops are served with coconut rice, ginger, squid, and
Downtown squid-ink oil. On weekends, Atlántico offers "Latino dim sum," tapas-size portions of dishes such as duck confit with passion-fruit oil, pineapple shavings, and plantain powder. À la carte, the plates are $3 to $9, but for $35 you can get a deluxe tasting menu ($25 for a vegetarian tasting menu). The bar makes mean cocktails with *cachaça,* a liquor distilled from sugarcane juice. You are unlikely to find a more extensive selection of South American wines anywhere in the city. At Minibar, a six-stool bar on the second floor, you can explore an $95 tasting menu of about 30 creative morsels, such as a foie-gras "lollipop" coated with cotton candy, conjured up before your eyes. ■TIP➔**Minibar is arguably the most adventurous dining experience in the city, which means you have to reserve at least a week in advance. The space generally closes from mid-August to mid-September.** ✉ *405 8th St. NW, Downtown,* ☎ *202/393–0812* ☜ *Reservations essential* ⊟ *AE, DC, MC, V* Ⓜ *Archives/Navy Memorial.* ✛ *2:D3*

¢–$ **Café Dalat.** In the heart of Arlington's "Little Saigon," you can find
VIETNAMESE low-priced Vietnamese fare in far-from-fancy but clean and pleasant
Arlington, VA Café Dalat, where service is extremely speedy. The sugarcane shrimp

is excellent, and *da ram gung* is a sinus-clearing dish of simmered chicken and ginger. All the appetizers are winners, in particular the crispy spring rolls and the tangy Vietnamese shrimp salad in lemon vinaigrette. ⊠ *3143 Wilson Blvd., Arlington, VA* ☎ *703/276–0935* ▤ *MC, V* Ⓜ *Clarendon.* ✛ *2:A5*

$
TURKISH
Georgetown

Cafe Divan. This small Turkish restaurant with walls of windows on three sides is a gathering spot for D.C.'s Turkish community as well as Georgetown's Euro population. You make a meal of meze, small plates with such morsels as cigar-shaped cheese-filled filo pastries and rice and currant–stuffed grape leaves, or pace yourself and leave room for main courses like Iskender kebab, thin slices of veal and lamb piled on crisped pita chips with drizzles of yogurt and tomato sauce. The unconventional Turkish-style pizzas from the wood oven are wonderful as well. ⊠ *1834 Wisconsin Ave. NW, Georgetown* ☎ *202/338–1747* ▤ *AE, MC, V* Ⓜ *Dupont Circle.* ✛ *1:A2*

$$$
ITALIAN
Georgetown

Cafe Milano. By night you're likely to rub shoulders with local socialites, sports figures, visiting celebrities, and the Euro-crowd at Cafe Milano's cheek-by-jowl bar. Expect authentic, sophisticated Italian cooking and a pricey wine list. Specialties are fried stuffed olives and smelts, thin-crust pizzas, pasta dishes such as lobster with linguine and orecchiette with anchovies, air-dried ricotta, and the type of beautifully composed and dressed salads favored by ladies who lunch. ⊠ *3251 Prospect St. NW, Georgetown* ☎ *202/333–6183* ▤ *AE, D, DC, MC, V* ✛ *1:A5.*

$$$–$$$$
ASIAN
Downtown

Café MoZU. Banks of windows with views of the Potomac and a spare Japanese sensibility set the tone for this airy dining room at the Mandarin Oriental. The food has a Eurasian bent, with dishes such as oysters six ways, Kobe rib-eye steak with citrus sauce, and sautéed black cod with miso. The witty black-and-white martini shake sparks the most interest on the dessert roster. The café regularly serves tea with offerings way beyond the usual Earl Grey (every evening from 6 to 10:30, though the times change often), and an à la carte sushi menu is the ticket for those on the run. Though almost every seat in the house is a good one, the banquettes are most in demand. ⊠ *Mandarin Oriental, 1330 Maryland Ave. SW, Downtown* ☎ *202/787–6868* ▤ *AE, D, DC, MC, V.* ✛ *2:B6*

¢–$
AFRICAN
U Street

Café Nema. Somali, North African, and Middle Eastern cuisines are combined to form simple but flavorful entrées at Café Nema. Grilled chicken, lamb, and beef kebabs and salmon steak are paired with fresh vegetables and an outstanding curried basmati-rice pilaf that has bits of caramelized onion, cloves, and raisins. *Sambousa* (flaky fried triangles of dough filled with curried vegetables or meat) and hummus appetizers are well prepared. There's a good selection of pastas, salads, and sandwiches. Live jazz plays on Thursday. ⊠ *1334 U St. NW, U Street corridor* ☎ *202/667–3215* ▤ *AE, D, DC, MC, V* Ⓜ *U St./Cardozo.* ✛ *1:H2*

$$$
STEAK
Downtown

Capital Grille. A few blocks from the U.S. Capitol, this New England–tinged steak house is a favorite among Republican congressmen. Politics aside, the cuisine, wine list, and surroundings are all top-shelf. Don't let the meat hanging in the window distract you from the fact that this restaurant has a lot more to offer than fine dry-aged porterhouse cuts and delicious cream-based potatoes. For instance, don't miss the panfried calamari with hot cherry peppers. A second location in Tysons Corner has the same menu but a slightly different wine list. ✉*601 Pennsylvania Ave. NW, Downtown* ☎*202/737–6200* ⊕*www. thecapitalgrille.com* ⚷*Reservations essential* ▭*AE, D, DC, MC, V* ◷*No lunch Sun.* Ⓜ *Archives—Navy Memorial* ✉*1861 International Dr., McLean, VA* ☎*703/448–3900* ▭*AE, D, DC, MC, V* ◷*No lunch weekends.* ✛ *2:D4*

$$
NEW
AMERICAN
Arlington, Va

Carlyle Grand Café. Whether you eat at the bustling bar or in the dining room upstairs, you'll find an imaginative, generous interpretation of Modern American cooking. Start with the blue crab fritter or the house-made potato chips drizzled with blue cheese, then move on to entrées such as pecan-crusted trout, veal meat loaf, and roast pork tenderloin with a citrus glaze. The warm flourless chocolate–macadamia nut waffle with vanilla ice cream and hot fudge sauce has become a local classic. You can even buy a loaf of the bread at the restaurant's own bakery, the Best Buns Bread Company, next door. ✉*4000 S. 28th St., Arlington, VA* ☎*703/931–0777* ▭*AE, D, DC, MC, V* ✛ *2:A6.*

$$–$$$
AMERICAN
Adams-Morgan

Cashion's Eat Place. Walls are hung with family photos, and tables are jammed with regulars feasting on up-to-date, home-style cooking. Founder and capital cuisine superstar Ann Cashion recently sold the spot to her longtime sous chef, but the Eat Place has remained a neighborhood favorite. The menu changes daily, but roast chicken, steak, and seafood are frequent choices. Side dishes, such as garlicky mashed potatoes, sometimes upstage the main course. If it's available, order the chocolate terrine layered with walnuts, caramel, mousse, and ganache. ▪**TIP**➜**At Sunday brunch, many entrées are a fraction of the normal price.** ✉*1819 Columbia Rd. NW, Adams-Morgan* ☎*202/797–1819* ⚷*Reservations essential* ▭*AE, MC, V* ◷*Closed Mon. No lunch* Ⓜ *Woodley Park/Zoo.* ✛ *1:F1*

$$$$
CONTINENTAL
Downtown

Caucus Room. Here's the quintessential Washington political restaurant. The limited partnership that owns it includes a Democratic super-lobbyist and a former Republican National Committee chairman. The dark wood and rich leather within make it perfect for business lunches or dinners, and the many private dining rooms are popular for political fund-raising events. The menu changes about three times a year, but you can count on prime meats and seafood dishes including sea bass and seared tuna. ✉*401 9th St. NW, Downtown* ☎*202/393–1300* ▭*AE, D, DC, MC, V* ◷*Closed Sun. No lunch weekends* Ⓜ *Navy Archives.* ✛ *2:D4*

$$–$$$
LATIN
AMERICAN
Downtown

Ceiba. At this very popular Latin restaurant you'll probably want to start with a mojito or a pisco sour cocktail, then taste the smoked-swordfish carpaccio or Jamaican crab fritters. This is a menu meant for grazing, but the main courses, like rib eye with chimichurri sauce and *feijoada* made from pork shanks, still satisfy. Also stellar are desserts such as Mexican vanilla-bean cheesecake with guava jelly, and cinnamon-dusted churros to dip in Mexican hot chocolate. Island-theme murals, angular cream banquettes, an open kitchen, and vaulted ceilings set the scene. ✉*701 14th St. NW, Downtown* ☎*202/393–3983* ▭*AE, D, DC, MC, V* ◷*Closed Sun. No lunch Sat.* Ⓜ *Metro Center.* ✛ *2:B2*

6

$$–$$$
FRENCH
Downtown

Central Michel Richard. French powerhouse chef Michel Richard has set up camp downtown with this semi-casual bistro offering up Franco-American spin-offs like fried chicken, leek-and-mussel chowder, and a ginger-flecked tuna burger. Rows of hams hang in a glass case. Light fixtures are subtly stamped with the word "Central." A jazzy portrait of Richard (think Andy Warhol) stares down from one wall. The mood is playful and low key; cocktails and champagne flow. And there are even a few carryovers from Richard's more formal Citronelle in Georgetown like "Le Kit Kat," the chef's take on a Kit Kat bar. ⊠ *1001 Pennsylvania Ave. NW, Downtown* ☎ *202/626–0015* ⌕ *Reservations essential* ⊟ *AE, D, MC, V* ⊗ *Closed Sun. No lunch Sat.* Ⓜ *Metro Center.* ⊹ *2:C3*

$$$$
STEAK
Capitol Hill

Charlie Palmer Steak. It's hard not to feel like a master of the universe when ensconced in this coolly elegant dining room with a drop-dead view of the Capitol. Oversize floral arrangements, tones of blue-gray, a dramatic glass-enclosed wine cellar, and quasi-Danish modern furniture form a backdrop to the contemporary cuisine. Dry-aged rib eye, marinated hanger steak, and filet mignon with roasted shallots are the meaty choices. But soft-shell crabs and butter-steeped lobster make a good showing, too, as do sides such as mashed Yukon Golds and goat-cheese tubetti that seems like deluxe macaroni and cheese. The lemon pound cake finishes things off nicely. ⊠ *101 Constitution Ave., Capitol Hill* ☎ *202/547–8100* ⊟ *AE, D, DC, MC, V* ⊗ *No lunch Sat.* Ⓜ *Union Station.* ⊹ *2:F4*

$$$$
FRENCH
Georgetown
Fodor'sChoice
★

Citronelle. See all the action in the glass-front kitchen at chef Michel Richard's flagship California-French restaurant. Appetizers might include foie gras with lentils prepared three ways, and main courses run to lobster medallions with lemongrass, saddle of lamb crusted with herbs, and breast of squab. Desserts are luscious: a crunchy napoleon with filamentlike pastry and the very special "chocolate bar," Richard's dense, rich take on a Snickers candy bar. A chef's table in the kitchen gives you a ringside seat (reserve at least a month ahead). The fixed-price menu costs $155, or $230 with wine pairings. The bar menu ($$–$$$) has morsels such as mushroom "cigars" and Serrano ham. ⊠ *Latham Hotel, 3000 M St. NW, Georgetown* ☎ *202/625–2150* ⌕ *Reservations essential Jacket required* ⊟ *AE, D, DC, MC, V* ⊗ *No lunch* ⊹ *1:B5.*

$$$$
AMERICAN
Downtown

CityZen. The Mandarin Hotel's rarefied dining room has fast become a destination for those serious about food. In a glowing space with soaring ceilings, chef Eric Zeibold, formerly of Napa Valley's famed French Laundry, creates luxe fixed-price meals from the finest ingredients. Unexpected little treasures abound, such as scrambled eggs with white truffles shaved at the table and buttery miniature Parker House rolls. Main courses could include black bass over caramelized cauliflower, and braised veal shank with potato gnocchi, and desserts such as Meyer lemon soufflé seem spun out of air. A three-course meal is $75, and the tasting menus run $90–$105. ⊠ *Mandarin Oriental, 1330 Maryland Ave. SW, Downtown* ☎ *202/787–6868* ⌕ *Reservations essential* ⊟ *AE, D, DC, MC, V* ⊗ *Closed Sun. and Mon. No lunch.*

$–$$
ITALIAN
U Street

Coppi's Organic Restaurant. An Italian bicycling motif permeates this restaurant, from the posters, photographs, and gear hanging on the walls to the monogrammed racing shirts worn by the staff. The wood oven–

baked pizzas are always good, but the frequently changing menu also includes antipasti, fresh pastas, meat, and fish—all made with organic ingredients. Look for items such as asparagus, English peas, and favas gently sautéed with butter and mint, or pastas such as gnocchi with black-truffle pesto, and *trenette* with porcini and strip steak. For dessert there's biscotti made in the brick oven and a sweet calzone filled with Nutella. ⊠*1414 U St. NW, U Street corridor* ☎*202/319–7773* ⊟*AE, D, DC, MC, V*⊗*No lunch* Ⓜ*U St./Cardozo.* ✛ *1:H2*

$$–$$$
SEAFOOD
Downtown

DC Coast. Chef Jeff Tunks's menu at this sophisticated downtown spot brings the foods of three coasts—Atlantic, Gulf, and Pacific—to Washington. Come for lunch to try his savory version of crab cakes; if you call ahead of time, you can order them for dinner. If you're homesick for New Orleans, try the gumbo (served only at lunch). For Pacific Rim cooking, you can't beat the smoked lobster. ■**TIP➔The bar scene is one of the liveliest in the downtown area.** ⊠*1401 K St. NW, Downtown* ☎*202/216–5988* ⌂*Reservations essential* ⊟*AE, D, DC, MC, V*⊗*Closed Sun. No lunch Sat.* Ⓜ*McPherson Sq.* ✛ *2:B1*

$$$$
AMERICAN
Downtown
Fodor'sChoice
★

Equinox. Virginia-born chef-owner Todd Gray looks to area purveyors for hard-to-find heirloom and local foodstuffs at his low-key American eatery. The furnishings and the food are simple and elegant. The fresh ingredients speak for themselves: grilled quail with a truffle reduction, rare duck breast served on a cabbage salad, crab cakes with diced mango, and barbecued salmon with a sauce of roasted peppers and corn. There are three fixed-price multicourse dinners; an à la carte menu ($$) is available at lunch. ⊠*818 Connecticut Ave. NW, Downtown* ☎*202/331–8118* ⌂*Reservations essential* ⊟*AE, DC, MC, V*⊗*No lunch weekends* Ⓜ*Farragut W.* ✛ *2:A2*

$
AFRICAN
U Street

Etete. The best of the city's Ethiopian restaurants, Etete doesn't hold back on the spices. Savory pastries known as *sambusas* are filled with fiery lentils, and ginger brightens a stew of vegetables. The sharing of dishes and the mode of eating—rather than using utensils diners tear off pieces of *injera*, a spongy pancake-like bread to scoop up stews and sautées—make for exotic and adventurous dining at this style-conscious eatery. ⊠*1942 9th St. NW, U Street* ☎*202/232–7600* ⊟*AE, D, DC, MC, V* Ⓜ*U St./African-American Civil War Memorial/Cardozo.* ✛ *1:H2*

$$–$$$
AFRICAN
Alexandria, VA

Farrah Olivia. The crossing of French, American, and African cooking makes for offbeat flavors and textures that often soar. And the chocolate-brown space with striking white "branches" on the walls and a giraffe motif behind the bar are just as stunning. Seared tuna with red wine and spicy peach accompaniments and pork with tandoori pork rinds are the sort of flights of fancy Ivory Coast–born chef Mourou Ouattara deals in. This is a daring restaurant with a personal touch—it's named for the chef's daughter. ⊠*600 Franklin St., Alexandria, VA* ☎*703/778–2233* ⊟*AE, D, MC, V*⊗*Closed Mon.* Ⓜ*King St.* ✛ *2:A6*

$–$$
AMERICAN
Dupont Circle

Firefly. The backlighted, amber bar and birch-log wall create a warm and natural look at this showcase for contemporary American bistro food. Start with roasted beets and goat cheese or roasted turnip soup. More standard comfort food includes grilled pork tenderloin with Dijon mustard, and roast chicken with bacon-braised cabbage

6

and prunes. The small wine list, made up mostly of California boutique labels, is well chosen and priced fairly. ⊠*Hotel Madera, 1310 New Hampshire Ave. NW, Dupont Circle* ☎*202/861–1310*☐*AE, D, DC, MC, V* Ⓜ*Dupont Circle.* ⊹ *1:E4*

¢
AMERICAN
Georgetown
☺

Five Guys. One of the quirky traditions of this homegrown fast-food burger house is to note on the menu board where the potatoes for that day's fries come from, be it Maine, Idaho, or elsewhere. The place gets just about everything right: from the grilled hot dogs and hand-patted burger patties—most folks get a double—to the fresh hand-cut fries with the skin on and the high-quality toppings such as sautéed onions and mushrooms. Add an eclectic jukebox to all of the above and you've got a great burger experience. ⊠*1335 Wisconsin Ave. NW, Georgetown* ☎*202/337–0400*☐*MC, V.* ⊠*1645 Connecticut Ave. NW, Dupont Circle*☎*202/328–3483* Ⓜ*Dupont Circle* ⊹ *1:B4*

$–$$
CHINESE
Chinatown

Full Kee. Many locals swear by this standout from the slew of mediocre local Chinese joints. Addictively salty shrimp or scallops in garlic sauce cry out for a doggie bag to enjoy again later, as do the wide assortment of Cantonese-style roasted meats. ■**TIP→Order from the house specialties, not the tourist menu; the meal-size soups garnished with roast meats are the best in Chinatown.** Tried-and-true dishes include the steamed dumplings, crispy duck, eggplant with garlic sauce, and sautéed leek flower. ⊠*509 H St. NW, Chinatown* ☎*202/371–2233*☐*No credit cards* Ⓜ*Gallery Pl./Chinatown.* ⊹ *2:D2*

$–$$
SOUTHERN
Downtown

Georgia Brown's. An elegant New South eatery and a favorite hangout of local politicians, Georgia Brown's serves shrimp Carolina-style (head intact, with steaming grits on the side); thick, rich crab soup; and such specials as grilled salmon and slow-cooked green beans with bacon. Fried green tomatoes are filled with herb cream cheese, and a pecan pie is made with bourbon and imported Belgian dark chocolate. ■**TIP→The Sunday "jazz brunch" adds live music and a decadent chocolate fondue fountain to the mix.** The airy, curving dining room has white honeycomb windows and unusual ceiling ornaments of bronze ribbons. ⊠*950 15th St. NW, Downtown* ☎*202/393–4499*☐*AE, D, DC, MC, V*⊜*Reservations essential*☉*No lunch Sat.* Ⓜ*McPherson Square.* ⊹ *2:A2*

$
BELGIAN
Capitol Hill

Granville Moore's Brickyard. This Belgian beer hall with a gourmet soul is worth a visit despite its location in D.C.'s Atlas District, an area that can be seedy after dark. Snag a seat at the bar or at one of the first-come, first-served tables, and linger over unfiltered artisanal brews that range from Chimay to the obscure, lip-smacking Brasserie des Rocs. The food is terrific, specifically the pots of steamed mussels served with crunchy, twice-fried frîtes paired with homemade dipping sauces. The bison burger and chicken with prosciutto are downright decadent. ⊠*1238 H St. NE, Capitol Hill* ☎*202/399–2546* ☐*AE, MC, V.* ⊜*No reservations* ☉*No lunch.* ⊹ *2:H2*

$–$$
SEAFOOD
Dupont Circle
Fodor$Choice
★

Hank's Oyster Bar. The watchword is simplicity at this popular and chic take on the shellfish shacks of New England. A half-dozen oyster varieties are available daily on the half shell, both from the West Coast and local Virginia waters, alongside another half-dozen daily fish specials. An amuse-bouche of cheddar Goldfish crackers adds a touch of whimsy. Don't be shy about asking for seconds on the complimentary baking chocolate presented along with your check —the kitchen doesn't serve sweets, but it doesn't need to. ⊠*1624 Q St. NW, Dupont Circle* ☎*202/462-4265* ☐*AE, MC, V.* ☮*Dupont Circle.* ⊠*1026 King St., Alexandria, VA* ☎*703/739–4265* Ⓜ*King St.* ✦ *1:G3*

$-$$
INDIAN
Glover Park

Heritage India. You feel like a guest in a foreign land dining at this restaurant: there's incredible attention to detail in everything from the tapestried chairs to the paintings of India and the traditional tandoori and curry dishes. *Tahli* is a variety plate of six or seven curry, lamb,

or chicken dishes with rice and bread, served in small bowls or com-partments on a silver platter. Wine is presented in a small glass pitcher. Whatever you choose, the experience is as fascinating as the meal. ⊠*2400 Wisconsin Ave. NW, Glover Park* ☎*202/333–3120* ⚘*Res-ervations essential*☐*AE, D, MC, V.* ⊠*1337 Connecticut Ave. NW, Dupont Circle* ☎*202/331–1414* Ⓜ *Dupont Circle* ✦ *1:A2.*

$$$
SEAFOOD
Georgetown
Fodor's Choice
★

Hook. The old guard of Georgetown gourmands got a heavenly surprise last year when Barton Seaver, the young and charming chef at Café Saint-Ex on U Street, opened this ode to the "sustainable seafood" movement. From weakfish to yahoo, all of the uncommon fish on the menu are caught using environmentally friendly methods that preserve overfished seafood populations like swordfish and salmon. Consciousness aside, your palate is in for a thrill for lunch, brunch, or dinner. Seaver recently handed over his toque to longtime sous chef Joshua Whigham, but the kitchen has not missed a beat. Pastry chef Heather Chittum's fresh basil ice cream and homemade donuts stuffed with Nutella are also not to be missed. ⊠ *3241 M St. NW, Georgetown* ☎*202/625-4488* ⚘*Reserva-tions essential*☐*AE, MC, V.*☮*No lunch Mondays.* ✦ *1:B5*

$$$
ECLECTIC
Downtown

Indebleu. Visual drama and culinary fun are the twin concepts at this res-taurant where French technique meets American foodstuffs and Indian spices. Quaff mangotinis while lounging on orange futons in the noisy, high-energy bar, or head for one of the two stylish dining rooms upstairs. You can make a meal of starters such as the tower of crab and lobster spiked with curry oil, or go the more traditional route with a main course like striped bass with a mussel bouillabaisse. Leave room for the sweet "spaghetti and meatballs," made with saffron-cardamom ice cream and warm Indian milk balls. ⊠*707 G St. NW, Downtown* ☎*202/333–2538*☐*AE, D, MC, V*☮*No lunch weekends*Ⓜ*Gallery Pl.* ✦ *2:D2*

$$$$
AMERICAN
Washington, VA
Fodor's Choice
★

Inn at Little Washington. A 90-minute drive from the District takes you past hills and farms to this English country manor, where the service matches the setting. A seven-course dinner (without wine) is $138 Mon-day to Thursday, $148 on Friday and Sunday, and $168 on Saturday. After a first course of tiny canapés such as a mini-BLT on house-made bread, soup follows—perhaps chilled fruit or creamy leek. Braised duck and seared foie gras over watercress might come next, then squab over garlic polenta. Desserts, including the "palette" of pastel-hue sorbets, are fanciful, or choose the cheese plate, delivered on a life-size, mooing faux cow. ⊠*Middle and Main Sts., Washington, VA* ☎*540/675–3800* ⚖*Reservations essential* ☰*MC, V* ⊙*Closed Tues. in Jan.–Mar., July, and Aug.* ♣ *2:A6*

$$–$$$
SPANISH
Downtown

Jaleo. You are encouraged to make a meal of the long list of tapas at this lively Spanish bistro, although entrées such as paella are just as tasty. Tapas highlights include the *gambas al ajillo* (sautéed garlic shrimp), fried potatoes with spicy tomato sauce, and the grilled chorizo. Adventurers are encouraged to sample the octopus with paprika, and sweet tooths should save room for the crisp apple charlotte and the chocolate hazelnut torte. ⊠*480 7th St. NW, Downtown* ☎*202/628–7949* ☰*AE, D, DC, MC, V* Ⓜ*Gallery Pl./Chinatown.* ♣ *2:D3*

¢
AMERICAN
Capitol Hill
⊙

Jimmy T's Place. This D.C. institution is tucked in the first floor of an old row house only five blocks from the Capitol. Sassy waiters, talkative regulars, and this small diner's two boisterous owners, who run the grill, pack the place daily. Soak in the local culture or read the paper as you enjoy favorites such as grits, bacon, omelets, or the homey eggs Benedict, made with a toasted English muffin, a huge piece of ham, and lots of hollandaise sauce. The anything-goes atmosphere makes it a great place for kids. Breakfast is served all day. ⊠*501 E. Capitol St. SE, Capitol Hill* ☎*202/546–3646* ☰*No credit cards* ⊙*Closed Mon. and Tues. No dinner* Ⓜ*Eastern Market.* ♣ *2:H5*

$$
SEAFOOD
Capitol Hill

Johnny's Half Shell. A move from Dupont Circle to more spacious quarters on Capitol Hill may have diminished the neighborhood charm of this seafood bar, but at least it's easier to get a table these days. ■**TIP➜For a less buttoned-down vibe, head to the tiny taco joint next door, Taqueria Nationale, for the fish tacos that have Senate staffers raving.** The Southern-tinged mid-Atlantic fare—pristine Kumamoto oysters, flavorful seafood stews, fried oyster po'boys, and a stellar pickled-onion-and-blue-cheese-topped hot dog—is still as wonderful as ever. And a new pastry chef is turning out a worthy coconut cake. Not surprisingly, the crowd is heavy on politicos drawn as much by the buzz and big band tunes. ⊠*400 N. Capitol St. NW, Capitol Hill* ☎*202/737–0400* ☰*AE, MC, V* ⊙*Closed Sun.* Ⓜ*Union Station.* ♣ *2:F3*

$$
JAPANESE
Downtown

Kaz Sushi Bistro. Traditional Japanese cookery is combined with often inspired improvisations ("freestyle Japanese cuisine," in the words of chef-owner Kaz Okochi) at this serene location. For a first-rate experience, sit at the sushi bar and ask for whatever is freshest and best. The chef's years of experience preparing *fugu*—the potentially poisonous blowfish, available only in winter—means you're in good hands, though the experience is pricey at $150 per person. It's not all sushi here; innovations include sake-poached scallops with lemon-cilantro dressing. ⊠*1915 I St. NW, Downtown* ☎*202/530–5500* ☰*AE, DC, MC, V* ⊙*Closed Sun. No lunch weekends* Ⓜ*Farragut W.* ♣ *1:F6*

$$–$$$
SEAFOOD
Foggy Bottom

Kinkead's. This multichambered restaurant has a recently updated raw bar downstairs and more formal dining rooms upstairs, but the mood of quiet elegance remains. The open kitchen upstairs allows you to watch chef Bob Kinkead and company turn out an eclectic menu of mostly seafood dishes inspired by Kinkead's New England roots and by the cooking of Asia and Latin America. Don't miss the signature dish—salmon encrusted with pumpkin seeds and served with a ragout of crab, shrimp, and corn. Save room for dessert, because the chocolate and caramel sampler, which includes a chocolate-and-caramel soufflé, is a knockout. ⊠ *2000 Pennsylvania Ave. NW, Foggy Bottom* ☎ *202/296–7700* ⌂ *Reservations essential* ⊟ *AE, D, DC, MC, V* ⊘ *No lunch weekends* Ⓜ *Foggy Bottom/GWU.* ✛ *1:E6*

> ## WORD OF MOUTH
>
> "I have to recommend Komi. It's a small restaurant, and I think business casual would be fine. I warn you though - it's very expensive, but it's worth every penny. I took my husband here for his birthday, and we are still talking about our meal."
>
> —SavTrav

$$$$
NEW
AMERICAN
Dupont Circle
Fodor's Choice
★

Komi. Johnny Monis, the young, energetic chef-owner of this small, personal restaurant, offers one of the most adventurous dining experiences in the city. The five-course prix-fixe is $74 and showcases contemporary fare with a distinct Mediterranean influence. ■ **TIP→Reservations open 30 days in advance—and the longer you wait, the smaller your chance at a coveted table.** Star plates include fresh sardines with pickled lemons, suckling pig over apples and bacon with polenta, and mascarpone-filled dates with sea salt. ⊠ *1509 17th St., Dupont Circle* ☎ *202/332–9200* ⌂ *Reservations essential* ⊟ *AE, D, MC, V* ⊘ *Closed Sun. and Mon. No lunch* Ⓜ *Dupont Circle.* ✛ *1:E4*

$
CAFE
Dupont Circle
☾

Kramerbooks & Afterwords. This popular bookstore-cum-café is a favorite neighborhood breakfast spot. ■ **TIP→It's also a late-night haunt on weekends, when it's open around the clock.** There's a simple menu with soups, salads, and sandwiches, but many people drop in just for cappuccino and dessert. The "dysfunctional family sundae"—a massive brownie soaked in amaretto with a plethora of divine toppings—is a local favorite, and especially popular with kids. Catch a live music performance—everything from rock to the blues—here, Wednesday through Saturday from 8 PM to midnight. ⊠ *1517 Connecticut Ave. NW, Dupont Circle* ☎ *202/387–1462* ⊟ *AE, D, MC, V* Ⓜ *Dupont Circle.* ✛ *1:F4*

$$
FRENCH
Adams-Morgan

La Fourchette. On a block in Adams-Morgan where restaurants seem to open and close weekly, La Fourchette has stayed in business for nearly a quarter of a century by offering good bistro food at reasonable prices. Most of the menu consists of daily specials such as venison with shallots and pepper sauce, chicken in beurre blanc, or sweetbreads in a mushroom-cream sauce. This place looks as a bistro should, with an exposed-brick wall, a tin ceiling, bentwood chairs, and vaguely Postimpressionist murals. ⊠ *2429 18th St. NW, Adams-Morgan* ☎ *202/332–3077* ⊟ *AE, DC, MC, V* Ⓜ *Woodley Park/Zoo.* ✛ *1:F1*

$
MIDDLE
EASTERN
Woodley Park

Lebanese Taverna. Arched ceilings, cedar panels etched with leaf patterns, woven rugs, and brass lighting fixtures give the Taverna a warm elegance. Start with an order of Arabic bread baked in a wood-burning oven. Lamb, beef, chicken, and seafood are either grilled on kebabs, slow roasted, or smothered with a garlicky yogurt sauce. A group can make a

6

meal of the meze platters—a mix of appetizers and sliced *shawarma* (spit-roasted lamb). ⊠*2641 Connecticut Ave. NW, Woodley Park* ☎*202/265–8681* ⊟*AE, MC, V* ☉*No lunch Sun.* Ⓜ*Woodley Park/Zoo.* ✛ *1:D1*

$$ **Leopold's Kafe & Konditorei.** Forget all the clichés about heavy Austrian fare served by waiters in lederhosen. Leopold's is about as Euro trendy as it gets with an all-day coffee and drinks bar, an architecturally hip dining space, and a chic little patio complete with a spewing minifountain. Food is pared down Mitteleuropean: wine soup, crisp Wiener schnitzel paired with peppery greens, a spaetzle casserole that tastes like luxe mac 'n' cheese. In the middle of design-obsessed Cady's Alley, the café draws both an artsy city crowd that's content to sit and watch the scene evolve, just as it's done in Europe. ⊠*3318 M St. NW, Georgetown* ☎*202/965–6005* ⊟*AE, DC, MC, V.* ✛ *1:A5*

AUSTRIAN
Georgetown

$–$$ **Locanda.** Political combatants of all stripes lay down their arms at day's end for an easygoing, welcoming meal at this new standby, minutes from the House of Representatives office buildings. The decor is minimalist, throwing the spotlight onto traditional Italian dishes that are rendered feather-light by Mediterranean accents. The grilled octopus starter is punched up by piquant fresh chorizo, braised pork coasts onto your fork with a coat of lentils, and the house-made pasta is simply revelatory. The frutti di mare is an emerald-green stunner that joins its shrimp and mussels with irresistible looped spaghetti, made from a squid-based dough. ⊠ *633 Pennsylvania Ave. SE, Capitol Hill* ☎*202/547-0002* ⊟*AE, D, DC, MC, V.* ☉*Closed Sun. and Mon.* Ⓜ*Eastern Market.* ✛ *2:H6*

ITALIAN
Capitol Hill

$ **Malaysia Kopitiam.** The decor of this subterranean hideaway may be Gilligan's Island meets Kon-Tiki, but the voluminous menu has Malaysian treasures to spare. Though menus with photos are usually cheesy, the binder here is quite helpful, since Malaysian cuisine is less well known than, say, Chinese or Japanese. Sticky rice with minced shrimp and chicken, okra and eggplant curry with tamarind, and crazy salads like the rojak (tofu, peanuts, egg, and shrimp fritters) are among the stars on a roster with dozens of choices. The place is a hit with groups despite its smallish size, because of its rock-bottom prices and the lively communal dining approach. ⊠*1827 M St. NW, Dupont Circle* ☎*202/833–6232* ⊟*AE, D, DC, MC, V* Ⓜ*Dupont Circle.* ✛ *1:F5*

MALAYSIAN
Dupont Circle

$$$ **Marcel's.** Chef Robert Wiedmaier trained in the Netherlands and Belgium, and in this, his first solo venture, his French-inspired Belgian cooking focuses on robust seafood and poultry preparations. Start with mussels, if they're available, and move on to perfectly seared diver scallops with a fennel puree. The roast chicken is a marvel, white and dark cooked separately to perfect tenderness and moistness. In season, be sure to order the fig tart with citrus crème anglaise and honey-cinnamon ice cream. ⊠*2401 Pennsylvania Ave. NW, Foggy Bottom* ☎*202/296–1166* ⌗*Reservations essential* ⊟*AE, DC, MC, V* ☉*No lunch* Ⓜ*Foggy Bottom/GWU.* ✛ *1:D5*

BELGIAN
Foggy Bottom

¢–$ **The Market Lunch.** A walk around the Capitol, a stroll through Eastern Market, and then a hefty pile of blueberry pancakes from Market Lunch make for a perfect Saturday morning or afternoon on the Hill. The casual counter service and informal seating make it ideal for kids. Locals wait in long lines to dine on ham, eggs, grits, or pan-

AMERICAN
Capitol Hill
☾

cakes in the morning or crab cakes, fried shrimp, or fish for lunch –and owner Tom Glasgow earned that loyalty by setting up a temporary location after historic Eastern Market was decimated by a fire last spring. But don't be mistaken: eating here has never been a leisurely experience. On Saturday you must be in line by noon. ■ TIP→**Follow convention and order quickly, eat, and give up your seat for the next customer.** ✉ *Tent hall across the street from Eastern Market, 306 7th St. SE, Capitol Hill* ☎ *202/547–8444* 🖃 *No credit cards* ⊘ *Closed Mon. No dinner* Ⓜ *Eastern Market.* ✛ *2:H6*

> ### DID YOU KNOW?
>
> As if Washingtonians needed any more reason to cozy up to each other at Mie n Yu, pop princess Christina Aguilera confirmed its aphrodisiac powers when she told *Marie Claire* magazine that her baby was conceived the weekend she and hubby shared a plate here. Rumor has it they chose the decadent birdcage table for the best view.

\$\$
BELGIAN
U Street

Marvin. Eric Hilton, a D.C. local who became a national celebrity as half of the DJ supergroup Thievery Corporation, owns this quirky club and restaurant named after soul singer Marvin Gaye. Inspired by Gaye's sojourn in Belgium in the 1980s, the menu combines soul food with traditional French classics—think chicken and waffles and steak frîtes. The food is so good it'll bust your belt. After dinner, sample a Belgian beer and shake your booty on the upstairs dance floor. ✉ *2007 14th St. NW, U Street* ☎ *202/797-7171.* 🖃 *AE, MC, V.* ⊘ *No lunch* Ⓜ *U St./Cardozo.* ✛ *1:H2*

\$–\$\$
AMERICAN
Downtown
Ⓒ

Matchbox. The miniburgers, served on toasted brioche buns with a huge mound of fried onion strings, get the most press, but the main clue to what to order at this convivial triple-decker bar-restaurant is the glowing woodburning pizza oven. The personal pizzas are "New York–style," with a thin, crisp crust. You probably won't mistake them for the very best of New York, but the pizza margherita is good nevertheless. Homey plates such as grilled filet mignon with horseradish potatoes and spicy pecancrusted chicken add substance to the menu. There's a great lineup of draft beers and oddball martinis. ✉ *713 H St. NW, Downtown* ☎ *202/289-4441* ⊘ *Closed Sun.* Ⓜ *Gallery Pl./Chinatown.* ✛ *2:D2*

\$\$\$
ASIAN
Georgetown

Mie n Yu. Exotic romance abounds at this palatial retreat inspired by the Europe-to-Asia journey of explorer Marco Polo. The menu matches Polo's route along the Silk Road and takes on multiple ethnic personalities: nowhere else in the capital can you find a Thai pu-pu platter of beef satay and sugarcane pork alongside Chinese prawn toast and Indianinspired banana hummus with naan bread. If you'd like to take your dining adventure even further, try the chef's tasting menu and take your seat inside a giant birdcage at the center of the dining room where chic couples head for special nights. ✉ *3125 M St. NW, Georgetown* ☎ *202/333-6122* 🖃 *AE, DC, MC, V.* ⊘ *Closed for lunch Mon.-Tues.* ✛ *1:B5*

¢–\$
VIETNAMESE
Georgetown

Miss Saigon. Shades of mauve and green, black art deco accents, and potted palms decorate this Vietnamese restaurant, where attention is lavished on the food and its presentation. Begin with crisp egg rolls or chilled spring rolls, and then proceed to exquisite salads of shredded green papaya topped with shrimp or beef. Daily specials include imaginative

6

preparations of the freshest seafood. In addition, "caramel"-cooked and grilled meats are standouts. Prices are moderate, especially for lunch, but you may have to order several dishes to have your fill. ⊠*3057 M St. NW, Georgetown* ☎*202/333–5545*☰*AE, DC, MC, V.* ✛ *1:B5*

$–$$
FRENCH
Capitol Hill

Montmartre. With its sidewalk café, cheerful yellow walls, fresh flowers, and lusty yet chic fare, Montmartre evokes the Left Bank of Paris. Here's an unpretentious bistro that straddles classic and modern effort-lessly with dishes like cream of chestnut soup, braised rabbit with olives and shiitake mushrooms, hanger steak with caramelized shallots, and cod with homemade spaetzle. It's a politicians' hangout, but you'd never know it by the cozy, rustic feel of the place. ⊠*327 7th St. SE, Capitol Hill* ☎*202/544–1244*⌃*Reservations essential*☰*AE, DC, MC, V*☽*Closed Mon.* Ⓜ*Eastern Market.* ✛ *2:H6*

$$$$
STEAK
Georgetown

Morton's of Chicago. Enjoy a steak on the patio at the downtown location of this national chain, one block from the Renaissance Mayflower, a D.C. landmark hotel. In classic steak-house tradition, the emphasis is on quantity as well as quality; the New York strip and porterhouse steaks are well over a pound each. If you have an even larger appetite (or you plan to share), there's a 48-ounce porterhouse for $88. Prime rib, lamb, veal, chicken, lobster, and grilled fish are also on the menu. ⊠*3251 Prospect St., Georgetown* ☎*202/342–6258*⌃*Reservations essential*☰*AE, D, DC, MC, V*☽*No lunch.* ⊠*1050 Connecticut Ave. NW, Downtown* ☎*202/955–5997*☰*AE, D, MC, V*Ⓜ*Farragut N.* ✛ *1:f6*

$$–$$$
NEW AMERICAN
Woodley Park

New Heights. This inviting restaurant has 11 large windows that over-look nearby Rock Creek Park. The sophisticated contemporary cooking blends bold world flavors into the traditional American dishes. Truffled potato-leek soup gets dolled up with a cheddar cheese pierogi; king salmon wrapped in *katifi* (shredded wheat) is one of the more unusual entrées. Chocophiles will appreciate the chocolate mousse torte with strawberry coulis. ⊠*2317 Calvert St. NW, Woodley Park* ☎*202/234–4110*⌃*Reservations essential*☰*AE, D, DC, MC, V*☽*Closed Mon. and Tues.* Ⓜ*Woodley Park/Zoo.* ✛ *1:D1*

¢–$
ASIAN
Dupont Circle

Nooshi. Always packed, with long lines waiting for tables and takeout, this attractive Pan-Asian noodle house has remarkably good Chinese, Japanese, Thai, Indonesian, Malaysian, and Vietnamese dishes. Try the Thai drunken noodles, which are soused in sake; gado-gado, a "cooked" Filipino salad; or the Vietnamese rice noodles with grilled chicken. After the restaurant added its extensive sushi menu, it changed its name to Nooshi (noodles plus sushi). ⊠*1120 19th St. NW, Dupont Circle* ☎*202/293–3138*⌃*Reservations essential*☰*AE, MC, V*☽*No lunch Sun.* Ⓜ*Farragut N.* ✛ *1:F5*

$$–$$$
AMERICAN
Dupont Circle

Nora. Chef and founder Nora Pouillon helped pioneer the sustainable-food revolution with the first certified organic restaurant in the country, and her seasonal, sustainable ingredients are out of this world. Settle into the sophisticated and attractive quilt-decorated dining room and start with the mushroom, leek, and Brie tart or a locally grown salad. Entrées such as pepper-crusted steak and roasted salmon with parsnips emphasize the well-

balanced, earthy ingredients. ⊠2132 Florida Ave. NW, Dupont Circle ☎202/462–5143 ⚑Reservations essential▤AE, D, MC, V☾Closed Sun. No lunch Ⓜ Dupont Circle. ✛1:E3

$$$$
ITALIAN
Dupont Circle

Obelisk. Come here for eclectic Italian cuisine. The five-course prix-fixe ($65), your only option, changes every day, combining traditional dishes with chef Peter Pastan's innovations. Representative main courses are lamb with garlic and sage, and braised grouper with artichoke and thyme. The minimally decorated dining room is tiny, with closely spaced tables. ⊠2029 P St. NW, Dupont Circle ☎202/872–1180 ⚑Reservations essential▤DC, MC, V☾Closed Sun. and Mon. No lunch Ⓜ Dupont Circle. ✛1:E4

$$–$$$
AMERICAN
Downtown

Occidental Grill. One of the most venerable restaurants in the city covers its walls with photos of politicians and other notables who have come here for the food and the attentive service. The standbys are best—chopped salad, grilled tuna or swordfish, lamb shank, veal meat loaf. More than half of the menu is seafood. ⊠Willard InterContinental, 1475 Pennsylvania Ave. NW, Downtown ☎202/783–1475 ⚑Reservations essential▤AE, DC, MC, V Ⓜ Metro Center. ✛2:B3

$$–$$$
SEAFOOD
Downtown

Oceanaire Seafood Room. This link in a Minneapolis-based chain is a beautiful throwback to another era, with dark-wood paneling, semicircular red booths, white tablecloths, and a pink glow that makes everybody look great. Oceanaire distinguishes itself primarily with first-rate ingredients; you see it at its best by ordering simply, picking from the list of fresh fish that heads the menu—perhaps walleye pike or local rockfish. The portions are often big enough to feed a family of four. This place is a good time, and even better if you go with a group. ⊠1201 F St. NW, Downtown ☎202/347–2277 ⚑Reservations essential▤AE, D, DC, MC, V☾No lunch weekends Ⓜ Metro Center. ✛2:C3

$$–$$$
AMERICAN
Downtown

Old Ebbitt Grill. People flock here to drink at the several bars, which seem to go on for miles, and to enjoy well-prepared buffalo wings, hamburgers, and Reuben sandwiches. The Old Ebbitt also has Washington's most popular raw bar, which serves farm-raised oysters. Pasta is homemade, and daily fresh fish or steak specials are served until 1 AM. Despite the crowds, the restaurant never feels cramped, thanks to its well-spaced, comfortable booths. ■TIP→Service can be slow at lunch; if you're in a hurry, try the café-style Ebbitt Express next door. ⊠675 15th St. NW, Downtown ☎202/347–4800▤AE, D, DC, MC, V Ⓜ Metro Center. ✛2:B3

$$
MEDITER-
RANEAN
Downtown

Olives. Celebrity chef Todd English's D.C. outpost seems always to have a crowded dining room at lunch and dinner. The upstairs room, which overlooks the open kitchen, is where the action is, but the spacious downstairs dining room is more comfortable, albeit formal. Hearty starters include English's special butternut squash–stuffed tortelli and flatbread with goat cheese and escargots. Most plates have so much going on that there are bound to be some hits and some misses, but the spit-roasted chicken is done very well. ⊠ *1600 K St. NW, Downtown* ☎ *202/452–1866* ⟐ *Reservations essential* ▤ *AE, D, DC, MC, V* ⊘ *Closed Sun. No lunch Sat.* Ⓜ *Farragut N.* ✛ *1:G6*

¢ **Oohhs & Aahhs.** No-frills soul food is what you can find at this friendly
SOUTHERN   eat-in/take-out place where the price is right and the food is delicious.
U Street   Ultra-rich macaroni and cheese, perfectly fried chicken, and smoky-sweet beef ribs just beg to be devoured. Sides like collard greens have a healthy bent, cooked with vinegar and sugar rather than the traditional salt pork. Smack in the middle of the U Street area, the place is both a neighborhood hangout and destination for those missing the perennial dishes that Mama always made best.. ⊠ *1005 U St. NW, U Street* ☎ *202/667–7142* ⊘ *Closed Sun. and Mon.* Ⓜ *U St./African-American Civil War Memorial/Cardozo.* ✛ *1:H2*

¢–$ **Oyamel.** The specialty at this Mexican stunner is antojitos, literally trans-
MEXICAN   lated as "little dishes from the street." But the high ceilings, gracious ser-
Chinatown   vice, and gorgeous Frida Kahlo-inspired decor are anything but street, and even the smallest of dishes is bigger than life when doused with chocolatey mole poblano sauce or piquant lime-cilantro dressing. Standouts include house-made margaritas topped with a clever salt foam, the Veracruz red snapper in a hearty olive-tomato confit, and grasshopper tacos. Yes, those are bugs basted in tequila and pepper sauce—and they're delightful. ⊠ *401 7th St. NW, Downtown* ☎ *202/628-1005* ▤ *AE, D, MC, V.* Ⓜ *Archives/Navy Memorial.* ✛ *2:D3*

$$–$$$ **Palena.** Chef Frank Ruta and pastry chef Ann Amernick met while
NEW AMERICAN   working in the White House kitchens. At their contemporary American
Cleveland Park   restaurant, the French- and Italian-influenced menu changes seasonally.
Fodor's Choice   Among the can't-miss presentations are kabocha squash ravioli with
★   goat cheese, poached scallops with roasted beets, and a venison chop with andouille sausage. Comforting desserts such as a tangy German apple cake or a chocolate torte are a perfect match for the earthy cooking. ■ TIP➔ **Tasting menus are $58 for three courses, $67 for four courses, and $76 for five courses.** Reservations are not accepted for the equally fabulous lounge, where the inexpensive menu includes a cheeseburger with truffles, foie-gras terrine, and an extravagant platter of fries, onion rings, and paper-thin fried Meyer lemon slices. ⊠ *3529 Connecticut Ave. NW, Cleveland Park* ☎ *202/537–9250* ⟐ *Reservations essential* ▤ *AE, D, MC, V* ⊘ *Closed Sun. and Mon. No lunch* Ⓜ *Cleveland Park.* ✛ *1:D1*

$$–$$$ **Palette.** Sophisticated American fare is served in this slick gallerylike
AMERICAN   dining room of pale wood and frosted glass at the Madison Hotel.
Downtown   On the changing menu, appetizer highlights have included asparagus salad with a quail egg on brioche, and foie gras served in a funnel cake with pink peppercorn apple slaw and Riesling syrup. Skin-on Atlantic salmon and grilled Colorado lamb chops are worthy examples in the main course lineup. ⊠ *Madison Hotel, 1177 15th St. NW, Downtown* ☎ *202/587–2700* ▤ *AE, D, DC, MC, V* Ⓜ *McPherson Sq.* ✛ *1:G5*

$$$
STEAK
Dupont Circle

Palm. A favorite lunchtime hangout of power brokers, the Palm has walls papered with caricatures of the famous patrons who have dined there. Main attractions include gargantuan steaks and Nova Scotia lobsters, several kinds of potatoes, and New York cheesecake. One of Palm's best-kept secrets is that it's also a terrific old-fashioned Italian restaurant. Try the veal marsala for lunch or, on Thursday, the tasty shrimp in marinara sauce. ✉ *1225 19th St. NW, Dupont Circle* ☎ *202/293–9091* ⚓ *Reservations essential* ▭ *AE, D, DC, MC, V* ✪ *No lunch weekends* Ⓜ *Dupont Circle.* ✛ *1:F5*

¢–$
ITALIAN
Adams-Morgan

Pasta Mia. Patrons don't seem to mind waiting their turn to eat in this affordable, 40-seat trattoria. Pasta Mia's southern Italian appetizers and entrées all cost around $10. Large bowls of steaming pasta are served with a generous layer of freshly grated Parmesan. Some best sellers are fusilli with broccoli and whole cloves of roasted garlic, rich spinach fettuccine, and penne *arrabbiata* (in a spicy marinara sauce with olives). Tiramisu, served in a teacup, is a civilized way to finish your meal. ✉ *1790 Columbia Rd. NW, Adams-Morgan* ☎ *202/328–9114* ▭ *No credit cards* ✪ *Closed Sun. and Mon. No lunch* Ⓜ *Woodley Park/Zoo.* ✛ *1:F1*

$
ITALIAN
Dupont Circle
☺

Pizzeria Paradiso. A trompe-l'oeil ceiling adds space and light to a simple interior at the ever-popular Dupont Circle Pizzeria Paradiso. The restaurant sticks to crowd-pleasing basics: pizzas, panini, salads, and desserts. Although the standard pizza is satisfying, you can enliven it with fresh buffalo mozzarella or unusual toppings such as potatoes, capers, and mussels. Wines are well chosen and well priced. The intensely flavored gelato is a house specialty. At the larger location in Georgetown, a new Ratskeller-style beer pub on the lower level opened in 2006. ✉ *2029 P St. NW, Dupont Circle* ☎ *202/223–1245* ▭ *DC, MC, V* Ⓜ *Dupont Circle.* ✉ *3282 M St. NW, Georgetown* ☎ *202/337–1245* ▭ *D, DC, MC, V.* ✛ *1:E4*

¢–$
AMERICAN
U Street

Polly's Café. Tables can be hard to come by on weekend nights at Polly's Café, a cozy oasis with a fireplace. That's when locals arrive ready to swill beer, eat better-than-average bar food such as smoked mozzarella salad, and enjoy jukebox favorites from every era. Nightly specials such as grilled tuna with ginger-sesame vinaigrette are among the more substantial plates. The hearty brunch, available every day, is one of Washington's best values. ✉ *1342 U St. NW, U Street corridor* ☎ *202/265–8385* ▭ *MC, V* Ⓜ *U St./Cardozo.* ✛ *1:H2*

$$
NEW AMERICAN
Downtown

Poste. Inside the trendy Hotel Monaco, Poste woos diners with a towering skylighted space that until 1901 was the General Post Office. Homing in on Modern American brasserie fare, chef Robert Weland conjures up such satisfying dishes as foie-gras terrine with cognac jelly, and pan-roasted sirloin with truffled frites. In season, panfried softshell crabs are not to be missed. For dessert, there's a dream of a bourbon pecan tart topped with caramel sauce and ice cream. In warmer months, the neoclassical courtyard is a serene spot for cocktails and light fare. Year-round, the lively bar inside attracts scenesters with booths on raised platforms. ✉ *Hotel Monaco, 555 8th St. NW, Downtown* ☎ *202/783–6060* ▭ *AE, D, DC, MC, V* Ⓜ *Gallery Pl./Chinatown.* ✛ *2:D3*

6

$$
NEW AMERICAN
Chinatown

PS 7's. This restaurant manages to be at once swanky yet youthful, and its bar scene is hip but low-key, with inventive cocktails and nibbles like tuna tartare sliders, fried oysters with souffléd bacon mousse, and veal "chips." In the elegant sunken dining room, the menu reads like a tasting menu and the portions are tiny. The diner calls the shots. Veal is done three ways—a cheek, sweetbreads, the loin—all in petite portions. And the place is not without a touch of whimsy courtesy of portholelike fish tanks filled with goldfish in the restrooms. ☒777 I St. NW, Chinatown ☎202/742–8550 ▤AE, MC, V☉No lunch weekends Ⓜ Chinatown/Gallery Pl. ✛ 2:D2

$$–$$$
INDIAN
Chinatown
Fodor'sChoice
★

Rasika. This trendy Indian restaurant pairs an adventurous wine list with spicy fare in a super-sleek setting. The chef, London export Vikram Sunderam (from Bombay Brasserie), comes from a town where curries never get short shrift. He has prepared a menu of traditional delights, like a fiery chicken green masala, alongside newer, more inspired ones, like lamb miniburgers, tiny crab cakes with Indian spices, and fried spinach leaves with sweet yogurt sauce. Libations at the bar are concocted with as much creativity as the food. Muted shades of cream, apple-green, and cinnabar and dangling crystals evoke the subcontinent but in a stylish, modern way. ☒633 D St. NW, Chinatown ☎202/637–1222 ▤AE, D, DC, MC, V☉Closed Sun. No lunch weekends Ⓜ Archives/Navy Memorial. ✛ 2:D3

$$$
AMERICAN
Alexandria, VA
Fodor'sChoice
★

Restaurant Eve. Diners who visit star chef Cathal Armstrong's understated restaurant in charming Old Town pick between sitting in the bistro or the chef's tasting room. Comfortably contemporary in shades of pale moss and cinnamon, the bistro is known for plates such as bacon, egg, and cheese salad and pork belly confit. Glossy wood floors and buttercup-yellow couches set the scene in the more intimate, expensive tasting room, where a five-course meal is $95 and a nine-course meal $125 per person. Here, look for the distinctive lobster crème brûlée, butter-poached halibut with leek cream, and fried apple with ricotta tart. Even a Bloody Mary gets new life here, with lemongrass and chilies. ☒110 S. Pitt St., Alexandria, VA ☎703/706–0450 ▤AE, D, MC, V☉Closed Sun. No lunch Sat. Ⓜ King St. ✛ 2:A6

¢–$
BARBECUE
Alexandria, VA
☾

Rocklands. This homegrown barbecue stop is known for its flavorful pork ribs smoked over hickory and red oak. Sides like silky corn pudding, rich mac 'n' cheese, and crunchy slaw are as good as the meats, which cover everything from beef brisket and chopped pork barbecue to chicken and fish. Come early for dinner: they close at 8 PM daily. The Georgetown outpost does mostly takeout, but the restaurants in Alexandria, and Arlington cater to more of a sit-down, family crowd. ☒25 S. Quaker La., Alexandria, VA ☎703/778–9663 ▤AE, MC, V. ☒2418 Wisconsin Ave. NW, Georgetown ☎202/333-2558. ✛ 1:A2

¢–$
THAI
Dupont Circle

Sala Thai. Who says Thai food has to be sweat-inducing? Sala Thai makes the food as spicy as you wish, because this chef is interested in flavor, not fire. Among the subtly seasoned dishes are *panang goong* (shrimp in curry-peanut sauce), chicken sautéed with ginger and pineapple, and flounder with a choice of four sauces. Mirrored walls and warm lights soften this small dining room, as do the friendly service and largely local clientele. The Dupont and U Street locations are most

Cherry blossoms along the Tidal Basin

(top left) One arm of the Awakening sculpture in East Potomac Park. (top right) The Authority of the Law, outside the Supreme Court. (bottom) Tulip season at the Capitol.

(top) Homes along the C&O Canal in Georgetown. (bottom) Union Station---a good spot for shopping, as well as catching a train.

(top) Beneath the Capitol's magnificent dome. (bottom) A member of the Old Guard, standing watch at the Tomb of the Unknowns in Arlington National Cemetery.

(top) Washington's most coveted address, 1600 Pennsylvania Ave. (below) A concert at the Tidal Basin.

(top) The lobby scene between acts at the Kennedy Center. (bottom) Getting a feel for modernism at the Smithsonian American Art Museum.

(top) One of the more than 120 million specimens at the National Museum of Natural History. (bottom) Two faces from the collection of National Gallery of Art.

A Fourth of July picnic beside the Washington Monument.

popular, but Arlington, Bethesda, and the Upper Northwest neighborhood all host winning Sala locations. ✉2016 P St. NW, Dupont Circle ☎202/872–1144☲AE, D, DC, MC, V Ⓜ Dupont Circle. ✉1301 U St. NW, U Street corridor ☎202/462–1333 Ⓜ U St./Cardozo ✛ 1:E4.

$$$–$$$$
STEAK
Dupont Circle
Sam and Harry's. Cigar-friendly Sam and Harry's is understated, genteel, and packed at lunch and dinner. Miniature crab cakes are a good way to begin, but the real draws are prime meats such as porterhouse and New York strip steak served on the bone. Seafood specials change daily; Maine lobster is one possibility. End the meal with warm pecan pie laced with melted chocolate or a "turtle cake" of caramel and chocolate that is big enough for two. ✉1200 19th St. NW, Dupont Circle ☎202/296–4333 ⚒Reservations essential☲AE, D, DC, MC, V☣Closed Sun. No lunch Sat. Ⓜ Dupont Circle. ✛ 1:F5

$–$$
MIDDLE
EASTERN
Dupont Circle
Skewers–Café Luna. As the name implies, the focus at Skewers is on kebabs, here served with almond-flaked rice or pasta. Lamb with eggplant and chicken with roasted peppers are the most popular variations, but vegetable kebabs and skewers of filet mignon and seasonal seafood are equally tasty. With nearly 20 choices, the appetizer selection is huge. You can enjoy the cheap eats (chicken-and-avocado salad, mozzarella-and-tomato sandwiches, vegetable lasagna, pizza) downstairs at Café Luna or the reading room–coffeehouse upstairs at Luna Books. ✉1633 P St. NW, Dupont Circle ☎202/387–7400 Skewers, 202/387–4005 Café Luna☲AE, D, DC, MC, V Ⓜ Dupont Circle. ✛ 1:G4

$$–$$$
AMERICAN
Capitol Hill
Sonoma. This chic multilevel wine bar has pours aplenty (in both tasting portions and full glasses) along with well-thought-out charcuterie boards piled with prosciutto, bresaola with house-made condiments like pickled ramps, and figs braised in wine. There's more conventional fare, too, like a juicy Wagyu burger with Taleggio cheese and grilled onions. By day the crowd skews to Senate staffers, by night the place becomes a hipster scene in the bar on the second level—think low tables and sofas—while a youngish crowd shares cheese plates in the crowded street-level dining room. ✉223 Pennsylvania Ave. SE, Capitol Hill ☎202/544–8088 ⚒Reservations essential☲AE, D, DC, MC, V☣No lunch weekends Ⓜ Capitol S. ✛ 2:H5

$–$$
JAPANESE
Georgetown
Sushi-Ko. At one of the city's best Japanese restaurants, daily specials are always innovative: sesame oil-seasoned trout layered with crisp wonton crackers, and a sushi special might be salmon topped with a touch of mango sauce and a sprig of dill. You won't find the restaurant's delicious ginger, mango, or green-tea ice cream at the local Baskin-Robbins. ✉2309 Wisconsin Ave. NW, Georgetown ☎202/333–4187 ⚒Reservations essential☲AE, D, MC, V☣No lunch Sat.–Mon. ✛ 1:A2

$$–$$$
NEW AMERICAN
Dupont Circle
Tabard Inn. Fading portraits and overstuffed furniture make the lobby lounge look like an antiques store, but this hotel restaurant's culinary sensibilities are thoroughly modern. The menu, which changes daily, consistently offers interesting seafood and vegetarian options. A popular entrée is the branzino, a flaky white fish, served with artichokes, preserved lemon, and lentils in an olive sauce. A vegetarian option might be porcini risotto with kalamata olives, Roma tomatoes, and pesto. ■TIP➔In good weather you can dine in the courtyard. ✉Hotel Tabard Inn, 1739 N St. NW, Dupont Circle ☎202/331–8528☲AE, DC, MC, V Ⓜ Dupont Circle. ✛ 1:F4

$$–$$$
SPANISH
Downtown

Taberna del Alabardero. A lovely formal dining room, skillful service, and sophisticated cooking make this restaurant one of Washington's best. Start with tapas: piquillo peppers stuffed with *bacalao* (salt cod) or roasted leg of duck in a phyllo pastry pouch. Proceed to a hefty bowl of gazpacho or white garlic soup and venture on to authentic paella and fine Spanish country dishes. French-toast-like *torrijas* are a light ending to this rich fare. The plush interior and handsome bar make things romantic and help attract a well-heeled clientele. ✉ *1776 I St. NW, at 18th St., Downtown* ☎ *202/429–2200* ✍ *Reservations essential* 🖃 *AE, D, DC, MC, V* ⊗ *Closed Sun. No lunch Sat.* Ⓜ *Farragut W.* ✛ *1:F6*

> ### WORD OF MOUTH
>
> "For a special dinner, I LOVE Tenpenh—if you like Asian food, I'd highly recommend it. A few blocks away is '701', which has a good wine list and a piano player. If you like tapas, go to Jaleo's or Zaytina's (for a mediterrean spin on them)."
>
> —kaudrey

¢
JAPANESE
Downtown
Fodor's Choice
★
☾

Teaism. This informal teahouse stocks more than 50 teas (black, white, and green) imported from India, Japan, and Africa, but it also serves healthful and delicious Japanese, Indian, and Thai food as well as tea-friendly sweets like ginger scones, plum muffins, and salty oat cookies. You can mix small dishes—tandoori kebabs, tea-cured salmon, Indian flat breads—to create meals or snacks. There's also a juicy ostrich burger or *ochazuke,* green tea poured over seasoned rice. The smaller Connecticut Avenue branch (enter around the corner, on H Street; closed on weekends) is tucked neatly on a corner adjacent to Lafayette Park and the White House, a casual reprieve from neighboring high-priced restaurants. It's a perfect spot to grab lunch after touring the nation's power center. Breakfast is served daily. ✉ *400 8th St. NW, Downtown* ☎ *202/638–7740* 🖃 *D, MC, V* Ⓜ *Archives/Navy Memorial* ✉ *800 Connecticut Ave. NW, Downtown* ☎ *202/835–2233* Ⓜ *Farragut West.* ✉ *2009 R St. NW, Dupont Circle* ☎ *202/667–3827* 🖃 *D, MC, V* Ⓜ *Dupont Circle.* ✛ *1:E3, 2:D3*

$$–$$$
ITALIAN
Downtown

Teatro Goldoni. Named for an 18th-century Venetian playwright, this restaurant with a colorful interior is a showcase for chef Fabrizio Aielli's modern-meets-traditional Italian cooking. For a first course, try an unusual pasta dish, such as chocolate pappardelle with a royal boar ragù. At the center of the menu is a selection of fresh fish, which may be grilled, roasted, or cooked in parchment paper Venetian-style. There's also a wide selection of vegetarian entrées. Listen to live jazz here on Friday and Saturday. ✉ *1909 K St. NW, Downtown* ☎ *202/955–9494* 🖃 *AE, D, DC, MC, V* ⊗ *Closed Sun. No lunch Sat.* Ⓜ *Farragut N.* ✛ *1:F6*

$$–$$$
ASIAN
Downtown

TenPenh. One of the closest restaurants to the White House, this hopping venue is always buzzing with socialites, political junkies, and politicians. Chef Jeff Tunks's menu draws from many Asian cuisines—Chinese, Thai, Vietnamese, and Filipino. Main courses range from the chef's distinctive Chinese smoked lobster to tea-rubbed beef tenderloin. A pound cake served with Yuzu huckleberries and kaffir-lime coconut sorbet is one creation from pastry chef Norman Messer. ☒ *10th St. and Pennsylvania Ave. NW, Downtown* ☎ *202/393–4500* ⌕ *Reservations essential* ▭ *AE, D, DC, MC, V* �l *Closed Sun.* Ⓜ *Navy Archives.* ✛ *2:C3*

¢–$
LATIN
AMERICAN
Capitol Hill

Tortilla Cafe. A short hop from the bustling temporary location of the Eastern Market, this tiny take-out restaurant with just a few tables serves the best *pupusas* (cornmeal dough rounds stuffed with meat, cheese, or corn) in town. The menu is a mix of mostly Salvadoran and Mexican fare with favorites such as tamales, Peruvian seviches, and fried plantains served with sour cream and refried beans. If it's available, order the homey Salvadoran stew made with large chunks of beef, celery, carrots, and potatoes. The café is open 9–7 weekdays, 7–7 Saturday, and 7–7 Sunday. ☒ *210 7th St. SE, Capitol Hill* ☎ *202/547–5700* ⌕ *Reservations not accepted* ▭ *AE, D, MC, V* Ⓜ *Eastern Market.* ✛ *2:H5*

$$–$$$
ITALIAN
Downtown

Tosca. Chef Cesare Lanfranconi spent several years in the kitchen at Galileo, Washington's dearly departed favorite Italian restaurant, before starting the sleek, sophisticated Tosca with restaurateur Paolo Sacco. The food draws heavily from Lanfranconi's native Lake Como region, but isn't limited by it. Former standouts include polenta topped with wild mushrooms, and a tasty ravioli stuffed with ricotta and crushed amaretto cookies. Save room for dessert, particularly the chef's version of tiramisu, served in a martini glass. ☒ *1112 F St. NW, Downtown* ☎ *202/367–1990* ⌕ *Reservations essential* ▭ *AE, D, DC, MC, V* �l *Closed Sun. No lunch weekends* Ⓜ *Metro Center.* ✛ *2:C3*

$$–$$$
SOUTHERN
Dupont Circle

Vidalia. There's a lot more to Chef Jeffrey Buben's distinguished restaurant than the sweet Vidalia onion, which is a specialty in season. Inspired by the cooking and the ingredients of the South and the Chesapeake Bay region, Buben's version of New American cuisine revolves around the best seasonal fruits, vegetables, and seafood he can find. Try the five-onion soup made with duck broth, the shrimp on yellow grits, or the sensational lemon chess pie. The sleek modern surroundings, including a wine bar, are equal to the food. ☒ *1990 M St. NW, Dupont Circle* ☎ *202/659–1990* ▭ *AE, D, DC, MC, V* �l *No lunch weekends* Ⓜ *Dupont Circle.* ✛ *1:F5*

$$
NEW AMERICAN
Foggy Bottom

Westend Bistro by Eric Ripert. Where else but the Ritz-Carlton Hotel would you find the chef of New York City's award-winning restaurant Le Bernardin? Eric Ripert is wowing the swells of Foggy Bottom with comfort food such as fish burgers with saffron aïoli and a salad of local greens gussied up with truffle vinaigrette. Two caveats: side dishes must be ordered à la carte, and the handmade cocktails are a skyscraping $12 per glass. The pomegranate-spiked West End cocktail and a tangerine tequila named after the chef are particularly irresistible. ☒ *1190 22nd St. NW, Foggy Bottom* ☎ *202/974-4900* ⌕ *Reservations essential.* ▭ *AE,D, MC, V.* �l *No lunch weekends* Ⓜ *Foggy Bottom/ GWU.* ✛ *1:E5*

$$$
NEW AMERICAN
Downtown

Wolfgang Puck's The Source. Wolfgang Puck's first foray into Washington, D.C., provides diners with two dining experiences. The downstairs area is home to an intimate lounge where guests can order specialty cocktails, hand-rolled pizza crowned by homemade sausage, and a juicy quartet of miniature burgers with feather-light fries or tempura onion straws. Upstairs the focus is on haute cuisine: think curry red snapper

6

with lemongrass, and suckling pig tender enough to fall off your fork. The service is so dedicated it borders on slavish. Don't miss the lacquered duck with huckleberries and the mango soufflé dessert. ⊠ *575 Pennsylvania Ave. NW, Downtown* ☎*202/637-6100* ⚑*Reservations essential* ▤*AE, MC, V.* ⊘ *Closed Sun. No lunch* Ⓜ*Archives/Navy Memorial.* ✛ *2:D4*

$$
MIDDLE
EASTERN
Chinatown
Fodor'sChoice
★

Zaytinya. This sophisticated urban dining room with soaring ceilings is a local favorite for meeting friends or dining with a group. Zaytinya, which means "olive oil" in Turkish, devotes practically its entire menu to Turkish, Greek, and Lebanese small plates, known as meze. To get the full experience, make a meal of three or four of these, such as the popular braised lamb with eggplant puree and cheese, or the locally made goat cheese wrapped in grape leaves with tomato marmalade. ■**TIP→So many options make this a great choice for vegetarians and meat lovers alike.** Reservations for times after 6:30 are not accepted; come prepared to wait on Friday and Saturday nights. Bellydancers perform on Wednesday nights. ⊠*701 9th St. NW, Downtown* ☎*202/638–0800*▤*AE, DC, MC, V*Ⓜ*Gallery Pl./Chinatown.* ✛ *2:D2*

$–$$
SOUTHERN
Downtown

Zola. Swanky and chic, Zola channels a 1940s vibe with its snug banquettes, oval bar carts, and dramatic red flourishes. Food is fun without being over-the-top, and dishes have a Southern bent. Crisp rock shrimp spill over honeyed corn bread, a veal steak sidles up to polenta fritters, and rainbow chard gets a hit of applewood-smoked bacon. Dessert follows suit with sweets such as lemon chiffon pudding and chocolate fondue with Rice Krispies treats. Cocktail names reflect the restaurant's location inside the Spy Museum; there are daily wine flights as well. The bar menu includes a burger and a (slightly glammed-up) lobster roll. ⊠*800 F St. NW, Downtown* ☎*202/654–0999*▤*AE, D, DC, MC, V*⊘*No lunch weekends* Ⓜ*Gallery Pl./Chinatown.* ✛ *2:D3*

Washington, D.C. Dining & Lodging Atlas

KEY
☐ Hotels
■ Restaurants
🄻 Restaurant in Hotel
Ⓜ Subway Station

Map 1

- Adams Morgan
- Dupont Circle
- Georgetown
- West End
- Foggy Bottom

■ Ashby Inn
■ Bethesda Crab House
□ Embassy Suites

New Heights ■
Omni Shoreham ■

■ Lebanese Taverna

Ardeo ■
Dino ■
Indique ■
Nam-Viet ■
Palena ■
Politics & Prose ■
Spices ■

■ 2 Amys
■ Black Salt
■ Heritage India
■ Rocklands
■ Sushi-Ko
□ Holiday Inn Georgetown

Kalorama Guest House –Woodley Park □
Marriott Wardman Park □
Woodley Park Guest House □

Kalorama Road

Wyoming Avenue
Jurys Normandy Inn □

Tracy Place

■ Cafe Divan

BURLEITH/HILLANDALE

Dumbarton Oaks Park

S Street

■ Bistrot Lepic

R Street

S Street

Decatur Place

Montrose Park

R Street

Dent Place

Q Street

Q Street

Volta Place

■ Leonidas Fresh Belgian Chocolates

GEORGETOWN

P Street

P Street

■ Thomas Sweet Ice Cream

O Street

O Street

■ Five Guys

Dumbarton Ave.

Georgetown Inn □

N Street

WEST END

Olive Ave.

■ Cafe Milano

Fairmont Washington

Park Hyatt □

■ Leopold's Kafe & Konditonei

Bistro Français ■
Hook ■ Mie n Yu ■ ■ Miss Saigon

M Street

M Street

Blue Duck Tavern ■

← 1789 Restaurant

■ Latham
Citronelle

□ Four Seasons

Papa Razzi ■ ■ Filomena's

■ Ching Ching Cha

Georgetown Suites □

Pennsylvania Avenue

Washington Suites Georgetown □

■ Marcel's

The Melrose

One Washington Circle

K Street

WASHINGTON CIRCLE

Potomac River

FOGGY BOTTOM

■ Nick's Riverside Grill ■ Tony and Joe's Seafood Place
■ Sequoia

George Washington University Inn

Rosslyn

■ 2941 Restaurant

■ Notti Bianche

□ Doubletree Guest Suites

Map 2

- Northeast
- Chinatown
- The Mall
- Capitol Hill
- Penn Quarter

THOMAS CIRCLE

Vegetate

M Street NW

15th Street NW

14th St. NW

13th Street NW

12th Street NW

11th Street NW

10th Street NW

9th Street NW

7th Street NW

6th Street NW

5th Street NW

1

L Street NW

Morrison-Clark Inn

DC Coast

Brasserie Beck

Henley Park

Vermont Avenue NW

K Street NW

McPherson Square

Hostelling International

The Renaissance

MOUNT VERNON SQUARE

BLT Steak

Georgia Brown's

I Street NW

DOWNTOWN

CHINATOWN

PS 7's

2

Equinox

H Street NW

Matchbox

Full Kee

LAFAYETTE SQUARE

New York Avenue NW

Marriott @ Metro

Five Guys

On the Fly

Pennsylvania Avenue NW

W Executive Ave.

E Executive Ave.

Ceiba

Metro Center

Grand Hyatt Washington

Zaytinya

Indebleu

Old Ebbitt Grill

Oceanaire Seafood Room

Harrington

Cowgirl Creamery

Proof

Gallery Place/Chinatown

Zola

Oyamel

3

Occidental Grill

Tosca

Monaco Poste

6th Street

5th Street

Willard InterContinental

J.W. Marriott Pennsylvania Avenue

D Street NW

FreshFarm Farmers Market

Indiana Avenue

Jaleo

Café Atlántico

Rasika

13th Street NW

12th St. NW

11th Street NW

10th Street NW

9th St.

8th St.

7th St.

PENN QUARTER

TenPenh

1

THE ELLIPSE

14th Street NW

Central Michel Richard

Caucus Room

Teaism

Wolfgang Puck's The Souce

Pennsylvania Avenue

Archives/Navy Memorial

The Capital Grille

4

Constitution Avenue NW

Federal Triangle

Madison Drive NW

12th Street NW

9th Street NW

7th Street SW

Café Dalat

THE MALL

Jefferson Drive SW

5

Smithsonian

Tidal Basin

Inn at Little Washington

Carlyl Grand Café

10th Street SW

9th Street SW

L'Enfant Plaza

Maryland Avenue SW

6

Restaruant Eve

Farrah Olivia

Mandarin Oriental, D.C

Café MoZU

CityZen

| A | B | C | D |

Restaurants

1789 Restaurant, 1:A5
2Amys, 1:A2
2941 Restaurant, 1:A6
Ardeo, 1:D1
Ashby Inn, 1:B1
Banana Café, 2:H6
Bardia's New Orleans Café, 1:F1
Belga Cafe, 2:H6
Ben's Chili Bowl, 1:H2
Bethesda Crab House, 1:A1
Bistro Bis, 2:F3
Bistro Français, 1:B5
Bistrot du Coin, 1:E3
Bistrot Lepic, 1:A3
Black Salt, 1:A2
Blue Duck Tavern, 1:D5
BLT Steak, 2:A2
Bombay Club, 1:G6,
Brasserie Beck, 2:C1
Bread Line, 1:F6
Busboys and Poets, 1:H2
Café Atlántico, 2:D3
Café Dalat, 2:A5
Café Divan, 1:A2
Cafe Milano, 1:A5
Café MoZU, 2:B6
Café Nema, 1:H2
Café Saint-Ex, 1:H3
CakeLove, 1:G2
Capital Grille, The, 2:D4
Carlyle Grand Café, 2:A6
Cashion's Eat Place, 1:F1
Caucus Room, 2:D4
Ceiba, 2:B2
Central Michel Richard, 2:C3
Charlie Palmer Steak, 2:F4
Ching Ching Cha, 1:B5
Citronelle, 1:B5
CityZen, 2:B6
Coppi's Organic Restaurant, 1:H2
Cowgirl Creamery, 2:C3
DC Coast, 2:B1
Dino, 1:D1
Equinox, 2:A2
Etete, 1:H2
Farrah Olivia, 2:A6
Filomena Restaurant, 1:B5
Firefly, 1:E4
Five Guys, 1:B4, 2:D2
Full Kee, 2:D2
Georgia Brown's, 2:A2
Granville Moore's Brickyard, 2:H2
Hank's Oyster Bar, 1:G3

Hawk and Dove, 2:H5
Heritage India, 1:A2
Hook, 1:B5
Indebleu, 2:D2
Indique, 1:D1
Inn at Little Washington, 2:A6
Jaleo, 2:D3
Jimmy T's Place, 2:H5
Johnny's Half Shell, 2:F3
Kaz Sushi Bistro, 1:F6
Kinkead's, 1:E6
Komi, 1:G4
Kramerbooks & Afterwords, 1:F4
La Fourchette, 1:F1
Lebanese Taverna, 1:D1
Leonidas Fresh Belgian Chocolates, 1:A4
Leopold's Kafe & Konditorei, 1:A5
Local 16, 1:G2
Locanda, 2: H6
Malaysia Kopitiam, 1:F5
Marcel's, 1:D5
Market Lunch, The, 2:H6
Marvin, 1:H2
Matchbox, 2:D2
Mie n Yu, 1:B5
Miss Saigon, 1:B5
Monocle, The, 2:G3
Montmartre, 2:H6
Morton's of Chicago, 1:F6
Nam-Viet, 1:D1
New Heights, 1:D1
Nick's Riverside Grill, 1:B6
Nooshi, 1:F5
Nora, 1:E3
Notti Bianche, 1:D6
Obelisk, 1:E4
Occidental Grill, 2:B3
Oceanaire Seafood Room, 2:C3
Old Ebbitt Grill, 2:B3
Olives, 1:G6
On the Fly, 2:D2
Oohs & Aahs, 1:H2
Oyamel, 2:D3
Palace of Wonders, 2:H2
Palena, 1:D1
Palette, 1:G5
Palm, 1:F5
Papa Razzi, 1:B5
Pasta Mia, 1:F1
Pizzeria Paradiso, 1:E4
Politics & Prose, 1:D1
Polly's Café, 1:H2
Poste, 2:D3
Proof, 2:D2

PS 7's, 2:D2
Pug, The, 2:H2
Rasika, 2:D3
Red & The Black, The, 2:H2
Restaurant Eve, 2:A6
Rockland's, 1:A2
Rosemary's Thyme Bistro, 1:F3
Sala Thai, 1:E4
Sam and Harry's, 1:F5
Sequoia, 1:B6
Skewers–Café Luna, 1:G4
Sonoma, 2:H5
Spices Asian Restaurant & Sushi Bar, 1:D1
Starfish Café, 2:H6
Sushi-Ko, 1:A2
Tabard Inn, 1:F4
Taberna del Alabardero, 1:F6
Teaism, 1:E3; 2:D3
Teatro Goldoni, 1:F6
TenPenh, 2:C3
Thomas Sweet Ice Cream, 1:B4
Tony and Joe's Seafood Place, 1:B6
Tortilla Cafe, 2:H5
Tosca, 2:C3
Trattoria Alberto, 2:H6
Tune Inn, 2:H5
Vegetate, 2:C1
Vidalia, 1:F5
Westend Bistro by Eric Ripert, 1:E5
Wonderland Ballroom, 1:H1
Wolfgang Puck's The Source, 2:D4
Zaytinya, 2:D2
Zola, 2:D3

Lodging

Adam's Inn, 1:F1
Akwaaba, 1:G3
Best Western Capitol Skyline, 2:F6
Bricbseller Inn, 1:E4
Churchill Hotel, 1:D3
DC Guest House, 1:H4
Doubletree Guest Suites, 1:D6
Embassy Suites, 1: D5; 1:A1
Fairmont Washington, 1:D5
Fairfax Embassy Row, 1:E4
Four Seasons Hotel, 1:C5
George Washington University Inn, 1:D6

Georgetown Inn, 1:A5
Georgetown Suites, 1:B5
Grand Hyatt Washington, 2:C2
Hay-Adams Hotel, 1:G6
Henley Park Hotel, 2:C1
Holiday Inn Capitol, 2:H6
Holiday Inn Georgetown, 1:A2
Holiday Inn on the Hill, 2:F3
Hostelling International–Washington D.C, 2:C1
Hotel George, 2:F3
Hotel Harrington, 2:C3
Hotel Helix, 1:H4
Hotel Lombardy, 1:E6
Hotel Madera, 1:E4
Hotel Monaco, 2:D3
Hotel Palomar, 1:E4
Hotel Rouge, 1:G4
Hotel Tabard Inn, 1:F4
Hyatt Regency Washington on Capitol Hill, 2:F3
Inn at Dupont Circle South, The, 1:F4
J.W. Marriott Pennsylvania Avenue, 2:B3
Jurys Normandy Inn, 1:D2
Jurys Washington Hotel, 1:F4
Kalorama Guest House—Adams Morgan, 1:E1
Kalorama Guest House—Woodley Park, 1:D1
Latham Hotel, 1:B5
L'Enfant Plaza, 1:D6
Madison, The, 1:G5
Mandarin Oriental Washington, D.C, 2:B6
Mansion on O Street, 1:E4
Marriott Residence Inn, 1:E4
Marriott Wardman Park, 1:D1
Marriott Washington at Metro Center, 2:C2
Melrose Hotel, The, 1:D6
Morrison-Clark Inn, 2:C1
Omni Shoreham Hotel, 1:C1
One Washington Circle Hotel, 1:D5
Park Hyatt, 1:D5
Phoenix Park Hotel, 2:F3
Quincy, The, 1:F5
Renaissance Mayflower Hotel, 1:F5
Renaissance Washington D.C. Hotel, 2:D2

Ritz-Carlton Washington, D.C., 1:E5
Sofitel Lafayette Square Washington, 1:H6
St. Gregory, 1:E5
St. Regis Washington, D.C., 1:G6
State Plaza Hotel, 1:E6
Swann House, 1:F3
Topaz Hotel, 1:F4
Washington Court Hotel, 2:F3
Washington Doubletree Hotel, 1:G4
Washington Suites Georgetown, 1:D5
Willard InterContinental, 2:B3
Windsor Inn, 1:G3
Woodley Park Guest House, 1:D1
Wyndham Washington, D.C., 2:B1

Where to Stay

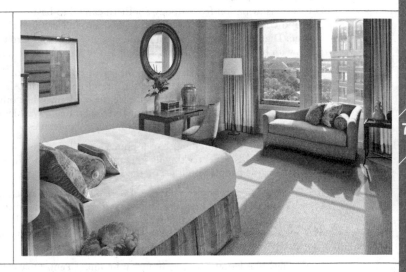

Mandarin Oriental

WORD OF MOUTH

"Please stay near a Metro line and don't bring the car at all. Parking is expensive and can be difficult to find; traffic is bad and the routes are confusing. Just wear sneakers and enjoy the fact you're burning off pounds.

–Thank you, the Commuters"
–kgh8m

THE SCENE

Updated by
Beth Kanter

D.C.'s transformation from stodgy Southern capital to bastion of culture and cool is well underway, and hotels here reflect the welcome change. Dignified lodgings fit for presidents and royalty share these pages with blingy boutique hotels straight out of New York or L.A.

This wave or renovation has led to a variety of options, so you'll do well to be choosy. Some hotels, like the brand new Westin Alexandria and Hotel Palomar Arlington embrace the modern. While others, like the newly restored Omni Shoreham and the St. Regis Washington, gracefully combine historic character with modern amenities.

If you crave people-watching, bar-hopping, and chic restaurants all within walking distance, try staying in Dupont Circle. Rooms here are as diverse as the people you'll see on the sidewalks.

If you are looking for more of a *The American President* experience, book a room on Capitol Hill. The Hill will put you in filibuster distance of the Capitol, the National Mall with all its museums, and The Library of Congress. Tony Georgetown, with a Four Seasons and a boutique-style Ritz-Carlton, is another option for an upscale experience.

Funky digs like Hotel Monaco in up-and-coming Penn Quarter put you near Chinatown, the International Spy Museum, high-end restaurants, and shopping. For a quieter stay, try Foggy Bottom, and for the best rates, head over the border to either Bethesda, Maryland, or suburban Virginia. New water-taxi service from Old Town Alexandria will help make the trip across the Potomac more scenic, not to mention more fun.

Whichever neighborhood you unpack your suitcase in, remember that another one is never far away on the Metro. There are many appealing options in places you might not think to look. We've listed them in the pages that follow.

WHERE SHOULD I STAY?

	Neighborhood Vibe	Pros	Cons
Adams-Morgan	Diverse area with lively bar-and-club scene. The city's center of late-night activity, filled with students and young professionals.	Wide selection of restaurants, bars, and offbeat shopping options. Filled with 19th-century architecture. Stylish budget sleeps.	Some areas are dodgy after dark; it's a 15-minute walk to the Metro; street parking is in short supply. Few nearby monuments.
Capitol Hill	Charming residential blocks of Victorian row houses populated by members of Congress and their staffers.	Convenient to Union Station and the Capitol. Stylish (if not cheap) hotels. Fine assortment of restaurants and shops.	Some streets iffy at night; parking takes some work; hotels are pricey. Chock-full of tourists and high-priced hotels.
Downtown	This once-abandoned part of town is undergoing a renaissance. It's packed during the day, and a little lonely at night.	Right in the heart of the Metro system; easy access to the White House. Large hotel selection.	Can feel desolate at night; few browse-worthy shops; daytime street parking near impossible.
Dupont Circle	D.C.'s most cosmopolitan neighborhood, filled with stylish bars, restaurants, and shops.	Modern design hotels... and lots of them; plentiful nightlife; easy Metro access.	Few budget options; limited street parking; very crowded in summer months.
Georgetown	Wealthy neighborhood bordered by the Potomac and a world-class university. Filled with students and upscale shops and eateries.	Safe area. Historic charm on every tree-lined street. Wonderful walking paths along river.	Crowded; no nearby Metro access; lots of traffic. Lodging options are limited and tend to be expensive.
Southwest	The outer frontier of visitors' Washington, near the Smithsonian museums and the Mall.	Near the Mall; family-friendly hotels; easy Metro access; great river views.	Not much going on other than federal offices; may be too quiet for some travelers.
West End & Foggy Bottom	Charming residential and office area along Pennsylvania Ave. Stately early-20th-century buildings.	Safe area; walking distance to Georgetown, State Department, and the Kennedy Center; good Metro access.	Paltry dining options and lots of traffic. Far from tourist attractions. Older hotels with few budget rates.
Woodley Park	A pleasant residential neighborhood with a lively strip of good restaurants.	Safe and quiet; an easy walk to the Zoo, Metro, and restaurants; street parking easier than Downtown.	A long ride to attractions other than the Zoo; feels almost suburban. Few new hotels.

7

WHERE TO STAY PLANNER

Where Should We Stay?

With hundreds of D.C.-area hotels, it may seem like a daunting question. But fret not—our expert writers and editors have done most of the legwork. The 80-plus selections here represent the best this city has to offer—from the best budget motels to the sleekest designer hotels.

Scan "Best Bets" on the following pages for top recommendations by price and experience. Or find a review quickly in the listings. Search by neighborhood, then alphabetically. Happy hunting!

Hotel Extras

Hotels in the nation's capital work hard to provide extras as varied as their clientele. Almost all inside-the-Beltway properties have Wi-Fi, work desks, sleek gyms (or health-club passes), and morning coffee for the lobbyist on the go. At family-friendly hotels you can often find swimming pools, zoo packages, bath toys, babysitting referrals, and kid-friendly fare on room-service and restaurant menus. Top hotels here offer everything from butler service to in-room spa treatments to evening canapés.

Need a Reservation?

With more than 92,000 guest rooms available in the area, you can usually find a place to stay—though it's always prudent to reserve. Hotels often fill up with convention-eers, politicians in transit, families, and, in spring, school groups. Hotel rooms in D.C. can be particularly hard to come by during the Cherry Blossom Festival in late March or early April, and also in May, when many graduate from college. Late October's Marine Corps Marathon also increases demand for rooms. Expect the city to be packed on and around Inauguration Day, Tuesday, January 20, 2009.

The **Washington DC Convention and Tourism Corporation** (☎ 800/422–8644 ⊕ www.washington.org) runs a reservation service. Many participating hotels are among the best in town.

Traveling with Kids

From the free Smithsonian museums on the Mall to the cuddly pandas at the National Zoo, D.C. is an eminently family-friendly town. Major convention hotels (and those on the waterfront) don't see many families, so we recommend looking Downtown, in Foggy Bottom, or Upper Northwest, where many hotels offer special panda packages for the zoo bound. Also, the closer your hotel is to a Metro stop, the more quickly you can get on the sightseeing trail. The Metro itself often ranks as a favorite attraction among the under-12 set. Consider a stay at an all-suites hotel. This will allow you to spread out and, if you prepare your meals in a kitchenette, to keep costs down. It gives the grown-ups the option of staying up past bedtime, too. A pool may well be essential for a stay with children, especially during D.C.'s notoriously humid summer months.

A number of well-known chains, including **Embassy Suites**, **Fairmont**, **Four Seasons**, **Ritz-Carlton**, and **St. Regis** also offer special programs for kids and usually have babysitting services. **Holiday Inns** allow kids (typically under 12) to eat free.

In the listings, look for the ☺, which indicates a property that we recommend for when you're traveling with little ones.

Facilities

We always list a property's facilities, but not whether you'll be charged extra to use them; when pricing accommodations, ask what's included. You can assume that all rooms have private baths, phones, TVs, and air-conditioning unless otherwise noted, and that all hotels operate on the European Plan (with no meals) unless we specify that they use the Continental Plan (CP, with a Continental breakfast), Breakfast Plan (BP, with a full-cooked breakfast), Modified American Plan (MAP, with breakfast and dinner), or the Full American Plan (FAP, with all meals).

Parking

Hotel parking fees range from free to $30 (plus tax) per night. This sometimes involves valet parking, with its implied additional gratuities. Street parking is free on Sunday and usually after 6:30 PM. But there are often far more cars searching than there are spaces available, particularly Downtown, in Georgetown, and in the upper Connecticut Avenue area.

During weekday rush hours many streets are unavailable for parking; illegally parked cars are towed, and reclaiming a car is expensive and very inconvenient. *Read signs carefully*; some are confusing, and the ticket writers are quick.

Prices

If you're interested in visiting Washington at a calmer, less-expensive time—and if you can stand semitropical weather—come in August, during the congressional recess. Rates also drop in late December and January, except around an inauguration. Weekend, off-season, and special rates (such as AARP discounts and Web-only promotions) can also make rooms more affordable. A little bit of research can pay off in big savings.

WHAT IT COSTS

FOR TWO PEOPLE

¢	$	$$	$$$	$$$$
under $125	$125–$210	$211–$295	$296–$399	over $400

Prices are for a standard double room in high season, excluding room tax (14.5% in D.C., 12.5% in MD, and 10.15% in VA).

In This Chapter

7

BEST BETS FOR D.C. LODGING

Fodor's offers a selective listing of quality lodging experiences at every price range, from the city's best budget motel to its most sophisticated luxury hotel. Here we've compiled our top recommendations by price and experience. The very best properties—those that provide a particularly remarkable experience in a price range—are designated in the listings with a Fodor's Choice logo.

ADAMS-MORGAN

$ **Jurys Normandy Inn.** On a quiet street in the embassy area of Connecticut Avenue stands this small Irish chain hotel. Cozy rooms, attractively decorated with colonial reproduction furniture, include free Wi-Fi, coffeemakers, and complimentary newspapers. Breakfast is served in an intimate parlor, and each Tuesday evening a wine-and-cheese reception is held for guests. **Pros:** Free Wi-Fi in lobby; quiet location; often runs good online deals. **Cons:** Smallish rooms; no room service; no restaurant. ⊠*2118 Wyoming Ave. NW, Adams-Morgan* ☎*202/483–1350 or 800/424–3729* ⊕*www.jurys-washingtondc-hotels.com* ⇆*75 rooms* ⚒*In-room: safe, refrigerator, Ethernet. In-hotel: laundry facilities, public Wi-Fi, parking (fee), no-smoking rooms* ⊟*AE, D, DC, MC, V* ⑩*CP* Ⓜ*Dupont Circle.* ✛ *1:D2*

¢   **Kalorama Guest House—Adams-Morgan.** Like its sister property in Woodley Park, this Adams-Morgan location has been created out of early-20th-century Victorian town houses. The rooms, which vary in size, include 19th-century antiques and cozy furnishings. Some have shared baths, and only the suites offer phones and TVs. **Pros:** Cozy alternative to a big hotel; walking distance to many restaurants. **Cons:** Not all rooms have private baths; limited privacy. ⊠*1854 Mintwood Pl. NW, Adams-Morgan* ☎*202/667–6369* ⊕*www.kaloramaguesthouse. com* ⇆*24 rooms, 9 with bath, 5 suites* ⚒*In-room: no phone (some), no TV (some). In-hotel: parking (fee), no-smoking rooms* ⊟*AE, D, DC, MC, V* ⑩*CP* Ⓜ*Woodley Park/Zoo.* ✛ *1:E1*

CAPITOL HILL

$–$$ **Holiday Inn on the Hill.** The "Bubble Wall" in the innovative lobby, ☾ accompanied by background jazz music, is your first indication that this is not your ordinary Holiday Inn. Rooms are unexpectedly stylish: silky blue comforters grace the beds, bathrooms have black granite countertops and Swiss bath amenities, and ergonomic chairs accompany the glass-topped desks. Rooms also provide free high-speed Internet access. If you stay in summertime, ask the friendly staff—dressed in jet-black-and-cobalt uniforms—to direct you to the rooftop swimming pool. In addition to sending your kids for a swim, you'll be happy to know that children under 12 eat free here. **Pros:** Rooftop pool, kids eat free. **Cons:** High parking fees, some people may feel uncomfortable walking alone at night in the area. ⊠*415 New Jersey Ave. NW, Capitol Hill* ☎*202/638–1616 or 800/884–7202* ⊕*www.holiday-inn. com* ⇆*343 rooms, 4 suites* ⚒*In-room: Ethernet. In-hotel: restaurant, room service, bar, pool, gym, parking (fee), no-smoking rooms* ⊟*AE, D, DC, MC, V* Ⓜ*Union Station.* ✛ *2:F3*

$$$$ **Hotel George.** Rooms at this cool boutique hotel offer duvet-covered **Fodor'sChoice** beds with the softest Egyptian cotton sheets, granite-topped desks, silk-★ screen prints, CD players, and seating areas with a lounge chair and ottoman. Most have marble bathrooms and terry robes, and each room comes with a complimentary in-room television "yoga program" (mat, block, and strap provided). Portraits of America's first president, by Andy Warhol protégé Steve Kaufman, adorn public areas. Bistro Bis

7

serves updated versions of classic French dishes. **Pros:** Stylish hotel; popular restaurant; men's and women's steam rooms. **Cons:** Expensive; some reports of street noise; ultra-modern feel not everyone's cup of tea. ⊠*15 E St. NW, Capitol Hill* ☎*202/347–4200 or 800/576–8331* ⊕*www.hotelgeorge.com* ⇗*138 rooms, 1 suite* ⛶*In-room:safe, DVD, Ethernet. In-hotel: restaurant, room service, bar, gym, concierge, laundry service, parking (fee), some pets allowed, no-smoking rooms.* ⊟*AE, D, DC, MC, V* Ⓜ*Union Station.* ✦ *2:F3*

$$$–$$$$ **Hyatt Regency Washington on Capitol Hill.** A favorite for political events, fundraising dinners, and networking meetings, this property is a solid choice if you're planning on spending a lot of time on the Hill. Expect to find the hotel abuzz with groups getting ready to participate in the political process. The Hyatt often serves as home base for lobbying days, where organizations bring in busloads of people to meet with lawmakers. The hotel is within walking distance of Union Station, home to Amtrak, the Metro, shops, a food court, and restaurants. ■**TIP→The Old Town Trolley picks you up right in front of the hotel to visit Washington's key tourist destinations. Pros:** Indoor pool; quick walk to Union Station; near the Capitol. **Cons:** Busy; lots of groups; escalator in lobby. ⊠*400 New Jersey Ave. NW, Capitol Hill* ☎*202/737–1234 or 800/233–1234* ⊕*www.washingtonregency.hyatt.com* ⇗*802 rooms, 32 suites* ⛶*In-room: Ethernet, Wi-Fi. In-hotel: restaurant, room service, bar, pool, gym, concierge, laundry service, executive floor, parking (fee), no-smoking rooms* ⊟*AE, D, DC, MC, V* Ⓜ*Union Station.* ✦ *2:F3*

$$$–$$$$ **Phoenix Park Hotel.** If you prefer to be near the Hill but not in a big meeting hotel, Phoenix Park may be for you. Guest rooms at this hotel named for a Dublin park were spruced up in 2006 during a $3 million upgrade that brought with it new beds, bedding, and updated public spaces. It's also across the street from Union Station. At the always-packed Dubliner Pub, which provides in-room dining, Irish entertainers perform nightly. **Pros:** Across from Union Station; recently updated guest rooms. **Cons:** No swimming pool; small rooms. ⊠*520 N. Capitol St. NW, Capitol Hill* ☎*202/638–6900 or 800/824–5419* ⊕*www. phoenixparkhotel.com* ⇗*141 rooms, 7 suites* ⛶*In-room: Ethernet, Wi-Fi . In-hotel: restaurant, room service, bar, gym, concierge, laundry service, parking (fee), public Wi-Fi, no-smoking rooms* ⊟*AE, D, DC, MC, V* Ⓜ*Union Station.* ✦ *2:F3*

$$$ **Washington Court Hotel.** Marble stairs lead you into a contemporary atrium lobby with a skylight, waterfall, and glass elevator. Each Deluxe room has a spacious work desk, a lounge chair and ottoman, and marble bathroom. The larger Executive King rooms offer expanded sitting areas with a pull-out sofa bed. Convenient to Union Station, the hotel has a wonderful view of the Capitol. **Pros:** Good location; Capitol views from many rooms. **Cons:** Mixed service; expensive parking. ⊠*525 New Jersey Ave. NW, Capitol Hill* ☎*202/628–2100 or 800/321–3010* ⊕*www.washingtoncourthotel.com* ⇗*252 rooms, 12 suites* ⛶*In-room: Ethernet. In-hotel: restaurant, room service, bar, gym, concierge, laundry service, parking (fee), no-smoking rooms* ⊟*AE, D, DC, MC, V* Ⓜ*Union Station.* ✦ *2:F3*

DOWNTOWN

$$–$$$ **DC Guest House.** Grand and gorgeous as this double town house is, it's hard to imagine it as a private home, which it was until 2002. Now its eclectic magnificence is yours to enjoy, along with a terrific collection of African antiquities adorning sitting and guest rooms. Original 1867 wood floors are throughout; much of the rest has been salvaged from local antiques furnishers as this neighborhood has gentrified. Sleeping quarters are roomy, with satin coverlets, huge closets, high ceilings and the same selective, just-so taste that blesses the sitting and dining rooms. Two of the rooms share a bath—they can be booked as a suite, or bathless for a lower price. ■ **TIP→Make sure to read the fine print on the strict cancellation policy: they charge a 10 percent fee if you cancel 15–30 days out and no refund if you cancel during the two weeks prior to your stay.** Pros: Utterly charming host; terrific design and decor; full cooked breakfast in gorgeous dining room. **Cons:** Transitional neighborhood; small bathrooms; may be too personal for some. ⊠ *1337 10th St. NW, Downtown* ☎ *202/332–2502* ⊕ *www.dcguesthouse.com* 🛏 *6 rooms, 4 with bath* ⅏ *In-room: DVD, Wi-Fi. In-hotel: no elevator, public Wi-Fi, parking (no fee), no kids under 12, no-smoking rooms* ▤ *AE, D, DC, MC, V* ⏍ *BP* Ⓜ *Convention Center.* ✛ *1:H4*

$$$ **Grand Hyatt Washington.** In this fanciful high-rise hotel's atrium, a player piano sits on a small island surrounded by a waterfall-fed blue lagoon. You can enter Metro Center, the hub of D.C.'s subway system, directly from the lobby. The hotel houses one of the city's more popular martini bars, the Butler's Lounge. Guest rooms have been upgraded with pillow-top mattresses, thick down comforters, and plush pillows on the beds, and marble baths that offer Portico spa products. Weekend brunch at this giant hotel is very popular. **Pros:** Right at Metro; location great for sightseeing and shopping; often runs good weekend deals. **Cons:** Big business and meeting hotel with a lot going on inside and out; with almost 900 rooms it can feel impersonal. ⊠ *1000 H St. NW, Downtown* ☎ *202/582–1234 or 800/233–1234* ⊕ *www.grandwashington.hyatt.com* 🛏 *851 rooms, 37 suites* ⅏ *In-room: Wi-Fi, refrigerator. In-hotel: 4 restaurants, room service, bars, pool, gym, concierge, laundry service, executive floor, parking (fee), public Wi-fi, no-smoking rooms* ▤ *AE, D, DC, MC, V* Ⓜ *Metro Center.* ✛ *2:C2*

$$$ **Hay-Adams Hotel.** Two famous Americans—statesman John Hay and
Fodor's Choice historian Henry Adams—once owned homes on the site where this Ital-
★   ian Renaissance mansion now stands, next to Lafayette Park and the White House. Since 1927 the elegant boutique hotel has prided itself on outstanding personalized service. White House views from rooms on the sixth, seventh, and eighth floors are stunning. Other rooms, dressed in beige and pale sage-green, face St. John's church or the interior, and are less expensive. The Lafayette serves exquisite American cuisine, and the hotel's bar is one of the most sophisticated you will find anywhere. **Pros:** Plush guest rooms; personalized service; almost in the shadow of the White House. **Cons:** Expensive; no pool. ⊠ *One Lafayette Sq. NW, Downtown* ☎ *202/638–6600 or 800/424–5054* ⊕ *www.hayadams. com* 🛏 *125 rooms, 20 suites* ⅏ *In-room: refrigerator (some), Wi-Fi. In-hotel: restaurant, room service, bar, concierge, laundry service, parking*

7

(fee), some pets allowed, public Wi-Fi, no-smoking rooms ▭*AE, D, DC, MC, V* Ⓜ*McPherson Sq. or Farragut N.* ✛ *1:G6*

$$$ **Henley Park Hotel.** A Tudor-style building adorned with gargoyles, this National Historic Trust hotel has the cozy charm of an English country house. Rooms, decorated with Edwardian-style furnishings, are amply fitted with modern amenities. ■**TIP**➙**Complimentary sedan service is provided to all Washington locations weekday mornings, and afternoon tea is offered at 4** PM. The highly acclaimed Coeur de Lion restaurant serves regional American dishes. **Pros:** Listed on Historic Hotels of America registry; workout room recently added; free wireless throughout hotel. **Cons:** Street parking; reports of street noise. ✉*926 Massachusetts Ave. NW, Downtown* ☎*202/638–5200 or 800/222–8474* ⊕*www.henleypark.com* ⇆*83 rooms, 13 suites* ☖*In-room: safe, Wi-Fi. In-hotel: Wi-Fi, restaurant, room service, bar, parking (fee), no-smoking rooms* ▭*AE, D, DC, MC, V* Ⓜ*Metro Center.* ✛ *2:C1*

¢ **Hostelling International–Washington D.C.** This well-kept hostel has a living room with a big-screen TV, a communal kitchen, a small gift shop, and Internet access. Rooms are generally dormitory-style, without private bathrooms, but families can have their own room if the hostel is not full. Towels and linens are included in the rates, as is continental breakfast. ■**TIP**➙**The maximum stay is 14 days, and reservations are highly recommended.** College-age travelers predominate, and July and August are the busiest months. The hostel's environmentally friendly outlook would make Al Gore smile. The facility uses earth-friendly paint, carpeting, and light bulbs, and stocks its kitchen with reusable goods rather than paper and plastic ones. Beginning in April 2008, the hostel also started purchasing Renewable Energy Credits. **Pros:** Price can't be beat; free Wi-Fi. **Cons:** Little privacy; crowded during college breaks, which makes getting a reservation difficult in the summer. ✉*1009 11th St. NW, Downtown* ☎*202/737–2333* ⊕*www.hiwashingtondc.org* ⇆*250 beds without bath* ☖*In-room: no phone, no TV, Wi-Fi. In-hotel: laundry facilities, public Wi-Fi no-smoking rooms* ▭*MC, V* Ⓜ*Metro Center.* ✛ *2:C1*

¢ **Hotel Harrington.** One of Washington's oldest continuously operating hotels, the Harrington doesn't offer many frills, but it does have low prices and a location right in the center of everything. It's very popular with springtime high-school bus tours and with families who like the two-bedroom, two-bathroom deluxe suites. **Pros:** Bargain prices; convenient location. **Cons:** No real amenities; shabby but not chic. ✉*436 11th St. NW, Downtown* ☎*202/628–8140 or 800/424–8532* ⊕*www.hotel-harrington.com* ⇆*250 rooms* ☖*In-room: refrigerator (some). In-hotel: 3 restaurants, room service, bar, laundry facilities, parking (fee), some pets allowed, no-smoking rooms* ▭*AE, D, DC, MC, V* Ⓜ*Metro Center.* ✛ *2:C3*

$$$ **Hotel Helix.** In the District's Logan Circle neighborhood, the Helix combines attitude with colorful hospitality. The theme here is fame, with blown-up photos of pop culture figures ranging from Martin Luther King Jr. to Little Richard. Lava lamps, psychedelic prints, and other objects create a back to the '60s feel. Some suites have bunk beds and flat-screen TVs. Wireless access and an evening champagne hour are

included. The Helix Lounge serves American comfort food such as grilled-cheese sandwiches. **Pros:** Funky Brady Bunch vibe makes for a groovy stay; fun extras like Pop Rocks and wax lips in the minibar; good service. **Cons:** A bit of a schlep to the Metro; no pool; small gym. ✉ *1430 Rhode Island Ave. NW, Downtown* ☎ *202/462–9001 or 866/508–0658* ⊕ *www.hotelhelix. com* 🛏 *160 rooms, 18 suites* ⚐ *In-room: safe, DVD, Wi-Fi. In-hotel:restaurant, room service, bar, gym, laundry service, Wi-Fi, concierge, parking (fee), some pets allowed, no-smoking rooms* ☰ *AE, D, DC, MC, V* Ⓜ *McPherson Sq.* ✛ *1:H4*

\$\$–\$\$\$ **Hotel Monaco.** The 1839 Tariff Building, originally designed by Robert Mills (of Washington Monument fame), was one of the leading neoclassical buildings of its day. The brilliantly restored interior introduces a colorful, playful design to the landmark edifice. Rooms have 15-foot vaulted ceilings, eclectic furnishings, and minibars with martini kits; the "Monte Carlo Tall Rooms" accommodate those needing extra bed space. Upon request, the hotel will deliver companion goldfish to your room for the duration of your stay. The fashionable Poste Brasserie serves contemporary American cuisine, and the Verizon Center is right across the street. **Pros:** Fun location next to Spy Museum; near great restaurants and shops and Metro. **Cons:** Not a quiet part of town; pricey; no pool. ✉ *700 F St. NW, Penn Quarter* ☎ *202/628–7177 or 877/202–5411* ⊕ *www.monaco-dc.com* 🛏 *167 rooms, 16 suites* ⚐ *In-room: safe, DVD, Wi-Fi. In-hotel: restaurant, room service, gym, concierge, laundry service, parking (fee), some pets allowed, no-smoking rooms* ☰ *AE, D, DC, MC, V* Ⓜ *Gallery Pl./Chinatown.* ✛ *2:D3*

\$–\$\$ **Hotel Lombardy.** Home to Washington's last hand-operated elevator, the Lombardy's original art deco styling dates from 1929, when the hotel was built as a posh apartment building. Reincarnated as a hotel, its rooms still feel like an elegant city home, with Chinese antiques, original oil paintings, and tiled bathrooms that almost feel cozy. Separate dressing areas and windows that open for fresh air complete the picture. In summer, ask for free passes to the pool at the nearby Washington Plaza hotel. **Pros:** Homey rooms; beautiful lounge; three blocks from the White House. **Cons:** Old-fashioned; expensive breakfast; on busy Pennsylvania Avenue. ✉ *2019 Pennsylvania Ave. NW, Downtown* ☎ *202/828-2600* ⊕ *www.hotellombardy.com* 🛏 *114 rooms 22 suites* ⚐ *In-room: kitchen, refrigerator, Ethernet. In-hotel: restaurant, room service, bar, gym, laundry service, parking (fee), no-smoking rooms* ☰ *AE, D, DC, MC, V* Ⓜ *Foggy Bottom-GWU.* ✛ *1:E6*

\$\$\$\$ **JW Marriott Pennsylvania Avenue.** From the location near the White House to the (literally) monumental views from the top floors, it's hard to forget you are in the nation's capital when you stay here. A recent room renovation brought with it plush linens, new signature beds, and modern technology that will keep business travelers plugged in. The lobby is also new following a $20 million facelift in 2007. **Pros:** In the heart of town; recently updated rooms, elevators, and lobby. **Cons:** With more than 700 rooms not an intimate hotel, pricey. ⊠ *1331 Pennsylvania Ave. NW, Downtown* ☎ *202/393–2000 or 800/228–9290* ⊕ *www.jwmarriottdc.com* ⊐ *729 rooms, 33 suites* △ *In-room: safe, Ethernet, Wi-Fi. In-hotel: 2 restaurants, room service, bars, pool, gym, concierge, laundry service (fee), executive floor, parking (fee), no-smoking room* ▭ *AE, D, DC, MC, V* Ⓜ *Metro Center.* ✛ *2:B3*

WORD OF MOUTH

"The Mandarin is a great hotel—I've done meetings there several times. The rooms are beautiful and the food/service impeccable. But—it could be closer to the sights. I agree with the Hay Adams as a more central location."

—nytraveler

$$$ **The Madison.** Luxury and meticulous service prevail at the stately Madison, which is why the signatures of presidents, prime ministers, sultans, and kings fill the guest register. Deceptively contemporary on the outside, the 15-story building, four blocks from the White House, is an elegant blend of Georgian, Federal, and American Empire styles. Guest rooms maintain the conservative, formal atmosphere of the hotel; get one facing M Street for the best views. The staff is eager to accommodate special requests. **Pros:** Detail-oriented service; elegant hotel. **Cons:** Pricey; may feel too formal. ⊠ *1177 15th St. NW, Downtown* ☎ *202/862–1600 or 800/424–8577* ⊕ *www.themadisondc.com* ⊐ *311 rooms, 42 suites* △ *In-room: refrigerator (some), dial-up. In-hotel: 2 restaurants, room service, bar, gym, concierge, parking (fee), minibar* ▭ *AE, DC, MC, V* Ⓜ *McPherson Sq.* ✛ *1:G5*

$$$–$$$$ **Mandarin Oriental Washington, D.C.** The sophisticated Mandarin Oriental lies at the juncture of the Potomac Tidal Basin and Washington Channel next to the Jefferson Memorial. Beautiful rooms decorated with soft Asian touches overlook either the Mall or the waterfront. All rooms have HDTV flat-screen TVs and other high-tech amenities, as well as Aromatherapy-brand bath products and kimono-style robes and slippers. The Mandarin has a stunning art collection, a gorgeous (but expensive) spa, and refined service. Its gourmet CityZen is one of Washington's hottest restaurants. Despite its impressive view of the waterways, the hotel is slightly out of the way from many of Washington's central attractions. **Pros:** The spa will ruin you for all other spas; beautiful hotel with beautiful views; during cherry-blossom season you can walk to the blooms. **Cons:** Expensive; a bit out of the way; not many dining options in the neighborhood. ⊠ *1330 Maryland Ave. SW, Downtown* ☎ *202/554–8588 or 888/888–17788999* ⊕ *www.mandarinoriental.com* ⊐ *347 rooms, 53 suites* △ *In-room: safe, Ethernet. In-hotel: 2 restaurants, room service, bar, pool, gym, spa, concierge, laundry service, executive floor, parking (fee), no-smoking rooms* ▭ *AE, D, DC, MC, V* Ⓜ *Smithsonian.* ✛ *2:B6*

$$$–$$$$ **Marriott Washington at Metro Center.** Near the White House, the MCI Center, and the Smithsonian museums, the Marriott has numerous

virtues, including a marble lobby, commissioned artwork, and the popular Metro Center Grille, Plaza Stop Café, and Regatta Raw Bar. Rooms were redone in 2006 and have all the bells and whistles typical of others in the Marriott chain. The indoor pool and health club are among the best in town. **Pros:** Great location; spa and health club are top notch; popular restaurants.

> **GREEN POOL**
>
> The Marriott Washington at Metro Center recently switched to a saline swimming pool, an environmentally friendly alternative to chemically treated pools. Added bonus: no red eyes or green hair from dunking under.

Cons: busy location; big chain hotel. ✉ *775 12th St. NW, Downtown* ☎ *202/737–2200 or 800/228–9290* ⊕ *www.marriott.com/wasmc* 🛏 *454 rooms, 2 suites* ♿ *In-room: Wi-Fi. In-hotel: Wi-Fi, 2 restaurants, room service, bar, pool, gym, concierge, laundry service, executive floor, parking (fee), no-smoking rooms* ▭ *AE, D, DC, MC, V* Ⓜ *Metro Center.* ✛ *2:C2*

$$$ **Morrison-Clark Inn.** The elegant merging of two 1864 Victorian town houses, this inn (the only inn in D.C. listed on the National Register of Historic Places) functioned as the Soldiers', Sailors', Marines', and Airmen's Club in the early 1900s. The antiques-filled public rooms have marble fireplaces, bay windows, 14-foot pier mirrors, and porch access, and one house has an ornate Chinese porch from 1917. Rooms have neoclassical, French country, or Victorian furnishings, and six have fireplaces. American cuisine with Southern and other regional accents is served at the inn's highly regarded restaurant, which has an outstanding wine selection. Wireless access is complimentary throughout the hotel. **Pros:** Charming alternative to big cookie-cutter hotels; historic feel throughout. **Cons:** Some noise issues reported; a bit of a walk to Metro; not ideal for young children. ✉ *1015 L St. NW, Downtown* ☎ *202/898–1200* ⊕ *www.morrisonclark.com* 🛏 *34 rooms, 20 suites* ♿ *In room: Wi-Fi. In-hotel: restaurant, room service, gym, laundry service, parking (fee), no-smoking rooms* ▭ *AE, D, DC, MC, V* ⏺️ *CP* Ⓜ *Metro Center.* ✛ *2:C1*

$–$$ **The Quincy.** Although a little short on personality, the Quincy makes up for blandness by offering the right price in the right place. The convenient location two blocks from the Farragut North and Farragut West stops puts you within Metro distance of the whole city, and the brand-new rooms are slicker than you'd imagine for such a reasonable price. Expect pillowtop beds and microfiber suede sectional sofas; bathrooms are cramped, but some rooms have a small attached kitchen. There's a popular Irish pub on the ground floor. **Pros:** Central location convenient to Metro; good value; small breakfast included. **Cons:** Much of the area shuts down at end of the work day; few amenities; nondescript. ✉ *1823 L St. NW, Downtown* ☎ *202/223–4320 or 800/424–2970* ⊕ *www.quincysuites.com* 🛏 *99 rooms* ♿ *In-room: kitchen (some), refrigerator. In-hotel: restaurant, laundry facilities, parking (fee), some pets allowed, no-smoking rooms* ▭ *AE, D, DC, MC, V* Ⓜ *Farragut N. or Farragut W.* ✛ *1:F5*

THE MAYFLOWER HOTEL: DID YOU KNOW?

■ President Franklin D. Roosevelt wrote, "The only thing we have to fear is fear itself" in room 776.

■ J. Edgar Hoover ate lunch at the Mayflower restaurant almost every weekday for 20 years. He almost always brought his own diet salad dressing.

■ Walt Disney once dined on the Mayflower's roof.

■ The state dinner celebrating the 1979 Arab-Israeli peace treaty was held here.

■ Winston Churchill sat for a portrait here.

■ Members of the House interviewed Monica Lewinsky in the 10th-floor Presidential Suite while pursuing the impeachment of President Bill Clinton.

■ Former New York Governor Eliot Spitzer (aka "Client 9") was allegedly visited by high-priced call girl "Kristen" in room 871 on February 13, 2008. The resulting scandal caused him to resign.

$$$ **Renaissance Mayflower Hotel.** The magnificent block-long lobby with its series of antique crystal chandeliers and gilded columns is a destination in and of itself. Guest rooms at this grande dame hotel, which opened its doors in 1925 for Calvin Coolidge's inauguration, have been treated to a recent makeover and are done in soothing yellows, green, tans and blues. Town and Country, the hotel's inside-the-Beltway power bar, has been a place for political wheeling and dealing for nearly as long as the hotel. Sam the bartender mixes up 101 martinis to keep guests happily in the drink. Work off the booze and the crab cakes, a favorite on the menu at the hotel's elegant Café Promenade, in the new spa-like fitness center. **Pros:** Gorgeous lobby; new fitness center with natural light and new equipment; a few steps from the Metro. **Cons:** Rooms vary in size; recent upgrade stopped short of flat-screen TVs and Wi-Fi in the guest rooms; no pool. ⊠ *1127 Connecticut Ave. NW, Downtown* ☎ *202/347–3000 or 800/228–9290* ⊕ *www.marriott. com* ☞ *580 rooms, 74 suites* ♿ *In-room: Ethernet. In-hotel: public Wi-Fi, restaurant, room service, bar, gym, concierge, laundry service, executive floor, parking (fee), no-smoking rooms* ▤ *AE, D, DC, MC, V* Ⓜ *Farragut N.* ✚ *1:F5*

$$–$$$ **Renaissance Washington D.C. Hotel.** Close to the Washington Convention Center and MCI Center, the Renaissance offers extensive business services and guest rooms with special mattresses and linens to help you get a good night's rest. The hotel includes a 10,000-square-foot fitness center and indoor lap pool. The casual restaurant, 15 Squares, serves regional American food; the Presidents' Sports Bar is decorated with black-and-white photos of U.S. presidents at play; Starbuck's serves its signature brew in the lobby. **Pros:** Convenient to convention center; near Metro; guest rooms updated in 2006. **Con:** Busy convention hotel. ⊠ *999 9th St. NW, Downtown* ☎ *202/898–9000 or 800/228–9898* ⊕ *www.marriott.com* ☞ *775 rooms, 26 suites* ♿ *In-hotel: public Wi-Fi, 2 restaurants, room service, bar, pool, gym, concierge, laundry ser-*

vice, parking (fee), some pets allowed, no-smoking rooms =AE, D, DC, MC, V ⓂGallery Pl./Chinatown. ✛ 2:D2

$$$$
Fodor's Choice
★

St. Regis Washington, D.C. Don't forget to look up and admire the ornate, hand-painted ceiling in the newly restored lobby of the St. Regis, a 1926 landmark hotel that reopened in January 2008 after an extensive 16-month restoration. Pratesi linens dress the beds, a 15-inch LCD TV is recessed behind the bathroom mirror in every guest room, and personal butlers now carry BlackBerrys, so while you're out you can e-mail requests like "Please pack my bags." Just two blocks from the White House, this Italian Renaissance–style hotel attracts a formal business crowd. If you check in with kids, hotel staff will give them F.A.O. Schwarz teddy bears and bring mini-robes to your room. The concierge also keeps a selection of toys and games on hand and can arrange babysitting. A new health club and restaurant are slated for late 2008. **Pros:** Two blocks from White House; newly renovated historic property; exceptional service. **Cons:** No pool; most rooms don't have great views; pricey. ✉923 16th and K Streets, NW, Downtown ☎202/638-2626 or 877/787-3447 ⊕www.stregis.com/washington ⇆175 rooms, 25 suites ⌂ In-room: safe, refrigerator (some), DVD (some), Ethernet, Wi-Fi. In hotel: restaurant, room service, bar, gym, spa, laundry service, concierge, public Wi-Fi, parking (fee), some pets allowed, no-smoking rooms. =AE, D, DC, MC,V ⓂFarragut N. ✛ 1:G6

$$$–$$$$
Fodor's Choice
★

Sofitel Lafayette Square Washington. The French could not have landed a better location for the Sofitel, a minute's walk from the White House. The boutique hotel has maintained the 1920s style of the original Shoreham office building, with an understated, sophisticated lobby and chic, though slightly small, guest rooms with beautiful marble bathrooms. The multilingual staff caters to Europeans and Americans, and Cafe 15 serves artful French dishes under the direction of an award-winning chef. **Pros:** Prestigious location; highly reviewed restaurant. **Cons:** Lobby on the small side; expensive parking. ✉806 15th St. NW, Downtown ☎202/730–8800 ⊕www.sofitel.com ⇆221 rooms, 16 suites ⌂In-room: safe, Wi-Fi. In-hotel: restaurant, room service, bar, gym, concierge, laundry service, some pets allowed, no-smoking rooms =AE, D, DC, MC, V ⓂMcPherson Sq. ✛ 1:H6

$
☾

Washington Doubletree Hotel. Just off Scott Circle, the Doubletree offers spacious guest rooms that have recently been renovated, with comfortable beds, well-equipped workstations, CD players, coffeemakers, and robes. An American bistro, 15 Ria, brings a New York sensibility to the hotel, which is only six blocks from the White House. **Pros:** Child-friendly; good location; updated rooms and fitness center. **Cons:** No pool; limited street parking at times. ✉1515 Rhode Island Ave. NW, Downtown ☎202/232–7000 or 800/222–8733 ⊕www.washington. doubletree.com ⇆181rooms, 39 suites ⌂In-room: safe, Ethernet, refrigerator. In-hotel: public Wi-Fi, restaurant, gym, concierge, parking (fee) =AE, D, DC, MC, V ⓂDupont Circle. ✛ 1:G4

$$$$

Willard InterContinental. The historic Willard has long been a favorite of American presidents and other newsmakers. Superb service and a wealth of amenities are hallmarks of the hotel, two blocks from the White House. The spectacular Beaux-Arts lobby showcases great col-

7

umns, sparkling chandeliers, mosaic floors, and elaborate ceilings. Period detail is reflected in the rooms, which have elegant, Federal-style furniture and sleek marble bathrooms. The hotel's formal restaurant, the Willard Room, has won nationwide acclaim for its modern take on French and American dishes. The Willard has opened its own history gallery, which chronicles the hotel's legendary past with photos, newspaper articles, and artifacts. There's also an outstanding spa and fitness center. **Pros:** Luxurious hotel; great location; noted restaurant. **Cons:** Expensive; no pool. ⊠*1401 Pennsylvania Ave. NW, Downtown* ☎*202/628–9100 or 800/827–1747* ⊕*www.washington.interconti. com* ⤶*292 rooms, 40 suites* ⑂*In-room: safe, Ethernet. In-hotel: 3 restaurants, room service, bar, gym, concierge, laundry service, parking (fee), some pets allowed, minibar, no-smoking rooms* ▤*AE, D, DC, MC, V* Ⓜ*Metro Center.* ✛ *1:D2*

DUPONT CIRCLE

$ **Akwaaba.** Celebrating African-American literary heritage in a guesthouse is the brainchild of Essence editor-turned-hotelier Monique Greenwood, and the result is DC's best place to curl up with a good book. Rooms named for authors feature collections of their work, and individual decor meant to evoke their spirits. The Langston Hughes Suite channels its namesake's 1920s style with a massive antique writing desk, while Toni Morrison's love of Africa is reflected in fabrics and designs in the room that bears her name. The bright-red and glamorous Zora Neale Hurston room features a sexy two-person Jacuzzi tub. **Pros:** Lots of personality; busy location; breakfast included. **Cons:** Very personal; neighborhood recently gentrified; smallish bathrooms. ⊠*1708 16th St. NW, Dupont Circle,* ☎*866/INN–DULJ* ⊕*www.akwaaba. com* ⤶*8 rooms* ⑂ *In-hotel: DVD (some), VCR (some), no-smoking rooms* ▤*AE, D, DC, MC, V* ⦿*BP* Ⓜ*Dupont Circle.* ✛ *1:G3*

¢   **Brickskeller Inn.** Run by the same family for 50 years, this 1912 building channels the spirit of a cheap European pension: shared (but clean) baths, tacky linens, and the lowest prices in the neighborhood, if not the city. For some, shag carpeting may be unthinkable at any price, but if you're looking to save on lodging without skimping on location, look no further. The friendly owners are full of sightseeing tips—first stop, their downstairs bar and restaurant, which serves food until 1 am. **Pros:** Rock-bottom price; convenient location; bar downstairs. **Cons:** Shared bath; run-down rooms; bar downstairs. ⊠*1523 22nd St. NW, Dupont Circle* ☎*202/293–1885* ⊕*www.thebrickskeller.org* ⤶*30 rooms, 2 with bath* ⑂*In-room: no TV (some), no a/c (some), Ethernet. In-hotel: restaurant, bar, laundry facilities, no-smoking rooms* ▤*AE, D, DC, MC, V* Ⓜ*Dupont Circle.* ✛ *1:E4*

$$ **Churchill Hotel.** This historic Beaux-Arts hotel offers comfort and elegance right outside Dupont Circle. Spacious rooms have recently gotten a face-lift and include a small work and sitting area. The building's hilltop location means that many guest rooms have excellent views of Washington. The staff goes out of its way to be helpful, and complimentary morning coffee is offered in the lounge. **Pros:** Friendly service;

good-sized rooms; frequent guest program. **Cons:** Far walk to Metro; uphill from Metro to hotel; elevators sometimes run slow. ✉*1914 Connecticut Ave. NW, Dupont Circle* ☎*202/797–2000 or 800/424–2464* ⊕*www.thechurchillhotel.com* ⬤*91 rooms, 82 suites* ⬡*In-room: kitchen (some), Wi-Fi. In-hotel: Wi-Fi, restaurant, room service, bar, gym, concierge, laundry service, parking (fee), minibar* ▭*AE, D, DC, MC, V* Ⓜ*Dupont Circle.* ✛ *1:D3*

$$–$$$
Fodor'sChoice
★
Hotel Madera. The unique Hotel Madera sits in a quiet part of town southwest of Dupont Circle. Innovative guest rooms with art nouveau styling have CD players, complimentary high-speed or wireless Internet access, and minibars. ■**TIP→** **Check in with a hybrid car and park for free.** Extra-spacious "specialty rooms" are decorated in rich earthy tones with finer furnishings, although the bathrooms remain small. The adjoining American bistro, Firefly, has a massive fake oak tree in the center of its dining room. The tree is hung with candles that resemble flickering fireflies. **Pros:** Fun hotel in fun location. **Cons:** No pool or gym; small bathrooms. ✉*1310 New Hampshire Ave. NW, Dupont Circle,* ☎*202/296–7600 or 800/368–5691* 🖷*202/293–2476* ⊕*www.hotelmadera.com* ⬤*82 rooms* ⬡*In-room: safe, kitchen (some), refrigerator (some), DVD, Wi-Fi. In-hotel: restaurant, bar, parking (fee), pets allowed, no-smoking rooms* ▭*AE, D, DC, MC, V* Ⓜ*Dupont Circle.* ✛ *1:E4*

$$$$
Hotel Palomar. The Palomar is winning hearts and minds with space, style, and a pro-pets policy that recently brought an anteater and an orangutan together in the otherwise subdued lobby. Perhaps accordingly, standard rooms here are some of the largest in town. Kimpton's signature animal prints make the scene in tiger-striped robes, crocodile-patterned carpets, and faux-lynx throws; plush purple and fuschia furnishings splash color on muted chocolate-beige rooms. Although bathrooms are surprisingly small, L'Occitane toiletries ease the blow; other up-to-the-minute details include laptop-sized safes and iPod docking stations. **Pros:** Spacious rooms; outdoor pool; fun extras. **Cons:** Smallish baths; busy public areas not cozy for sitting. ✉*2121 P St. NW, Dupont Circle* ☎*202/448–1800* ⊕*www.hotelpalomar-dc.com* ⬤*315 rooms, 20 suites* ⬡ *In-room: safe, refrigerator, DVD, Ethernet, Wi-Fi. In-hotel: restaurant, room service, bar, pool, gym, laundry service, parking (fee), pets allowed, no-smoking rooms* ▭*AE, D, DC, MC, V,* Ⓜ*Dupont Circle.* ✛ *1:E4*

$$$
Fodor'sChoice
★
Hotel Rouge. This gay-friendly postmodern hotel bathed in red succeeds at bringing Florida's South Beach club scene to D.C. Guest rooms, some with specialty themes such as "chill, chow, or chat," are decorated with swanky eye-catching furniture. In the hip lobby lounge the bartenders are always busy concocting sweet new drinks. Bar Rouge, the cocktail lounge, attracts club-going denizens at all hours. **Pros:** Great lounge scene; fun hotel; good location. **Cons:** No pool; the scene is not for everybody. ✉*1315 16th St. NW, Dupont Circle* ☎*202/232–8000 or 800/368–5689* ⊕*www.rougehotel.com* ⬤*137 rooms* ⬡*In-room: safe, kitchen (some), refrigerator (some), DVD. In-hotel: Wi-Fi, room service, bar, gym, concierge, parking (fee), pets allowed, no-smoking rooms* ▭*AE, D, DC, MC, V* Ⓜ*Dupont Circle.* ✛ *1:G4*

7

¢–$ **Hotel Tabard Inn.** Three Victorian town houses were consolidated to form the Tabard, one of the oldest hotels in D.C. Although the wooden floorboards creak and room sizes vary considerably (some share bathrooms), the dimly lighted hotel feels like an Old World inn, with alluring nooks and crannies inside and a brick-walled garden outside. The Tabard Inn's fireside bar may be one of the city's coziest winter retreats, and the restaurant

remains a favorite among locals. Free passes are provided to the nearby YMCA, which has extensive fitness facilities. **Pros:** Affordable choice; lots of character; Sunday night jazz in the hotel lounge. **Cons:** Some shared bathrooms; limited privacy. ⊠ *1739 N St. NW, Dupont Circle* ☎ *202/785–1277* ⊕ *www.tabardinn.com* ⇩ *40 rooms, 25 with bath* ♨ *In-room: no TV (some), Wi-Fi. In-hotel: Wi-Fi, restaurant, bar, laundry facilities, some pets allowed, no-smoking rooms* ⊟ *AE, D, DC, MC, V* ⏃○⏃*CP* Ⓜ *Dupont Circle.* ✛ *1:F4*

$–$$
Fodor's Choice
★
The Inn at Dupont Circle South. This is the inn where everybody knows your name. Innkeeper Carolyn jokes that her guests are "her babies," and the personal attention shows: there are many repeat customers here, and some keep in touch even when they are not in town. Most rooms have private baths; all have TVs, featherbeds, and typical inn decor complete with doilies, bric-a-brac, and Impressionist posters. Carolyn serves a hot breakfast in the parlor or on the sun porch. ▪**TIP**➔ **The Nook Room is aptly named and budget friendly at $95 per night. Pros:** Personable innkeeper; personalized service; great Dupont location across from Metro; children welcome. **Cons:** Older home complete with creaking floors; no elevator; not all rooms have private baths. ⊠ *1312 19th St. NW, Dupont Circle* ☎ *202/467–6777 or 866/467–2100* ⊕ *thedupontcollection.com* ⇩ *8 rooms* ♨ *In room: safe, refrigerator, Wi-Fi. In-hotel: no elevator, laundry facilities, public Wi-Fi, airport shuttle, parking (fee), no-smoking rooms* ⊟ *AE, MC, V.* ⏃○⏃*BP* Ⓜ *Dupont Circle.* ✛ *1:F4*

$$–$$$
Jurys Washington Hotel. The Irish-run Jurys chain has breathed new life into this older building on Dupont Circle. Half the guest rooms here were updated several years ago with a more modern flair in the spirit of the hotel's shining white marble lobby. At check-in it's a good idea to request one of the newer rooms, but whichever room you wind up with you'll be right in the heart of hip and urban Dupont Circle. Rooms have writing desks, coffeemakers, hair dryers, and complimentary newspaper delivery. Biddy Mulligan's, the hotel bar, draws a Guinness-guzzling crowd. **Pros:** Free Wi-Fi; great location; fun neighborhood bar. **Cons:** Busy area, no pool. ⊠ *1500 New Hampshire Ave. NW, Dupont Circle* ☎ *202/483–6000 or 866/534–6835* ⊕ *www.jurysdoyle.com* ⇩ *314 rooms, 6 suites* ♨ *In-room: safe, Wi-Fi. In-hotel: Wi-Fi, restaurant,*

room service, bar, gym, concierge, laundry service, parking (fee), no-smoking rooms ☰AE, D, DC, MC, V Ⓜ*Dupont Circle.* ✛ *1:F4*

$$$–$$$$ **Mansion on O Street.** Rock 'n' roll palace meets urban thrift shop in this utterly oddball supper club–cum-guesthouse, a scramble of five side-by-side town houses crammed with art, junk, and everything in between. Nothing here suggests a hotel: from a two-story log-cabin suite with fish tanks and pony-skin chairs to the John Lennon–theme room with a signed guitar case and hologrammed bathroom floor, this is the most unusual sleep in town. Squander your evenings shooting pool in the billiards room, or pick up one of the ubiquitous guitars and write a song about the place—you won't be the first. Breakfast (included) is self-service in the giant, funky turquoise kitchen, and 24-hour room service is now available—just tell the chef what you are in the mood for and wait for the knock on your door. Watch for secret doorways, some left from when the Mansion was a dorm for Hoover's G-Men. **Pros:** One-of-a-kind; serious about privacy; glamorous common areas. **Cons:** Layout makes for many dark rooms; eccentric staff and service; expensive. ✉*2020 O St. NW, Dupont Circle* ☎*202/496–2020* ⊕*www.omansion.com* 🛏*18 rooms, 11 suites* ◊ *In-room: DVD (some), VCR (some), Ethernet, Wi-Fi. In-hotel: room service, bar, laundry service, parking (fee), no-smoking rooms* ☰AE, D, DC, MC, V ⍾*BP* Ⓜ*Dupont Circle.* ✛ *1:E4*

$$$ **Marriott Residence Inn.** It's remarkable that a commercial chain can feel so cozy, but this Residence Inn does just that by offering a small fireplace sitting room right off the lobby. The hotel has studios and one-and two-bedroom suites, excellent for business travelers or families. An evening reception (Monday through Thursday) is offered with complimentary snacks, and STARS Bistro and Bar next door has an innovative bar with piano and cabaret-style singing on weekends and half-price wine nights on Mondays and Tuesdays. **Pros:** Breakfast buffet included; good choice for families. **Cons:** Standard chain hotel; no unique touches. ✉*2120 P St. NW, Dupont Circle* ☎*202/466–6800 or 800/331–3131* ⊕*www.marriott.com/wasri* 🛏*107 suites* ◊ *In-room: kitchen, Ethernet. In-hotel: Wi-Fi, restaurant, room service, gym, laundry facilities, parking (fee), no-smoking rooms* ☰AE, D, DC, MC, V ⍾*CP* Ⓜ*Dupont Circle.* ✛ *1:E4*

$$–$$$ **Swann House.** From breakfast under the antique crystal chandelier to
Fodor'sChoice evening sherry by the fire, the days pass grandly in this sumptuous 1883
★ mansion. Equidistant from Dupont Circle's establishment scene and U Street's antiestablishment one, the location is convenient for much of D.C.'s nightlife. But like the local couples who come here for romantic weekends, you might be tempted to stay in, particularly if you've booked a room with a Jacuzzi or a two-person claw-foot tub. The Lighthouse Room, in one of the mansion's round turrets, is small, but three huge windows flood it with light, and there's an engaging view of the dog park across the street. A small swimming pool beckons in hot weather. **Pros:** Location, location, location; beautiful and lavish rooms; fireplaces in winter, a pool in summer. **Cons:** It is a B&B—you may find yourself sharing a breakfast table; cheaper rooms are small. ✉*1808 New Hampshire Ave. NW, Dupont Circle* ☎*202/265-4414* Ⓜ*Dupont*

7

Circle ⊕*www.swannhouse.com*
⟋*9 rooms, 3 suites* ⌂ *In-room:*
DVD (some), VCR (some), Wi-Fi.
In-hotel: pool, no elevator, public
Wi-Fi, parking (fee), no kids under
12, no-smoking rooms ⊟*AE, D,*
DC, MC, V ⦿*CP.* ✛ *1:F3*

WORD OF MOUTH

"I stayed [at the Topaz Hotel] for a business trip in December, 2005. I thought it was great. The room was spacious, the staff was accommodating and the decor was a bit edgier than what you'd find in your standard chain hotel. If you get a chance, join the Kimpton "In Touch" rewards program on their web site before you leave. I was upgraded to a larger room and found a personalized note in my room when I arrived thanking me for choosing the hotel for my stay."

—nycuwsapt

$$$ **Topaz Hotel.** A night at the Topaz is akin to a slumber party at a New Age dance club. The hotel's mystical theme is expressed through the colorful walls and art, allusions to different forms of enlightenment, and the fruity "power shakes" served in the morning. Creatively themed guest rooms, which were spruced up in 2007 with new bedding, carpeting, and furniture, may come with exercise equipment or yoga mats. The popular (and loud) Topaz Bar draws people from all over town. **Pros:** Hybrid cars park free; good service; far from a cookie-cutter hotel experience. **Cons:** Funky style not for everyone; no pool. ⊠*1733 N St. NW, Dupont Circle* ☎*202/393–3000 or 800/775–1202* ⊕*www.topazhotel.com* ⟋*91 rooms, 8 suites* ⌂*In-room: safe, DVD, Wi-Fi. In-hotel: bar, laundry service concierge, public WiFi, parking (fee), some pets allowed no-smoking rooms* ⊟*AE, D, DC, MC, V* Ⓜ*Dupont Circle.* ✛ *1:F4*

$$–$$$ **Fairfax Embassy Row.** At this writing, the hotel was undergoing a major renovation but did not close during the process. The childhood home of Al Gore, the former Westin at Embassy Row has an English hunt-club theme. The intimate guest rooms are furnished with brocade draperies and reproduction antiques from late-1800s Washington. It is near Dupont Circle, Georgetown, and the Kennedy Center. **Pros:** newly renovated historic hotel; charming property; great Dupont Circle location. **Cons:** no pool; challenging street parking. ⊠*2100 Massachusetts Ave. NW, Dupont Circle* ☎*202/293–2100 or 888/625–5144* ⊕*www. westin.com/embassyrowwashingtondc* ⟋*160 rooms, 46 suites* ⌂*In-room: safe, Ethernet, minibar. In-hotel: 2 restaurants, room service, bar, gym, concierge, laundry service, parking (fee), some pets allowed (fee)* ⊟*AE, D, DC, MC, V* Ⓜ*Dupont Circle.* ✛ *1:E4*

¢–$ **Windsor Inn.** Near tree-lined New Hampshire Avenue, this bed-and-breakfast is in one of Washington's most attractive neighborhoods. The Phillips Collection and the restaurants and shops of Dupont Circle lie within six blocks. The three-story inn is actually two buildings, and neither has an elevator. Rooms are tastefully decorated but small, and most have showers only. There are some amenities expected of larger hotels, such as hair dryers and a morning newspaper. Three nights per week, sherry or wine is served in the downstairs lobby and a continental breakfast is out in the mornings. **Pros:** Guest rooms on the small side; pretty location; short walk to Metro. **Cons:** Some rooms could use updating; no elevator. ⊠*1842 16th St. NW, Dupont Circle* ⊕*www. windsor-inn-dc.com* ☎*202/667–0300 or 800/423–9111* ⇔*36 rooms, 10 suites* ⌂*In-room: refrigerator (some), Wi-Fi. In-hotel: no elevator, public Wi-Fi, no-smoking rooms* ⊟*AE, DC, MC, V* ⍟*CP* Ⓜ*Dupont Circle.* ✛ *1:G3*

GEORGETOWN

$$$$ **Four Seasons Hotel.** Having completed a whopping $40 million renova-
Fodor'sChoice tion in 2005, the Four Seasons has reasserted its role as Washington's
★ leading hotel. Impeccable service and a wealth of amenities have long
☺ made this a favorite with celebrities, hotel connoisseurs, and families.
Luxurious, ultramodern rooms offer heavenly beds, flat-screen digital
TVs with DVD players, and French limestone or marble baths with
separate showers and sunken tubs. A 2,000-piece original art collection
graces the walls, and a walk through the corridors seems like a visit
to a wing of the MoMA or the Met. The formal Seasons restaurant
offers traditional dishes with an elegant twist, as well as a popular
Sunday brunch. The sophisticated spa here is one of the best in town.
Pros: Edge of Georgetown makes for a fabulous location; lap of luxury
feel; Four Seasons service. **Cons:** Expensive; challenging street parking,
expensive ($42 a night) valet service. ⊠*2800 Pennsylvania Ave. NW,
Georgetown* ☎*202/342–0444 or 800/332–3442* ⊕*www.fourseasons.
com/washington* ⇔*160 rooms, 51 suites* ⌂*In-room: safe, Ethernet.
In-hotel: restaurant, room service, bar, pool, gym, concierge, children's
programs (ages 5–16), parking (fee), some pets allowed, no-smoking
rooms* ⊟*AE, D, DC, MC, V* Ⓜ*Foggy Bottom.* ✛ *1:C5*

$ **Georgetown Inn.** Reminiscent of a gentleman's sporting club, this quiet,
Federal-era, redbrick hotel seems like something from the 1700s. The
spacious guest rooms are decorated in a colonial style. The hotel, in the
heart of historic Georgetown, lies near shopping, dining, galleries, and
theaters. The publike Daily Grill restaurant serves American cuisine.
Pros: Shoppers will love the location; good price for the neighborhood.
Cons: A hike to Metro; crowded area. ⊠*1310 Wisconsin Ave. NW,
Georgetown* ☎*202/333–8900 or 800/368–5922* ⊕*www.georgetown
collection.com* ⇔*86 rooms, 10 suites* ⌂*In-room: Wi-Fi. In-hotel: Wi-
Fi, restaurant, room service, bar, gym, parking (fee)* ⊟*AE, D, DC,
MC, V* Ⓜ*Foggy Bottom.* ✛ *1:B5*

$–$$ **Georgetown Suites.** If you consider standard hotel rooms cramped and
☺ overpriced, you'll find this establishment a welcome surprise. Consist-
ing of two buildings a block apart in the heart of Georgetown, the
hotel has suites of varying sizes. All have fully equipped kitchens and
separate sitting rooms, and include free local calls and continental
breakfast. **Pros:** All suites; good price; good choice for a family that
wants to spread out. **Cons:** Parking can be challenging at times; not a
lot of character. ⊠*1111 30th St. NW, Georgetown* ☎*202/298–7800
or 800/348–7203* ⊕*www.georgetownsuites.com* ⇔*216 suites* ⌂*In-
room: kitchen, Wi-Fi. In-hotel: gym, laundry facilities, laundry service,*

7

public Wi-Fi, parking (fee), no-smoking rooms ⊟*AE, D, DC, MC, V* ⏍❘*CP* Ⓜ*Foggy Bottom.* ✢ *1:B5*

$–$$ **Holiday Inn Georgetown.** On the edge of Georgetown, this Holiday Inn is a short walk from dining, shopping, Dumbarton Oaks, the National Cathedral, and Georgetown University. Many guest rooms offer a scenic view of the Washington skyline. There's a free shuttle service to the Metro. ■ **TIP➜Kids under 12 eat free, and rooms offer video games. Pros:** Quiet neighborhood; walk to Whole Foods and a selection of restaurants. **Cons:** Not near a Metro; a bit off-the-beaten path for downtown sightseeing. ⊠*2101 Wisconsin Ave. NW, Georgetown* ☎*202/338–4600 or 800/465–4329* ⊕*www.higeorgetown.com* ⊅*281 rooms, 4 suites* ⚿*In-room: Ethernet. In-hotel: restaurant, room service, bar, pool, gym, laundry facilities, parking (fee), no-smoking rooms* ⊟*AE, D, DC, MC, V* Ⓜ*Foggy Bottom.* ✢ *1:A2*

$ **Latham Hotel.** Many of the small, beautifully decorated rooms at this Fodor'sChoice elegant boutique hotel offer treetop views of the Potomac River and ★ the C&O Canal. The polished-brass-and-glass lobby leads to Citronelle, one of the city's most acclaimed (and expensive) French restaurants—make a reservation before you arrive. You'll find a number of Washington's most illustrious personalities here for dinner, with many diplomats overnighting at the hotel. Be prepared for occasional street noise in some rooms, as the Latham lies on Georgetown's fashionable main avenue. **Pros:** Fun location; lots of charm; great restaurant. **Cons:** Street noise; busy area especially at night and on weekends. ⊠*3000 M St. NW, Georgetown,* ☎*202/726–5000 or 866/481–9126* ⊕*www. georgetowncollection.com* ⊅*133 rooms, 9 suites* ⚿*In-room: Wi-Fi. In-hotel: restaurant, room service, bar, pool, public Wi-Fi, parking (fee), no-smoking rooms* ⊟*AE, D, DC, MC, V* Ⓜ*Foggy Bottom.* ✢ *1:B5*

$$$–$$$$ **The Melrose Hotel.** This European-style boutique hotel has a convenient address between Georgetown and the White House. Bellboys in top hats greet you in the lobby, which connects to the Landmark restaurant and intimate Library bar. The gracious rooms have desks in their own nooks, small marble bathrooms, and high-tech amenities—some have been renovated in the past year. Rooms facing K Street are quieter. **Pros:** Nice alternative to big conference hotels; good location; walk to Georgetown for meals and shopping. **Cons:** Street noise and noise from the corridors an issue in some rooms. ⊠*2430 Pennsylvania Ave. NW, Georgetown* ☎*202/955–6400 or 800/635–7673* ⊕*www.melrosehotel. com* ⊅*207 rooms, 33 suites* ⚿*In-room: safe, Wi-Fi. In-hotel: restaurant, room service, bar, gym, concierge, laundry service, public Wi-Fi, parking (fee), no-smoking rooms* ⊟*AE, D, DC, MC, V.* ✢ *1:D6*

$$$$ **Park Hyatt.** A study in stylish neutrality, the brand-new Park Hyatt is all clean lines, natural wood, and sun-warmed glass. Nominally Americana-themed, Zen-spare rooms are enlivened by duck decoys and Shaker accents; delicate white Frette linens make up wide, luxurious beds. Deluxe rooms are worth the extra cost, with separate living rooms and spacious, spa-style stone bathrooms equipped with rain showers. Free car service from the hotel is offered daily 7 AM to 7 PM. Downstairs, the Blue Duck Tavern is recommended. **Pros:** Spacious rooms; good for entertaining, tea cellar with rare and vintage teas an unusual touch;

lull you to sleep beds. **Cons:** Expensive valet parking; not convenient to Metro. ✉*1201 24th St. NW, Georgetown* ☎*202/789–1234* ⊕*www. parkhyattwashington.com* ⇌*196 rooms, 19 suites* ♻*In-room: safe, refrigerator, Ethernet, Wi-Fi. In-hotel: restaurant, room service, bar, indoor pool, gym, laundry service, concierge, public Wi-Fi, parking (fee), no-smoking rooms* ▭*AE, D, DC, MC, V.* ✢ *1:D5*

\$\$–\$\$\$ **Washington Suites Georgetown.** Just outside the center of Georgetown, this older all-suites accommodation offers families and long-stay travelers an alternative to standard hotel rooms. Each suite has a fully equipped kitchen, a small living and dining area, and a separate bedroom and bath. ■**TIP**➔**Stock your fridge at the Trader Joe's across the street.** Fresh pastries, juices, and cereal are served each morning in the breakfast room. Many of the staff members have worked at the hotel for years and know regular guests by name. **Pros:** Friendly staff; good for long-term stays; good value. **Cons:** No-frills; breakfast room can be crowded when hotel is full. ✉*2500 Pennsylvania Ave. NW, Georgetown* ☎*202/333–8060 or 877/736–2500* ⊕*www.washingtonsuitesgeorgetown.com.* ⇌*124 suites* ♻*In-room: kitchen, Ethernet. In-hotel: gym, laundry facilities, parking (fee), no-smoking rooms* ▭*AE, D, DC, MC, V* ▯◎▯ *CP* Ⓜ*Foggy Bottom.* ✢ *1:D5*

SOUTHWEST

\$–\$\$ **Best Western Capitol Skyline.** Who could believe that a Best Western, built ♻ in the 1960s near I–395, would make a 21st-century comeback? Yet the Capitol Skyline has done just that. The hotel is a cool retro embodiment of its earlier heritage, with a gleaming lobby and inviting rooms done in red, white, and blue (some with views of the U.S. Capitol). Children staying here will enjoy the summertime pool, and the restaurant offers a kids' menu. The hotel lies in an area considered a last frontier in Washington's development, and you will need to wait for the hotel's free shuttle, hail a cab, or hop on the Metro to reach major tourist attractions. **Pros:** Big outdoor pool; large rooms; good value. **Cons:** Area sketchy at night; out-of-the-way; restaurant has uneven food and slow service. ✉*10 I St. SW, Southwest* ☎*202/488–7500 or 800/458–7500* ⊕*www.bestwesterncapitolskyline.com* ⇌*197 rooms, 6 suites* ♻*In-room: safe, Wi-Fi. In-hotel: restaurant, pool, laundry service, parking (fee), no-smoking rooms* ▭*AE, D, DC, MC, V* Ⓜ*Navy Yard.* ✢ *1:F6*

\$–\$\$ **Holiday Inn Capitol.** One block from the National Air and Space Museum, ♻ this family-friendly hotel is also well equipped for business travelers, including free Wi-Fi. Newly renovated rooms have upgraded beds, granite vanities in the bathrooms, and include coffeemakers and hair dryers. The downtown sightseeing trolley stops here, and you can buy discount tickets for the National Air and Space Museum's IMAX movies at the front desk. Kids under 19 stay free, and those under 12 eat for free at Smithson's Restaurant. **Pros:** Family-friendly; rooftop pool; close to museums. **Cons:** Limited restaurants nearby; not much going on in the neighborhood at night. ✉*550 C St. SW, Southwest* ☎*202/479–4000 or 877/477–4674* ⊕*www.holidayinncapitol.com* ⇌*532 rooms, 13* *suites* &*In-room: Ethernet, Wi-Fi. In-hotel: restaurant, room service, bar, pool, gym, laundry facilities, parking, no-smoking rooms (fee)* ⊟*AE, D, DC, MC, V* |◉|*BP* Ⓜ*L'Enfant Plaza.* ✛ *2:H6*

$$-$$$ **L'Enfant Plaza.** An oasis of calm above a Metro stop and a shopping mall, L'Enfant Plaza lies two blocks from the Smithsonian museums and has spectacular views of the river, the Capitol, and the monuments. A heated, rooftop pool is open year-round. Business travelers in particular take advantage of its proximity to several government agencies (USDA, USPS, and DOT). All rooms have coffeemakers. **Pros:** Short walk to Smithsonian; pet friendly; good views from top floors. **Cons:** Business area that's sleepy at night; not many nearby restaurants; pricey. ⊠*480 L'Enfant Plaza SW, Southwest* ☎*202/484–1000 or 800/635–5065* ⊕*www.lenfantplazahotel.com* ⥥*348 rooms, 22 suites* &*In-room: Wi-Fi In-hotel: 3 restaurants, room service, bar, pool, gym, concierge, laundry service, public Wi-Fi, parking (fee), some pets allowed, no-smoking rooms* ⊟*AE, D, DC, MC, V* Ⓜ*L'Enfant Plaza.* ✛ *1:D6*

WEST END & FOGGY BOTTOM

$$-$$$ **Doubletree Guest Suites.** Among the row houses on this stretch of New Hampshire Avenue, you might not realize at first how close you are to the Kennedy Center and Georgetown. This all-suites hotel has a tiny lobby, but its roomy one- and two-bedroom suites have full kitchens and living-dining areas with desks, dining tables, and sofa beds. The rooftop pool provides a place to relax after summertime sightseeing. You receive chocolate-chip cookies upon arrival. **Pros:** Near Metro and supermarket; quiet neighborhood; good online deals sometimes available. **Cons:** Far from the museums and major attractions; rooms could use some renovation. ⊠*801 New Hampshire Ave. NW, Foggy Bottom* ☎*202/785–2000 or 800/222–8733* ⊕*www.doubletree.com* ⥥*105 suites* &*In-room: kitchen, Wi-Fi. In-hotel: room service, pool, laundry facilities, laundry service, public Wi-Fi, parking (fee), some pets allowed, no-smoking rooms* ⊟*AE, D, DC, MC, V* Ⓜ*Foggy Bottom/GWU.* ✛ *1:D6*

$$-$$$ **Embassy Suites.** Plants cascade over balconies beneath a skylight in this modern hotel's atrium, which is filled with classical columns, plaster lions, wrought-iron lanterns, waterfalls, and tall palms. Within walking distance of Georgetown, the Kennedy Center, and Dupont Circle, the suites here are suitable for both business travelers and families. Beverages are complimentary at the nightly manager's reception, and the rate includes cooked-to-order breakfast. There's a kids' corner with movies and games, and the Italian restaurant, Trattoria Nicola's, serves lunch and dinner. **Pros:** Family-friendly; all suites; pool to keep the little ones—and sweaty tourists—happy. **Cons:** Not a lot of character; museums not in walking distance. ⊠*1250 22nd St. NW, West End* ☎*202/857–3388 or 800/362–2779* ⊕*www.embassysuites. com* ⥥*318 suites* &*In-room: refrigerator, Wi-Fi. In-hotel: restaurant, room service, bar, pool, gym, laundry service, parking (fee), no-smok-*

ing rooms ⊟*AE, D, DC, MC, V* ⏀|*BP* Ⓜ*Foggy Bottom/GWU or Dupont Circle.* ✚ *1:D5*

$$$$ Fairmont Washington. The large glassed-in lobby and about a third of the bright, spacious rooms overlook the Fairmont's central courtyard and gardens. Rooms are comfortable, if not the city's most modern. The informal Juniper restaurant serves mid-Atlantic fare and has courtyard dining; there's a champagne brunch on Sunday in the Colonnade Room. ■**TIP→The health club is one of the best in the city.** Families have access to the pool, kids' menus and crayons in the restaurant, and a babysitting referral service. The Fairmont also offers family packages, such as the "Panda Package," a trip to visit the pandas at the National Zoo. **Pros:** Fitness-focused guests will love the health club; lots of kid-friendly features. **Cons:** Pricey; not many attractions in walking distance. ✉*2401 M St. NW, Foggy Bottom* ☎*202/429–2400 or 877/222–2266* ⊕*www.fairmont.com* ⇄*406 rooms, 9 suites* ⚘*In-room: safe, Ethernet. In-hotel: restaurant, room service, bar, pool, gym, concierge, executive floor, parking (fee), some pets allowed, no-smoking rooms* ⊟*AE, D, DC, MC, V* Ⓜ*Foggy Bottom/GWU.* ✚ *1:D5*

$ George Washington University Inn. This boutique hotel is in a quiet neighborhood a few blocks from the Kennedy Center, the State Department, and George Washington University. Wrought-iron gates lead through a courtyard to the hotel's front entrance, where beveled-glass doors open onto a small lobby with a gray marble floor. Rooms, which vary in size and configuration, have colonial-style furniture and complimentary high-speed Internet access. Guests also receive free entry to the nearby Bally Total Fitness club. **Pros:** Good price; close to Metro. **Cons:** Not many amenities; far from museums. ✉*824 New Hampshire Ave. NW, Foggy Bottom* ☎*202/337–6620 or 800/426–4455* ⊕*www. gwuinn.com* ⇄*64 rooms, 31 suites* ⚘*In-room: safe, kitchen (some), refrigerator, Wi-Fi. In-hotel: restaurant, bar, laundry facilities, laundry service, parking (fee), no-smoking rooms* ⊟*AE, DC, MC, V* Ⓜ*Foggy Bottom/GWU.* ✚ *1:D6*

$$–$$$ One Washington Circle Hotel. Given its location near the State Department and George Washington University, this all-suites business hotel is a relative bargain. The suites have modern, vibrant furnishings and feature separate bedrooms, living rooms, dining areas, and walk-out balconies; some have full kitchens. The American-style Circle Bistro is popular with locals. **Pros:** All suites; balconies; near Metro. **Cons:** Some street noise; small bathrooms. ✉*1 Washington Circle NW, Foggy Bottom,* ☎*202/872–1680 or 800/424–9671* ⊕*www.thecirclehotel.com* ⇄*151 suites* ⚘*In-room: kitchen, Ethernet. In-hotel: Wi-Fi, restaurant, room service, bar, pool, gym, laundry facilities, laundry service, parking (fee), no-smoking rooms* ⊟*AE, D, DC, MC, V* Ⓜ*Foggy Bottom/GWU.* ✚ *1:D5*

$$$$ Ritz-Carlton Washington, D.C. The more traditional of Washington's two Ritz-Carltons, this elegant hotel pampers guests with formal, attentive service and luxurious amenities. It is slated to renovate its deluxe rooms beginning in the summer of 2008; they already feature separate showers and marble tubs, portable phones, and beds with goose-down pillows, Egyptian cotton linens, and hypoallergenic pillows—in fact, it would be difficult to find more comfortable beds than those at the Ritz. Hotel guests have lobby access to the 100,000-square-foot Sports Club/LA for a fee. **Pros:** Attentive service; convenient to several parts of town; great health club. **Cons:** Pricey room rates; expensive valet parking. ⊠ *1150 22nd St. NW, Foggy Bottom* ☎*202/835–0500 or 800/241–3333* ⊕*www.ritzcarlton.com/hotels/washington_dc* ⇙*275 rooms, 25 suites* ⌂*In-room: safe, Wi-Fi. In-hotel: Wi-Fi, restaurant, room service, bar, pool, gym, spa, concierge, executive floor, parking (fee),* ⊟*AE, D, DC, MC, V* Ⓜ*Foggy Bottom/GWU.* ✛ *1:E5*

$$–$$$ **St. Gregory.** Once the FCC building, the handsome St. Gregory caters to business and leisure travelers who appreciate the spacious accommodations that include fully stocked kitchens. All rooms include turndown service, a newspaper, and shoe shine. The modern lobby, which has a sculpture of Marilyn Monroe in her *Seven Year Itch* pose, connects to the M Street Bar & Grill. **Pros:** Big rooms; good for long-term stays. **Cons:** Far from the Mall and museums; area is sleepy at night. ⊠*2033 M St. NW, West End* ☎*202/530–3600 or 800/829–5034* ⊕*www. stgregoryhotelwdc.com* ⇙*54 rooms, 100 suites* ⌂*In-room: kitchen (some), Ethernet. In-hotel: restaurant, room service, gym, concierge, laundry service, executive floor, parking (fee), no-smoking rooms* ⊟*AE, D, DC, MC, V* Ⓜ*Dupont Circle.* ✛ *1:E5*

$$ **State Plaza Hotel.** No Washington hotel gets you quicker access to the State Department, which sits across the street. There's nothing distinguishing about the lobby, but the spacious guest rooms have kitchenettes and lighted dressing tables, and the hotel staff is friendly and attentive. Guests receive a complimentary newspaper and a shoe shine. Nightly turndown service is provided. **Pros:** All suites; free Internet access; walk to Metro. **Cons:** Far from museums; not a lot of character. ⊠*2117 E St. NW, Foggy Bottom* ☎*202/861–8200 or 800/424–2859* ⊕*www.stateplaza.com* ⇙*214 rooms, 16 suites* ⌂*In-room: kitchen, Ethernet. In-hotel: restaurant, room service, gym, laundry service, parking (fee), no-smoking rooms* ⊟*AE, D, DC, MC, V* Ⓜ*Foggy Bottom/GWU.* ✛ *1:E6*

WOODLEY PARK & UPPER NORTHWEST

¢–$ **Adam's Inn.** This cozy B&B spreads through three residential town houses near Adams-Morgan, the Zoo, and Dupont Circle. The Victorian-style rooms are small but comfortable. Many share baths, but those that do also have a sink in the room. A communal kitchen and limited garage parking are available. Rooms don't come with phones or TVs, but there are pay phones, cable TV, and free Wi-Fi in the public areas. A two-night stay is required on weekends, but the hotel is flexible on that rule in the off-season. **Pros:** Affordable; nearby Metro; lively neighborhood. **Cons:** No elevator; some shared baths; two-day stay required over Saturday nights. ⊠*1746 Lanier Pl. NW, Woodley Park* ☎*202/745–3600 or 800/578–6807* ⊕*www.adamsinn.com* ⇙*26 rooms, 16 with bath* ⌂*In-room: no phone, no TV. In-hotel: laundry facilities, parking (fee), no-smoking rooms* ⊟*AE, D, DC, MC, V* ❐*CP* Ⓜ*Woodley Park/Zoo.* ✛ *1:F1*

$-$$ Embassy Suites. You can feel good about your carbon footprint as you enjoy the newly renovated suites at this green hotel. The hotel cut its energy usage by a third in 2007 and boasts efficient heating and cooling systems in every suite, energy star appliances, a saline pool, and even prints with soy-based ink. Families will love the free breakfast and afternoon reception, two-room suites, and being attached to two shopping malls complete with dining and movie theaters. You can hop on the Metro without ever stepping outside. **Pros:** Eco and family-friendly; in a mall; chain hotel. **Cons:** Family-friendly; in a mall; chain hotel. ⊠*4300 Military Rd., Upper Northwest* ☎*202/362–9300 or 800/760–6120* ⊕*www.embassysuitesdc.com* ⤶*198 suites* ♿*In-room: refrigerator, Ethernet. In-hotel: room service, bar, pool, gym, laundry service, parking (fee), no-smoking rooms* ▭*AE, D, DC, MC, V* ⍾*BP* Ⓜ*Friendship Heights.* ✛ *1:A1*

¢ Kalorama Guest House—Woodley Park. Two elegantly restored Victorian town houses make for comfortable and convenient lodging near the National Cathedral. The cozy rooms, which have just been renovated, are furnished with 19th-century antiques and vary in size. Those in search of a television, Wi-Fi, or a phone will need to visit one of the original house parlors, where sherry and tea are available around the clock. **Pros:** Continental breakfast included; close to Metro; walk to some restaurants. **Cons:** Limited privacy; no in-room phones; far from the Mall. ⊠*2700 Cathedral Ave. NW, Woodley Park* ☎*202/328–0860 or 800/974–9101* ⊕*www.kaloramaguesthouse.com* ⤶*18 rooms, 12 with bath, 3 suites* ♿*In-room: no phone, no TV. In-hotel: Wi-Fi, laundry facilities, parking (fee), no kids under 6, no-smoking rooms* ▭*AE, D, DC, MC, V* ⍾*CP* Ⓜ*Woodley Park/Zoo.* ✛ *1:D1*

$$$ Marriott Wardman Park. You almost get the sense that you stepped into a mini city when you first enter the Marriott Wardman Park. The hotel, housed in a hard-to-miss redbrick Victorian building behind the Woodley Park Metro, just got a $100 million upgrade, leaving all guests rooms with splashes of bright colors typical of many a Marriott these days. Rooms in the decidedly quieter 1918 Wardman Tower have not been renovated yet, but some will prefer its lower-key energy. The hotel's ground level has tons of seating, food choices, a full-service Starbucks, and lots of places to plug in. Kids will love the outdoor pool and the proximity to the pandas. **Pros:** On top of Metro; light-filled sundeck; pretty residential neighborhood with some good ethnic restaurants. **Cons:** Busy; loud; lines at restaurants when hotel is at capacity. ⊠*2660 Woodley Rd. NW, Woodley Park* ☎*202/328–2000 or 800/228–9290* ⊕*www.marriott.com* ⤶*1,171 rooms, 145 suites* ♿*In-room: safe, kitchen (some), refrigerator (some), Ethernet. In-hotel: 2 restaurants, room service, 3 bars, pool, gym, spa, laundry service, concierge, executive floor, public Wi-Fi, parking (fee), some pets allowed, no-smoking rooms* ▭*AE, D, DC, MC, V* Ⓜ*Woodley Park/Zoo.* ✛ *1:D1*

$$$-$$$$
Fodor's Choice
★
☺
Omni Shoreham Hotel. A $15 million dollar facelift has enhanced this already elegant hotel overlooking Rock Creek Park, and the historic property is aging gracefully. The light-filled guest rooms have a soothing garden palette and feature flat-screen TVs and marble bathrooms. The vast art deco-and-Renaissance–style lobby welcomes visitors, who in the past have ranged from The Beatles to heads of state (the hotel has played host

> **EVERYTHING'S COMING UP TULIPS**
>
> In a city known for its blossoms, the Marriott Wardman Park ranks high. Each spring some 45,000 brightly colored tulip bulbs bloom in front of the Woodley Park hotel creating a garden that puts a smile on many an early morning commuter's face.

to inaugural balls since its 1930 opening). There is even a resident ghost said to haunt Suite 870. Families will love the larger-than-typical guest rooms, kiddie pool, bird-watching, bike rentals, and movie nights. ■TIP➔Parents: Ask the concierge about story time and cuddles with the guide dog for the blind who trains at the hotel. **Pros:** Newly renovated historic property; great outdoor pool and sundeck; good views from many rooms. **Cons:** Not downtown; big. ⊠*2500 Calvert St., NW, Woodley Park* ☎*202/234–0700 or 800/545–8700* ⊕*www.omnihotels.com* ➪*818 rooms, 16 suites* ⚷*In-room: safe, refrigerator (some), DVD (some), VCR (some), Wi-Fi. In-hotel: restaurant, room service, bar, pool, gym, spa, bicycles, children's programs (ages 3-13), concierge, laundry service, parking (fee), some pets allowed, no-smoking rooms* ⊟*AE, D, DC, MC, V* Ⓜ*Woodley Park/Zoo.* ✛ *1:C1*

¢–$
Fodor's Choice
★
Woodley Park Guest House. This warm, peaceful B&B on a quiet residential street lies near the entrance to the Metro nearest the Zoo and close to Adams-Morgan and Rock Creek Park. Antiques-filled rooms are individually decorated, and some have private baths. Conversation between guests is encouraged at the communal breakfast, which includes a fresh fruit salad, cereal, yogurt, and homemade pastries. A two-night minimum stay is required, with few exceptions. **Pros:** Close to Metro; near the Zoo; breakfast included. **Cons:** Metro ride to downtown; some shared baths; limited privacy. ⊠*2647 Woodley Rd. NW, Woodley Park* ☎*202/667–0218 or 866/667–0218* ⊕*www.woodleyparkguesthouse.com* ➪*18 rooms, 11 with bath* ⚷*In-room: no TV, Wi-Fi. In-hotel: laundry service, parking (fee), no kids under 12* ⊟*AE, MC, V* ❑CP Ⓜ*Woodley Park/Zoo.* ✛ *1:D1*

SUBURBAN MARYLAND

$–$$
Bethesda Court Hotel. Bright burgundy awnings frame the entrance to this comfortable, intimate, three-story inn, where there's a lovely, well-tended courtyard. The relaxed hotel is two blocks from the Bethesda Metro and set back from busy Wisconsin Avenue. Nearby downtown Bethesda is home to restaurants, shops, and an independent movie theater. ■TIP➔Evening tea with cookies is complimentary, as are limousine service and shuttles to the National Institutes of Health. **Pros:** Free Wi-Fi, close to Metro, basic continental breakfast included. **Cons:** Far

from downtown and major attractions; small rooms; no room service. ✉ *7740 Wisconsin Ave., Bethesda, MD* ☎301/656–2100 or 800/874–0050 ⊕*www.bethesdacourtwashdc.com* ⛫*74 rooms, 1 suite* ♿*In-room: safe, refrigerator, Wi-Fi. In-hotel: Wi-Fi, gym, laundry facilities, parking (fee)* ☰*AE, D, DC, MC, V* ⍟*CP* Ⓜ*Bethesda.*

$$–$$$ **Doubletree Hotel Bethesda.** Newly renovated in 2007, the Doubletree has guest rooms that are larger than those at comparable hotels, with firm, comfortable beds, ample working space, and free morning newspaper delivery. The hotel caters to business travelers with a free shuttle to the nearby Metro (about five blocks on foot), the National Institutes of Health, and the Naval Medical Center. **Pros:** Rooftop pool; hypo-allergenic rooms available with allergy-free pillows and bedding, in-room air purification systems, unscented and anti-microbial products used; good value. **Cons:** Outside the city; far from major attractions; a bit of a walk to Metro and downtown Bethesda. ✉ *8120 Wisconsin Ave., Bethesda, MD* ☎301/652–2000 or 888/465–4329 ⊕*www.doubletree bethesda.com* ⛫*269 rooms, 7 suites* ♿*In-room: safe, Wi-Fi. In-hotel: restaurant, bar, pool, gym, laundry facilities, laundry service, parking (fee)* ☰*AE, D, DC, MC, V.* Ⓜ*Bethesda.*

$$$ **Hyatt Regency Bethesda.** This hotel stands atop the Bethesda Metro station on Wisconsin Avenue, the main artery between Bethesda and Georgetown; downtown Washington is a 15-minute Metro ride away. Well-equipped guest rooms have sleigh beds and mahogany furnishings, as well as large workstations for business travelers. They also include 32-inch TVs and marble baths. The rooftop fitness center and indoor pool are welcome retreats from a busy day in the city. **Pros:** On top of Metro; walk to dozens of restaurants and two movie theaters; indoor pool. **Con:** Reports of noise traveling up from the atrium. ✉ *1 Bethesda Metro Center, 7400 block of Wisconsin Ave., Bethesda, MD* ☎301/657–1234 or 800/233–1234 ⊕*www.bethesda.hyatt.com* ⛫*391 rooms, 7 suites* ♿*In-room: Wi-Fi. In-hotel: Wi-Fi, 3 restaurants, room service, 2 bars, pool, gym, concierge, laundry service, parking (fee)* ☰*AE, D, DC, MC, V* Ⓜ*Bethesda.*

$$–$$$ **Marriott Residence Inn Bethesda Downtown.** In the heart of downtown Bethesda, this all-suites hotel caters primarily to business travelers who stay for several nights. If you're looking for an affordable home away from home, this is a sensible option. The comfortably (though slightly blandly) furnished one- and two-bedroom suites come with fully equipped kitchens with a standard-size refrigerator and dishwasher, plates, and utensils. ■**TIP➜The many complimentary services include grocery shopping, a breakfast buffet, and evening cocktail and dessert receptions.** Tons of restaurants are within walking distance. **Pros:** Rooftop pool; large rooms; walk to Metro and restaurants. **Cons:** Far from monuments, museums, and airports. ✉ *7335 Wisconsin Ave., Bethesda, MD* ☎301/718–0200 or 800/331–3131 ⊕*www.residence innbethesdahotel.com* ⛫*187 suites* ♿*In-room: kitchen, Ethernet. In-hotel: pool, gym, laundry facilities, parking (fee), no-smoking rooms* ☰*AE, D, DC, MC, V* ⍟*BP* Ⓜ*Bethesda.*

7

SUBURBAN VIRGINIA

$$–$$$ **Embassy Suites Old Town Alexandria.**
Ⓒ Adjacent to Alexandria's landmark George Washington Masonic Temple sits this modern all-suites hotel, which is also across the street from the Metro station and around the corner from the Amtrak station. A free shuttle is available to transport you to the scenic Alexandria riverfront, which has shops and restaurants. The cooked-to-order breakfast is complimentary, as is the cocktail reception every evening. There's also a playroom for children. **Pros:** All suites; free made-to-order breakfast; across from Metro station. **Cons:** Outside city; small pool which is often crowded; popular with school groups. ✉1900 Diagonal Rd., Alexandria, VA ☎703/684–5900 or 800/362–2779 ⊕www.embassysuites.com ⟳268 suites ☖In-room: kitchen (some), refrigerator, Wi-Fi, Ethernet. In-hotel: Wi-Fi, restaurant, pool, gym, laundry facilities, laundry service, parking (fee) ▭AE, D, DC, MC, V ⍟BP Ⓜ King Street.

$$$ **Hilton Arlington and Towers.** Traveling downtown is easy from this hotel just above a Metro stop. Guest rooms offer "serenity" beds, work desks, and comfy chairs, and the hotel's service is friendly and responsive. Plans are underway for an on-site fitness center. The hotel also has direct access via skywalk to the Ballston Common Mall and National Science Foundation. **Pros:** Easy Metro access; big rooms; online check-in for HHonors members. **Cons:** Far from attractions; high-rise building; no pool. ✉950 N. Stafford St., Arlington, VA ☎703/528–6000 or 800/445–8667 ⊕www.hiltonarlington.com ⟳204 rooms, 5 suites ☖In-room: Wi-Fi. In-hotel: Wi-Fi, restaurant, bar, laundry service, concierge, executive floor, parking (fee) ▭AE, D, DC, MC, V Ⓜ Ballston.

$–$$ **Holiday Inn Arlington at Ballston.** You can get in and out of Washington quickly from this hotel three blocks from a Metro station. Especially comfortable for business travelers, rooms have spacious workspaces, plus tea/coffeemakers. Sightseers can take advantage of the hotel's proximity to Arlington National Cemetery and the Iwo Jima and downtown monuments and museums. Kids 12 and under eat free. **Pros:** Free high-speed Internet access; free parking on Friday and Saturday nights; near the Metro. **Cons:** Outside the city; typical chain-style guest rooms. ✉4610 N. Fairfax Dr., Arlington, VA ☎703/243–9800 or 888/465–4329 ⊕www.hiarlington.com ⟳219 rooms, 2 suites ☖In-room: Wi-Fi, Ethernet. In-hotel: Wi-Fi, restaurant, room service, bar, pool, gym, laundry facilities, parking (fee) ▭AE, D, DC, MC, V Ⓜ Ballston.

$–$$ **Hotel Monaco Alexandria.** When you walk into Old Town's new Hotel Monaco you might feel bad for those poor souls who made reservations elsewhere. But don't worry, the Adriatic blue walls, European and Moroccan travel props, and the cheerful and committed staff will cheer you back up in no time. Inviting guest rooms pick up on this

Kimpton hotel's theme of "history" with fun details like faux snake-skin walls and chairs done in upholstery with the image of a local vintage map. While the Old Town location puts you outside the District, this historic neighborhood holds its own. Stroll down to the water and admire the D.C. view. ■**TIP➡ Water bowls runneth over at the hotel's doggie happy hour on Tuesday and Thursday nights in the summer:** ⊕*www.doggiehappyhour.com.* **Pros:** Hotel restaurant Jackson 20 is getting good early reviews; bend-over-backwards attitude toward service; in the heart of Old Town with its many restaurants, shops, and history. **Cons:** Not in DC; long walk to Metro. ⊠*489 King, Old Town Alexandria* ☎*703/549-6080* ⊕*www.monaco-alexandria.com* ⟲*231 rooms, 10 suites* ⌂*In room: safe, kitchen (some), refrigerator, DVD, Ethernet, Wi-Fi. In-hotel: restaurant, room service, pool, gym, laundry service, concierge, public Wi-Fi, airport shuttle, parking (fee), some pets allowed, no-smoking rooms* ▭ *AE, D, DC, MC, V.*

$$ **Hyatt Arlington.** The renovations gods have recently kissed this Hyatt, leaving it a solid over-the-Potomac choice. Most guest room are large and modern and have new mattresses. The hotel's restaurant, Mezza9, serves Mediterranean cuisine, and the lobby bar is a good place to relax with an early-evening martini or late-night drink. Jogging paths and golf courses can be found nearby. **Pros:** Free Internet access; across from Metro. **Cons:** Outside the city; Rosslyn not known for its quaint charm. ⊠*1325 Wilson Blvd., Arlington, VA* ☎*703/525-1234 or 800/908-4790* ⊕*www.arlington.hyatt.com* ⟲*294 rooms, 8 suites* ⌂*In-room: Wi-Fi. In-hotel: restaurant, room service, bar, gym, concierge, laundry service, parking (fee)* ▭*AE, D, DC, MC, V.*

$$$ **Key Bridge Marriott.** If you don't mind being across the Potomac, this ☾ hotel is a good alternative to downtown. Newly renovated guest rooms sparkle, and the views from the hotel's Potomac side are camera-phone worthy. Although the property carries a Virginia zip code, you can walk over the Key Bridge into Georgetown, and the Rosslyn Metro is about four blocks away. Added bonus: one of the few hotels in town with an indoor-outdoor pool. **Pros:** Good choice if traveling with kids; can walk across the bridge to Georgetown; about four blocks from the Metro. **Cons:** Outside the city; not much of note happening in the immediate area, especially at night. ⊠*1401 Lee Hwy., Arlington, VA* ☎*703/524-6400 or 800/228-9290* ⊕*www.marriott/waskb-key-bridge* ⟲*568 rooms, 14 suites* ⌂*In-room: safe, refrigerator (some,) Ethernet. In-hotel: 2 restaurants, room service, bar, pool, gym, spa, laundry service, concierge, public Wi-Fi, parking (fee), no-smoking rooms* ▭*AE, D, DC, MC, V* Ⓜ*Rosslyn.*

$$–$$$ **Marriott Residence Inn Arlington Pentagon City.** The view across the Potomac of the D.C. skyline and the monuments is magnificent from this all-suites high-rise. Adjacent to the Pentagon, it's two blocks from the Pentagon City Fashion Centre mall, which has movie theaters, a food court, 150 shops, and a Metro stop. ■**TIP➡All suites include full kitchens with dishwashers, ice-makers, coffeemakers, toasters, dishes, and utensils.** Complimentary services include grocery shopping, daily newspaper delivery, full breakfast, light dinner Monday to Wednesday, and movies, popcorn, and ice cream on Thursday evening. **Pros:** All-

LODGING ALTERNATIVES

APARTMENT RENTALS

D.C. is a notoriously transient town, with people hopping on and off the campaign trail on a moment's notice often leaving their apartments in the sublets and long-term rental columns of local newspapers and Web sites. If you can't stomach the idea of another family vacation with you and the kids squeezed into a single hotel room with no kitchen or if you are traveling with others, a furnished rental might be for you. Often these rentals wind up saving you money—especially on meals and snacks. Be warned, the allure of a full kitchen and room to spread out might get you hooked on apartment rentals for life. Here are some Web sites to help you find hotel alternatives, short-term apartment rentals, and apartment exchanges.

⊕ www.vrbo.com

⊕ www.washingtondc.craigslist.org

⊕ thehill.com/classifieds.html

⊕ www.militarybyowner.com

⊕ www.dcdigs.com

⊕ www.remington-dc.com

⊕ www.cyberrentals.com

⊕ thedupontcollection.com/brook-land.html

International Agents Hideaways International (⊠ 767 Islington St., Portsmouth, NH ☎ 603/430–4433 or 800/843–4433 ⊕ www.hide-aways.com), membership $185.

Rental Listings Washington Post (⊕ www.washingtonpost.com). **Washington CityPaper** (⊕ www.washingtoncitypaper.com).

B&BS

To find reasonably priced accommodations in small guesthouses and private homes, try **Bed and Breakfast Accommodations, Ltd.** (☎ 413/582–9888 or 877/893–3233 ⊕ www.bedandbreakfastdc.com) which is staffed weekdays 10–5. It handles about 45 different properties in the area.

HOME EXCHANGES

If you would like to exchange your home for someone else's, join a home-exchange organization, which will send you its updated listings of available exchanges for a year and include your own listing in at least one of them. It's up to you to make specific arrangements.

Exchange Clubs HomeLink International (☎ 813/975–9825 or 800/638–3841 ⊕ www.homelink.org); $80 for a listing published in a directory and on Web sites. Intervac U.S. (☎ 800/756–4663 ⊕ www.intervacus.com); $126 yearly for a listing, online access, and a catalog; $78.88 without catalog.

HOSTELS

No matter what your age, you can save on lodging costs by staying at hostels. **Hostelling International—USA** (⊠ 8401 Colesville Rd., Suite 600, Silver Spring, MD ☎ 301/495–1240 ⊕ www.hiusa.org) offers single-sex, dorm-style beds and, at many hostels, rooms for couples and family accommodations. Membership allows you to stay in HI-affiliated hostels at member rates; one-year membership is about $28 for adults, and hostels charge about $10–$30 per night. Members have priority if the hostel is full.

suites setup a plus for families; easy walk to Metro. **Cons:** Outside of D.C.; neighborhood dead at night. ⊠*550 Army Navy Dr., Arlington, VA* ☎*703/413–6630 or 800/331–3131* ⊕*www.marriott.com/hotels/ travel/waspt-residence-inn-arlington-pentagon-city* ⤶*299 suites* ⅊*In-room: kitchen, Ethernet. In-hotel: pool, gym, laundry facilities, laundry service, public Wi-Fi, airport shuttle, parking (fee), some pets allowed (fee)* ⊟*AE, D, DC, MC, V* ⅋⊙*BP* Ⓜ*Pentagon City.*

$$$–$$$$
Fodor'sChoice
★

Morrison House. The architecture, parquet floors, crystal chandeliers, decorative fireplaces, and furnishings of Morrison House are so faithful to the Federal period (1790–1820) that it's often mistaken for a renovation rather than a structure built from scratch in 1985. The elegant hotel blends Early American charm with modern conveniences. Rooms are individually furnished, and some offer decorative fireplaces and four-poster beds. The popular Elysium Restaurant serves contemporary American cuisine. The hotel sits in the heart of Old Town Alexandria, eight blocks from the train and Metro stations. **Pros:** Attentive staff; the in-hotel Grille restaurant has a great piano bar; lots of charm. **Cons:** Outside the city; no pool. ⊠*116 S. Alfred St., Alexandria, VA* ☎*703/838–8000 or 866/834–6628* ⊕*www.morrisonhouse.com* ⤶*46 rooms, 3 suites* ⅊*In-room: Wi-Fi. In-hotel: Wi-Fi, restaurant, room service, bar, concierge, parking (fee)* ⊟*AE, DC, MC, V* Ⓜ*King St.*

$$$
Palomar Arlington. From the mood lighting to the burnt-orange marble reception to the fantastically funky living room off the lobby, you might think you woke up in Manhattan or South Beach rather than Rosslyn, Virginia. Complimentary coffee, tea and newspapers are in the living room every morning, and all meals are served at the hotel's yummy Italian restaurant, Domaso, which overlooks the city. The Metro is a short walk away, and you can stroll over the Key Bridge to Georgetown from this new Kimpton property. **Pros:** Sleek modern hotel with attention to detail; comfy beds; local wines and art featured in the hotel and wine gift shop. **Cons:** Hip hotel in an un-hip location; some noise from National Airport's flight path above; no swimming pool. ⊠*1121 North 19th Street, Rosslyn* ☎*703/351-9170* ⊕*www.hotelpalomar-arlington.com* ⤶*142 rooms, 12 suites* ⅊*In-room: safe, refrigerator, DVD, Ethernet, Wi-Fi. In-hotel: restaurant, gym, laundry services, concierge, public Wi-Fi, parking (fee), some pets allowed, no-smoking rooms* ⊟*AE, D, DC, MC, V* Ⓜ*Rosslyn.*

$$$$
Ritz-Carlton Pentagon City. A 2007 renovation of this Ritz has successfully achieved a more contemporary feel than one might traditionally associate with the luxury chain. The large guest rooms now shine in a gold, yellow, and blue, and coffeemakers have been placed in all rooms. Attached to a shopping mall, this Ritz-Carlton is a quick cab ride from both Ronald Reagan National Airport and downtown D.C. Afternoon tea remains popular among both guests and locals. Metro can be accessed through the mall. **Pros:** Indoor walk to Metro; newly renovated guest rooms and restaurant; indoor pool. **Cons:** Outside D.C.; slightly less ritzy than other Ritz-Carlton properties in town. ⊠*1250 S. Hayes St., Arlington, VA* ☎*703/415–5000 or 800/241–3333* ⊕*www. ritzcarlton.com/en/Properties/PentagonCity* ⤶*345 rooms, 21 suites* ⅊*In-room: safe, Wi-Fi. In-hotel: restaurant, room service, bar, pool,*

7

gym, concierge, laundry service, executive floor, airport shuttle, park-ing (fee) ⊟*AE, D, DC, MC, V* Ⓜ*Pentagon City.*

$$$–$$$$ **The Westin Alexandria.** The staff seems genuinely happy to see you come through door at this brand-new hotel plopped down in a recently devel-oped section of Old Town. Done in blues, wood tones, and imported Jerusalem stone, the lobby and public areas have something of a Frank Lloyd Wright feel, while the rooms offer standard Westin features like the Heavenly Bed and Baths and flat-screen TVs. It's a good option to get more for your travel dollar if you don't need or want to be in D.C., but it will take you around 25 minutes to get downtown by Metro and the closest stop is about four blocks away. **Pros:** New hotel complete with new hotel smell; rooms with pretty views of either the Masonic Temple or Old Town; close to Ronald Reagan National Airport and Metro. **Cons:** Outside the city; half-hour walk to waterfront. ✉*400 Courthouse Square, Alexandria, VA* ☎*703/253-8600* ⊕*www.westin. com/alexandria* ⤃*309 rooms, 10 suites* ⋔*In-room: safe, refrigera-tor (some), Wi-Fi. In-hotel: restaurant, room service, bar, children's programs (ages 4-12), pool, gym, laundry service, concierge, execu-tive floor, public Wi-Fi, parking (fee), some pets allowed, no-smoking rooms* ⊟*AE, D, DC, MC, V.*

Nightlife

Iota Club and Cafe band

WORD OF MOUTH

"Penn Quarter is definitely the new 'hot' nightlife neighborhood for the over-30 crowd."

—MikeT

"I LOVE the Capitol Steps. They lampoon anyone and everyone."

—SuzieTrue

NIGHTLIFE PLANNER

The Price of Admission

Most bars in D.C. have cover charges for bands and DJs, especially those performing on Friday and Saturday. Expect to pay from $10 to $20 for most dance clubs. Jazz and comedy clubs often have higher cover charges along with drink minimums.

Dress Code

Most bars and clubs require men to wear a shirt with a collar (polo shirts are fine) and dress shoes. No sneakers or Timberlands allowed. Jeans are acceptable if they are not torn or baggy. Shirts with logos are often not allowed. The code is less strict for women. "Dress to impress" or you won't get in.

Last Call

Last call in D.C. is 2 AM, and most bars and clubs close by 3 AM on the weekend and between midnight and 2 AM during the week. The exceptions are after-hours dance clubs and bars with kitchens that stay open late.

Five Great Nightlife Experiences

Ben's Chili Bowl: Chili has become a condiment at this late-night spot beloved of U Street revelers.

Café Saint-Ex: There's an upstairs and downstairs for your wild and mild sides.

Blues Alley: D.C.'s classiest jazz club is the place to enjoy jazz tunes and Cajun food in an intimate setting.

Chi-Cha Lounge: It's like your living room, only hipper, and they serve sangria and hookah.

Ibiza: This warehouse-tuned-mega club in Northeast D.C., is the place to go wild with VIP terraces, waterfalls, seven bars, a 50,000 LED light wall on the dance floor, and a 3 AM closing time.

Where to Find What's Going On

To survey the local scene, consult Friday's "Weekend" section in the *Washington Post* and the free weekly *Washington CityPaper*. The free publications *Metro Weekly* and the *Washington Blade* offer insights on gay and lesbian nightlife.

Local blogs DCist (⊕ *www.dcist.com*) and Free Ride (⊕ *www.readexpress.com/freeride.php*) post daily on D.C. events. It's a good idea to call clubs ahead of time, as last week's punk-rock party might be this week's merengue marathon.

Signs of Life in the Burbs

The city's suburbs have a nightlife of their own, in part thanks to Washington's Metro system, which runs until 3 AM on weekends. Near the Bethesda stop in downtown Bethesda, Maryland, there's a relaxed nightlife scene. In Northern Virginia, to which droves of young people in search of cheaper rent have decamped, bars and clubs heat up the areas surrounding the Clarendon and Courthouse Metro stations.

ADAMS-MORGAN
18th and Columbia is a nightlife nexus

U STREET
live rock and jazz, hipster bars

GEORGETOWN
college kids and well-heeled grownups

DUPONT CIRCLE
gay-friendly; trendy clubs

DOWNTOWN
upscale drinking and dancing

CAPITOL HILL
casual bars where staffers unwind

Columbia Rd.
Florida Ave.
18th St.
Florida Ave.
New Hampshire Ave.
Vermont Ave.
Sheridan Circle
Massachusetts Ave.
Dupont Circle
Logan Circle
Rock Creek
Connecticut Ave.
Scott Circle
Rhode Island Ave.
M St.
Thomas Circle
M St.
Washington Circle
Whitehurst Fwy.
K St.
New York Ave.
23rd St.
Pennsylvania Ave.
15th St.
14th St.
FOGGY BOTTOM
Theodore Roosevelt Island
Virginia Ave.
Constitution Ave.
THE MALL
Reflecting Pool
Independence Ave.
THE MONUMENTS
Arlington Memorial Br.
Columbia Island
Tidal Basin
Potomac River
Francis Case Memorial Br.
Washington Canal

VIRGINIA

0   500 yards
0   500 meters

Updated by
Mitchell Tropin

From buttoned-down political appointees who've just arrived to laid-back folks who've lived here their whole lives, Washingtonians have plenty of options when they head out for a night on the town. Most places are clustered in several key areas, making a night of bar-hopping relatively easy.

Georgetown's dozens of bars, nightclubs, and restaurants radiate from the intersection of Wisconsin and M streets. The crowds tend to include older adults and college students. Georgetown is also the safest place in D.C., with a large police presence on weekends. Parking, however, is a scarce commodity, and there is no nearby Metro station. Taxis are often the best choice.

In contrast, the 18th Street strip in Adams-Morgan between Columbia Road and Kalorama Avenue offers a wide variety of places that feature hip-hop DJs, Latin music, and everything in between. If you're looking for off-beat spots that don't take themselves too seriously, you're in the right place.

For serious dance action, head to Northeast. Huge crowds and loud music ranging from hip-hop and Latin to techno and trance await you at the ever popular warehouse-turned-mega clubs like Love and Ibiza. This is a rougher part of town, so be cautious. Make use of the clubs' limited premium parking—for about $20—that will put you close to their entrances. Even parking a few blocks away on neighborhood streets is risky at night. Taxis are another good option, as there is no nearby Metro. More intimate dance clubs can be found around F Street, near Chinatown, such as the Ultrabar and Platinum.

The U Street corridor (U Street NW between 12th and 16th streets), once D.C.'s hippest neighborhood and a regular stop for jazz greats, is now undergoing a revival, with bars that appeal to all types.

The stretch of Pennsylvania Avenue between 2nd and 4th streets has a half-dozen Capitol Hill bars. And thanks to massive recent development, Penn Quarter is burgeoning with squeaky clean new bars.

BARS & LOUNGES

When it comes to the bar scene, Washington can feel like a college town—senators are even referred to as "junior" and "senior." Residents go out regularly, and they're served by a large number and wide variety of watering holes, most packed with people of all ages and interests. If you're into going out, you can find what you're looking for here.

CAPITOL HILL

Dubliner. A Washington institution that offers cozy paneled rooms, rich pints of Guinness, and nightly live Irish entertainment make this place popular among Capitol Hill staffers and Georgetown law students. It is located in the Phoenix Park Hotel, near Union Station. ✉*4 F St. NW, Capitol Hill* ☎*202/737–3773* ⊕*www.dublinerdc.com* Ⓜ*Union Station.*

Hawk and Dove. The regulars at this friendly bar—in the shadow of the Capitol—include politicos, lobbyists, and disgruntled interns. Conversation is ripe with overexcitement or rage at the political events of the day, although some just come to watch sports on the TVs above the bar. ✉*329 Pennsylvania Ave. SE, Capitol Hill* ☎*202/543-3300* ⊕*www.hawkanddoveonline.com* Ⓜ*Eastern Market.*

Mr. Henry's Capitol Hill. You'll find great local singers and musicians at this long-time Washington favorite where Roberta Flack was discovered. ✉*601 Pennsylvania Ave. SE, Capitol Hill* ☎*202/546–8412* ⊕*www.mrhenrysrestaurant.com* Ⓜ*Eastern Market.*

DOWNTOWN

Fadó Irish Pub. Designed by Irish craftspeople with authentic Irish materials, dark and warm Fadó is really four pubs in one: the Library, the Victorian Pub, the Gaelic, and the Cottage. The pub's name comes from an old Irish expression meaning "long ago." Live Irish acoustic music is performed every Sunday afternoon, and there's live Celtic rock on Wednesday and Saturday nights. Monday night is quiz night. Fadó often pulls a crowd from the nearby Verizon Center. ✉*808 7th St. NW, Chinatown* ☎*202/789–0066* ⊕*www.fadoirishpub.com* Ⓜ*Gallery Pl./Chinatown.*

Gordon Biersch Brewery. This brewery-restaurant in the revived Chinatown neighborhood offers great pub food and lively crowds. Beer fans will savor the many German-style brews that are made according to the "Reinheitsgebot"—the German Purity Law of 1516 ✉*900 F St. NW, Chinatown* ☎*202783–5454* ⊕*wwwgordonbiersch.com* Ⓜ*Gallery Pl./Chinatown.*

Indebleu. Dressed in vivid red and orange, this ultracool lounge has one of the most popular bar menus in town. Not only does it include a large list of hot cocktails, it has the imagination to logically arrange them on a D.C. Metro map. This club has earned an international reputation, so expect crowds. ✉*707 G St. NW, Chinatown* ☎*202/333–2538* ⊕*www.tantradc.com* Ⓜ*Gallery Pl./Chinatown.*

8

GEORGETOWN

The center of Georgetown is a good 15-minute walk from the nearest Metro (Foggy Bottom), but flagging down a cab is never a problem.

Degrees. Inside what was once the Georgetown Incinerator, this modern bar in the Ritz-Carlton is a breath of fresh air in the neighborhood's rather monotone scene. With an extensive wine and cocktail selection behind the black granite bar and a hip, well-dressed set of patrons in front of it, Degrees exudes elegance from all corners. If there's too much attitude in the bar, head out to the hotel's lovely lobby and sit by the fireplace. ⊠ *3100 South St. NW, Georgetown* ☎ *202/912–4100* ⊕ *www.ritzcarlton.com.*

J Paul's. This is a great neighborhood saloon and a terrific place to for a beer and a game. The menu is extensive, but stick to the great seafood dishes and hamburgers. J Paul attracts a diverse crowd from students to lobbyists and politicians. ⊠ *3218 M St. NW, Georgetown* ☎ *202/333–3450.*

DUPONT CIRCLE

Brickskeller. Its selection of more than 1,000 varieties of beer from around the world landed Brickskeller in *Guinness World Records 2003.* Other draws include the cozy, although slightly grungy, cellar location; the diverse clientele; the tasty burgers; and the adept servers, who actually have to attend "beer school" to get a job here. ⊠ *1523 22nd St. NW, Dupont Circle* ☎ *202/293–1885* ⊕ *www.thebrickskeller. com* Ⓜ *Dupont Circle.*

Fodor's Choice **Eighteenth Street Lounge (ESL).** Home to Washington's chic set, ESL's
★ unmarked visage might be intimidating, but this multilevel club's array of sofa-filled hardwood coves makes it seem like the city's chillest house party. On the top floor of this former mansion, jazz musicians often entertain loungers seated nearby. Fans of techno music flock here, because it's the home of the ESL record label and the renowned musicial duo Thievery Corporation. ■TIP→The dress code here is strictly enforced by the doorman; no khakis, baseball caps, sneakers, or light-colored jeans. ⊠ *1212 18th St. NW, Dupont Circle* ☎ *202/466–3922* ⊕ *www.eslmusic.com* Ⓜ *Dupont Circle.*

Gazuza. The bar, whose name means "lust" in Castilian Spanish, draws an attractive local crowd that attempts to chat over the throbbing house music. The tiny interior, done in an aggressively modern style, fills up early, spilling patrons onto the spacious balcony, a prime people-watching spot. ⊠ *1629 Connecticut Ave. NW, Dupont Circle* ☎ *202/667–5500* ⊕ *www.latinconcepts.com/gazuza* Ⓜ *Dupont Circle.*

ADAMS-MORGAN

Chief Ike's Mambo Room. This is a favorite spot for a friendly, laid-back evening. Chief Ike's is known for attracting a wild and eccentric crowd—the drinks may not be anything special, but the person sitting next to you may very well be. There's plenty of room to hang out, chat, and sip a cool cocktail with dancing downstairs. You can't miss Chief Ike's gaudy entrance. ⊠ *1725 Columbia Rd. NW, Adams-Morgan* ☎ *202/332–2211* Ⓜ *Woodley Park/Zoo.*

D.C.'S PARTY ANIMALS: INTERNS

GENERAL DESCRIPTION
Migratory species, aged 16 to 25, present in the region in great abundance in summer.

IDENTIFYING MARKS
Eager expression, hangover. Can be confused with law student, but interns are almost always spotted in groups of four or more, do not carry books, and wear badges marked INTERN—a dead giveaway. The male is nearly uniform in khakis, blazer, and tie. Female shows greater variety of plumage, but look for sundresses in spring and summer and pearls year-round.

DIET
A fairly regular daily diet of Starbucks in the morning, Chinese takeout at lunch, and pizza, burritos, and the like in the evening is enriched by great quantities of draft beer, often consumed by groups of interns, from pitchers.

HABITAT
During the day, interns flock with other political species to the Capitol and White House, and are most easily spotted inside these buildings, Republican and Democratic subspecies sometimes intermingling. After hours, they congregate both at Hill bars like **Capital Lounge** (mostly Republicans) and the **Hawk and Dove** (mostly Democrats), and also farther afield, at **Third Edition** in Georgetown. On weekends, look for interns at **Open City** in Woodley Park, gathering in great numbers to feed on pancakes.

BEHAVIOR
When among their own, Washington interns are known for late-night parties and beer pong. In the presence of other political species (staffers, legislators), behavior is markedly more subdued. Interns are nearly always single while in Washington, and their mating rituals are particularly showy; coupling up between Republican and Democratic subspecies is not unusual, and occasional interns have been known to pair temporarily with legislators and others.

Habana Village. Mojito anyone? This popular nightspot in Adams-Morgan captures the sounds, tastes, and smells of Cuba in a friendly environment. The menu offers exquisite Cuban dishes. ✉ *1834 Columbia Rd., Adams-Morgan* ☎*202462–6310* ⊕*www.habanvillage.com* Ⓜ *Woodley Park/Zoo.*

Madam's Organ. Neon lights behind the bar, walls covered in kitsch, and works from local artists add to the gritty, bayou feel that infuses Madam's Organ. Its three levels play host to an eclectic clientele that shoots pool, listens to live music performed every night on the lower level, and soaks up rays on the roof deck. There are some who dislike Madam's Organ for its popularity, but, for most, it's a place that's hard not to like. Rolling Rock is half-price for redheads. ✉*2461 18th St. NW, Adams-Morgan* ☎*202/667–5370* ⊕*madamsorgan.com* Ⓜ *Woodley Park/Zoo.*

Tryst. Bohemian and unpretentious, this coffeehouse-bar serves fancy sandwiches and exotic coffee creations. Comfy chairs and couches fill the big open space, where you can sit for hours sipping a cup of tea—or a martini, in the evening—while chatting or clacking away at your laptop. Tryst is best in the warm months, when the front windows swing open and the temperature matches the temperament. ✉ *2459 18th St. NW, Adams-Morgan* ☎ *202/232–5500* ⊕ *www.trystdc.com* Ⓜ *Woodley Park/Zoo.*

U STREET/CARDOZO

★ **Café Saint-Ex.** Themed after the life of Antoine de Saint-Exupéry, French pilot and author of *The Little Prince,* this bi-level bar has a split personality. The upstairs brasserie has pressed-tin ceilings and a propeller hanging over the polished wooden bar. Downstairs is the Gate 54 nightclub, designed to resemble an airplane hangar with dropped corrugated-metal ceilings and backlit aerial photographs. The DJs draw twentysomethings nightly. ✉ *1847 14th St. NW, Logan Circle* ☎ *202/265–7839* ⊕ *www.saint-ex.com* Ⓜ *U St./Cardozo.*

★ **Chi-Cha Lounge.** Insular groups of young professionals relax on sofas and armchairs in this hip hangout while Latin jazz mingles with Peruvian and Bolivian folk music in the background and old movies run silently behind the bar. This lounge, modeled after an Ecuadorian hacienda, gets packed on weekends, so come early to get a coveted sofa along the back wall. Down the tasty tapas as you enjoy the namesake drink—think sangria with a bigger kick. For a price, you can smoke a hookah filled with imported honey-cured tobacco. ✉ *1624 U St. NW, U Street corridor* ☎ *202/234–8400* ⊕ *www.latinconcepts.com/chicha* Ⓜ *U St./Cardozo.*

Helix Lounge. Despite feeling like someone's lounged-out basement, Helix caters to a mixed, completely non-Hill crowd—an oddity in D.C. Locals, who sit on couches and overstuffed ottomans, sip specialty cocktails and chat among themselves. Most are well dressed, but it's definitely not a scene. ✉ *Hotel Helix, 1430 Rhode Island Ave. NW, Logan Circle* ☎ *202/462–9001* ⊕ *www.hotelhelix.com/heldini* Ⓜ *U St./Cardozo.*

The Saloon. A classic watering hole, the Saloon has no TVs, no light beer, and no martinis. What you can find are locals engaged in conversation—a stated goal of the owner—and some of the world's best beers, including the rare Urbock 23, an Austrian beer that is rated one of the tastiest and strongest in the world, with 9.6 percent alcohol content (limit one per customer). ✉ *1207 U St. NW, U Street corridor* ☎ *202/462–2640* Ⓜ *U St./Cardozo.*

SOUTHWEST/WATERFRONT

★ **Zanzibar on the Waterfront.** Featuring Caribbean and African-influenced food, this addition to the traditional seafood restaurants on D.C.'s Southwest waterfront caters to well-dressed professionals in their thirties. Live entertainment is offered as well as multiple dance floors. Zanzibar also schedules special events, such as performances by Jamaica's Elephant Man and R&B singer Melba Moore. ✉ *700 Water St. SW, Waterfront* ☎ *202/554–9100* ⊕ *www.zanzibar-otw.com* Ⓜ *L'Enfant Plaza.*

VIRGINIA

Carpool. "Andy Warhol meets General Motors" is how one magazine described this former-garage-turned-bar. Enjoy a brew and food from a kitchen run by Rocklands, which makes some of the best barbecue

D.C.'S PARTY ANIMALS: STAFFERS

GENERAL DESCRIPTION

Prolific species endemic to the Washington area; similar species are present in state capitals throughout the country, but the Washington staffer is notably more rapacious. Republican and Democratic subspecies are distinct; Senate, Congressional, White House, and Departmental varieties are less so, due in part to migration between offices every two to four years.

IDENTIFYING MARKS

BlackBerry; security badge, usually worn around neck; males tend toward dark suits but females are often seen in red. Republican subspecies tends to be heavier, and the males have extremely neat hair; Democratic subspecies is svelter and hairier in both sexes, but dress is less predictable. Both subspecies are distinguishable from lawyers only by badge.

DIET

The bulk of the staffer's diet is coffee, but it also consumes takeout and martinis. While staffers are technically omnivores, their actual intake depends on their environment and which other species are present. A staffer may eat lo mein with legislators or foie gras with lobbyists, or both, in the same day.

HABITAT

Like other political species, staffers tend to stick close to the Capitol and White House during the day, although they can also be spotted at the **Red River Grille** and the **Capital Grille** at lunchtime. After hours, the best places to watch Republican staffers are **Bullfeathers** and **Tortilla Coast,** both on the Hill. Democratic staffers are also present on the Hill at the **Hawk and Dove,** and farther afield, on V Street at **Busboys and Poets.** As populations of GOP and Democratic staffers shift, turf wars sometimes erupt; observe Democratic staffers moving in on Republican territory at the **Capital Lounge** on the Hill, and the reverse at **Stetson's,** in Adams-Morgan.

BEHAVIOR

Remarkably intelligent and adaptable, staffers are some of Washington's most interesting species to observe. It is not uncommon to observe a staffer simultaneously sending e-mails on its BlackBerry, talking on a cell phone, and ordering in a restaurant or bar (the scientific name for this behavior is formulating policy). Staffers are gregarious among their own, but can become obsequious and competitive when in the presence of legislators.

8

in the area. Carpool, which serves a local clientele, has 16 pool tables, four dartboards, and a cigar room with a walk-in humidor. ✉*4000 Fairfax Dr., Arlington, VA* ☎*703/532–7665* ⊕*www.carpoolweb.com* Ⓜ*Ballston.*

Fishmarket. There's something different in just about every section of this multilevel, multiroom space, from a piano-bar crooner to a ragtime piano shouter and a guitar strummer. The thirty- and fortysomething crowd is boisterous. If you really like beer, order the largest size; it comes in a glass big enough to put your face in. ✉*105 King St., Old Town Alexandria, VA* ☎*703/836–5676* ⊕*www.fishmarketoldtown. com* Ⓜ*King St.*

Iota. The bands at Iota play alt-country or stripped-down rock to unpretentious, attentive crowds who come mainly because they like good music. Expect to fight your way to the bar—it gets crowded quickly. There's a cover that ranges from $5 to $17, depending on the act. ✉2832 Wilson Blvd., Arlington, VA ☎703/522–8340 ⊕www.iotaclubandcafe.com Ⓜ Clarendon.

State Theatre. This is the place to go to see famous bands from the past like Leon Russell, the Smithereens, and Jefferson Starship. You have the choice of sitting or standing in this renovated movie theatre, which is about 10 miles south of D.C. ✉220 N. Washington Blvd., Falls Church, VA ☎703/237–0300 ⊕wwwthestatetheatre.com Ⓜ East Falls Church.

GAY & LESBIAN BARS

Washington's gay population has traditionally congregated in Dupont Circle. 17th Street between P Street and R Street is an especially active scene.

Halo. At this Logan Circle hangout you won't have to elbow for room or shout to be heard—a rarity in nearby gay bars. Sleek and stylish, the bar uses dramatic lighting to make the most of its tunnel-like space, where well-dressed men lounge on modern leather furniture. ✉1435 P St. NW, Logan Circle ☎202/797–9730 Ⓜ Dupont Circle.

> ### WORD OF MOUTH
>
> "[Dupont Circle] is a wonderful and vibrant part of the city and I would hate for someone to decide not to visit it because they thought it was the 'gay area' and they would be uncomfortable. . . . That said, if it does make you uncomfortable you may not want to visit the Tuesday before Halloween, when the drag queens run their high heel race on 17th St."
>
> —hlg22

JR's Bar & Grill. On the 17th Street strip, JR's packs in a mostly male, young professional crowd. Patrons shoot pool, play video games, gaze at videos on the big screen, and chat with their neighbors. ✉1519 17th St. NW, Dupont Circle ☎202/328–0090 ⊕www.jrswdc.com Ⓜ Dupont Circle.

Phase One. An eclectic, mostly female clientele frequents this longtime neighborhood hangout. The small dance floor and pool tables in the back make it an intimate and comfortable spot, although sometimes the place gets very crowded. ✉525 8th St. SE, Capitol Hill ☎202/544–6831 ⊕www.phase1dc.com Ⓜ Eastern Market.

MUSIC CLUBS

At the junction between the North, the South, and the Rust Belt, D.C. has become somewhat of a crossroads for folk, rock, and jazz acts. The high number of venues, sustained by a hard-working, hard-playing population, entices many of them to stay and play. Also, as the nation's capital D.C. often pulls the biggest acts for special events and celebra-

D.C.'S PARTY ANIMALS: LOBBYISTS

GENERAL DESCRIPTION

Though currently plentiful, the lobbyist is a threatened species in Washington. Ironically, recent legislation about and public awareness of the species have only deepened its endangerment.

IDENTIFYING MARKS

Lobbyists may look familiar to New Yorkers, due to their marked resemblance to investment bankers (the latter are extremely rare in Washington). Easy to identify by custom-made suits, stylish haircuts, and the occasional suspender or cigar (males only), they are distinguishable from lawyers by their habit of picking up the check.

DIET

Studies of lobbyists' expense reports indicate a particularly voracious appetite, heavy on red meat, sushi, and fine wine. It is interesting to note, however, that lobbyists take virtually all their meals in restaurants, and thus have a limited ability to find food on their own; without an expense account, the lobbyist may starve.

HABITAT

The lobbyist's habitat is shrinking rapidly, and is a source of some concern. Washington lobbyists are native only to K Street, but in recent years their normal range had extended to the Capitol, with a vast migratory range encompassing Scottish golf courses, Mississippi casinos, and the Mariana Islands. As pressure increases on the species, it is being driven back to K Street, but can still be reliably spotted at **Charlie Palmer, Capital Grille, La Colline, The Monocle,** and **The Capitol Hill Club.** Follow the sommelier.

BEHAVIOR

Lobbyists coexist symbiotically with legislators, each reliant on the other for protection and sustenance. Thus, the two species are often spotted together: the lobbyist feeding the legislator with food, trips, and campaign cash, the legislator reciprocating with spending bills. In such company, the lobbyist is at its most resplendent—charming and expansive. When alone or with members of their own species, however, lobbyists can be gruff and temperamental. Watch for them on cell phones in expensive restaurants.

tions. Stay tuned with the *Washington Post*, the *Washington Citypaper*, and *DCist* (⊕ *www.dcist.com*).

ACOUSTIC, FOLK & COUNTRY MUSIC CLUBS

Fodor'sChoice **The Birchmere.** A legend in the D.C. area, the Birchmere is one of the best
★ places outside of the Blue Ridge Mountains to hear acoustic folk, country, and bluegrass. Enthusiastic crowds have enjoyed performances by artists such as Mary Chapin Carpenter, Lyle Lovett, Leon Redbone, and Emmylou Harris. Recently, the club has expanded its offerings to

WORD OF MOUTH

"My favorite live music place is the Birchmere, which is in Alexandria but not in Old Town"

—allison04

include jazz performers such as Diane Schuur and Al Jareau, and blues artists like Robert Cray and Buddy Guy. ✉3701 Mt. Vernon Ave., Alexandria, VA ☎703/549–7500 ⊕www.birchmere.com.

Folklore Society of Greater Washington. At more than 200 events a year, the society presents folk and traditional musicians and dancers from all over the country. Venues around the D.C. area host FSGW events ranging from contra dancing to storytelling to open-mike singing. ☎202/546–2228 ⊕www.fsgw.org.

JAZZ & BLUES CLUBS

The **D.C. Blues Society** (⊕www.dcblues.org)is a clearinghouse for information on upcoming shows, festivals, and jam sessions in the metropolitan area. It also publishes a monthly newsletter.

Fodor'sChoice **Blues Alley.** Head here for a classy evening in an intimate setting, com-
★   plete with great music and outstanding New Orleans–style grub. The cover charge is typically $25 for well-known performers such as Moses Allison, and more for top acts like Wynton Marsalis. There is also a $10 food or drink minimum. ■TIP➔You can come for just the show, but those who enjoy a meal get better seats. ✉1073 Wisconsin Ave. NW, near M St., Georgetown ☎202/337–4141 ⊕www.bluesalley.com Ⓜ Foggy Bottom.

Bohemian Caverns. The low-ceiling stairway delivers you to a performance space made to look like a cave, a complete and accurate renovation of the Crystal Caverns, once a mainstay of D.C.'s "Black Broadway" and the place to see Miles Davis and Charlie Parker. The club rightfully calls itself "the Sole Home for Soul Jazz." These days Friday and Saturday are given over to jazz; blues acts headline on Thursday; and open-mike night on Wednesday brings jazz-influenced poets to the stage. ✉2001 11th St. NW, U Street corridor ☎202/299–0801 ⊕www.bohemiancaverns.com Ⓜ U St./Cardozo.

Columbia Station. This unpretentious neighborhood bar attracts an eclectic crowd, many of whom were pulled in off the street by the good vibes emanating from this place. Amber lights and morphed musical instruments adorn the walls, and high-quality live local jazz and blues fills the air. The large, open windows up front keep the place cool in summer months. ✉2325 18th St. NW, Adams-Morgan ☎202/462–6040 Ⓜ Woodley Park/Zoo.

★   **HR-57.** Named after a congressional resolution proclaiming jazz a "rare and valuable national treasure," HR-57 isn't just a club, it's also a nonprofit cultural center. The warm, inviting center spotlights musicians based in the D.C. area, many of whom have national followings. Fried chicken and collard greens are on the menu; beer and wine are available, or bring your own bottle (corkage is $3 per person). ✉1610 14th St. NW, Logan Circle ☎202/667–3700 ⊕www.hr57.org Ⓜ U St./Cardozo.

Mr. Henry's. This laid-back club is the last holdout of a once-thriving live-music scene on Capitol Hill. Roberta Flack got her start in the upstairs performance space, where a dozen or so tables are scattered around the wood-paneled room. There's never a cover. ✉601 Pennsylvania Ave.

SE, Capitol Hill ☎*202/546–8412* Ⓜ*Eastern Market.*

New Vegas Lounge. Dr. Blues doesn't allow any soft-jazz-bluesy-fusion in his house. Even during the weekly open-jam session at this longtime favorite, it's strictly no-nonsense wailing guitar rhythms by seasoned local players. ✉*1415 P St. NW, Dupont Circle* ☎*202/483–3971* ⊕*www.thenewvegaslounge.com* Ⓜ*Dupont Circle.*

Takoma Station Tavern. Beside the subway stop that lends it its name, the Takoma hosts such local favorites as Marshall Keys and Keith Killgo, with the occasional nationally known artist stopping by to jam. The jazz happy hours starting at 6:30 PM Thursday and Friday pack the joint. There's reggae on Saturday and comedy on Monday. Sneakers and athletic wear are not allowed. ✉*6914 4th St. NW, Takoma Park* ☎*202/829–1999* ⊕*www.takomastation.com* Ⓜ*Takoma.*

Twins Jazz. Twin sisters Kelly and Maze Tesfaye have made this cozy space a haven for some of D.C.'s strongest straight-ahead jazz players, as well as for groups from New York City. On the club's menu are tasty Ethiopian appetizers along with such staples as nachos, wings, and burgers. ✉*1344 U St. NW, U Street corridor* ☎*202/234–0072* ⊕*www.twinsjazz.com* Ⓜ*U St./Cardozo.*

> ### EARLY TO BED
>
> During a performance at Georgetown's Blues Alley, the headliner noted that the 8 PM shows at the club sell out, while the later 10 PM shows beg for patrons. She attributed this to the fact that "people in Washington have to get up at 5:30 AM every morning and turn on the TV to see what is happening with the world." That remark is close to the truth, and explains a sometimes lackluster nightlife during the workweek in D.C.

ROCK & POP CLUBS

Fodor's Choice ★ **Black Cat.** Come here to see the latest local bands as well as indie stars such as Neko Case, Modest Mouse, and Clinic. Dave Grohl, lead singer of the Foo Fighters and formerly of Nirvana, owns a stake in the club. The post-punk crowd whiles away the time in the Red Room, a side bar with pool tables, an eclectic jukebox, and no cover charge. The club also is home to Food for Thought, a legendary vegetarian café. ✉*1811 14th St. NW, U Street corridor* ☎*202/667–7960* ⊕*www.blackcatdc.com* Ⓜ*U St./Cardozo.*

DC9. With live music seven days a week, this two-story rock club hosts up-and-coming indie rock bands and the occasional nationally known act. There's a narrow bar on the ground floor and a humongous concert space upstairs. ✉*1940 9th St. NW, U Street corridor* ☎*202/483–5000* ⊕*www.dcnine.com* Ⓜ*U St./Cardozo.*

★ **9:30 Club.** When they come to town, the best of the nonstadium performers, and a few of the bigger acts, play this large but cozy space wrapped by balconies on three sides. Recent acts have included current sensations as well as groups with a long history, such as the B-52s, Reconteurs, Lou Reed, Crowded House, and Joe Jackson ■TIP➔**For the best seats, arrive at least an hour before the doors open, typically at**

7:30. ⊠*815 V St. NW, U Street corridor* ☎*202/393–0930* ⊕*www.930. com* Ⓜ*U St./Cardozo.*

Rock and Roll Hotel. In the revived H St. corridor, this venue offers some of the nation's best indie acts. Housed in a former funeral home, the multiple dance floors can get very crowded when well-known bands or DJ's perform. Live acts are in the main room and DJs spin on the second floor, called the Hotel Bar. Notable acts include the Walkmen, Andrew W.K., and Juliette and the Licks. ■**TIP**➜**Take the Atlas Courtesy Shuttle, a 12-passenger van, from the Union Station Metro to the club. The shuttle is free, operating every Friday and Saturday, 10 PM–2:30 AM. Call** ☎ *301/751–1802* **for pickup.** ⊠*1353 H St NE, H Street corridor* ☎*202/388–7625* ⊕*www.rockandrollhoteldc.com* Ⓜ*Potomac Avenue.*

Velvet Lounge. Squeeze up the narrow stairway and check out the eclectic local and national bands that play at this unassuming neighborhood joint. Performers ranging from indie mainstays to acclaimed up-and-comers rock the house with psychobilly, alt-country, and indie pop. ⊠*915 U St. NW, U Street corridor* ☎*202/462–3213* ⊕*www.velvet loungedc.com* Ⓜ*U St./Cardozo.*

DANCE CLUBS

Washington's dance clubs seem constantly to be re-creating themselves. A club might offer heavy industrial music on Wednesday, be host to a largely gay clientele on Thursday, and thump to the sounds of '70s disco on Friday. Club-hoppers can choose from five hubs: Georgetown, Adams-Morgan, Dupont Circle, U Street, and along 9th Street NW near Gallery Place Metro station.

Five. House music is what draws the crowds to this three-story club near Dupont Circle. And the sound track is constantly morphing—the house, hip-hop, and drum-and-bass tracks the DJs play on Wednesday become deep house and disco on Saturday. On Thursday the place echoes until the early morning with a Latin groove. ⊠*1214-B 18th St. NW, Dupont Circle* ☎*202/331–7123* ⊕*www.fivedc.com* Ⓜ*Dupont Circle.*

Fur. This multi-level entertainment mecca offers a variety of electronic, Latin, and hip-hop music with some nights devoted to a music specialty. The dance floor is large, accommodating over 2,000 people with state-of-the-art sound and lighting systems. The club enforces its dress code, requiring shirts with collars and no sneakers or Timberlands. ⊠*33 Patterson St. NE, Northeast* ☎*202/842–3401* ⊕*wwwfurnight club.com.*

★ **Habana Village.** No matter what the temperature is outside, it's always balmy inside the unpretentious Habana Village. The tiny dance floors are packed nightly with couples moving to the latest live salsa and merengue tunes. When it's time to cool down, you can head to one of several lounges in this converted four-story town house and sip the house specialty: a *mojito* garnished with sugarcane. ⊠*1834 Columbia*

D.C.'S PARTY ANIMALS: LEGISLATORS

GENERAL DESCRIPTION

The legislator's life cycle is one of migration, from its home state to Washington and back, during weekends, Congressional recesses, and finally, election years. Natural selection has made it thus a particularly hardy and dynamic species; its struggles for dominance are among Washington's most dramatic and powerful.

IDENTIFYING MARKS

Prominent smile, entourage. Legislators are rarely alone, but outside of the Capitol, seldom in the company of other legislators, preferring the company of staffers, lobbyists, and sometimes, interns. They often travel in black SUVs and tend to be hard to catch, but can sometimes be lured by cameras and microphones. The Senate variety is almost exclusively white and largely male; the House variety is more diverse and vocal.

DIET

While in Washington, legislators eat a rich diet of porterhouse steak, Chinese takeout, and French fries (n.b., some of the Republican subspecies prefer Freedom fries). But in election years a legislator's epic journey of campaign migration results in significant culinary hardship, and during this time many subsist on donuts and pie.

HABITAT

Observe legislators in the Capitol itself, and around the Hill and White House at **TenPenh**, **Capital Grille**, and **The Caucus Room**, as well as in Georgetown at **Café Milano** and **Citronelle**. On Friday afternoons and Monday mornings you may catch a glimpse of legislators migrating through Reagan National Airport. In election years their habitat changes dramatically, and while hard to find in Washington, they're easy to spot at county fairs and senior citizens' homes.

BEHAVIOR

This species is known for noisy and complex displays of principle, called speechifying. These displays are meant to simultaneously attract voters and intimidate competitors; occasionally, they also result in legislation.

Rd. NW, Adams-Morgan ☎202/462–6310 ⊕www.habanavillage.com Ⓜ Woodley Park/Zoo.

Ibiza. Since its re-launch in 2007, Ibiza has become a hugely popular dance club. Noted for its 3 AM closing, the club attracts a more diverse crowd. It has 30,000 square feet of space, seven bars, and a rooftop deck—a rarity in D.C. ✉ *225 First St. NE., Northeast* ☎202/234—9225 ⊕ *www.dcclubhost.com* Ⓜ *New York Ave-Florida Ave.-Gallaudet.*

★ **Love.** This four-story dance powerhouse looms over the industrial Northeast corridor far from downtown D.C. Elegant and minimalist, Love makes the most of its former warehouse home. Washington Wizards players and other celebrities are frequently spotted in the VIP areas. The music changes from night to night, and from floor to floor, but you're sure to sample salsa, house, and trance. This wood-paneled club attracts a primarily upscale, but diverse clientele. The dress code is strictly enforced. Love also has occasional concerts from performers

The Low Down on Late Night Eats

Top off a night of bar-hopping with a stop at one of these delicious late-night haunts.

ADAMS MORGAN

The menu at **Amsterdam Falafelshop** (✉ 2425 18th St. NW 20009 ☎ 202/234-1969 ⊕ www.falafelshop.com/index.html Ⓜ Woodley Park-Zoo, Adams Morgan) might consist of only three items—falafels in pita, Dutch-style french fries, and brownies–but the choices are far from limited. At this cash-only spot, choose from nearly 20 different garnishes and a variety of dipping sauces.

As the bars clear out after last call, make your way off crowded and chaotic 18th Street and into the pleasantly low-key **El Tamarindo** (✉ 1785 Florida Ave., NW ☎ 202/238-3660 Ⓜ Dupont Circle) for cheap heaping portions of Mexican and Salvadoran cuisine. You can enjoy a full sit-down meal at 3:00 AM, including chile con queso, quesadillas, enchiladas, Salvadoran-style *pupusas* (tortillas stuffed with cheese and other fillings), and soups.

DUPONT CIRCLE

It's not only the literati who flock to the charming **Kramerbooks & Afterwards** (✉ 1517 Connecticut Ave., NW ☎ 202/387-3825 Ⓜ Dupont Circle) for a book and brew. This all-inclusive bookstore, bar, and café is a popular after-hours destination attracting hip, young Washingtonians. Open 24 hours on Friday and Saturday, and late at night during the week, this is the perfect place to wind down after a long night. The dinner menu offers classic American dishes from bacon cheeseburgers to crab-cake sandwiches and decadent home-made cakes and pies.

Once known as a popular gay hangout, **Annie's Paramount Steak House** (✉ 1609 17th St. NW ☎ 202/232-0395 Ⓜ Dupont Circle) now attracts a more varied crowd. Anyone who craves steak and eggs in the middle of the night will appreciate this reliable and relatively cheap steak house, open 24 hours on Friday and Saturday.

GEORGETOWN

After a night of hobnobbing with politicos, stop in at **Five Guys Famous Burger and Fries** (✉ 1335 Wisconsin Ave., NW ☎ 202/337-0400 Ⓜ Foggy Bottom). It's famous for a reason—their award-winning ground-beef burgers with all the fixings and crispy, twice-fried fries hit the spot. If you're going to fill up on the free peanuts, make sure to select the "little" burger, which is one patty instead of the usual two.

Amid all the hubbub of Georgetown's M Street is **Mon Cheri Café** (✉ 3015 M St., NW 20007 ☎ 202/338-2745 Ⓜ Foggy Bottom), a sandwich-to-go shop. What it lacks in ambience, it makes up for in the food. Serving everything from burgers to gyros to cheesesteaks, this unpretentious café is a nice departure from its somewhat haughty surroundings.

The name says it all at Georgetown's **Bistro Français** (✉ 3128 M St. NW ☎ 202/338-3830 Ⓜ Foggy Bottom), where you can expect straightforward French fare. Open until 3 AM Tuesday through Thursday and until 4 AM Friday through Sunday, this neighborhood landmark is where many local chefs relax when they're finished cooking.

–Carolyn Galgano

such as Wyclef Jean and Alicia Keys. ■TIP→Shuttle service is available from 18th and M streets, a boon, considering Love's isolated, industrial locale. ⊠*1350 Okie St. NE, Northeast* ☎*202/636–9030* ⊕*www. lovetheclub.com*

Modern. A small, underground club with lowered bar and high-backed booths, Modern is cozy and familiar. The DJs spin songs you know, from Madonna to Outkast, and the crowd dresses up to match the swank surroundings. ⊠*3287 M St. NW, Georgetown* ☎*202/338–7027.*

Platinum. This upscale dance venue has retained the columns, grand staircase, and high ceilings from its previous life as a bank. The DJs play techno, hip-hop, house, and Latin music for three dance floors and a VIP lounge. ⊠*915 F St. NW, Downtown* ☎*202/393–3555* ⊕*www. platinumclubdc.com* Ⓜ*Metro Center.*

Ultrabar. Relatively intimate, this bar offers a fun and luxurious environment. The club offers the metallic interior of Croma, a VIP room, warm wood paneling in the Bedroom, andspectacular lasers on the Main Floor, with multiple dance floors featuring hip-hop, Latin, and international music. ⊠*911 F St. NW, Downtown* ☎*202/638–4663* ⊕*www.platinumclubdc.com* Ⓜ *Metro Center.*

GAY & LESBIAN DANCE CLUBS

Apex. At this prime hot spot for gay men, a light show, mirrors, and fog enhance the experience on the dance floor. It's a bit easier to get a drink at the upstairs bar. A room in the back shows '80s music videos. A long-time fixture on the P St corridor, the club was formerly known as Badlands. There's less attitude here than at larger clubs. ⊠*1415 22nd St. NW, Dupont Circle* ☎*202/296–0505* ⊕*www.apex-dc.com* Ⓜ*Dupont Circle.*

Chaos. It's hard to miss this subterranean club on Friday and Saturday, with its strobe lights and thumping music. A young, chic lesbian crowd takes over on Wednesday, and Thursday is Latin night. Tuesday means drag bingo—a favorite of gays and straights alike. ⊠*1603 17th St. NW, Dupont Circle* ☎*202/232–4141* ⊕*www.chaosdc.com* Ⓜ*Dupont Circle.*

Cobalt. Stop for a martini in the swank second-floor 30 Degrees lounge before heading upstairs to the dance floor. The Tuesday night "Flashback" parties are always fun, although most of the songs are older than the twentysomethings who pack the place. Management cautions that the bar attracts a wild, younger crowd, saying the place is not meant to be a neighborhood bar for quiet conversation; weekend parties are known to be wild. ⊠*1639 R St. NW, Dupont Circle* ☎*202/462–6569* ⊕*www.cobaltdc.com* Ⓜ*Dupont Circle.*

Remington's. Country-western dancing is all the rage at this cavernous club on Capitol Hill. Check out the "dance floor etiquette" online in advance. On Sunday there are dance lessons from 5 to 7 and a women's tea dance from 5 to 9:30. ⊠*639 Pennsylvania Ave. SE, Capitol Hill* ☎*202/543–3113* ⊕*www.remingtonswdc.com* Ⓜ*Eastern Market.*

8

COMEDY CLUBS

With perhaps the richest of all subjects to mine—the machinations of government and those who try to run it—D.C.'s political satirists thrive. Jon Stewart's a Johnny-come-lately in this town. Countless open-mike nights in bars all over town even let Hill staffers lampoon themselves. But Washington is a one-horse town: few top stand-up acts visit, but those who do come to the Improv.

Capitol Steps. Putting the "mock" in democracy, the musical political satire of this group of current and former Hill staffers is presented in the amphitheater of the Trade Center every Friday and Saturday at 7:30 PM and occasionally at other spots around town. Ronald Reagan was said to have been a big fan of the Steps, who remain one of D.C.'s favorite groups. Tickets are available through Ticketmaster. ⊠ *Ronald Reagan Bldg. and International Trade Center, 1300 Pennsylvania Ave. NW, Downtown* ☎ *703/683–8330* ⊕ *www.capsteps.com* Ⓜ *Federal Triangle.*

↻ **ComedySportz.** Located south of D.C. in the Ballston Commons Mall, two teams of comedians compete in this skit-based improv competition Thursday, Friday, and Saturday nights. There is an early family show where no obscenities are allowed and a late-night adults-only show with more mature material on Friday and Saturday. ⊠ *Ballston Common Mall, 4238 Wilson Blvd., Arlington, VA* ☎ *703/294–5233* ⊕ *www.cszdc.com* Ⓜ *Ballston.*

DC Improv. Most comedy clubs have bitten the dust in D.C., but the Improv, as everyone calls it, continues to offer a steady menu of well-known and promising stand-up headliners. Recent acts have included Kevin Nealon, Colin Quinn, and a bevy of funny amateurs. ⊠ *1140 Connecticut Ave. NW, Downtown* ☎ *202/296–7008* ⊕ *www.dcimprov.com* Ⓜ *Farragut N.*

Gross National Product. This nonpartisan comedy troupe has been aiming its barbs at sitting presidents for years. Past shows include *Clintoons, All the President's Women,* and *Son of a Bush.* GNP's "Scandal Tours" offer a cross-city look at Washington's low points. ☎ *202/783–7212* ⊕ *www.gnpcomedy.com.*

Washington Improv Theater (WIT). Refreshingly, WIT doesn't focus on Beltway politics, instead relying heavily on audience suggestions. Their smart, irreverent humor is performed to sell-out crowds at the black-box theater of Flashpoint in Chinatown. The troupes Improv Nation and Jackie also fall under WIT's umbrella. ⊠ *Flashpoint, 916 G St. NW, Chinatown* ☎ *202/315–1315* ⊕ *www.dcwit.com.*

The Performing Arts

Yo Yo Ma with the Baltimore Symphony Orchestra

WORD OF MOUTH

"Note that the Kennedy Center has a free concert on its Millennium Stage every night of the year at 6:00 PM—check their website to see what's playing when you are there, and get there 5:30-5:45 if you want a seat. Afterward, you might enjoy walking around/ grabbing a bite to eat in Georgetown; the waterfront area is very lively if it is warm."

—MoonGirl

PERFORMING ARTS PLANNER

Tickets: The Standard Sources

Tickets to most events are available by calling or visiting the venue's box office or through the following ticket agencies:**Ticketmaster** (☎ 202/397–7328, 703/573–7328, or 410/547–7328 ⊕ www.ticketmaster.com) sells tickets for events at most venues. You can buy by phone, on the Web, or in person at Macy's department stores and the D.C. Visitor Information Center. **Tickets.com** (☎ 800/955–5566 ⊕ www.tickets.com) takes online reservations for a number of events around town and has outlets in some Olsson's Books & Records.

Tickets: On the Cheap

TICKETplace (✉ Old Post Office Pavilion, 407 7th St. NW, Downtown ☎ 202/842–5387 ⊕ www.ticketplace.org Ⓜ Archives/Navy Memorial) sells half-price, day-of-performance tickets for select shows. They don't operate on Sunday or Monday; tickets for events on those days are sold at the booth on Saturday. The service charge is 12% at the booth and 17% online.

Find Out What's Happening

To sift through the flurry of events, check out these resources:
■ The daily "Guide to the Lively Arts" and the Friday "Weekend" sections in the *Washington Post*
■ The Thursday *Washington Times* "Washington Weekend" section
■ The free weekly *Washington CityPaper* (⊕ www.washingtoncitypaper.com), published on Thursday
■ The "City Lights" section in the monthly *Washingtonian* magazine
■ Online, the *Post* (⊕ www.washingtonpost.com/cityguide), *Times* (⊕ www.washingtontimes.com/activityguide), and *Washingtonian* (⊕ www.washingtonian.com/inwashington) all publish entertainment guides. Two of D.C.'s most popular local blogs, DCist (⊕ www.dcist.com) and Free Ride (⊕ www.readexpress.com/freeride.php), post daily on D.C. events

Free Events

The abundance of freebies in Washington extends to the arts. Highlights among the no-charge events include:
■ The Shakespeare Theatre Free for All, a two-week run of performances every June
■ The Millennium Stage at the Kennedy Center, where there are free performances daily at 6 PM
■ The National Cathedral, which hosts frequent concerts
■ Screen on the Green, a showing of classic films on the Mall every Monday in July and August
■ The National Academy of Sciences, which shows off its acoustically advanced auditorium with concerts of chamber music on Sunday afternoons from fall through spring
■ The Fort Dupont Summer Theater's jazz series Saturday nights in July and August

Updated by
Mitchell Tropin

In the past 40 years D.C. has gone from being a cultural desert to a thriving arts center. The arts scene has exploded to meet the demands of educated young professionals who flock here for opportunities in government. Visitors have the opportunity to view incredible theater, music, and dance in fresh, dynamic facilities. When you include the old steadfasts—the Kennedy Center, the Washington National Opera, and the National Theatre—it's clear that Washington's arts scene is now a major draw of talent on the East Coast and one of the top reasons to visit.

PERFORMANCE VENUES

9

Though most of the very best out-of-town performers flock to the Kennedy Center or the Verizon Center, Washington is also peppered with dozens of small and medium-size venues. Performance halls tend to showcase musicians, but there's no shortage of dance and theater troupes, or stand-up comedians. Don't go looking for a theater district: the venues are spread across town and in the Maryland and Virginia suburbs.

Atlas Performing Arts Center. Known as the "People's Kennedy Center," this relatively new performance venue is community-based, encompassing four theaters and three dance studios. Located in a restored historic movie theater, the Atlas presents performances by the dance troupe Joy of Motion, the light opera company Washington Savoyards, the African Continuum Theatre, and the Capital City Symphony. Atlas is not Metro-accessible; the nearest cab stand is at Union Station, where a free shuttle bus also runs on Friday and Saturday nights. Parking is available on the street. ⊠ *1333 H St. NE, Northeast* ☎ *202/399–7993* ⊕ *www.atlasarts.org.*

Five Great Arts Experiences

■ **Kennedy Center:** The gem of the D.C. arts scene, this is the one performance venue you would take with you if you were stranded on a desert isle.

■ **National Gallery of Art garden concerts:** These are classy events where you're actually encouraged to take off your shoes.

■ **Screen on the Green:** Not even your neighbor the lobbyist (or the neighborhood multiplex) has a screen this big.

■ **Shakespeare Theatre:** Among the top Shakespeare companies in the world, this troupe excels at both classical and contemporary interpretations.

■ **Woolly Mammoth:** This remarkable theater company stages some of the most creative and entertaining new plays from the nation's best playwrights.

Center for the Arts. This state-of-the-art performance complex on the suburban Virginia campus of George Mason University satisfies music, ballet, and drama patrons with regular performances in its 1,900-seat concert hall, the 500-seat proscenium Harris Theater, and the intimate 150-seat black-box Theater of the First Amendment. The 9,500-seat Patriot Center, site of pop acts and sporting events, is also on campus. ⊠*Rte. 123 and Braddock Rd., Fairfax, VA* ☎*888/945–2468* ⊕*www. gmu.edu/cfa.*

Clarice Smith Performing Arts Center at Maryland. The 17-acre center, on the College Park campus of the University of Maryland, presents a wide range of music, dance, and drama in half a dozen striking but cozy venues. Shuttle service to the center is available at the College Park Metro station during the academic year. ⊠*University Blvd. and Stadium Dr., College Park, MD* ☎*301/405–2787* ⊕*www.claricesmithcenter.umd. edu* Ⓜ*College Park.*

DAR Constitution Hall. Acts ranging from Jamie Foxx to Clay Aiken to B. B. King perform at this 3,700-seat venue, one of Washington's grand old halls. ⊠*1776 D St. NW, Downtown* ☎*202/628–4780* ⊕*www. dar.org/conthall* Ⓜ*Farragut West.*

D.C. Jewish Community Center. The DCJCC hosts the Washington Jewish Music Festival and the Washington Jewish Film Festival, along with periodic musical performances by groups such as the Arab-Israeli Orchestra of Nazareth. The JCC is also the home of Theatre J. ⊠*1529 16th St. NW, Downtown* ☎*202/518–9400* ⊕*www.washingtondcjcc. org* Ⓜ*Dupont Circle.*

FodorsChoice
★ **John F. Kennedy Center for the Performing Arts.** On the bank of the Potomac River, the gem of the D.C. arts scene is home to the National Symphony Orchestra, the Washington Ballet, and the Washington National Opera. The best out-of-town acts perform at one of three performance spaces—the Concert Hall, the Opera House, or the Eisenhower Theater. Eclectic performers can be found at the Center's smaller venues, including the Terrace Theater, showcasing chamber groups and experimental works; the Theater Lab, home to cabaret-style performances like the

audience-participation hit *Sheer Madness*; the KC Jazz Club; and a 320-seat family theater. But that's not all. On the Millennium Stage in the center's Grand Foyer you can catch free performances almost any day at 6 PM. ■TIP➔On performance days, a free shuttle bus runs between the Center and the Foggy Bottom/GWU Metro stop. ⊠*New Hampshire Ave. and Rock Creek Pkwy. NW, Foggy Bottom* ☎*202/467–4600 or 800/444–1324* ⊕*www.kennedy-center.org* Ⓜ*Foggy Bottom/GWU.*

Lisner Auditorium. A 1,500-seat theater on the campus of George Washington University in downtown D.C., Lisner hosts pop, classical, and choral music shows, modern dance performances, and musical theater. ⊠*730 21st St. NW, Foggy Bottom* ☎*202/994–6800* ⊕*www.lisner.org* Ⓜ*Foggy Bottom/GWU.*

FodorŚChoice **Music Center at Strathmore.** Located ½ mi outside the Capital Beltway
★ in North Bethesda, this concert hall receives praise for its acoustics and its audience-friendly design. Major national folk, blues, pop, jazz, Broadway, and classical artists perform here. The center is home to the Baltimore Symphony Orchestra and the National Philharmonic. More-intimate performances are held in the 100-seat Dorothy M. and Maurice C. Shapiro Music Room. ■TIP➔Consider taking the Metro to Strathmore; the center is less than a block from the Grosvenor Metro station. ⊠*5301 Tuckerman La., North Bethesda* ☎*301/581–5200* ⊕*www.strathmore.org* Ⓜ*Grosvenor/Strathmore.*

★ **National Gallery of Art.** Since 1942 the National Gallery has offered a variety of music. On Friday from Memorial Day through Labor Day, local jazz groups perform from 5 to 9 PM to a packed sculpture garden. Loyal listeners dip their weary feet in the fountain, sip sangria, and let their week wash away. From October to June, free concerts by the National Gallery Orchestra and performances by visiting recitalists and ensembles are held in the West Building's West Garden Court on Sunday nights. Entry is first-come, first-served, with doors opening at 6 PM and concerts starting at 6:30 PM. ⊠*6th St. and Constitution Ave. NW, The Mall* ☎*202/737–4215* ⊕*www.nga.gov* Ⓜ*Archives/ Navy Memorial.*

9

Smithsonian Institution. Jazz, musical theater, and popular standards are performed in the National Museum of American History. In the museum's third-floor Hall of Musical Instruments, musicians occasionally play period instruments from the museum's collection. The Smithsonian's annual Folklife Festival, held on the Mall, highlights the cuisine, crafts, and day-to-day life of several different cultures. The Smithsonian Associates sponsor programs that offer everything from a cappella groups to Cajun Zydeco bands; all events require tickets, and locations vary. ⊠*1000 Jefferson Dr. SW, The Mall* ☎*202/357–2700, 202/633-1000 recording, 202/357–3030 Smithsonian Associates* ⊕*www. si.edu* Ⓜ*Smithsonian.*

> **WORD OF MOUTH**
>
> "Each summer the Smithsonian sponsors a folklife festival which features the food, music, dance, history, culture, etc. of several countries/states/groups. . . . I haven't been to the festival in years, but as both a Texan and a space nut, I'll have to head over this summer!"
>
> —longhorn55

Verizon Center. In addition to being the home of the Washington Capitals hockey and Washington Wizards basketball teams, this 19,000-seat arena also plays host to D.C.'s biggest concerts, ice-skating events, and the circus. Parking can be a problem, but several Metro lines converge at an adjacent station. ⊠ *601 F St. NW, Chinatown* ☎ *202/661–5000* ⊕ *www.verizoncenter.com* Ⓜ *Gallery Place/Chinatown.*

Wolf Trap National Park for the Performing Arts. Wolf Trap is the only national park dedicated to the performing arts. June through September, the massive, outdoor Filene Center hosts close to 100 performances, ranging from pop and jazz concerts to dance and musical theater productions. In summer, the National Symphony Orchestra is based here, and the Children's Theatre-in-the-Woods delivers 70 free performances. During the colder months, the intimate, indoor Barns at Wolf Trap fill with the sounds of musicians playing folk, country, and chamber music, along with myriad other styles. The park is just off the Dulles Toll Road, about 20 mi from downtown. ■ TIP➔**When the Filene Center hosts an event, Metrorail operates a $5 round-trip shuttle bus—exact change only—from the West Falls Church Metro station. The bus leaves 20 minutes after the show or no later than 11 PM, whether the show is over or not.** ⊠ *1645 Trap Rd., Vienna, VA* ☎ *703/255–1900, 703/938–2404 Barns at Wolf Trap* ⊕ *www.wolftrap.org* Ⓜ *Vienna.*

MUSIC

With dozens of acoustically superior venues and majestic backdrops around town, D.C. sets a lofty stage for its musicians, who have the talent to match. Whether it's the four armed services bands marching in the footsteps of John Philip Sousa, opera singers performing under the direction of Plácido Domingo, or chamber players performing Renaissance pieces on period instruments, this city's musicians consistently lay down a fitting soundtrack.

CHAMBER MUSIC

Coolidge Auditorium at the Library of Congress. Over the past 81 years the Coolidge has hosted most of the 20th-century's greatest performers and composers, including Copland and Stravinsky. Today it draws musicians from all genres, including classical, jazz, and gospel, and it continues to wow audiences with its near-perfect acoustics and sightlines. ⊠ *Library of Congress, Jefferson Bldg., 101 Independence Ave. SE, Capitol Hill* ☎ *800/551–7328* ⊕ *www.loc.gov* Ⓜ *Capitol South.*

Corcoran Gallery of Art. Hungary's Takács String Quartet and the Klavier Trio Amsterdam are among the chamber groups that have appeared in the Corcoran's Musical Evening Series, held one night each month from October to May and periodically in summer. ■ TIP➔**Concerts are followed by a reception with the artists.** ⊠ *500 17th St. NW, Downtown* ☎ *202/639–1700* ⊕ *www.corcoran.org* Ⓜ *Farragut West.*

Dumbarton Concerts. Dumbarton United Methodist Church, a fixture in Georgetown since 1772 (in its current location since 1850), sponsors this concert series, which has been host to musicians such as the

American Chamber Players, the St. Petersburg String Quartet, and the Thibaud String Trio. ✉*Dumbarton United Methodist Church, 3133 Dumbarton Ave. NW, Georgetown* ☎*202/965–2000* ⊕*www.dumbartonconcerts.org* Ⓜ*Foggy Bottom.*

Folger Shakespeare Library. The library's internationally acclaimed resident chamber music ensemble, the Folger Consort, regularly presents medieval, Renaissance, and baroque pieces performed on period instruments. The season runs from October to May. ✉*201 E. Capitol St. SE, Capitol Hill* ☎*202/544–7077* ⊕*www.folger.edu* Ⓜ*Union Station or Capitol South.*

National Academy of Sciences. Free Sunday afternoon performances are given fall through spring in the academy's 670-seat auditorium. ✉*2100 C St. NW, Downtown* ☎*202/334–2436* ⊕*www.nationalacademies. org/arts* Ⓜ*Foggy Bottom/GWU.*

Phillips Collection. Duncan Phillips's mansion is more than an art museum. On Sunday afternoons from October through May, chamber groups from around the world perform in its long, dark-paneled Music Room. ■TIP➡**Concerts begin at 4 PM; arrive early for decent seats.** ✉*1600 21st St. NW, Dupont Circle* ☎*202/387–2151* ⊕*www. phillipscollection.org* Ⓜ*Dupont Circle.*

CHORAL MUSIC

Basilica of the National Shrine of the Immaculate Conception. Choral and church groups occasionally perform at the largest Catholic church in the Americas. ✉*400 Michigan Ave. NE, Catholic University* ☎*202/526–8300* ⊕*www.nationalshrine.com* Ⓜ*Brookland/CUA.*

Choral Arts Society of Washington. The 200-voice Choral Arts Society choir performs a variety of classical pieces at the Kennedy Center from fall to spring. Three Christmas sing-alongs are scheduled each December, along with a popular tribute to Martin Luther King Jr. on his birthday. ☎*202/244–3669* ⊕*www.choralarts.org.*

Washington National Cathedral. Choral and church groups frequently perform in this grand church. Admission is usually free. ✉*Massachusetts and Wisconsin Aves. NW, Cleveland Park* ☎*202/537–6207* ⊕*www. cathedral.org/cathedral* Ⓜ*Tenleytown/AU.*

> **WORD OF MOUTH**
>
> "A concert at the National Cathedral is enthralling and magnificent. On the 4th of July we went to the organ concert there—it was spectacular (and free!) . . . we also attended *The Messiah* last December, which was thrilling (but not free)."
>
> –vivi

OPERA

The *Washington Post* "Weekend" section is a good source for information on opera and classical performances.

In Series. Trademark cabaret, experimental chamber opera, and Spanish musical theater (also known as *zarzuela*) are among the hallmarks of this burgeoning nonprofit company, which performs at venues around the city. ☎*202/518–0152* ⊕*www.inseries.org*.

☾ **Opera Theatre of Northern Virginia.** Four times a year this company stages an opera at an Arlington community theater. The winter production is geared to young audiences. ☎*703/528–1433* ⊕*www.novaopera.org*.

Summer Opera Theater Company. An independent professional troupe, the Summer Opera Theater Company stages one opera in June and one in July. ⊠*Hartke Theater, 3801 Harewood Rd. NE, Catholic University* ☎*202/319–4000* ⊕*www.summeropera.org* Ⓜ*Brookland/CUA*.

Fodor'sChoice **Washington National Opera.** Under the directorship of Plácido Domingo,
★ the Washington National Opera presents eight operas in the fall and spring at the Kennedy Center Opera House. The operas, presented in their original languages with English supertitles, are often sold out to subscribers, but you can purchase returned tickets an hour before curtain time. ∎TIP➔For standing-room tickets to each week's performances, inquire at the box office starting the preceding Saturday. ☎*202/295–2400 or 800/876–7372* ⊕*www.dc-opera.org*.

ORCHESTRAS

Baltimore Symphony Orchestra. When the 2,000-seat Music Center at Strathmore opened in 2005, the world-renowned Baltimore Symphony Orchestra relocated to the Greater Washington area. It now performs year-round at the center, a half-mile outside the Beltway in North Bethesda. The nearest Metro station is less than a block away. ⊠*5301 Tuckerman La., North Bethesda* ☎*877/276–1444* ⊕*www. bsoatstrathmore.org* Ⓜ*Grosvenor/Strathmore*.

National Symphony Orchestra. Under the direction of Leonard Slatkin, the NSO performs from September to June at the Kennedy Center Concert Hall. In summer the NSO performs at Wolf Trap and gives free concerts at Rock Creek Park's Carter Barron Amphitheatre. On Memorial and Labor Day weekends and July 4, the orchestra performs on the West Lawn of the Capitol. ⊠*New Hampshire Ave. and Rock Creek Pkwy. NW, Foggy Bottom* ☎*202/462–4600* ⊕*www.kennedy-center.org/nso*.

PERFORMANCE SERIES

Armed Forces Concert Series. From June to August, bands from the four armed services perform Monday, Tuesday, Wednesday, and Friday evenings on the East Terrace of the Capitol. Other performances occur at 8 PM from June to August, on Tuesday, Thursday, Friday, and Sunday nights at the **Sylvan Theater** (⊠*Washington Monument grounds, 14th St. and Constitution Ave., The Mall* ☎*202/426–6841* Ⓜ*Smithsonian*). Concerts usually include marches, patriotic numbers, and some classical music. The Air Force celebrity series features popular artists such as Earl Klugh and Keiko Matsui on Sundays in February and March at DAR Constitutional Hall. ☎*202/767–5658 Air Force, 703/696–3718 Army, 202/433–4011 Marines, 202/433–2525 Navy*.

Carter Barron Amphitheatre. On Saturday and Sunday nights from June to September this 3,750-seat outdoor theater hosts pop, jazz, gospel, and rhythm-and-blues artists such as Chick Corea and Nancy Wilson. The National Symphony Orchestra also performs here, and for two weeks the Shakespeare Theatre presents a free play. ⊠*Rock Creek Park, 4850 Colorado Ave. NW, Upper Northwest* ☎*202/426–0486* ⊕*www.nps. gov/rocr/cbarron.htm.*

Fort Dupont Summer Theater. The National Park Service presents national and international jazz artists at 8 PM on Saturday evenings from July to August at the outdoor Fort Dupont Summer Theater. Wynton Marsalis, Shirley Horne, and Ramsey Lewis are among the artists who have performed free concerts here. ⊠*Minnesota Ave. and Randall Circle SE, Southeast* ☎*202/426–5961* ⊕*www.nps.gov/fodu.*

Institute of Musical Traditions. Emerging, near-famous, and celebrated folk performers such as Si Kahn, John McCutcheon, and the Kennedys, perform at the Institute's concerts, most often held at the St. Mark Presbyterian Church. ⊠*10701 Old Georgetown Rd., Rockville, MD* ☎*301/754–3611* ⊕*www.imtfolk.org.*

Transparent Productions. Composed of a small group of dedicated jazz connoisseurs, this nonprofit organization regularly brings acclaimed avant-garde jazz musicians to intimate clubs and university stages. Past performers have included the Ethnic Heritage Ensemble, bassist William Parker, and saxophonist Steve Coleman. ■ TIP→**Tickets are usually in the $10 range, and all proceeds go directly to the artists.** ☎*No phone* ⊕*www.transparentproductions.org.*

Washington Performing Arts Society. This nonprofit organization books high-quality classical music, jazz, gospel, modern dance, and performance art into halls around the city. Past artists include the Alvin Ailey American Dance Theater, Yo-Yo Ma, the Chieftains, Sweet Honey in the Rock, and Cecilia Bartoli. ☎*202/833–9800* ⊕*www.wpas.org.*

THEATER & PERFORMANCE ART

Perhaps as a counterbalance to all the political theater in town, D.C.'s playhouses, large and small, have grown into a force to be reckoned with over the past few years. Nearly every major theater in town has recently renovated its performance spaces or is in the process of doing so, and new small theaters are popping up all the time. If all that weren't enough, D.C. often hosts some of the best touring companies from the East Coast and beyond.

LARGE THEATERS

★ **Arena Stage.** The first regional theater company to win a Tony Award, Arena Stage performs mainly American theater, reviving some classic plays and showcasing the country's best new writers. While its historic waterfront location undergoes a $120 million renovation, Arena Stage will hold its performances a few miles south in Crystal City at the Crystal Forum. Toward the end of 2009 the Arena plans to return to its home in Southwest D.C. ✉*1800 S. Bell St., Crystal City* ☎*202/488–3300* ⊕*www.arenastage.org* Ⓜ*Crystal City* .

☾ **Ford's Theatre.** Looking much as it did when President Lincoln was shot at a performance of *Our American Cousin*, Ford's primarily hosts patriotic musicals, most with family appeal. Dickens's *A Christmas Carol* is staged every year. The theater is now maintained by the National Park Service, which has spent $8.5 million to make it more comfortable for audiences. ✉*511 10th St. NW, Downtown* ☎*202/426–6925* ⊕*www.fordstheatre.org* Ⓜ*Metro Center*.

Lincoln Theatre. Once the host of such notable black performers as Cab Calloway, Lena Horne, and Duke Ellington, the 1,250-seat Lincoln is part of the revitalized and lively U Street corridor. It presents movies, comedy shows, and musical performers such as Harry Belafonte, the Count Basie Orchestra, and the Harlem Boys and Girls Choir. ✉*1215 U St. NW, U Street corridor* ☎*202/328–6000* ⊕*www.thelincolntheatre.org* Ⓜ*U Street/Cardozo*.

☾ **National Theatre.** Though once destroyed by fire and rebuilt several times, the National Theatre has operated in the same location since 1835. It now hosts touring Broadway shows, such as *Spamalot* and *Movin' Out*. ■TIP→**From September through April, look for free children's shows Saturday morning and free Monday night shows that may include Asian dance, performance art, and a cappella cabarets.** ✉*1321 Pennsylvania Ave. NW, Downtown* ☎*202/783–3372* ⊕*www.nationaltheatre.org* Ⓜ*Metro Center*.

Fodor'sChoice **Shakespeare Theatre.** This acclaimed troupe, known as one of the world's
★ three great Shakespearean companies, crafts fantastically staged and acted performances of works by Shakespeare and his contemporaries. The theatre has undergone an amazing transformation. Complimenting the existing stage in the Lansburgh Theatre is the Sidney Harman Hall, which opened in October 2007. The new stage provides a 21st-century, state-of-the-art, mid-sized venue for an outstanding variety of performances, from Shakespeare's Julius Caesar to the hilarious Abridged History of America. For two weeks in late spring they perform Shakespeare for free at Carter Barron Amphitheatre. ✉*450 7th St. NW, Downtown* ☎*202/547–1122* ⊕*www.shakespearedc.org* Ⓜ*Gallery Pl./Chinatown or Archives/Navy Memorial*.

Warner Theatre. One of Washington's grand theaters, the Warner hosts road shows, dance recitals, pop music, and the occasional comedy act in its majestic art deco performance space. ✉*513 13th St. NW, Downtown* ☎*202/783–4000* ⊕*www.warnertheatre.com* Ⓜ*Metro Center*.

SMALL THEATERS & COMPANIES

Often performing in churches and other less-than-ideal settings, Washington's small companies present drama that can be every bit as enthralling as—and often more daring than—that offered by their blockbuster counterparts. No matter the size, all companies in town compete fiercely for the Helen Hayes Award, Washington's version of the Tony.

American Century Theatre. Devoted to staging overlooked or forgotten classic American plays, American Century has staged performances of Kurt Vonnegut's *Happy Birthday, Wanda June,* Orson Wells's *Moby Dick Rehearsed,* and even a rare Mel Brooks' production, *Archy and Mehitabel.* ✉*2700 Lang St., Arlington* ☎*703/998-4555* ⊕*www. americancentury.org*

District of Columbia Arts Center. Known by area artists as DCAC, this cross-genre space shows changing exhibits in its gallery and presents avant-garde performance art, improv, and experimental plays in its tiny black-box theater. ✉*2438 18th St. NW, Adams-Morgan* ☎*202/462–7833* ⊕*www.dcartscenter.org.*

Folger Shakespeare Library. The library's theater, a 250-seat re-creation of the inn-yard theaters with seating in the balcony popular in Shakespeare's time, hosts three to four productions a year of Shakespeare or Shakespeare-influenced works. Though the stage is a throwback, the sharp acting and staging certainly push the envelope. ✉*201 E. Capitol St. SE, Capitol Hill* ☎*202/544–7077* ⊕*www.folger.edu* Ⓜ*Union Station or Capitol S.*

Gala Hispanic Theatre. This company attracts outstanding Hispanic actors from around the world, performing works by leading Latino playwrights, such as Federico García Lorca and Mario Vargas Llosa. Plays are presented in English or in Spanish with instant English translations supplied through earphones. The company performs in the newly renovated Tivoli Theatre in Columbia Heights, a hot spot for Latino culture and cuisine. ✉*Tivoli Sq., 3333 14th St. NW, 14th and Park Rd., Columbia Heights* ☎*202/234–7174* ⊕*www.galatheatre.org* Ⓜ*Columbia Heights.*

☾ **Glen Echo Park.** The National Park Service has transformed this former amusement park into a thriving arts center. Every weekend the Adventure Theater puts on traditional plays and musicals aimed at children ages four and up. Families can spread out on carpeted steps. At the Puppet Company Playhouse, skilled puppeteers perform classic stories Wednesday through Sunday. ✉*7300 MacArthur Blvd., Glen Echo, MD* ☎*301/634–2222, 301/320–5331 Adventure Theater, 301/320–6668 Puppet Co.* ⊕*www.glenechopark.org.*

☾ **Imagination Stage.** Shows like Roald Dahl's classic story *The BFG,* and original fare such as Karen Zacarias and Deborah Wicks LaPuma's *Cinderella Likes Rice and Beans* are produced here for children ages four and up. The state-of-the-art center in Bethesda includes two theaters and a digital media studio. Make reservations in advance. ✉*4908 Auburn Ave., Bethesda, MD* ☎*301/961–6060* ⊕*www.imagination stage.org.*

Rorschach Theatre. A newcomer on the D.C. theatre scene, Rorschach stages some of the most creative plays in Washington, featuring intimate and passionate performances. The company offers lesser-known works by *Angels in America's* Tony Kusher and Russia's Mikhail Bulgakov, as well as stage adaptations of literary classics such as *Lord of the Flies.* ✉*1421 Columbia Road, Columbia Heights* ☎*202/452–5538* ⊕*www.rorschachtheatre.com* Ⓜ*Columbia Heights*

Round House Theatre. Each season on its Main Stage in Bethesda, Round House presents an eclectic body of work ranging from world premieres to great 20th-century works to contemporary adaptations of the classics. Round House's 150-seat black-box stage, home to more experimental works, is in Silver Spring, adjacent to the American Film Silver Theatre & Cultural Center. ✉*4545 East–West Hwy., Bethesda, MD* ☎*240/644–1099* ⊕*www.round-house.org* Ⓜ*Bethesda* ✉*8641 Colesville Rd., Silver Spring, MD* ☎*240/644–1099* Ⓜ*Silver Spring.*

Signature Theatre. Led by artistic director Eric Schaeffer, Signature has earned national acclaim for its presentation of contemporary plays and groundbreaking American musicals, especially those of Stephen Sondheim. In early 2007 the company moved into a dramatic new facility in Arlington, Virginia, with two performance spaces, the 299-seat MAX and the 99-seat ARK. ✉*2800 S. Stafford St., Arlington, VA* ☎*703/820–9771* ⊕*www.sig-online.org.*

★ **Studio Theatre.** One of the busiest groups in the city, this independent company produces an eclectic season of classic and offbeat plays in four spaces: the original Mead and Milton theaters, the newer 200-seat Metheny Theatre, and the experimental Stage 4. The theatre is part of the revitalized 14th Street corridor. ✉*1333 P St. NW, Dupont Circle* ☎*202/332–3300* ⊕*www.studiotheatre.org* Ⓜ*Dupont Circle.*

Theater J. In recent years Theater J has emerged as one of the country's most distinctive and progressive Jewish performance venues, offering an ambitious range of programming that includes work by noted playwrights, directors, designers, and actors. Performances take place in the Aaron and Cecile Goldman Theater at the D.C. Jewish Community Center (DCJCC). ✉*1529 16th St. NW, Downtown* ☎*202/518–9400* Ⓜ*Dupont Circle.*

Washington Stage Guild. This company performs neglected classics and foreign plays at its new beautiful and intimate venue, offering lesser-known works by Oscar Wilde and George Bernard Shaw, such as *Don Juan in Hell* and *Lord Arthur Savile's Crime*. The Guild also stages selections from the Lady Gregory plays, hilarious slices of Irish life that presage Yates and Beckett. George Bernard Shaw is a specialty. ✉ *E St. and Eighth Ave. NW, Penn Quarter* ☎*240/582–0050* ⊕*www. stageguild.org* Ⓜ*Gallery Pl./Chinatown or Archives/Navy Memorial.*

Fodor's Choice
★ **Woolly Mammoth.** Unusual avant-garde shows with edgy staging and solid acting have earned Woolly Mammoth top reviews and favorable comparisons to Chicago's Steppenwolf. The troupe's talent is accentuated by its new, modern, 265-seat theater in Penn Quarter near the MCI Center. ✉*641 D St. NW, Downtown* ☎*202/393–3939* ⊕*www.woollymammoth.net* Ⓜ*Gallery Pl./Chinatown or Archives/ Navy Memorial.*

DANCE

The solid performances of the Washington Ballet, generally considered one of the better troupes in the U.S., and those of smaller companies around town are complemented by frequent visits from some of the world's best companies, including the Kirov Ballet and the Alvin Ailey

American Dance Theater. Washington is also host to many festivals, and dance is often highlighted. The traditional Japanese dance featured during the Cherry Blossom Festival and the varied styles that come to town during the Smithsonian Folklife Festival are particular treats.

Dance Place. This studio theater showcases the best local dance talent in an assortment of modern and ethnic shows; performances take place most weekends. It also conducts dance classes daily. ⊠ *3225 8th St. NE, Catholic University* ☎ *202/269–1600* ⊕ *www.danceplace.org* Ⓜ *Catholic University.*

Joy of Motion. A dance studio by day, Joy of Motion is the home of several area troupes that perform in the studio's Jack Guidone Theatre, located in Northwest Washington. The resident Dana Tai Soon Burgess & Company (modern), CrossCurrents Dance Company (contemporary), and Silk Road Dance Company (traditional Middle Eastern and Central Asian) also perform at the Atlas Performing Arts Center, which is located on H Street in Northeast Washington. Two additional Joy of Motion studios in Dupont Circle and Bethesda offer classes only. ⊠ *5207 Wisconsin Ave. NW, Friendship Heights* ☎ *202/276–2599* ⊕ *www.joyofmotion.org* Ⓜ *Friendship Heights.*

★ **Washington Ballet.** Between September and May, this company presents classical and contemporary ballets, including works by choreographers such as George Balanchine, Choo-San Goh, and artistic director Septime Webre. Its main shows are mounted at the Kennedy Center. Each December the Washington Ballet performs *The Nutcracker* at the Warner Theatre. ☎ *202/362–3606* ⊕ *www.washingtonballet.org.*

FILM

D.C.'s countless foundations, embassies, national museums, and institutions offer the visiting cinephile an unexpected side benefit—quirky, long-forgotten, seldom-seen, and arcane films on as many topics as there are special interests.

Fodor$Choice **American Film Institute Silver Theatre and Cultural Center.** This three-screen,
★ state-of-the-art center for film is a restoration of architect John Eberson's art deco Silver Theatre, built in 1938. The AFI hosts film retrospectives, festivals, and tributes celebrating artists from Jeanne Moreau to Russell Crowe. The AFI Silver also hosts the annual Silver Docs festival, which features some of the world's best documentaries and appearances by some of the greatest filmmakers, such Martin Scorsese. ⊠ *8633 Colesville Rd., Silver Spring, MD* ☎ *301/495–6700* ⊕ *www. afi.com/silver* Ⓜ *Silver Spring.*

Arlington Cinema 'N' Drafthouse. The rules are relaxed at this second-run theater, where you can enjoy beer and nosh, like pizza and buffalo wings, while you watch yesterday's blockbuster. Smoking sections are provided for certain shows. Most matinee and early shows are totally no-smoking. The drafthouse also features stand-up comics, who perform on the old movie theater's stage. ∎**TIP→Minors (under 21) must be accompanied by a parent or guardian.** ⊠ *2903 Columbia Pike, Arlington, VA* ☎ *703/486–2345.*

9

Filmfest DC. An annual citywide festival of international cinema, the D.C. International Film Festival, or Filmfest, takes place in late April or early May at venues throughout the city. ☎202/628–3456 ⊕*www. filmfestdc.org.*

Hirshhorn Museum and Sculpture Garden. Avant-garde and experimental first-run documentaries, features, and short films are frequently screened here for free. ⊠*Independence Ave. and 7th St. SW, The Mall* ☎202/357–2700 ⊕*www.hirshhorn.si.edu* Ⓜ*Smithsonian or L'Enfant Plaza.*

Landmark's E Street Cinema. Specializing in independent, foreign, and documentary films, this theater has been warmly welcomed by D.C. movie lovers both for its selection and state-of-the-art facilities. Like its cousin in Bethesda, E Street has an impressive concession stand, stocked to please the gourmand, the health-conscious, and those who just want a jumbo box of Milk Duds. ⊠*555 11th St. NW, Downtown* ☎202/452–7672 Ⓜ*Metro Center.*

Loews Cineplex Uptown 1. Featuring the largest movie screen in town, the Uptown is a true movie palace with art deco flourishes; a wonderful balcony; and—in one happy concession to modernity—crystal-clear Dolby sound. It's home to Washington's biggest movie premieres. ⊠*3426 Connecticut Ave. NW, Cleveland Park* ☎202/966–5400 Ⓜ*Cleveland Park.*

National Archives. Historical films, usually documentaries, are shown here daily. Screenings range from the 1942 documentary by Robert Flaherty on the plight of migrant workers to archival footage of Charles Lindbergh's solo flight from New York to Paris. ⊠*Constitution Ave. between 7th and 9th Sts. NW, The Mall* ☎202/501–5000 ⊕*www. archives.gov* Ⓜ*Archives/Navy Memorial.*

National Gallery of Art, East Building. Free classic and international films, often complementing the exhibits, are shown in this museum's large auditorium. Pick up a film calendar at the museum or online. ⊠*Constitution Ave. between 3rd and 4th Sts. NW, The Mall* ☎202/842–6799 ⊕*www.nga.gov* Ⓜ*Archives/Navy Memorial.*

National Geographic Society. Documentary films with a scientific, geographic, or anthropological focus are shown regularly at National Geographic's Grosvenor Auditorium. ⊠*1600 M St., Dupont Circle* ☎202/857–7700 ⊕*www.nationalgeographic.com/nglive/washington* Ⓜ*Farragut North.*

★ **Screen on the Green.** Every July and August, this weekly series of classic films turns the Mall into an open-air cinema. People arrive as early as 5 PM to picnic, socialize, and reserve a spot. The show starts at dusk. ⊠*The Mall ✛at 7th St.* ☎877/262–5866 Ⓜ*Smithsonian.*

Sports & the Outdoors

Jogging along the mall with The Capitol in the distance

WORD OF MOUTH

"I second [visiting] the National Arboretum. My favorites are: the riverside park at the bottom of the Asian trail (just outside the fence) for a picnic; the overlooks in the dogwood areas; the Asia trail itself; the columns. The [Kenilworth] Aquatic Gardens (accessed off the Baltimore-Washington Parkway by car) are stunning in the month of July."

—bardo1

SPORTS & THE OUTDOORS PLANNER

Where the Pros Play

If you're going to a pro sports event, chances are you'll be headed to one of four venues. The perennially popular Redskins play football in the Maryland suburbs at **FedEx Field** (⊠*Arena Dr., Landover, MD*). The Redskins' home is the largest stadium in the National Football League, seating 91,000. Check the Washington Post want ads and Craig's List for tickets. Parking is a hassle, so arrive several hours early if you don't want to miss the kickoff.

Robert F. Kennedy Stadium (⊠*2400 E. Capitol St. NE, at 22nd St.,* M *Stadium*), the Redskins' former residence on Capitol Hill, is now home to Major League Soccer's D.C. United.

D.C.'s baseball team, the Nationals, play in the new spacious state-of-the-art ballpark, **Nationals Park** (⊠*1500 S. Capitol Street, SE,20003* M *Stadium*), on the Anacostia waterfront in Southwest Washington.

Verizon Center (⊠*601 F St. NW, between 6th and 7th Sts.,* M *Gallery Place/Chinatown*) hosts many sporting events, including hockey, basketball, and figure skating.

Five Great Outdoor Experiences

Visiting the pandas: The giant pandas at the National Zoo are quite simply the District's most beloved residents.

Picture-postcard motivation: Run or bike with Washington's monuments as a unique background.

Bird-watching on Theodore Roosevelt Island: Take in the spectacular scenery at the wildlife sanctuary.

One of Washington's loveliest places for a stroll: Walk through Dumbarton Oaks' many acres of distinctive gardens modeled after classic French, English, and Italian landscapes.

A new perspective on the cherry trees: Take a leisurely trip in a paddleboat around the Tidal Basin, surrounded by the famous blossoms in spring.

Washington for Every Season

With every change of the seasons, D.C. offers new pleasures for sports and outdoor enthusiasts:

In **winter** you can have an old-fashioned afternoon of ice-skating and hot chocolate in the National Gallery's sculpture garden, or go to the Verizon Center to see the Wizards play basketball or the Capitals play hockey.

Come **spring,** the city emerges from the cold with activities everywhere. Runners become a common sight on the Mall, and boating is available nearby.

In **summer,** baseball fans head to new Nationals Park to see the Nationals play, and Washington Redskins fans check out their favorite football stars at training camp in Ashburn, Virginia.

When **fall** arrives the seasonal colors of the trees in Rock Creek Park are a spectacular sight for bikers, hikers, and runners. Tickets to see the Redskins at FedEx Field are some of the city's most prized commodities.

Updated by
Mitchell Tropin

Washingtonians are an active bunch. The city's 69 square miles are in part a fantastic recreational backyard, with dozens of beautiful open spaces, and natives take full advantage of it, exploring by bike, running amid the monuments, and even sailing up the Potomac. They're also passionate about their local teams—especially the Redskins, whose games are sold out year after year.

Rock Creek Park has miles of wooded trails and paths for bikers, runners, and walkers that extend to almost every part of the city. The National Mall connects the Lincoln Memorial and the Capitol building. With the monuments as a backdrop, you can ride a bike or take a jog. Around the Tidal Basin, see the Jefferson Memorial from a paddleboat or run alongside the Potomac River. Theodore Roosevelt Island, a wildlife sanctuary that deserves to be better known, has several paths for hiking and enjoyable spots for a picnic.

PARKS & NATURE

10

ANIMALS

National Aquarium. The aquarium has an incongruous location inside the Commerce Department Building, near the massive Ronald Reagan Building. Established in 1873, it's the country's oldest public aquarium, with more than 1,200 fish and other creatures—such as eels, sharks, and alligators—representing 270 species of fresh- and saltwater life. The exhibits look somewhat dated, but the easy-to-view tanks, accessible touching pool (with crabs and sea urchins), low admission fee, and lack of crowds make this a good outing with small children. The Aquarium's cafeteria is also a great place to stop for a snack. ⊠ *14th St. and Constitution Ave. NW, East End* ☎ *202/482–2825* ⊕ *www.nationalaquarium.com* ⊠ *$5* ☉ *Daily 9–5, last admission at 4:30; sharks fed*

Mon., Wed., and Sat. at 2; piranhas fed Tues., Thurs., and Sun. at 2; alligators fed Fri. at 2 Ⓜ *Federal Triangle.*

Ⓒ **National Zoo.** For many years, the zoo's most famous resident was Smokey the Bear, but the top attractions nowadays are the giant pandas. Tian Tian and Mei Xiang came from China in 2000, and will stay here until 2010. In 2005 their cub, Tai Shan, was born, the first giant panda cub to survive from birth at the National Zoo and only the third to survive in the U.S. The pandas are stars, and their many fans cluster around their bamboo-filled compound.

Carved out of Rock Creek Park, the zoo is a series of rolling, wooded hills that complement the many innovative compounds showing animals in their native settings. Step inside the Great Flight Cage to observe the free flight of many species of birds; this walk-in aviary is open from May to October (the birds are moved indoors during the colder months). Between 10 and 2 each day you can catch the orangutan population traveling on the "O Line," a series of cables and towers near the Great Ape House that allows the primates to swing hand over hand about 35 feet over your head. The most ambitious addition to the zoo is Amazonia, an amazingly authentic reproduction of a South American rain-forest ecosystem. You feel as if you are deep inside a steamy jungle, with monkeys leaping overhead and noisy birds flying from branch to branch. Part of the Smithsonian Institution, the National Zoo is one of the foremost zoos in the world. Created by an Act of Congress in 1889, the 163-acre park was designed by landscape architect Frederick Law Olmsted, who also designed the U.S. Capitol grounds. Before the zoo opened in 1890, live animals used as taxidermists' models were kept on the Mall. ✉ *3001 Connecticut Ave. NW, Woodley Park* ☎ *202/673–4800 or 202/673–4717* ⊕ *www.si.edu/natzoo* 🎟 *Free, parking $16* ☉ *May–mid-Sept., daily 6 AM–8 PM; mid-Sept.–Apr., daily 6–6. Zoo buildings open at 10 and close before zoo closes* Ⓜ *Cleveland Park or Woodley Park/Zoo.*

GARDENS

Constitution Gardens. Many ideas were proposed to develop this 50-acre site near the Reflecting Pool and the Vietnam Veterans Memorial. It once held "temporary" buildings erected by the Navy before World War I and not removed until after World War II. President Nixon is said to have favored something resembling Copenhagen's Tivoli Gardens. The final design was plainer, with paths winding through groves of trees and, on the lake, a tiny island paying tribute to the signers of the Declaration of Independence, their signatures carved into a low stone wall. In 1986 President Reagan proclaimed the gardens a living legacy to the Constitution; in that spirit, a naturalization ceremony for new citizens now takes place here each year. ✉ *Constitution Ave. between 17th and 23rd Sts. NW,* ⊕ *www.nps.gov/coga* Ⓜ *Foggy Bottom.*

NEED A BREAK? At the circular snack bar just west of the Constitution Gardens lake you can get hot dogs, potato chips, candy bars, soft drinks, and beer at prices lower than those charged by most street vendors.

FodorsChoice **Dumbarton Oaks.** One of the loveliest places for a stroll in Washing-
★   ton is Dumbarton Oaks, the acres of enchanting gardens adjoining
Dumbarton House in Georgetown. Planned by noted landscape architect Beatrix Farrand, the gardens incorporate elements of traditional
English, Italian, and French styles such as a formal rose garden, an
English country garden, and an orangery (circa 1810). A full-time crew
of a dozen gardeners toils to maintain the stunning collection of terraces, geometric gardens, tree-shaded brick walks, fountains, arbors,
and pools. Plenty of well-positioned benches make this a good place for
resting weary feet, too. You enter the gardens at 31st and R streets.
In 1944 one of the most important events of the 20th century took
place at **Dumbarton House,** when representatives of the United States,
Great Britain, China, and the Soviet Union met in the music room to
lay the groundwork for the United Nations. Career diplomat Robert Woods Bliss and his wife Mildred bought the property in 1920
and tamed the sprawling grounds, and removed later 19th-century
additions that had obscured the Federal lines of the 1801 mansion. In
1940 the Blisses gave the estate to Harvard University, which maintains world-renowned collections of Byzantine and pre-Columbian art
here. Both collections are small but choice, reflecting the enormous
skill and creativity developed at roughly the same time in two very
different parts of the world. The Byzantine collection includes beautiful examples of both religious and secular items executed in mosaic,
metal, enamel, and ivory. Pre-Columbian works—artifacts and textiles
from Mexico and Central and South America by peoples such as the
Aztec, Maya, and Olmec—are arranged in an enclosed glass pavilion
designed by Philip Johnson. Normally on view to the public are the
lavishly decorated music room and selections from Mrs. Bliss's collection of rare illustrated garden books. ✉ *1703 32nd St. NW, George-*
town, ☎ *202/339–6401 or 202/339–6400* ✉ *Gardens: Apr.–Oct. $8,*
Nov.–Mar. free ☉ *Gardens: Apr.–Oct., Tues.–Sun. 2–6; Nov.–Mar.,*
Tues.–Sun. daily 2–5.

★   **Hillwood Estate, Museum and Gardens.** Cereal heiress Marjorie Merriweather Post purchased the twenty-five acre Hillwood Estate in 1955.
Post devoted equal attention to her gardens as she did to the 40-room
Georgian mansion: you can wander through thirteen acres of them,
including a Japanese rock and waterfall garden, a manicured formal
French garden, a rose garden, Mediterranean fountains, and a greenhouse full of orchids. The "Lunar Lawn," where she threw garden parties
that were the most coveted invitation in Washington society, is planted
with dogwood, magnolia, cherry, and plum trees, as well as azaleas,
camellias, lilacs, tulips, and pansies. The estate is best reached by taxi
or car (parking is available on the grounds). It's a 20 to 30-minute walk
from the Metro. ✉ *4155 Linnean Ave. NW, Northwest* ☎ *202/686–*
5807 or 202/686–8500 ⊕ *www.hillwoodmuseum.org* ✉ *House and*
grounds $12 ☉ *Feb.–Dec., Tues.–Sat. 10–5* Ⓜ *Van Ness/UDC.*

Tudor Place. A little more than a block from Dumbarton Oaks in Georgetown is this little-known gem, the former home of Martha Washington's
granddaughter. The house has 5½ acres of gardens that offer impressive
replications of Federal-period gardens and include 19th-century specimen

10

trees and boxwoods from Mount Vernon. Make time for a one-hour tour of the house itself, which features many rare possessions of George and Martha Washington. ✉ *1644 31st Pl. NW, Georgetown* 🕾 *202/965–0400* 🌐 *www.tudor-place.org* 🖃 *$6, garden $2* 🕙 *House tours: Tues.–Fri. 10, 11:30, 1, 2:30, Sat. on the hr 10–3, Sun. on the hr noon–3. Garden: Mon.–Sat. 10–4, Sun. noon–4* 🕙 *Closed Jan.* Ⓜ *Woodley Park or Dupont Circle.*

Kenilworth Aquatic Gardens. Exotic water lilies, lotuses, hyacinths, and other water-loving plants thrive in this 14-acre sanctuary of quiet ponds and marshy flats. The gardens' wetland animals include turtles, frogs, beavers, spring azure butterflies, and some 40 species of birds. ■ TIP➔ In July nearly everything blossoms; early morning is the best time to visit, when day-bloomers are just opening and night-bloomers have yet to close. The nearest Metro stop is a 15-minute walk away. ✉ *Anacostia Ave. and Douglas St. NE, Anacostia* 🕾 *202/426–6905* 🌐 *www.nps. gov* 🖃 *Free* 🕙 *Gardens and visitor center, daily 7–4; garden tours daily at 9, 10, and 11* Ⓜ *Deanwood.*

🕙 **United States Botanic Garden.** Established by Congress in 1820, this is the oldest botanic garden in North America. The recently renovated glass building, a Victorian design, sits at the foot of Capitol Hill, in the shadow of the Capitol building. It offers an escape from the stone and marble federal office buildings that surround it; inside are exotic rain-forest species, desert flora, and trees from all parts of the world. A special treat is the extensive collection of rare and unusual orchids. Walkways suspended 24 feet above the ground provide a fascinating view of the plants. A relatively new addition is the National Garden, which emphasizes educational exhibits. The two-year-old garden features the Rose Garden, Butterfly Garden, Lawn Terrace, First Ladies' Water Garden, and Regional Garden. ✉ *1st St. and Maryland Ave. SW, Capitol Hill* 🕾 *202/225–8333* 🌐 *www.usbg.gov* 🖃 *Free* 🕙 *Daily 10–5* Ⓜ *Federal Center SW.*

Fodor'sChoice ★ **United States National Arboretum.** During azalea season (mid-April through May), this 446-acre oasis is a blaze of color. In early summer, clematis, peonies, rhododendrons, and roses bloom. At any time of year the 22 original Corinthian columns from the U.S. Capitol, reerected here in 1990, are striking. For a soothing, relaxing walk, visit the Cryptomeria Walk and Japanese Stroll Garden, which are part of the Bonsai and Penjing Museum. On weekends a tram tours the Arboretum's curving roadways at 10:30, 11:30, 1, 2, 3, and 4; tickets are $4 for adults and $2 for children. The **National Herb Garden** and the **National Bonsai Collection** are also here. ✉ *3501 New York Ave. NE, Northeast* 🕾 *202/245–2726* 🌐 *www.usna.usda.gov* 🖃 *Free* 🕙 *Arboretum and herb garden daily 8–5, bonsai collection daily 10–3:30* Ⓜ *Weekends only, Union Station, then X6 bus (runs every 40 min); weekdays, Stadium/Armory, then B2 bus to Bladensburg Rd. and R St.*

PARKS

C&O Canal. This waterway kept Georgetown open to shipping after its harbor had filled with silt. George Washington was one of the first to advance the idea of a canal linking the Potomac with the Ohio River across the Appalachians. Work started on the Chesapeake & Ohio Canal in 1828, and when it opened in 1850 its 74 locks linked Georgetown with Cumberland, Maryland, 184.5 mi to the northwest (still short of its intended destination). Lumber, coal, iron, wheat, and flour moved up and down the canal, but it was never as successful as its planners had hoped it would be. Many of the bridges spanning the canal in Georgetown were too low to allow anything other than fully loaded barges to pass underneath, and competition from the Baltimore & Ohio Railroad eventually spelled an end to profitability. Today the canal is part of the National Park System; walkers follow the towpath once used by mules while canoeists paddle the canal's calm waters.

You can glide into history aboard a mule-drawn **canal boat ride.** The National Park service provides the hour-long rides from about mid-April through late October; tickets cost $7 and are available across the canal, next to the Foundry Building. The schedule varies by season, with limited rides in the spring and fall. In summer the boats run at least twice a day from Wednesday through Sunday. Call the visitor center for the exact schedule on the day of your visit. Canal-boat rides also depart from the Great Falls Tavern visitor center in Maryland. *For more information on the Great Falls segment of the park, see Chapter 12, Side Trips.* ⊠ *Georgetown Canal Visitor Center, 1057 Thomas Jefferson St. NW, Georgetown* ☎ *202/653–5190* ⊕ *www.nps.gov/choh* ☉ *Apr.–Oct., Wed.–Sun. 9–4:30; Nov.–Mar., weekends 10–4, staffing permitting.*

East Potomac Park. This 328-acre finger of land extends from the Tidal Basin between the Washington Channel to the east and the Potomac River to the west. There are playgrounds, picnic tables, tennis courts, swimming pools, a driving range, two 9-hole golf courses, miniature golf, and an 18-hole golf course. Double-blossoming cherry trees line Ohio Drive and bloom about two weeks after the single-blossoming variety that attracts throngs to the Tidal Basin each spring. *The Awakening* sculpture is on Hains Point, at the tip of the park, where the Anacostia River merges with the Potomac. ⊠ *Maine Ave. SW heading west, or Ohio Dr. heading south, follow signs carefully; Ohio Dr. closed to traffic on summer weekends and holidays 3* PM*–6* AM ☎ *202/619-7222* Ⓜ *Smithsonian.*

10

Pershing Park. A quiet, sunken garden honors General John J. "Black Jack" Pershing, the first to hold the title General of the Armies, a rank Congress created in 1919 to recognize his military achievements. Engravings on the stone walls recount pivotal campaigns from World War I, when Pershing commanded the American expeditionary force and conducted other military exploits. Ice-skaters glide on the square pool here in winter. ⊠*15th St. and Pennsylvania Ave., White House area* Ⓜ*McPherson Sq.*

Ⓒ **Rock Creek Park.** The 1,800 acres surrounding Rock Creek have provided a cool oasis for D.C. residents ever since Congress set them aside for recreational use in 1890. Bicycle routes and hiking and equestrian trails wind through the groves of dogwoods, beeches, oaks, and cedars, and 30 picnic areas are scattered about. Rangers at the **Nature Center and Planetarium** (⊠*South of Military Rd.,5200 Glover Rd. NW, Northwest* ☎*202/426–6829*) introduce visitors to the park and keep track of daily events; guided nature walks leave from the center weekends at 2. The center and planetarium are open Wednesday through Sunday from 9 to 5. The renovated 19th-century **Klingle Mansion**(⊠*3545 Willliamsburg La. NW, Northwest*) is used as the National Park Service's Rock Creek headquarters. Also in distant areas of the park are Fort Reno, Fort Bayard, Fort Stevens, and Fort DeRussy, remnants of the original ring of forts that guarded Washington during the Civil War, and the Rock Creek Park Golf Course, an 18-hole public course. Landscape architect Horace Peaslee created oft-overlooked **Meridian Hill Park** (⊠*16th and Euclid Sts., Adams-Morgan*), a noncontiguous section of Rock Creek Park, after a 1917 study of the parks of Europe. As a result, it contains elements of parks in France (a long, straight mall bordered with plants), Italy (terraces and wall fountains), and Switzerland (a lower-level reflecting pool based on one in Zurich). It's also unofficially known as Malcolm X Park in honor of the civil rights leader. Drug activity once made it unwise to visit Meridian Hill alone; it's somewhat safer now, but avoid it after dark.

Ⓒ **Tidal Basin.** This placid pond was part of the Potomac until 1882, when portions of the river were filled in to improve navigation and create additional parkland. At the **boathouse** (☎*202/479–2426*), on the northeast bank of the Tidal Basin, you can rent paddleboats during the warmer months. Rental cost is $8 per hour for a two-person boat, $16 per hour for a four-person boat. The boathouse is open from mid-March through October from 10 to 6.

Two grotesque sculpted heads on the sides of the Inlet Bridge can be seen as you walk along the sidewalk that hugs the basin. The inside walls of the bridge also feature two other interesting sculptures: bronze, human-headed fish that spout water from their mouths. The bridge was refurbished in the 1980s at the same time the chief of the park, Jack Fish, was retiring. Sculptor Constantine Sephralis played a little joke: these fish heads are actually Fish's head.

Once you cross the bridge, continue along the Tidal Basin to the right. This route is especially scenic when the **cherry trees** are in bloom. The first batch of these trees arrived from Japan in 1909. The trees were infected with insects and fungus, however, and the Department of Agriculture ordered them destroyed. A diplomatic crisis was averted when the United States politely asked the Japanese for another batch, and in 1912 First Lady Helen Taft planted the first tree. The second was planted by the wife of the Japanese ambassador, Viscountess Chinda. About 200 of the original trees still grow near the Tidal Basin. (These cherry trees are the single-flowering Akebeno and Yoshino variety. Double-blossom Fugenzo and Kwanzan trees grow in East Potomac Park and flower about two weeks after their more famous cousins.)

The trees are now the centerpiece of Washington's two-week **Cherry Blossom Festival,** held each spring since 1935. The festivities are kicked off by the lighting of a ceremonial Japanese lantern that rests on the north shore of the Tidal Basin, not far from where the first tree was planted. The once-simple celebration has grown over the years to include concerts, martial-arts demonstrations, and a parade. Park-service experts try their best to predict exactly when the buds will pop. The trees are usually in bloom for about 10–12 days in late March or early April. When winter refuses to release its grip, the parade and festival are held anyway, without the presence of blossoms, no matter how inclement the weather. And when the weather complies and the blossoms are at their peak at the time of the festivities, Washington rejoices. ⊠ *Bordered by Independence and Maine Aves., The Mall* Ⓜ *Smithsonian.*

West Potomac Park. Between the Potomac and the Tidal Basin, West Potomac Park is best known for its flowering cherry trees, which bloom for two weeks in late March or early April. During the rest of the year, West Potomac Park is just a nice place to relax, play ball, or admire the views at the Tidal Basin.

PARTICIPATION SPORTS

10

BICYCLING

The numerous trails in the District and its surrounding areas are well maintained and clearly marked.

For scenery, you can't beat the **C&O Canal Towpath** (⊕ *www.nps.gov/ choh*), which starts in Georgetown and runs along the C&O Canal into Maryland. You could pedal to the end of the canal, nearly 200 mi away in Cumberland, Maryland, but most cyclists stop at Great Falls, 13 mi from where the canal starts. The occasionally bumpy towpath, made of gravel and packed earth, passes through wooded areas of the C&O Canal National Historical Park. You can see 19th-century locks from the canal's working days, and if you're particularly lucky, you may catch a glimpse of mules pulling a canal barge. The barges now take passengers, not cargo.

Suited for bicyclists, walkers, rollerbladers, and strollers, the paved **Capital Crescent Trail** (☎ *202/234-4874 Capital Crescent Coalition*) stretches along the old Georgetown Branch, a B&O Railroad line that was completed in 1910 and was in operation until 1985. The 7½-mi route's first leg runs from Georgetown near Key Bridge to central Bethesda at Bethesda and Woodmont avenues. At Bethesda and Woodmont, the trail heads through a well-lighted tunnel near the heart of Bethesda's lively business area and continues into Silver Spring. The 3½-mi stretch from Bethesda to Silver Spring is gravel. The Georgetown Branch Trail, as this section is officially named, connects with the Rock Creek Trail, which goes to Rockville in the north and Memorial Bridge past the Washington Monument in the south. On weekends when the weather's nice, all sections of the trails are crowded.

Cyclists interested in serious training might try the 3-mi loop around the golf course in **East Potomac Park** (☎202/485–9874 *National Park Service*) at Hains Point, the southern area of the park (entry is near the Jefferson Memorial). It's a favorite training course for dedicated local racers and would-be triathletes. ■TIP➔ Going to the southernmost point in the park, where the Anacostia and Potomac rivers merge, you'll come face to face with one of Washington's most unusual and delightful sculptures, *The Awakening*, a half-buried giant. A must-see, this enormous hand and head contrast sharply with the usual statutes of generals and statesmen.

Each day, bicyclists cruise **The Mall** amid the endless throngs of runners, walkers, and tourists. There's relatively little car traffic, and bikers can take in some of Washington's landmarks, such as the Washington Monument, the Reflecting Pool, the Vietnam Memorial, and some of the city's more interesting architecture, such as the Smithsonian Castle and the Hirshhorn, the "Doughnut on the Mall."

Mount Vernon Trail, across the Potomac in Virginia, has two sections. The northern part, closest to D.C. proper, is 3½-mi long and begins near the causeway across the river from the Kennedy Center that heads to Theodore Roosevelt Island (➪ *Hiking*). It then passes Ronald Reagan National Airport and continues on to Old Town Alexandria. This section has slight slopes and almost no interruptions for traffic, making it a delightful, but challenging, biking route. Even relatively inexperienced bikers enjoy the trail, which provides wonderful views of the Potomac. To access the trail from the District, take the Theodore Roosevelt Bridge or the Rochambeau Memorial Bridge, also known as the 14th Street Bridge. South of the airport, the trail runs down to the Washington Marina. The final mile of the trail's northern section meanders through protected wetlands before ending in the heart of Old Town Alexandria. The trail's 9-mi southern section extends along the Potomac from Alexandria to Mount Vernon.

Rock Creek Park covers an area from the edge of Georgetown to Montgomery County, Maryland. The bike path there is asphalt and has a few challenging hills, but it's mostly flat. You can bike several miles without having to stop for cars (the roadway is closed entirely to cars on the weekend). The two separate northern parts of the trail, which begin in Bethesda and Silver Spring, merge around the Washington, D.C., line. Many bikers gather at this point and follow the trail on a path that goes past the Washington Zoo and eventually runs toward the Lincoln Memorial and Kennedy Center. Fifteen miles of dirt trails are also in the park; these are best for hiking.

> **BIKING THE MALL**
>
> A pleasant loop route begins at the Lincoln Memorial, going north past the Washington Monument, and turning around at the Tidal Basin. Along the way are small fountains and parks for taking a break and getting a drink of water.

INFORMATION
Washington Area Bicyclist Association (⊠*1803 Connecticut Ave., Northwest* ☎*202/518–0524* ⊕*www.waba.org*).

RENTALS & TOURS
Bicycle Pro Shop Georgetown (⊠*3403 M St. NW, Georgetown* ☎*202/337–0311*), near Georgetown University and Key Bridge by the Potomac River, rents city bikes for $20 per day.

Big Wheel Bikes, near the C&O Canal Towpath, rents multispeed bikes for $25 per day and $15 for three hours. A second location is near the Capital Crescent Trail. There's also an Alexandria branch if you want to ride the Mount Vernon Trail. ⊠*1034 33rd St. NW, Georgetown* ☎*202/337–0254* ⊠*3119 Lee Highway, Arlington, VA* ☎*301/652–0192* ⊠*2 Prince St., Alexandria, VA* ☎*703/739–2300*.

Bike the Sites (☎*202/966–8662* ⊕*www.bikethesites.com*) is a tour company that offers three-hour, 8-mi guided tours of downtown Washington. Costs range from $35 to $55, and bike rental is included. Advance reservations are required. Tours start from the Mall.

The Boathouse at Fletcher's Cove (⊠*4940 Canal Rd., at Reservoir Rd., Foxhall* ☎*202/244–0461*), next to the C&O Towpath and Capital Crescent Trail, rents fixed-gear bikes for $8 per hour and $19 per day.

Revolution Bikes (⊠*3411 M St. NW, Georgetown* ☎*202/965–3601*), near Georgetown University and Key Bridge by the Potomac River, rents city bikes for $20 per day.

Thompson's Boat Center (⊠*2900 Virginia Ave. NW, Foggy Bottom* ☎*202/333–4861*) allows easy access to the Rock Creek Trail and the C&O Towpath and is close to the monuments. All-terrain bikes are $8 per hour and $25 per day. Fixed-gear and children's bikes are $8 per hour and $15 per day. Children's trailers (attachments to adult bikes) rent for $4 per hour or $15 per day.

10

BOATING & SAILING

Canoeing, sailing, and powerboating are popular in the Washington, D.C., area. Several places rent boats along the **Potomac River** north and south of the city. You can dip your oars just about anywhere along the river—go canoeing in the C&O Canal, sailing in the widening river south of Alexandria, or even kayaking in the raging rapids at Great Falls, a 30-minute drive from the capital.

RENTALS

Belle Haven Marina (✉ *George Washington Pkwy., Alexandria, VA* ☎ *703/768–0018*), south of Reagan National Airport and Old Town Alexandria, rents three types of sailboats: Sunfish are $30 for two hours during the week and $35 for two hours on the weekend; Hobie Cat–style sailboats and Flying Scots are $46 for two hours during the week and $54 for two hours during the weekend. Canoes and kayaks are available for rent at $20 for two hours. Rentals are available from April to October.

The Boathouse at Fletcher's Cove (✉ *4940 Canal Rd., at Reservoir Rd., Foxhall* ☎ *202/244–0461*), just north of Georgetown, rents 17-foot rowboats for $11 per hour and $20 per day. Canoes are available for rent at $11 per hour and $21 per day.

Thompson's Boat Center (✉ *2900 Virginia Ave. NW, Foggy Bottom* ☎ *202/333–4861*) is near Georgetown and Theodore Roosevelt Island. The center rents canoes for $8 per hour and $22 per day. Single kayaks are $8 per hour and $24 per day, and double kayaks are $10 per hour and $30 per day. Rowing sculls are also available, but you must demonstrate prior experience and a suitably high skill level.

Tidal Basin (✉ *Bordered by Independence Ave. and Maine Ave., The Mall* ☎ *202/479–2426* Ⓜ *Farragut* W), in front of the Jefferson Memorial, rents paddleboats beginning in April and usually ending in September, depending on how cold the water gets. The entrance is at 1501 Maine Avenue SW, on the east side of the Tidal Basin. You can rent two-passenger boats at $8 per hour and four-passenger boats at $16 per hour.

HIKING

Hikes and nature walks are listed in the Friday "Weekend" section of the *Washington Post*. Several area organizations sponsor outings, and most are guided: the **Potomac-Appalachian Trail Club** (✉ *118 Park St. SE, Vienna, VA* ☎ *703/242–0965*) sponsors hikes—usually free—on trails from Pennsylvania to Virginia, including the C&O Canal and the Appalachian Trail. The **Sierra Club** (☎ *202/547–2326*) has many regional outings; call for details.

The **Billy Goat Trail** (⊠ *MacArthur Blvd., Potomac, MD* ☎ *301/413–0720* ⊕ *www.nps.gov/choh*) has some outstanding views of the wilder parts of the Potomac. This challenging 2-mi trail, which starts and ends at the C&O Canal Towpath below Great Falls, has some steep downhills and climbs.

Fodor's Choice ★ **Theodore Roosevelt Island** (⊠ *Foggy Bottom20037* ☎ *703/289–2552 or 703/289–2550* ⊕ *www.nps.gov/this*), designed as a memorial to the environmentally minded president, is a wildlife sanctuary off the George Washington Parkway on the Virginia side of the city. It can be reached by car by taking the Theodore Roosevelt Bridge or I–66. Hikers and bicyclists can easily reach it by taking the 14th Street Bridge. Many birds and other animals live in the island's marsh and forests.

A self-guided nature trail winds through **Woodend** (⊠ *8940 Jones Mill Rd., Chevy Chase, MD* ☎ *301/652–9188, 301/652–1088 for recent bird sightings* ⊕ *www.audubonnaturalist.org*), a verdant 40-acre estate, and around the suburban Maryland headquarters of the local **Audubon Naturalist Society**. The estate was designed in the 1920s by Jefferson Memorial architect John Russell Pope and has a mansion, also called Woodend, on its grounds. You're never far from the trill of birdsong here, as the Audubon Society has turned the place into something of a private nature preserve, forbidding the use of toxic chemicals and leaving some areas in a wild, natural state. Programs include wildlife identification walks, environmental education programs, and a weekly Saturday bird walk September through June. A bookstore stocks titles on conservation, ecology, and birds. The grounds are open daily sunrise to sunset, and admission is free.

A 1,460-acre refuge in Alexandria, **Huntley Meadows Park** (⊠ *3701 Lockheed Blvd., Alexandria, VA* ☎ *703/768–2525*) is made for birders. You can spot more than 200 species—from ospreys to owls, egrets, and ibis. Much of the park is wetlands, a favorite of aquatic species. A boardwalk circles through a marsh, enabling you to spot beaver lodges, and 4 mi of trails wend through the park, making it likely you'll see deer, muskrats, and river otters as well. The park is usually open daily dawn to dusk.

RUNNING

Running is one of the best ways to see the city, and several scenic trails wend through downtown Washington and nearby Northern Virginia. It can be dangerous to run at night on the trails, although the streets are fairly well lighted. Even in daylight, it's best to run in pairs when venturing beyond public areas or heavily used sections of trails. Most city streets are safe for runs alone during the day, especially around government buildings, museums, and monuments, where there's additional police protection. Many hotels offer maps of routes that include city landmarks.

The 89-mi-long **C&O Canal Towpath** (⊕ *www.nps.gov/choh*) in the C&O National Historical Park is a favorite of runners and cyclists. The path is mostly gravel and dirt, making it easy on knees and feet. The most popular loop, which goes from a point just north of the Key Bridge in Georgetown to the Boat House at Fletcher's Cove, is about 4 mi round-trip.

Fodor'sChoice
★
The most popular running route in Washington is the 4½-mi loop on **The Mall** around the Capitol and past the Smithsonian museums, the Washington Monument, the Reflecting Pool, and the Lincoln Memorial. At any time of day, hundreds of runners, speed walkers, bicyclists, and tourists make their way along the gravel pathways. For a longer run, veer south of the Mall on either side of the Tidal Basin and head for the Jefferson Memorial and East Potomac Park, the site of many races.

> ### KITE FLYING
>
> The Smithsonian's annual **Kite festival** (✉ *Downtown 20013* ☎ *202/357-3030* ⊕ *www.kite-festival.org* Ⓜ *Smithsonian*) at the National Mall gives kids and adults a chance to enjoy a day of kite flying on the National Mall. The granddaddy of kite festivals, held in connection with the Cherry Blossom Festival in April, also features kite battles and incredible kite-flying exhibitions.

Across the Potomac in Virginia is the **Mount Vernon Trail**. The 3½-mi northern section begins near the pedestrian causeway leading to Theodore Roosevelt Island (directly across the river from the Kennedy Center) and goes past Ronald Reagan National Airport and on to Old Town Alexandria. You can get to the trail from the District by crossing either the Theodore Roosevelt Bridge at the Lincoln Memorial or the Rochambeau Memorial Bridge at the Jefferson Memorial. South of the airport, the trail runs down to the Washington Marina. The 9-mi southern section leads to Mount Vernon.

Rock Creek Park has 15 mi of trails, a bicycle path, a bridle path, picnic groves, playgrounds, and the boulder-strewn rolling stream that gives it its name. The most popular run in the park is a trail along the creek from Georgetown to the National Zoo: about a 4-mi loop. In summer there's considerable shade, and there are water fountains and an exercise station along the way. The roadway is closed to traffic on weekends.

INFORMATION & ORGANIZATIONS

Group runs and weekend races around Washington are listed in the Friday "Weekend" section of the *Washington Post*. You can also check the Thursday calendar of events in the *Washington Times*. Comprehensive listings of running and walking events are posted online by the *Washington Running Report* (⊕*www.runwashington.com*) and *racePacket* (⊕*www.racepacket.com*). Other reliable sources for races and casual running gatherings are the Montgomery County Road Runners Club (⊕*www.mcrrc.org*), the nation's third-largest running club, and the D.C. Road Runners Club (⊕*www.dcroadrunners.com*).

Tuesday and Thursday evenings at 6:30 PM you can join the **Capitol Hill Runners** (☎*301/283–0821*) on a 6- to 8-mi run, which begins at the Reflecting Pool at the base of the Capitol's west side. Most Sunday mornings the **Fleet Feet Sports Shop** (✉1841 Columbia Rd. NW, Adams-Morgan ☎202/387–3888) sponsors informal runs through Rock Creek Park and other areas. The shop's owner and father of the city's mayor Phil Fenty leads the runs. The courses change at Phil's discretion and usually go from 5 to 7 mi. Call the **Gatorade and Road Runners Club of America Hotline** (☎703/683–7722) for general information about running and racing in the area.

SPECTATOR SPORTS

BASEBALL

Major League baseball has returned to D.C., where the **Washington Nationals** (✉Potomac and First Sts. SW 20003 ☎202/675–6287 ⊕ washingtonnationals.mlb.com Ⓜ Navy Yard) of the National League play in their new spectacular home, Nationals Park. Tickets range from $5 to $65. Individual game tickets may be purchased at the park or through the team's Web site. ■TIP➔ The Metro is a hassle-free and inexpensive way to get to the ball park. The closest and most convenient stop is the Navy Yard on the Green Line.

BASKETBALL

There are several top-flight college basketball teams here. Of the Division I men's college basketball teams in the area, the most prominent are the **Georgetown University Hoyas** (⊕guhoyas.collegesports.com), former NCAA national champions. The Hoyas became a national basketball powerhouse under their coach John Thompson III. Most home games are played at the **Verizon Center** (✉601 F St. NW, between 6th and 7th Sts., Downtown ☎202/628–3200, 202/432–7328 box office ⊕www.verizoncenter.com).

The WNBA's **Washington Mystics** (✉6th and F Sts., Downtown ☎202/432–7328 ⊕www.wnba.com/mystics Ⓜ Gallery Pl./Chinatown) play at the Verizon Center in downtown Washington. The Mystics perennially lead the WNBA in attendance, despite a losing record. The games are loud, boisterous events. Ticket prices range from $10 to $60, with courtside tickets for $115. You can buy tickets at the Verizon Center box office, from the team directly through its Web site, or through Ticketmaster. The women's basketball season runs from late May to August.

10

Fodor'sChoice ★ The NBA's **Washington Wizards** (✉6th and F Sts., Downtown ☎202/432–7328 ⊕www.nba.com/wizards Ⓜ Gallery Pl./Chinatown) play from October to April at the Verizon Center and feature superstar Gilbert Arenas. Tickets for individual games cost $40 to $850. The team also offers $10 seats in the upper level and courtside seats for a whopping $2,500. Buy tickets from the Verizon Center box office, from Ticketmaster, or directly from the team's Web site.

FOOTBALL

Whatever the vicissitudes of the season, one thing remains the same: tickets to watch the **Washington Redskins** (☎301/276–6000 FedEx Field stadium ⊕*www.redskins.com*) are difficult to get. Though FedEx Field is the largest football stadium in the NFL, all 91,000 seats are held by season-ticket holders. Occasionally you can find tickets advertised in the classifieds of the *Washington Post* or *Craig's List,* or buy them from online ticket vendors and auction sites—at top dollar, of course. Tickets can range from $175 to $300 for less popular opponents and go as high as $800 for elite teams, such as the New York Giants, or Washington's biggest rival, the Dallas Cowboys. ■**TIP**➜ **Tickets are difficult to get, but fans can see the players up close and for free at training camp, held in August.** The Redskins invite the public to attend their training camp in Ashburn, in nearby Loudoun County, Virginia. Camp begins in late July and continues through mid-August. The practices typically last from 90 minutes to two hours. Fans can bring their own chairs, and the players are usually available after practice to sign autographs. Call ahead to make sure the practices are open that day. A practice schedule is on the team's Web site.

HOCKEY

One of pro hockey's better teams, the **Washington Capitals** (✉*6th and F Sts., Downtown* ☎*202/432–7328* ⊕*www.washingtoncaps.com* Ⓜ*Gallery Pl./Chinatown*) play home games October through April at the Verizon Center and feature one of hockey's brightest new superstars, Alex Ovechkin. Seats on the main level range from $71 to $176, and those in the upper deck range from $10 to $55.50. Tickets are less expensive if you purchase a family pack. Tickets can be purchased at the Verizon Center box office, from Ticketmaster, or directly from the team's Web site.

SOCCER

Fodor'sChoice
★ **D.C. United** (✉*Robert F. Kennedy Stadium, 2400 E. Capitol St. SE, Capitol Hill* ☎*202/547–3134* ⊕*www.dcunited.com* Ⓜ*Stadium*) is one of the best Major League soccer (U.S. pro soccer) teams. International matches, including some World Cup preliminaries, are often played on RFK Stadium's grass field, dedicated exclusively to soccer play. Games are April through September. You can buy tickets, which generally cost $25–$65, with discounts for groups, at the RFK Stadium ticket office, through Ticketmaster, or through the team's Web site, which offers package deals for families.

Shopping

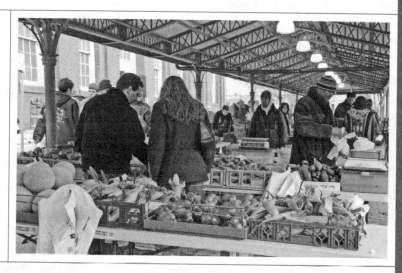

WORD OF MOUTH

"On Sunday we metro'd down to Eastern Market in the morning . . . there are actually cafes and shops on the main street. It's always a fun place to look around and my friends both purchased lovely earrings."

—Weespxx

"If all else fails, the Smithsonian gift shops are reeeaaally tempting, and bribery goes a long way."

—mooselywild

SHOPPING PLANNER

Beat the Heat

D.C.'s summertime humidity can take the starch out of any shopper. When it's sticky out, head to Georgetown, where stores are tightly packed and waterfront breezes drift up the side streets, and Dupont Circle, where you can duck inside for an iced coffee or ice cream between gallery stops.

Gallery Hopping

Washington has three main gallery districts—Downtown, Dupont, and Georgetown—though small galleries can be found all over in converted houses and storefronts. Whatever their location, many keep unusual hours and close entirely on Sunday and Monday. The *Washington Post* "Weekend" section and *Washington CityPaper* (published on Thursday) are excellent sources of information on current exhibits and hours.

Hours

Store hours vary greatly. In general, Georgetown stores are open late and on Sunday; stores downtown that cater to office workers close at 6 PM and may not open at all on weekends. Some stores extend their hours on Thursday.

Getting Around

Georgetown is the only neighborhood the Metro doesn't reach, so you can walk, drive (though parking is a challenge), take a taxi, or hop on the D.C. Circulator bus (the Georgetown-Union Station loop traverses the shopping strips on M Street and Wisconsin Avenue). Some locations in Friendship Heights on Connecticut Avenue are most easily reached by car.

Historic Walks

Shopping is the perfect opportunity to acquaint yourself with some of D.C.'s historic neighborhoods. A quick diversion down a side street in Georgetown reveals the neighborhood's historic charm and current glamour. Peer around a corner in Dupont or Capitol Hill to see a true D.C. architecture classic—the row house. Wandering downtown you are sure to bump into one of the nation's great neoclassical structures, whether it be the White House or the historic Hotel Monaco.

How to Save Money

If you're willing to dig a bit, D.C. can be a savvy shoppers dream. Upscale consignment stores like Secondi in Dupont Circle and discount outlets like Loehmann's in Friendship Heights provide an alternative to the surrounding luxury retail. Secondhand bookstores in Dupont and Georgetown provide hours of browsing and buying at welcoming prices.

Where to Find Unique Gifts

Museum shops are the best places to find unusual items, like the astronaut food on sale at the Air and Space Museum. Downtown galleries sell distinctive modern design gifts. Eastern Market and the surrounding Capitol Hill neighborhood offer local D.C. wares, including jewelry, political books, and even hot sauce.

FRIENDSHIP HEIGHTS/ WISCONSIN AVENUE
luxury & discount retailers in a suburban strip

ADAMS-MORGAN
eclectic bohemian rummaging

U STREET
small vintage, urban boutiques & chic home design stores

GEORGETOWN
retail chains, antiques & galleries, endless hours of cruising

DUPONT CIRCLE
books, coffee, galleries, perfect on the weekends

DOWNTOWN
modern home furnishings, gallery art, & specialty items

EASTERN MARKET
local weekend market & neighborhood stores for unique gifts

Sheridan Circle

Massachusetts Ave.

Columbia Rd.

Florida Ave.

Florida Ave.

New Hampshire Ave.

16th St.

Florida Ave.

Vermont Ave.

Dupont Circle

Logan Circle

Rhode Island Ave.

Scott Circle

Thomas Circle

M St.

Rock Creek

M St.

Connecticut Ave.

Washington Circle

K St.

New York Ave.

Whitehurst Fwy.

M St.

Pennsylvania Ave.

23rd St.

FOGGY BOTTOM

15th St.

14th St.

Virginia Ave.

Theodore Roosevelt Island

Constitution Ave.

Reflecting Pool

THE MONUMENTS

THE MALL

Independence Ave.

Arlington Memorial Br.

Columbia Island

Tidal Basin

Potomac River

Francis Case Memorial Br.

Washington Canal

VIRGINIA

0   500 yards

0   500 meters

Updated by
Mary Beth
Bohman

African masks that could have inspired Picasso; kitchenware as objets d'art; bargains on Christian Dior, Hugo Boss, and Burberry; paisley scarves from India; American and European antiques; books of every description; handicrafts from almost two dozen Native American tribes; music boxes by the thousands; busts of U.S. presidents; textiles by the armful; fine leather goods—all this and more can be found in the nation's capital.

Many of the smaller one-of-a-kind shops have survived urban renewal, the number of designer boutiques is on the rise, and interesting specialty shops and new shopping areas are springing up all over town. Weekdays, downtown street vendors offer a funky mix of jewelry; brightly patterned ties; buyer-beware watches; sunglasses; and African-inspired clothing, accessories, and art. Discriminating shoppers will find satisfaction at upscale malls on the city's outskirts. Of course, T-shirts and Capitol City souvenirs are always in plentiful supply, especially on the streets ringing The Mall.

ADAMS-MORGAN

Scattered among the dozens of Latin, Ethiopian, and international restaurants in this most bohemian of Washington neighborhoods are a score of eccentric shops. If quality is what you seek, Adams-Morgan and nearby Woodley Park can be a minefield; tread cautiously. Still, for the bargain hunter it's great fun. ■ TIP→If bound for a specific shop, you may wish to call ahead to verify hours. Adams-Morganites are often not clock-watchers, although you can be sure an afternoon stroll on the weekend will yield a few hours of great browsing. The evening hours bring scores of revelers to the row, so plan to go before dark unless you want to couple your shopping with a party pit stop.

How to get there is another question. Though the Woodley Park-Zoo/Adams-Morgan Metro stop is technically closer to the 18th Street strip (where the interesting shops are), getting off here means that you will have to walk over the bridge on Calvert Street. Five minutes longer, the walk from the Dupont Circle Metro stop is more scenic; you cruise north on 18th Street through tree-lined streets of row houses and embassies. You can also easily catch Metrobus 42 or a cab from Dupont to Adams-Morgan. ⊠ *18th St. NW between Florida Ave. and Columbia Ave., Adams-Morgan* Ⓜ *Woodley Park-Zoo/Adams-Morgan or Dupont Circle.*

NEED A BREAK?

Tryst Coffeehouse. Relax with a latte on one of the couches or cushiony chairs at this neighborhood hangout. They have a surprisingly large menu that includes sandwiches, bagels, pastries, and alcoholic drinks in addition to their coffee selections. Free Wi-Fi is an added bonus. ⊠ *2459 18th St. NW, Adams-Morgan* ☎ *202/232-5500* ⊕ *www.trystdc.com.*

SPECIALTY STORES

ANTIQUES & COLLECTIBLES

Fodor'sChoice ★

Miss Pixie's Furnishings and Whatnot. The well-chosen collectibles—handpicked by Miss Pixie herself—include gorgeous parasols and umbrellas, antique home furnishings, lamps and mirrors, glass- and silverware, and hardwood bed frames. The reasonable prices will grab your attention. ⊠ *2473 18th St. NW, Adams-Morgan* ☎ *202/232-8171* ⊕ *www.misspixies.com* ⊗ *Closed Wed.* Ⓜ *Woodley Park/Zoo.* **Toro Mata.** Stunning black-and-white pottery from the town of Chulucana is a specialty of this Peruvian gallery; they directly represent six different artisans living and working there. The walls of the gallery are lined with elegant handcrafted wood mirrors, colorful original paintings, alpaca apparel, and other imported Andean crafts. ⊠ *2410 18th St. NW, Adams-Morgan* ☎ *202/232-3890* ⊕ *www.toromata.com* ⊗ *Closed Mon.* Ⓜ *Woodley Park/Zoo.*

BOOKS

Idle Time Books. This multitier used-book store sells "rare to medium rare" books with plenty of meaty titles in all genres, especially out-of-print literature. ⊠ *2467 18th St. NW, Adams-Morgan* ☎ *202/232-4774.* ⊕ *www.idletimebooks.com* Ⓜ *Woodley Park/Zoo.*

CHOCOLATE

biagio. For chocoholics, this is one-stop shopping; biagio will feed your passions, with offerings both foreign—Valrhona from France—and domestic—Marie Bell from New York and Vosges Haut Chocolat from Chicago. Selections from D.C.-area chocolatiers make for tasty souvenirs or gifts. ⊠ *1904 18th St. NW, Adams-Morgan* ☎ *202/238-1506* ⊕ *www.biagiochocolate.com* ⊗ *Closed Mon.* Ⓜ *Dupont Circle.*

HOME FURNISHINGS

Skynear and Company. The owners of this extravagant shop travel the world to find the unusual, and their journeys have netted rich textiles, furniture, and home accessories. A staff of interior designers is on hand to help you identify and sort through the collection of treasures. ⊠ *2122 18th St. NW, Adams-Morgan* ☎ *202/797-7160* ⊕ *www.skynearonline.com* Ⓜ *Woodley Park/Zoo.*

MEN'S & WOMEN'S CLOTHING

Kobos. All the traditional and contemporary ethnic clothing and accessories at this neighborhood staple were imported from West Africa. ⊠ *2444 18th St. NW, Adams-Morgan* ☎ *202/332-9580* Ⓜ *Woodley Park/Zoo.*

FIVE GREAT SHOPPING EXPERIENCES

Apartment Zero, Downtown: The modern, international designs displayed at this home-furnishings store are the perfect counterpoint to the rich traditions of American history and art at the downtown museums.

Kramerbooks & Afterwords, Dupont Circle: Meeting up at Kramerbooks for a lazy Sunday afternoon of brunch and shopping is a quintessential D.C. experience.

Uncle Brutha's Gourmet Foods & Hot Sauce Emporium, Eastern Market: Step up to the tasting bar for a sinus-clearing sample in this friendly shop a block from historic Eastern Market.

Urban Chic, Georgetown: Looking for somewhere to begin in chocka-block Georgetown? Look no further.

Nana, U Street: Fashion is fun again at Nana, where the designers are up-and-coming and the knowledgeable staff is refreshingly attitude-free.

Meeps Fashionette. Catering to fans of shabby-chic and campy glamour, this shop at the bottom of the Adams-Morgan strip stocks a wide selection of vintage clothes and costumes for women and men from the 1940s through the '80s. There's also an expanding selection of new, original designs by local talent. ✉ *2104 18th St. NW, Adams-Morgan* ☎ *202/265–6546* ⊕ *www.meepsDC.com* ⊙ *Closed Mon.* Ⓜ *Dupont Circle.*

SHOES **Fleet Feet.** The expert staff at this friendly shop will assess your feet and your training schedule before recommending the perfect pair of new running shoes. Shoes, apparel, and accessories for running, swimming, soccer, and cycling crowd the small space, where you might just bump into Mayor Adrian Fenty (his parents own the shop). ✉ *1841 Columbia Rd. NW,, Adams-Morgan* ☎ *202/387-3888* ⊕ *www.fleetfeetdc.com* Ⓜ *Woodley Park/Zoo.*

Shake Your Booty. Trend-conscious Washingtoniennes come here for funky and affordable leather boots, fun flats, and dancing shoes. ✉ *2206 18th St. NW, Adams-Morgan* ☎ *202/518–8205* ⊕ *www.shakeyourbootyshoes.com* Ⓜ *Woodley Park/Zoo.*

CAPITOL HILL–EASTERN MARKET

As the Capitol Hill area has become gentrified, unique shops and boutiques have sprung up, many clustered around the redbrick Eastern Market. Inside are produce and meat counters, plus the Market Five art gallery. ■TIP➡The flea market, held on weekends outdoors, presents nostalgia and local crafts by the crateful. There's also a farmers' market on Saturday. Along 7th Street you can find a number of small shops selling such specialties as art books, handwoven rugs, and antiques. Cross Pennsylvania Avenue and head south on 8th Street for historic Barracks Row. Shops, bars, and restaurants inhabit the charming row houses leading toward the Anacostia River. The other shopping lure on the Hill is Union Station, D.C.'s gorgeous train station. Beautifully restored, it now houses both mall shops and Amtrak and commuter trains.

Keep in mind that Union Station and Eastern Market are on opposite sides of the Hill. The Eastern Market Metro stop is the midpoint between the Eastern Market strip and Barracks Row; Union Station is several blocks away. You can certainly walk to Union Station from the Eastern Market stop, but it might be taxing after the time already spent on your feet in the shops. ⊠ *7th and C Sts. SE, Capitol Hill* Ⓜ *Eastern Market or Union Station.*

NEED A BREAK?

The Market Lunch. Locals line up for pancakes and fried fish at this greasy grill next to the fish counter in Eastern Market's food bazaar. Try their specialty crab-cake sandwiches on Sunday. ⊠ *North corner of Eastern Market, 225 7th St. SE, Capitol Hill* ☎ *202/547-8444* ⊙ *Closed Mon.*

A MARKET & A MALL

Eastern Market. Vibrantly-colored produce and flowers; quality meat, poultry, and fish; fragrant cheeses; and tempting sweets are sold by independent vendors at this D.C. institution. On weekends a flea market and an arts and crafts market add to the fun. The redbrick building was gutted by fire in April 2007, but the community rallied around the beloved 134-year-old landmark and restoration work is underway. At this writing, it is scheduled for completion in 2009. In the interim, a temporary structure across the street houses vendors and the lunch counter, The Market Lunch. ⊠ *306 7th St. SE, Capitol Hill* ⊕ *www. easternmarketdc.com* ⊙ *Closed Mon.*

Union Station. This group of shops, resplendent with marble floors and gilded, vaulted ceilings, is inside a working train station. Upscale mall retailers include such familiar names as L'Occitane, Ann Taylor, and Nine West, as well as a bookstore, a multiplex movie theater, sit-down restaurants, and a food court. The east hall is filled with vendors of expensive domestic and international wares who sell from open stalls. ■ TIP➔ There's a tiny outpost of Vacarro's Italian Pastry Shop in the food court. The cannoli and biscotti are to die for. The Christmas season brings lights, a train display, and seasonal gift shops to Union Station. ⊠ *50 Massachusetts Ave. NE, Capitol Hill* ☎ *202/289–1908* ⊕ *www.unionstationdc. com* Ⓜ *Union Station.*

SPECIALTY STORES

BOOKS **Capitol Hill Books.** Pop into this three-story maze of books to browse through a wonderful collection of out-of-print history books, political and fiction writings, and modern first editions. ⊠ *657 C St. SE, Capitol Hill* ☎ *202/544–1621* ⊕ *www.capitolhillbooks-dc.com* Ⓜ *Eastern Market.*

Ⓒ **Fairy Godmother.** This specialty store features books for children, from infants through teens, in English, Spanish, and French. It also sells puppets, toys, craft sets, and CDs. ⊠*319 7th St. SE, Capitol Hill* ☎*202/547–5474* ♥*Closed Sun.* Ⓜ*Eastern Market.*

Trover Shop. A stone's throw from the Capitol, Trover is all about politics. Policy wonks and Hill staffers head to this independent for its excellent selection of political titles and for the book signings. Toys, cards, magazines, and newspapers round out the selection. Note that Trover is close to the Capitol Hill Metro and far from the other shops listed in this section. Stop in here after a visit to the Capitol, the Supreme Court, or the Library of Congress.. ⊠*221 Pennsylvania Ave. SE, Capitol Hill* ☎*202/547–2665* ⊕*www.trover.com* Ⓜ*Capitol S.*

CRAFTS & GIFTS

Fodor'sChoice

★

Alvear Studio. This popular design and imports store overflows with a colorful bounty from the worldwide travels of its owners. You can find Cambodian Buddhas happily seated on Southwestern cowhide rugs. There's also a good representation of local art, furniture, and jewelry. ⊠*705 8th St. SE, Capitol Hill* ☎*202/546–8434* ⊕*www.alvearstudio. com.*♥*Closed Mon. and Tues.* Ⓜ*Eastern Market.*

Homebody. Original artwork, contemporary rugs, delicious-smelling candles, modern kitchen items, and an eclectic mix of jewelry, bags, and wallets crowd this sophisticated and irreverent boutique. ⊠*715 8th St. SE, Capitol Hill* ☎*202/544–8445* ⊕*www.homebodydc.com* ♥*Closed Mon.* Ⓜ*Eastern Market.*

The Village Gallery. This collection of artsy gifts and women's clothing lives in a welcoming house and garden. The upstairs gallery showcases a permanent exhibit of work by D.C. painter Alan Braley, along with a changing roster of local, American, and international artists. ⊠*705 North Carolina Ave. SE, Capitol Hill* ☎*202/546–3040* ⊕*www.thevillageoncapitolhill.com* ♥*Closed Mon.* Ⓜ*Eastern Market.*

Woven History/Silk Road. Landmarks in this bohemian neighborhood, these connected stores sell handmade treasures from small villages around the world. Silk Road sells home furnishings, gifts, clothing, rugs, and accessories made in Asian mountain communities as well as such contemporary items as aromatherapy candles from New York City's not-so-rural Greenwich Village. Woven History's rugs are made the old-fashioned way, with vegetable dyes and hand-spun wool. ⊠*311–315 7th St. SE, Capitol Hill* ☎*202/543–1705* ⊕*www.wovenhistory.com* Ⓜ*Eastern Market.*

CHILDREN'S CLOTHING

⊙

Dawn Price Baby. The infant and toddler clothing at this friendly rowhouse boutique has been carefully selected with an eye for super-comfortable fabrics and distinct designs. They also stock toys, gifts, cribs, bedding, and coveted Bugaboo strollers. ⊠*325 7th St. SE, Capitol Hill* ☎*202/543–2920* ⊕*www.dawnpricebaby.com* ♥*Closed Mon.* Ⓜ*Eastern Market.*

FOOD & WINE

Uncle Brutha's Gourmet Foods & Hot Sauce Emporium. The overwhelming popularity of their stall at neighboring Eastern Market encouraged these entrepreneurs to become a permanent neighborhood fixture. At the hot-sauce tasting bar you can sample all products in the store—300 hot sauces, spices, condiments, and marinades—including the namesake, award-winning Uncle Brutha's Hot Sauce. ⊠*323 7th St. SE,*

11

Eastern Market ☎202/546–3473 ⊕*www.unclebrutha.com* Ⓜ*Eastern Market.*

WOMEN'S CLOTHING **Forecast.** If you like classic, contemporary styles, Forecast should be in your future. It sells silk sweaters and wool blends in solid, muted tones for women seeking elegant but practical clothing from brands like Yansi Fugel. The housewares and gifts selection on the first floor is colorful and of high quality. ✉*218 7th St. SE, Capitol Hill* ☎*202/547–7337* ☯*Closed Mon.* Ⓜ*Eastern Market.*

SPLENDID SHOE STORES
■ Church's, Downtown
■ Fleet Feet, Adams-Morgan
■ Sassanova, Georgetown
■ Wild Women Wear Red, U Street corridor

DOWNTOWN

Downtown D.C. is spread out and sprinkled with federal buildings and museums. Shopping options run the gamut, from the Gallery Place shopping center to small art galleries and bookstores. Gallery Place houses familiar chain stores like Urban Outfitters, Bed, Bath & Beyond, Ann Taylor Loft, and Aveda; it also has a movie theater and a bowling alley. Other big names in the downtown area include Macy's and chain stores like H&M and Banana Republic. With its many offices, downtown tends to shut down at 5 PM sharp, with the exception of the department stores and larger chain stores. A jolly happy-hour crowd springs up after working hours and families and fans fill the streets during weekend sporting events. The revitalized Penn Quarter has some of the best restaurants in town peppered among its galleries and specialty stores.

The worthwhile shops are not concentrated in one area, however. The Gallery Place Metro stop provides the most central starting point—you can walk south to the galleries and design shops, or west toward Metro Center and Farragut North, though this trek is only for the ambitious. Although Gallery Place is a nightlife hot spot, Metro Center and the Farragut area are largely silent after working hours. ✉*North of Pennsylvania Ave. between 7th and 18th Sts., up to Connecticut Ave. below L St., Downtown* Ⓜ*Archives/Navy Memorial, Farragut N and W, Gallery Pl., McPherson Sq., or Metro Center.*

■ NEED A BREAK? **Footnotes Cafe.** Cozy up inside of Olsson's Books at this simple café. Fresh sandwiches and soups named for famous authors fill Chapter 1 of the charming menu, which also has the typical caffeinated drinks and pastries. ✉**418 7th St. NW, Downtown** ☎ **202/638–4882** ⊕**www.footnotescafe.com.**

SPECIALTY STORES

ART GALLERIES The downtown art scene is concentrated on 7th Street between D and I streets. Redevelopment has meant that many artists have had to move their working studios from here to more affordable digs. The galleries, however, which bring foot traffic to area businesses, have managed to maintain a foothold, and new spaces open each year. ■TIP→On the

CLOSE UP

D.C.'s Museum Shops

Does someone in your life need a replica of the Hope diamond? It's waiting for you at the gift shop in the National Museum of Natural History. With a wide range of merchandise and price points, from inexpensive postcards to pricey pottery, museum gift shops allow you the flexibility to bring home a small memento of your visit to the nation's capital or to invest in a piece of American art or history. Museum gift shops offer everything from period jewelry reproductions to science kits for kids, not to mention prints and postcards of the masterpiece paintings in the permanent collections. If you don't want to carry around multiple shopping bags, rest assured that most of the items in museum shops can be purchased off the museum's Web site once you return home. Prices are no higher than you'd find in comparable stores. Another bonus: you won't pay tax on anything purchased in a public museum.

third Thursday of each month, the galleries extend their hours and offer light refreshments from 6 to 8.

Touchstone Gallery. All kinds of mediums are showcased at this 3,000-square-foot artist-owned cooperative. With a membership of more than 30 local artists represented by monthly rotations, the gallery shows a wide range of styles, prices, and quality. ⊠ *406 7th St. NW, Downtown* ☎ *202/347–2787* ⊕ *www.touchstonegallery.com* ⊙ *Closed Mon. and Tues.* Ⓜ *Gallery Pl./Chinatown or Archives/Navy Memorial.*

Zenith Gallery. Founded in 1978, the Zenith exhibits indoor and outdoor sculpture, mixed media, jewelry, and art furniture, as well as a large selection of paintings by national and international artists. ⊠ *413 7th St. NW, Downtown* ☎ *202/783–2963* ⊕ *www.zenith gallery.com* ⊙ *Closed Mon.* Ⓜ *Gallery Pl./Chinatown or Archives/ Navy Memorial.*

BOOKS   **Olsson's Books and Records.** This independent, locally owned D.C. favorite stocks a large and varied collection of books for readers of all ages, a good selection of classical, jazz, and alternative CDs, as well as an expanding choice of DVDs. The staff recommendations and bargain books make browsing here a treat. Check their Web site for author readings and discussion groups. There's another branch in Dupont Circle. ⊠ *418 7th St. NW, Downtown* ☎ *202/638–7610* ⊕ *www.olssons. com* Ⓜ *Archives/Navy Memorial* ⊠ *1307 19th St. NW, Dupont Circle* ☎ *202/785–1133* Ⓜ *Dupont Circle.*

CRAFTS &   **Fahrney's.** What began in 1929 as a repair shop and a pen bar—a place
GIFTS   to fill your fountain pen before setting out for work—is now a wonderland for anyone who loves a good writing instrument. You'll find pens in silver, gold, and lacquer by the world's leading manufacturers. ⊠ *1317 F St. NW, Downtown* ☎ *202/628–9525* ⊕ *www.fahrneyspens. com* ⊙ *Closed Sun.* Ⓜ *Metro Center.*

Indian Craft Shop. Jewelry, pottery, sand paintings, weavings, and baskets from more than 45 Native American tribes, including Navajo, Pueblo, Zuni, Cherokee, Lakota, and Seminole, are at your fingertips here … as long as you have a photo ID to enter the federal building. Items range from inexpensive jewelry (as little as $5) on up to collector-quality art pieces (more than $1,000). ✉*U.S. Department of the Interior, 1849 C St. NW, Room 1023, Downtown* ☎*202/208–4056* ☉*Closed weekends, except 3rd Sat. of each month* Ⓜ*Farragut W or Farragut N.*

Music Box Center. Listen to a total of 500 melodies on more than 1,500 music boxes at this exquisite—and unusual—store. One irresistible item: the Harry Potter music box that plays "That's What Friends Are For." ✉*1920 I St. NW, Downtown* ☎*202/783–9399* ☉*Closed Sun..* Ⓜ*Farragut W.*

FOOD & WINE

Fodor'sChoice

★

Cowgirl Creamery. A California original, this self-titled "cheese shop" has an educated staff that can help you find the perfect block (through many taste tests) as well as a matching wine or olive spread. Their artisan cheeses hail from the Bay area, from local cheese makers, and from points beyond. ✉*919 F St. NW, Downtown* ☎*202/393–6880* ⊕*www.cowgirlcreamery.com* ☉*Closed Sun..* Ⓜ*Gallery Pl.*

HOME
FURNISHINGS

Apartment Zero. This swank housewares store describes itself as the center of 21st-century design. If you're searching for pieces large or small to give your own house a downtown look, this is the place for you. A series of cultural and design-oriented events are regularly hosted in-store—call or check the Web site for more information. ✉*406 7th St. NW, Downtown* ☎*202/628–4067* ⊕*www.apartmentzero.com.* ☉*Closed Mon. and Tues.* Ⓜ*Gallery Pl./Chinatown or Archives/Navy Memorial.*

SHOES

Church's. This top-notch English company's handmade men's shoes are noted for their comfort and durability. ✉*1820 L St. NW, Downtown* ☎*202/296–3366* ☉*Closed Sun..* Ⓜ*Farragut N.*

WOMEN'S
CLOTHING

Alex. Looking for cutting-edge fashion from the latest designers? This jewel box of a shop delivers. In addition to the contemporary lines, Alex stocks a small collection of high-end vintage pieces. ✉*1919 Pennsylvania Ave. NW (entrance is on Eye St.), Downtown* ☎*202/296–2610* ⊕*www.alexboutiquedc.com* Ⓜ*Farragut W.*

Fodor'sChoice

★

Coup de Foudre. All of the upscale lingerie in this inviting, elegant boutique hails from France. Coup de Foudre—which translates to "love at first sight"—specializes in friendly, personalized bra fittings. ✉*1001 Pennsylvania Ave. NW, Downtown* ☎*202/393–0878* ⊕*www.coupdefoudre lingerie.com* ☉*Closed Sun..* Ⓜ*Metro Center.*

Rizik Bros. This tony, patrician Washington institution offers designer women's clothing and expert advice. The sales staff will help find just the right style from the store's inventory, which is particularly strong in formal dresses. Take the elevator up from the northwest corner of Connecticut Avenue and L Street. ✉*1100 Connecticut Ave. NW, Downtown* ☎*202/223–4050* Ⓜ*Farragut N.*

DUPONT CIRCLE

You might call Dupont Circle a younger, less staid version of Georgetown—almost as pricey but with more apartment buildings than houses. Its many restaurants, offbeat shops, and specialty book and record stores give it a cosmopolitan air. The street scene here is more urban than Georgetown's, with bike messengers and chess aficionados filling up the park. The Sunday farmers' market is a popular destination for organic food, fresh cheese, homemade soap, and hand-spun wool. To the south of Dupont Circle proper are several boutiques and familiar retail stores close to the Farragut and Farragut North Metro stops. Burberry and Thomas Pink both have stores in this area of Dupont. ✉ *Connecticut Ave. between M and S Sts.* Ⓜ *Dupont Circle.*

> ### OPEN HOUSE FOR ART
>
> On the "First Friday" of every month, the streets of Dupont Circle fill with wine-and-cheese-loving gallery hoppers, who are there to attend the joint open houses held by almost 20 galleries. Check out **The Galleries of Dupont Circle** (⊕ *www.dupontcirclegalleries.com*) for information on all events.

NEED A BREAK? **Kramerbooks & Afterwords.** Serving brunch in the morning, snacks in the afternoon, cocktails in the evening, and coffee all day long, Kramer's is the perfect spot for a break. Try to snag an outside table, drop your shopping bags, and watch the world go by. ✉ *1517 Connecticut Ave. NW, Dupont Circle* ☎ *202/387-1400* ⊕ *www.kramers.com* Ⓜ *Dupont Circle.*

SPECIALTY STORES

ANTIQUES & COLLECTIBLES **Geoffrey Diner Gallery.** A must for hard-core antiques shoppers on the hunt for 19th-, 20th-, and 21st-century wares, this store sells Tiffany lamps and Arts and Crafts pieces from pivotal designers from Europe and the United States. It's open Saturday and by appointment only. ✉ *1730 21st St. NW, Dupont Circle* ☎ *202/483-5005* ⊕ *www.dinergallery.com* ⊙ *Closed Sun.–Fri.* Ⓜ *Dupont Circle.*

ART GALLERIES **America, Oh Yes!** With one of the most extensive folk-art collections in the country, this gallery is also known for its reasonable prices. It represents more than 160 self-taught American artists. ✉ *1350 Connecticut Ave. NW, Suite 202, Dupont Circle* ☎ *202/721-0043* ⊕ *www.americaohyes.com* ⊙ *Closed weekends* Ⓜ *Dupont Circle.*

Burdick Gallery. John Burdick's cozy gallery focuses exclusively on Inuit art and sculpture of the Eskimo communities of Hudson Bay, Baffin Island, and the high central Canadian Arctic. Expect to find arresting, uniquely executed depictions of nature and home. ✉ *2114 R St. NW, Dupont Circle* ☎ *202/986-5682* ⊕ *www.burdickgallery.com* ⊙ *Closed Sun. and Mon.* Ⓜ *Dupont Circle.*

Burton Marinkovich Fine Art. You know you've reached this gallery when you spot the small front yard with two modern abstract sculptures (they're by Lesley Dill and Leonard Cave). The gallery has works on paper by modern and contemporary masters, including Ross Bleckner, Richard Diebenkorn, David Hockney, Kandinsky, Matisse, Miró, Motherwell, Picasso, and others. Rare modern illustrated books and British linocuts from the Grosvenor School are also specialties. ✉ *1506 21st*

St. NW, Dupont Circle 🕾*202/296–6563* ⊕*www.burtonmarinkovich. com* ⊘*Closed Sun. and Mon.* Ⓜ*Dupont Circle.*

Fodor'sChoice
★
Hemphill Fine Arts. This spacious gem of a contemporary gallery shows established artists in all mediums such as Jacob Kainen and William Christenberry as well as emerging ones like Colby Caldwell. ⊠*1515 14th St. NW, 3rd fl., Logan Circle* 🕾*202/234–5601* ⊕*www.hemphill finearts.com* ⊘*Closed Sun. and Mon.* Ⓜ*Dupont Circle.*

Irvine Contemporary. This bright and open gallery space showcases emerging regional and international artists. Noteworthy names include Teo Gonzalez, Paul D. Miller (DJ Spooky), and Dalek (James Marshall). ⊠*1412 14th St. NW, Dupont Circle* 🕾*202/332–8767* ⊕*www. irvinecontemporary.com* ⊘*Closed Sun. and Mon.* Ⓜ*Dupont Circle.*

BOOKS
Fodor'sChoice
★
Kramerbooks & Afterwords. One of Washington's best-loved independents, this cozy shop has a small but choice selection of fiction and nonfiction. Open 24 hours on Fridays and Saturdays, it's a convenient meeting place. Kramerbooks shares space with a café that has late-night dining and live music from Wednesday to Saturday. ∎**TIP→There's a computer with free Internet access available in the bar, though you'll have to stand up to use it.** ⊠*1517 Connecticut Ave. NW, Dupont Circle* 🕾*202/387–1400* ⊕*www.kramers.com* Ⓜ*Dupont Circle.*

Lambda Rising. Over the years, Lambda has grown beyond its local fame to national influence. Lambda Rising is *the* source for information and literature for and about the gay, lesbian, bisexual, and transgendered communities. The store isn't all business, though: check out the fun, colorful, and ever-changing window displays. ⊠*1625 Connecticut Ave. NW, Dupont Circle* 🕾*202/462–6969* ⊕*www.lambdarising.com* Ⓜ*Dupont Circle.*

★ **Second Story Books.** A used-books and -records emporium that stays open late, Second Story may lead bibliophiles to browse for hours. ⊠*2000 P St. NW, Dupont Circle* 🕾*202/659–8884* ⊕*www.second storybooks.com* Ⓜ*Dupont Circle.*

CHILDREN'S CLOTHING
©
Kid's Closet. If filling a little one's closet is on your list, stop here for high-quality contemporary infant and children's clothing and toys. They carry sizes 0-7 for boys and 0-16 for girls. ⊠*1226 Connecticut Ave. NW, Dupont Circle* 🕾*202/429–9247* ⊕*www.kidsclosetdc.com* ⊘*Closed Sun.* Ⓜ*Dupont Circle.*

CRAFTS & GIFTS
Beadazzled. A rainbow of ready-to-string beads fills the cases at this appealing shop. They also stock jewelry as well as books on crafts history and techniques. Check their Web site for a class schedule. ⊠*1507 Connecticut Ave. NW, Dupont Circle* 🕾*202/265–2323* ⊕*www. beadazzled.net* Ⓜ*Dupont Circle.*

The Chocolate Moose. This store is simple, sheer fun for adults and kids alike. Looking for clacking, windup teeth? You can find them here, along with unusual greeting cards, strange boxer shorts, and unique handcrafts. If playing with all those fun toys makes you hungry, you can pick up a select line of premium European chocolates. ⊠*1743 L St. NW, Dupont Circle* 🕾*202/463–0992* ⊕*www.chocolatemoosedc. com.*⊘*Closed Sun.* Ⓜ*Farragut N.*

Terra. Carved sugar bowls from Mozambique, baby socks by Trumpette, and luxury cashmere travel sets are among the eclectic offerings at Terra. Their globe-trotting collection of interesting design goods will supply fashionable gifts for all occasions. ⊠*1706 Connecticut Ave. NW* ☎*202//232–8581* ⊕*www.shopterradc.com.*

The Written Word. Not just a stationery store, the Written Word is more like a tribute to paper. In addition to a wide variety of handmade papers, there are journals, photo albums, and scrapbooks—all made out of unusual papers, as well as unique greeting cards. It's also one of the few places in D.C. that offer custom letterpress printing. ⊠*1427 P St. NW, Dupont Circle* ☎*202/223–1400* ⊕*www.writtenwordstudio. com* Ⓜ*Dupont Circle.*

HOME
FURNISHINGS
Dragonfly. Dragonfly's expert owner hand-selects antiques on her trips to Asia. Finds from eight provinces in China, Vietnam, and Mongolia fill this inviting shop. ⊠*1457 Church St. NW* ☎*202/265–3359* ⊕*www.dragonflydd.com.*♥*Closed Mon.-Tues.* Ⓜ*Dupont.*

Reincarnations. Reincarnations is a neighborhood favorite, partly because of its duo of imposing wooden soldiers at the doorway. It's hard to pinpoint one style that dominates—trendy, antique, funky—and everyone can find something to like here. ⊠*1401 14th St. NW, Logan Circle* ☎*202/319–1606* ⊕*www.reincarnationsfurnishings. com/* Ⓜ*Dupont Circle.*

Tabletop. Evoking a museum gift shop, this two-story row house is a delightful place to find bags by Swedish designer Lotta Jansdotter, Mari Mekko accessories, and daphne olive jewelry, as well as modern furniture, pillows, and rugs. ⊠*1608 20th St. NW, Dupont Circle* ☎*202/387–7117* ⊕*www.tabletopdc.com* Ⓜ*Dupont Circle.*

JEWELRY
Pampillonia Jewelers. Here you can find traditional designs in 18-karat gold and platinum as well as eye-catching contemporary designs. They also carry estate and antique jewelry and make repairs. The selection for men is particularly good. ⊠*1213 Connecticut Ave. NW, Farragut Square* ☎*202/628–6305* ⊕*www.pampillonia.com.*♥*Closed Sun.* Ⓜ*Farragut N.*

Tiny Jewel Box. Despite its name, this venerable D.C. favorite contains six floors of precious and semiprecious wares, including unique gifts, home accessories, vintage pieces, and works by well-known designers. ⊠*1147 Connecticut Ave. NW, Farragut Square* ☎*202/393–2747* ⊕*www.tinyjewelbox.com.*♥*Closed Sun.* Ⓜ*Farragut N.*

KITCHENWARE
Coffee and the Works. Coffee and tea lovers head to this charmingly cluttered shop for high-end kitchen gadgets, magnets, colorful ceramic pots, and other accessories, as well as the beans and leaves themselves. ⊠*1627 Connecticut Ave. NW, Dupont Circle* ☎*202/483–8050* Ⓜ*Dupont Circle.*

MEN'S
CLOTHING
J. Press. Like its flagship store, founded in Connecticut in 1902 as a custom shop for Yale University, this Washington outlet is resolutely traditional: Shetland and Irish wool sport coats are a specialty. ⊠*1801 L St. NW, Farragut Square* ☎*202/857–0120* ⊕*www.jpressonline.com* Ⓜ*Farragut N.*

WOMEN'S **Betsy Fisher.** Catering to women of all ages and sizes in search of con-
CLOTHING temporary and trendy styles, this store stocks one-of-a-kind accessories,
Fodor's Choice clothes, shoes, and jewelry by well-known designers like Diane Von
★ Furstenberg. A small selection of up-and-coming local designs is also
available. ✉ *1224 Connecticut Ave. NW, Dupont Circle* ☎*202/785–
1975* ⊕*www.betsyfisher.com* Ⓜ*Dupont Circle.*

Fodor's Choice **Secondi.** One of the city's finest consignment shops, Secondi carries a
★ well-chosen selection of women's designer and casual clothing, accessories, and shoes. The brands carried include Marc Jacobs, Louis Vuitton, Donna Karan, Prada, and Ann Taylor. ✉*1702 Connecticut Ave.
NW, 2nd fl., Dupont Circle* ☎*202/667–1122* ⊕*www.secondi.com*
Ⓜ*Dupont Circle.*

GEORGETOWN

Although Georgetown is not on a Metro line and street parking is
nonexistent, people still flock here, keeping it D.C.'s favorite shopping
area. This is also the capital's center for famous residents, as well as
being a hot spot for restaurants, bars, and nightclubs.

National chains and designer shops now stand side-by-side with the
specialty shops that first gave the district its allure, but the historic
neighborhood is still charming and its street scene lively. In addition to
housing tony antiques, elegant crafts, and high-style shoe and clothing
boutiques, Georgetown offers wares that attract local college students
and young people: books, music, and fashions from familiar names
such as Banana Republic, BCBG, Betsey Johnson, Kate Spade, and
Urban Outfitters. Most stores lie east and west on M Street and to the
north on Wisconsin Avenue. The intersection of M and Wisconsin is
the nexus for chain stores and big-name designer shops. The farther
you venture in any direction from this intersection, the more eclectic
and interesting the shops become. Some of the big-name stores are
worth a look for their architecture alone; several shops blend traditional Georgetown town-house exteriors with airy modern showroom
interiors.

Shopping in Georgetown can be expensive, but you don't have to add
expensive parking lot fees to your total bill. The nearest Metro, Foggy
Bottom/GWU, is a 10- to 15-minute walk from the shops. ■TIP➡**The
D.C. Circulator is your best bet for getting into and out of Georgetown,
especially if it's hot or if you are laden down with many purchases. This
$1 bus runs along M Street and up Wisconsin, passing the major shop-
ping strips.** ✉*Intersection of Wisconsin Ave. and M St., Georgetown*
Ⓜ*Foggy Bottom/GWU.*

**NEED A
BREAK?** **DolceZZa.** The hand-made gelato and sorbet at this all-white storefront are
divine, especially during the heat of summer. The flavors, such as Coconut
con Dulce de Leche, are endlessly inventive. Strawberry-, peach-, apple-, and
clementine-flavored sorbets are available seasonally. Espresso and churros
will warm winter afternoons. ✉*1560 Wisconsin Ave. NW, Georgetown20007*
☎*202/333-4646* ⊕*dolcezzagelato.com.*

MALL

Shops at Georgetown Park. Near the hub of the Georgetown shopping district is this posh tri-level mall, which looks like a Victorian ice-cream parlor inside. The pricey clothing and accessory boutiques and the ubiquitous chain stores draw international visitors in droves. Next door is a branch of the Dean & Deluca gourmet grocery and café. ✉ *3222 M St. NW, Georgetown* ☎ *202/298–5577* ⊕ *www.shopsat-georgetownpark.com* Ⓜ *Foggy Bottom/GWU.*

SPECIALTY STORES

ANTIQUES &
COLLECTIBLES

Cherub Antiques Gallery & Michael Getz Antiques. Two dealers have shared this Victorian row house for 24 years. Michael Getz Antiques carries fireplace equipment and silver. Cherub Antiques Gallery specializes in art nouveau and art deco. A glass case by the door holds a collection of over 100 cocktail shakers, including Prohibition-era pieces disguised as teakettles. ✉ *2918 M St. NW, Georgetown* ☎ *202/337–2224 Cherub Gallery, 202/338–3811 Michael Getz Antiques* Ⓜ *Foggy Bottom/GWU.*

Fodor'sChoice
★

Jean Pierre Antiques. Very Georgetown, this gorgeous shop sells antique furniture and gifts from France, Germany, and Italy. ✉ *2601 P St. NW, Georgetown* ☎ *202/337–1731.*

Marston Luce. House and garden accessories are in the mix here, but the emphasis is on 18th- and 19th-century French country furniture discovered by the owner on yearly buying trips in Europe. They also carry Scandinavian painted furniture. ✉ *1651 Wisconsin Ave. NW, Georgetown* ☎ *202/333–6800.* ⊙ *Closed Sun.* Ⓜ *Foggy Bottom/GWU.*

Miller & Arney Antiques. English, American, and European furniture and accessories from the 17th, 18th, and early 19th centuries make Miller & Arney Antiques look like a museum gallery. Asian porcelain adds splashes of color. ✉ *1737 Wisconsin Ave. NW, Georgetown* ☎ *202/338–2369.* ⊕ *www.millerarney.com* ⊙ *Closed Sun.* Ⓜ *Foggy Bottom/GWU.*

Old Print Gallery. Here you can find the capital's largest collection of old prints, with a focus on maps and 19th-century decorative prints (including Washingtoniana). ✉ *1220 31st St. NW, Georgetown* ☎ *202/965–1818* ⊕ *www.oldprintgallery.com* ⊙ *Closed Sun.* Ⓜ *Foggy Bottom/GWU.*

Opportunity Shop of the Christ Child Society. This Georgetown landmark, staffed by volunteers, sells fine antiques, crystal, silver, and porcelain on consignment. Prices are moderate, and profits go to a good cause—the Christ Child Society, which provides for the needs of local children and young mothers. ✉ *1427 Wisconsin Ave. NW, Georgetown* ☎ *202/333–6635.* ⊕ *www.christchilddc.org* Ⓜ *Foggy Bottom/GWU.*

Susquehanna. With three rooms upstairs, four rooms downstairs, and a garden full of benches, urns, and tables, Susquehanna is the largest antiques shop in Georgetown. The shop's true specialty is European and American furniture and decorative art from the 18th and 19th centuries. ✉ *3216 O St. NW, Georgetown* ☎ *202/333–1511* ⊕ *www. susquehannaantiques.com.* ⊙ *Closed Sun.* Ⓜ *Foggy Bottom/GWU.*

11

ART GALLERIES Many of Georgetown's galleries are on side streets. Their holdings are primarily work by established artists.

Addison Ripley. This well-respected gallery exhibits contemporary work by national and local artists, including painters Manon Cleary and Wolf Kahn and photographer Frank Hallam Day. ✉ *1670 Wisconsin Ave. NW, Georgetown* ☎ *202/338–5180* ⊕ *www.addisonripleyfineart.com* ⊙ *Closed Sun. and Mon.* Ⓜ *Foggy Bottom/GWU.*

Appalachian Spring. The glossy wooden jewelry boxes displayed here are treasures in their own right. Traditional and contemporary American-made crafts—including art glass, pottery, jewelry, and toys—fill this lovely shop. There's also an outpost in Union Station. ✉ *1415 Wisconsin Ave. NW, Georgetown* ☎ *202/337-5780* ⊕ *www.appalachianspring.com* ✉ *Union Station, East Hall, 50 Massachusetts Ave. NE, Capitol Hill* ☎ *202/682-0505.*

Galleries 1054. Several distinct galleries live under one roof at this location. **cross mackenzie ceramic art** (☎ *202/333–7970*) features vibrant and unusual ceramic pieces. **Parish** (☎ *202/944–2310*) features contemporary work in all mediums by African-American artists. **Alla Rogers** (☎ *202/333–8595*) has contemporary Eastern European, Russian, and American art and photography. ✉ *1054 31st St. NW, Georgetown* ⊙ *Closed Sun. and Mon.* Ⓜ *Foggy Bottom/GWU.*

BOOKS **Bartleby's Books.** Be a scholar and surround yourself with rare and precious books in this antiquarian book store. The Americana collection—organized by state—is particularly browsable; you might just find an unexpected souvenir from home. ✉ *1132 29th St. NW, Georgetown* ☎ *202/298-0486* ⊕ *www.bartlebysbooks.com* ⊙ *Closed Sun. and Mon.*

Bridge Street Books. This charming independent store focuses on politics, history, philosophy, poetry, literature, film, and Judaica. ✉ *2814 Pennsylvania Ave. NW, Georgetown* ☎ *202/965-5200* ⊕ *www.bridgestreetbooks.com* Ⓜ *Foggy Bottom/GWU.*

CHILDREN'S CLOTHING **Piccolo Piggies.** Chock-full of fun and educational toys as well as classic layette and children's clothing (up to size 14 for girls and 10 for boys), this warm store is a pleasure to browse through—even if you're a bit over the age limit. ✉ *1533 Wisconsin Ave. NW, Georgetown* ☎ *202/333–0123* ⊕ *www.piccolo-piggies.com.*

Yiro. One hundred percent organic, Yiro clothing (through age 10) is produced without chemicals and is colored only with natural dyes (and yes, the outfits are soft and attractive). A baby registry will help you pick the perfect gift for the environmentally conscious mom. ✉ *3236 P St. NW, Georgetown* ☎ *202/338-9476* ⊕ *www.yirostores.com.*

ALL AMERICAN GIFTS

- Appalachian Spring, Georgetown
- Bartleby's Books, Georgetown
- Cowgirl Creamery, Downtown
- Goodwood, U Street corridor

HOME
FURNITURE
Fodor's Choice
★
A Mano. The store's name is Italian for "by hand," and it lives up to its name, stocking colorful hand-painted ceramics, hand-dyed tablecloths, blown-glass stemware, and other home and garden accessories by Italian and French artisans. Items are now also available in their online catalog. ⊠*1677 Wisconsin Ave. NW, Georgetown* ☎*202/298–7200* ⊕*www.amano.bz.*

Theodore's. A Washington institution, Theodore's is the place to visit for ultramod housewares, from stylish furniture to accessories, leather, and upholstery that make a statement. There's an excellent selection of wall-storage units for almost all tastes. ⊠*2233 Wisconsin Ave. NW, Georgetown* ☎*202/333–2300* ⊕*www.theodores.com.*

MEN'S &
WOMEN'S
CLOTHING
Commander Salamander. This funky outpost sells clothes for punk kids and ravers. Retro aficionados will also find clothing and accessories for their wardrobes. Sifting through the assortment of leather, chains, toys, and candy-color makeup is as much entertainment as it is shopping.. ⊠*1420 Wisconsin Ave. NW, Georgetown* ☎*202/337–2265* Ⓜ*Foggy Bottom/GWU.*

The District Line. This premium casual men's and women's clothing outlet exclusively features threads from the other side of the pond. It's a one-stop shop for U.K. clothing lines, including Fred Perry (classic mod) and Boxfresh (London street style). ⊠*1250 Wisconsin Ave. NW, Georgetown* ☎*202/558–5508* ⊕*www.thedistrictline.com.*

relish. In the fashionable Cady Alley stretch, this dramatic space holds an expanding men and women's collection hand-picked seasonally by the owner. Modern, elegant, and practical selections include European classics as well as well-tailored modern designers, such as Miu Miu and Sigerson Morrison. ⊠*3312 Cady's Alley NW, Georgetown* ☎*202/333–5343* ⊕*www.relishdc.com* ⊙*Closed Sun.* Ⓜ*Foggy Bottom/GWU.*

SHOES
Fodor's Choice
★
Hu's Shoes. This cutting-edge shoe store would shine in Paris, Tokyo, or New York. Luckily for us, it brings ballet flats, heels, and boots from designers like Chloé, Proenza Schouler, Sonia Rykiel, and Viktor&Rolf right here to Georgetown. ⊠*3005 M St. NW, Georgetown* ☎*202/342–0202* ⊕*www.hushoes.com* Ⓜ*Foggy Bottom/GWU.*

Sassanova. There are high-end shoes in this girly shop for every occasion—be it a walk on the beach or through a boardroom. Brands carried include Lulu Guinness, Emma Hope, and Sigerson Morrison. Jewelry, bags, and shoes for kids round out the selection. ⊠*1641 Wisconsin Ave. NW, Georgetown* ☎*202/471–4400* ⊕*www.sassanova.com.*

SPAS &
BEAUTY
SALONS
Fodor's Choice
★
Blue Mercury. Hard-to-find skin-care lines—Laura Mercier, Trish McEvoy, and Paula Dorf are just a few—are what set this home-grown, now national, chain apart. The retail space up front sells soaps, lotions, perfumes, cosmetics, and skin- and hair-care products. Behind the glass door is the "skin gym," where you can treat yourself to facials, waxing, massage, and oxygen treatments. ⊠*3059 M St. NW, Georgetown* ☎*202/965–1300* ⊕*www.bluemercury.com* Ⓜ*Foggy Bottom/GWU* ⊠*1619 Connecticut Ave. NW, Dupont Circle* ☎*202/462–1300* Ⓜ*Dupont Circle.*

Sephora. Better than any department store perfume or cosmetic counter, this supplier of beauty products offers hundreds of fine fragrances, bath products, and cosmetics from all over the world—right at your fingertips. Sephora also carries its own line of beauty products, all exquisitely packaged and quite affordable. The black-clad salespeople are pleasantly low-key. ⊠*3065 M St. NW, Georgetown* ☎*202/338–5644* ⊕*www.sephora.com* Ⓜ*Foggy Bottom/GWU.*

WOMEN'S
CLOTHING

The Phoenix. Here you can find contemporary clothing in natural fibers by designers such as Eileen Fisher and Flax, as well as jewelry and fine- and folk-art pieces from Mexico. ⊠*1514 Wisconsin Ave. NW, Georgetown* ☎*202/338–4404* ⊕*www.thephoenixdc.com.*

Urban Chic. It's hard to imagine a fashionista who wouldn't find something she loved here—whether she could afford it might be another story. Gorgeous suits, jeans, cocktail dresses, and accessories from Catherine Malandrino, Ella Moss, Rebecca Taylor, and Susana Monaco are to be had. The handbags are a highlight. ⊠*1626 Wisconsin Ave. NW, Georgetown* ☎*202/338–5398* ⊕*www.urbanchiconline.com.*

Valise. Party-hopping Washingtoniennes pop by this tiny boutique for one-of-a-kind cocktail dresses and perhaps a trendy accessory to match. ⊠*1624 Wisconsin Ave. NW, Georgetown* ☎*202/333–3622* ⊕*www.shop-valise.com.*

Wink. While the clientele and styles skew toward the young and trendy, women of all ages shop in this subterranean space for coveted jeans and colorful, sparkly tops, dresses, and jewelry. Theory, Diane von Furstenberg, and Development are among the labels carried. ⊠*3109 M St. NW, Georgetown* ☎*202/338–9465* ⊕*www.shopwinkdc.com* Ⓜ*Foggy Bottom/GWU.*

U STREET

In the 1930s and '40s, U Street was known for its classy theaters and jazz clubs. After decades of decline following the 1968 riots, the neighborhood has been revitalized. The area has gentrified at lightning speed, but has retained a diverse mix of multiethnic young professionals and older, working-class African-Americans. At night the neighborhood's club, bar, and restaurant scene comes alive. During the day the street scene is more laid-back, with more locals than tourists occupying the distinctive shops. ■TIP→On the third Thursday of each month the area shops stay open late to offer light refreshments and special deals for the fun "Shopper Socials." ⊠*U St. between 12th and 17th Sts., U Street corridor* Ⓜ*U St./Cardozo.*

NEED A
BREAK?

Love Cafe. The sister store to the CakeLove bakery across the street, this is a casual community hot spot. The buttercream cupcakes are incredibly sweet, and the rosy atmosphere warms you on the inside. ⊠*1506 U St. NW, U Street corridor* ☎*202/588–7100* ⊕*www.cakelove.com* Ⓜ*U St./Cardozo.*

SPECIALTY STORES

ANTIQUES &
COLLECTIBLES

Goodwood. This friendly shop sells vintage and antique wood furniture, including wonderful 19th-century American pieces, along with stained glass, mirrors, and other decorative items—even a small but gorgeous collection of estate jewelry. ☒1428 U St. NW, U Street corridor ☎202/986-3640 ⊕www.goodwooddc.com ⊙Closed Mon.–Wed. Ⓜ U St./Cardozo.

FASHIONS FOR HER
■ Betsy Fisher, Dupont Circle
■ Coup de Foudre, Downtown
■ Nana, U Street corridor
■ relish, Georgetown

Millennium. This eclectic shop sells what it calls "20th-century antiques," a unique blend of high-end vintage mid-century modern housewares, clothing, and furniture ☒1528 U St. NW, downstairs, U Street corridor ☎202/483–1218 ⊙Closed Mon.–Wed. Ⓜ U St./Cardozo.

HOME
FURNISHINGS

Go Mama Go! This colorful, inviting store makes you feel like you're wandering through the stalls of a global marketplace. African, Asian, and Latin home furnishings and unique gifts dominate the wares. ☒1809 14th St. NW, U Street corridor ☎202/299–0850 ⊕www.gomamago.com Ⓜ U St./Cardozo.

Habitat Home Accents & Jewelry. This store sells artist-made jewelry and well-chosen desk sets, lamps, and tabletop items. ☒1510 U St. NW, U Street corridor ☎202/518-7222 ⊕www.habitatstyle.com ⊙Closed Tues. and Wed. in winter. Ⓜ U St./Cardozo.

Home Rule. Here you can find some of the latest design elements for the bath, bar, kitchen, and dining room from Europe as well as playful sink stoppers and other fun and affordable household items. ☒1807 14th St. NW, U Street corridor ☎202/797-5544 ⊕www.homerule.com. Ⓜ U St./Cardozo.

Muléh. Exquisite contemporary Indonesian and Filipino home furnishings and trendy clothes from L.A. and New York fill this expansive showroom. The furniture pieces, which are the primary focus of the store, are made from fine organic materials. It's sort of like wandering through a luxury resort in Southeast Asia and finding a fabulous clothing boutique tucked in the back. ☒1831 14th St. NW, U Street corridor ☎202/667-3440 ⊕www.muleh.com ⊙Closed Mon. Ⓜ U St./Cardozo.

Zawadi. The name means "gift" in Swahili, but you may want to buy the beautiful African art, textiles, home accessories, and jewelry for yourself. ☒1524 U St. NW, U Street corridor ☎202/232-2214 ⊕www.zawadidc.com Ⓜ U St./Cardozo.

WOMEN'S
CLOTHING

Moojoo Ken. To become a true D.C.-er, you should outfit yourself with the matching purses and shoes inspired by and named after the city streets found in this local luxury collection. ☒1512 U St. NW, U Street corridor ☎202/234-3140 ⊕www.moojooken.com Ⓜ U St./Cardozo.

Fodor'sChoice
★

Nana. A hip and friendly staff is one of the reasons why D.C. women love this store. Another is the stock of both new and vintage women's clothes at affordable prices, plus handmade jewelry and cool handbags. ✉*1528 U St. NW, upstairs, U Street corridor* ☎202/667–6955 ⊕*www.nanadc.com* Ⓜ*U St./Cardozo.*

Wild Women Wear Red. The unique footwear and handbags here, many of which are boldly hued, are for the adventurous. Featured designers include Bronx NY and Lisa Nading. ✉*1512 U St. NW, U Street corridor* ☎202/387–5700 ⊕*www.wildwomenwearred.com* Ⓜ*U St./Cardozo.*

FRIENDSHIP HEIGHTS

The major thoroughfare Wisconsin Avenue runs northwest through the city from Georgetown toward Maryland. It crosses the border in the midst of the Friendship Heights shopping district, which is also near Chevy Chase. Expensive department stores and designer shops stand cheek by jowl with major discount chains around the Friendship Heights Metro stop. Other neighborhoods in the District yield more interesting finds and more enjoyable shopping and sightseeing, but it's hard to beat Friendship Heights for sheer convenience and selection. Bloomingdale's is the latest addition to the upscale lineup, which includes Barneys CO-OP, Neiman Marcus, and Saks Fifth Avenue. Stand-alone designer stores like Jimmy Choo, Louis Vuitton, Christian Dior, and Cartier up the luxury quotient. Filene's Basement, Loehmann's, and T.J. Maxx hawk the designer names at much lower prices. Lord & Taylor and chains like the Gap, Ann Taylor Loft, and Williams Sonoma occupy the middle ground.

Tightly packed into a few blocks, the big-name area is self-explanatory. However, there are also a few local gems in the surrounding neighborhood. Some of these small shops are far from Metro stops, so call ahead for directions. ✉*Wisconsin Ave. between Jenifer St. NW and Western Ave.* Ⓜ*Friendship Heights.*

SPECIALTY STORES

BOOKS **Politics and Prose.** The calendar of this legendary independent is jam-packed with author events and signings, and their tables are endlessly browsable. There's a coffee shop downstairs where you can debate the issues of the day. The nearest Metro is 15 minutes away. ✉*5015 Connecticut Ave. NW, Friendship Heights* ☎202/364–1919 ⊕*www. politics-prose.com* Ⓜ*Friendship Heights.*

FOOD & WINE **Calvert Woodley Liquors.** This liquor store carries not only an excellent selection of wine and hard liquor, but also many kinds of cheese and other picnic and cocktail-party fare, as well as the legendary H&H bagels from New York. Its international offerings have made it a favorite pantry for embassy parties. ✉*4339 Connecticut Ave. NW, Tenleytown* ☎202/966–4400 ⊕*www.calvertwoodley.com.*☉*Closed Sun.* Ⓜ*Van Ness/UDC.*

Rodman's Discount Foods and Drugstore. The rare store that carries wine, cheese, and space heaters, Rodman's is a fascinating hybrid of Kmart and Dean & Deluca. The appliances are downstairs, the imported peppers and chocolates upstairs. ■TIP➡**It's also a working drugstore, so you can have a prescription filled or pick up some sinus medicine, bath bubbles,**

or a pair of sunglasses. ⊠*5100 Wisconsin Ave. NW, Friendship Heights* ☎*202/363–3466* Ⓜ*Friendship Heights.*

GIFTS **Periwinkle Inc.** Warm and welcoming, Periwinkle offers a panoply of gift options: boutique chocolates, cases of nutty and gummy treats, Stonewall Kitchen snacks, hand-designed wrapping paper, scented bath products, printed note cards, and Voluspa candles. ⊠*3815 Livingston St. NW, Friendship Heights* ☎*202/364–3076* Ⓜ*Friendship Heights.*

MEN'S & **Everett Hall.** D.C.'s own Everett Hall designs men's suits that are richly
WOMEN'S classic in their material and cutting-edge in their design, color, and
CLOTHING sensibility. Most suits are $1,000 and up. From NBA and NFL athletes to K-Street lawyers, men with verve and a sense of style covet Hall's designs. ⊠*Chevy Chase Pavilion, 5301 Wisconsin Ave. NW, Friendship Heights* ☎*202/362–0191* Ⓜ*Friendship Heights.*

Micmac Bis. Inside this boutique with eye-catching displays are clothes by Issey Miyake and Yohji Yamamoto, and cool Arche shoes. ⊠*5454 Wisconsin Ave. NW, Chevy Chase* ☎*301/654–8686* Ⓜ*Friendship Heights.*

Sahba. This avant-garde women's clothing boutique stocks an expertly selected cache of True Religion jeans, Robert Rodriguez tops, and Jamin Peuch handbags. ⊠*5300 Wisconsin Ave. NW, Friendship Heights* ☎*202/966–5080* Ⓜ*Friendship Heights.*

Side Trips

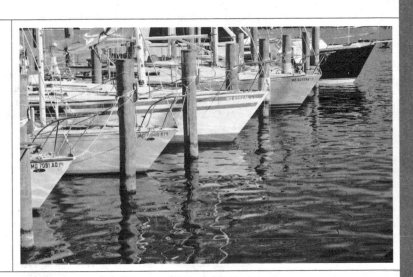

Sailboats in a marina at the Annapolis Yacht Club

WORD OF MOUTH

"Possibly my favorite thing to do in the whole D.C. area is to ride the Mt. Vernon Trail. You can cross over the Memorial Bridge from D.C. and hop right on the bike trail, which travels along the Potomac all the way to Mt. Vernon. I can't emphasize just how gorgeous this ride is. If you rent bikes, you'll just have to also be sure to rent bike locks, so when you reach Mt. Vernon, you can lock them up while you go into Mt. Vernon to see all the sights."

—RaymondLuxuryYacht

SIDE TRIPS PLANNER

If You Don't Have a Car

A car is a big help when visiting the sights outside of Washington, but you're not lost without one.

Of the places we cover here, Alexandria is the easiest car-free option, reachable by Metro at the King Street stop, about 25 minutes from Metro Center. Once you exit, it's a 10-block walk to the center of Old Town. To get to Annapolis, you can take one of the commuter buses, and to reach Mount Vernon, you use a combination of bus and Metro. The C&O Canal begins in Georgetown; from there it's an easy 13-mile bike ride (or a pleasant, but long, walk) along the canal towpath to Great Falls Tavern.

Four Places to Explore

ALEXANDRIA

Alexandria is across the Potomac and 7 mi downstream from Washington. As a commercial port, it competed with Georgetown in the days before Washington was a city. It's now a "big" small town loaded with historic homes, shops, and restaurants.

C&O CANAL & GREAT FALLS

The C&O Canal National Historic Park (on the Washington, D.C., and Maryland side of the Potomac) and the Great Falls Park (on the Virginia side) are both part of the National Park System. At a point about 9 mi west of the District line, the two parks face each other. It's here that the steep, jagged falls of the Potomac roar into a narrow gorge, providing one of the most spectacular scenic attractions in the East. Canoeing, bicycling, and fishing are popular in the parks.

MOUNT VERNON, WOODLAWN & GUNSTON HALL

Three splendid examples of plantation architecture remain on the Virginia side of the Potomac, 16 mi south of the District. Mount Vernon, the most-visited historic house in America, was the home of George Washington; Woodlawn was the estate of Washington's step-granddaughter; and Gunston Hall was the residence of George Mason, a patriot and author of the document on which the Bill of Rights was based.

ANNAPOLIS, MARYLAND

Maryland's capital is a popular destination for seafood lovers and boating fans. Warm, sunny days bring many boats to the City Dock, where they're moored against a background of waterfront shops and restaurants. The city has one of the country's largest assemblages of 18th-century architecture, with more than 50 pre–Revolutionary War buildings. Its nautical reputation is enhanced by the presence of the U.S. Naval Academy.

Updated by
Cathy Sharpe

Within an hour of D.C. are getaway destinations connected to the nation's first president, naval history, colonial events, and the Civil War. Alexandria was once a bustling colonial port, and Old Town preserves this flavor with its cobblestone streets, taverns, and waterfront. Cycle 7 mi downriver along the banks of the Potomac to get there, or hop on the Metro for a quick 30-minute ride.

For another active trip into the past, walk or bike along the 13-mi path that parallels a section of the Chesapeake & Ohio (C&O) Canal, past Glen Echo Park, to Great Falls Tavern on the Maryland side of the Potomac. This is one of Washington's favorite nearby destinations for weekend hiking. Mount Vernon, George Washington's plantation, is a mere 16 mi from D.C. on the Virginia side of the Potomac. Make a day of it, and visit the two other interesting plantation homes—Woodlawn and Gunston Hall—that are nearby.

Another option is to get out on the water in Annapolis, a major center for boating and home to the U.S. Naval Academy. Feast on the Chesapeake Bay's famous crabs, then watch the midshipmen parade on campus at the academy.

ALEXANDRIA

A short drive (or bike ride) from Washington, Alexandria provides a welcome break from the monuments and hustle-and-bustle of the District. Here you encounter America's colonial heritage. Founded in 1749 by Scottish merchants eager to capitalize on the booming tobacco trade, Alexandria became one of the most important colonial ports. Alexandria has been associated with the most significant personages of the colonial, Revolutionary, and Civil War periods. In Old Town this colorful past is revived through restored 18th- and 19th-century homes, churches, and taverns; on the cobbled streets; and on the revitalized waterfront, where clipper ships docked and artisans displayed

TOP EXPERIENCES AROUND D.C.

HISTORICAL SIGHTS

Of primal importance to the shaping of the United States are spots dear to George Washington: Mount Vernon and the mansions of his relatives. Bayside Annapolis, the country's first peacetime capital, is not to be missed for its port and its naval ties. A vast neighborhood of 18th-century architecture, which includes 50 pre–Revolutionary War buildings, is also here.

OUTDOOR ADVENTURES

There are vast areas for hikers in the Maryland and Virginia parks near the Great Falls. Those who fish can stake out the numerous riverbanks and salty shores. Bikers may ride for hundreds of miles on the area's excellent paved bicycle paths. One especially attractive route winds south along the Virginia shore of the Potomac. From it, you can view Georgetown and Washington's monuments on the opposite bank; Arlington National Cemetery; Ronald Reagan National Airport; and Old Town Alexandria. Before ending at Mount Vernon, the route runs through wildlife sanctuaries, and there are many fine picnic spots along the way.

their wares. Alexandria also has a wide variety of small to medium-size restaurants and pubs, plus a wealth of boutiques and antiques dealers vying for your time and money.

MAIN ATTRACTIONS

⓫ **Alexandria Black History Museum.** A museum, reading room, and park ★ comprise this nine-acre site that pays tribute to the African-American experience. The museum incorporates the Robert H. Robinson Library, a building constructed in the wake of a landmark 1939 sit-in protesting the segregation of Alexandria libraries. It recounts the history of African-Americans in Alexandria and Virginia from 1749 to the present. The federal census of 1790 recorded 52 free blacks living in the city, and Alexandria had two of the busiest slave markets in the South. Adjacent to the museum is the Watson Reading Room, filled with historical documents and videos highlighting the history and culture of African-Americans. Volunteers are on-hand to help visitors with research. You'll also want to stroll through Heritage Park which includes a 19th-century cemetery, sculptures commemorating the contributions of African-Americans to Alexandria, and a wetland area that is home to beavers, mallards and turtles. ⊠*902 Wythe St., Old Town* ☎*703/838–4356* ⊕*oha.alexandriava.gov/bhrc* ⊠*Free* ☉*Tues.–Sat. 10–4.*

❹ **Athenaeum.** One of the most noteworthy structures in Alexandria, the Athenaeum is a striking, reddish-brown Greek Revival edifice at the corner of Prince and Lee streets. It was built as a bank in the 1850s, and is now home to the Northern Virginia Fine Arts Association. The volunteer-staffed gallery showing ongoing art exhibits is open Wednesday to Friday afternoons from 11 to 3 and weekends from noon to 5. ⊠*201 Prince St., Old Town* ☎*703/548–0035w www.nvfaa.org.*

❼ **Carlyle House Historic Park.** The grandest of Alexandria's older houses, Carlyle House was patterned after a Scottish country manor house.

Old Town
Alexandria,
Virginia

12

Scottish merchant John Carlyle completed the structure in 1753. This was General Edward Braddock's headquarters, and the place where he met with five royal governors in 1755 to plan the strategy and funding of the early campaigns of the French and Indian War. ✉ *121 N. Fairfax St., Old Town* ☎ *703/549–2997* w *www.nvrpa.org/parks/carlylehouse* ✉*$4* ⊙ *Tues.–Sat. 10–4, Sun. noon–4, guided tours every ½ hr, last tours begin at 4.*

14 **Friendship Fire House.** Alexandria's showcase firehouse, home to the
🕭 area's first volunteer fire company beginning in 1774, is outfitted in typical 19th-century firefighting fashion. Artifacts include leather water buckets, axes, and hand- and steam-powered pumpers. ✉*107 S. Alfred St., Old Town* ☎*703/838–3891* ⊕*oha.alexandriava.gov/friendship* ✉*Free* ⊙*Fri. and Sat. 10–4, Sun. 1–4.*

8 **Gadsby's Tavern Museum.** This museum is housed in the old City Tavern
🕭 and Hotel, which was a center of political and social life in the late 18th century. A tour takes you through the taproom, dining room, assembly room, ballroom, and communal bedrooms. Friday evening tours visit the same rooms but are led by a costumed guide using a lantern. There also are a number of special events that vary from month to month, including "Tea with Martha Washington," lectures and programs for children and

families like "Swordsmen's Rendez-
vous." Check the Web site for a calendar of events. ✉*134 N. Royal
St., Old Town* ☎*703/838–4242* ⊕
oha.alexandriava.gov/gadsby 💲*$4,
$2 children 11–17, lantern tours $5*
🕙*Nov.–Mar., Wed.–Sat. 11–4, Sun.
1–4, last tour at 3:45; Apr.–Oct.,
Tues.–Sat. 10–5, Sun.–Mon. 1–5,*

> **CAPITAL FACTS**
>
> George Washington went to birth-
> day celebrations in the ballroom
> at the Gadsby Tavern.

*last tour at 4:45; tours 15 min before and after the hr. Lantern tours
June–Aug., Fri. 7–9:15, last tour departure.*

⑮ George Washington Masonic National Memorial. Alexandria, like Washington, has no tall buildings, so the spire of this memorial dominates
the surroundings. The building fronts King and Duke Streets, Alexandria's major east–west arteries; from the ninth-floor observation
deck you get a spectacular view of Alexandria, with Washington in
the distance. (Note: you cannot go above the mezzanine except on the
guided tour.) The building contains furnishings from the first Masonic
lodge in Alexandria, of which George Washington was a member; he
became a Mason in 1753 and was a Worshipful Master, a high rank, at
the same time he served as president. ✉*101 Callahan Dr., Old Town*
☎*703/683–2007* ⊕*www.gwmemorial.org* 💲*Free* 🕙*Daily 10–4; 50-
min guided tours of building and observation deck daily at 10, 11:30,
1:30, and 3.*

❶ Ramsay House. The best place to start a tour of Alexandria's Old Town
is at the **Alexandria Visitors Center,** in Ramsay House, a re-creation
of the home of the town's founder, a merchant and first lord mayor,
William Ramsay. The structure is believed to be on the site of the oldest house in Alexandria. Travel counselors here provide brochures
and maps for self-guided walking tours; tour companies give guided
walking tours that leave from here. Ticket prices vary, though most
are about $10. Call ahead to get guided tour times. ■**TIP➔They can
also give you a 24-hour permit for free parking at any two-hour metered
spot, even if you're visiting from elsewhere in Virginia.** ✉*221 King St.,
Old Town* ☎*703/838–4200 or 800/388–9119* ⊕*www.funside.com*
🕙*Daily 9–5.*

❻ Torpedo Factory Art Center. Torpedoes were manufactured here by the
★ U.S. Navy during World Wars I and II. Now the building houses the studios and workshops of about 85 artists and artisans, and has become
one of Alexandria's most popular attractions. You can view the workshops of printmakers, jewelry makers, sculptors, painters, and pot-
ters, and most of the art and the crafts are for sale. On the second
Thursday of every month the building hosts an Art Night, in which the
galleries stay open until 9. The Torpedo Factory also houses the **Alexandria Archaeology Museum** (☎*703/838–4399* ⊕*oha.alexandriava.gov/
archaeology*), a city-operated research facility devoted to urban archaeology and conservation. Artifacts from excavations in Alexandria are
on display here. Admission is free; hours are Tuesday through Friday
10–3, Saturday 10–5, and Sunday 1–5. ✉*105 N. Union St., Old Town*

☎703/838–4565 ⊕*www.torpedo-factory.org* ⬛*Free* ⊙*Daily 10–5; galleries open until 9 on 2nd Thurs. of month.*

ALSO WORTH SEEING

🔟 **Boyhood Home of Robert E. Lee.** The childhood home of the Commander in Chief of the Confederate forces of Virginia, Robert E. Lee, is a fine example of a 19th-century town house with Federal architecture. It's now a private home and is not

open to visitors. Some of the furnishings, however, are displayed at the Lyceum. You can visit the Web site for a virtual tour ✉*607 Oronoco St., Old Town* ⊕*www.leeboyhoodhome.com.*

⑤ **Captain's Row.** Many of Alexandria's sea captains once lived on this block. The cobblestones in the street were allegedly laid by Hessian mercenaries who had fought for the British during the Revolution and were held in Alexandria as prisoners of war. ✉*Prince St. between Lee and Union Sts., Old Town*

⑫ **Christ Church.** Both Washington and Lee were pewholders in this Episcopal church. (Washington paid 36 pounds and 10 shillings—a lot of money in those days—for Pew 60.) Built in 1773, Christ Church is a good example of Georgian church architecture. It has a fine Palladian window, an interior balcony, and an English wrought-brass-and-crystal chandelier. Docents give tours during visiting hours. ✉*118 N. Washington St., Old Town* ☎*703/549–1450* ⊕*www.historicchristchurch. org* ⬛*Free, $5 donation suggested* ⊙*Mon.–Sat. 9–4, Sun. 2–4.*

⑨ **Lee-Fendall House Museum.** The short block of Alexandria's Oronoco Street between Washington and St. Asaph streets is the site of two Lee-owned houses. One is the Lee-Fendall House, the home of several illustrious members of the Lee family, and the other is the boyhood home of Robert E. Lee. The house and its furnishings are those of a Lee home of the 1850–70 period. United Mine Workers leader John Lewis lived here from 1937 until his death in 1969. Weekend hours are irregular, so call ahead. ✉*614 Oronoco St., Old Town* ☎*703/548–1789* ⊕*www. leefendallhouse.org* ⬛*$4* ⊙*Tues., Thurs., Fri. and Sat. 10–4, Wed. and Sun. 1–4; sometimes closed weekends. Closed Jan.*

⑬ **Lyceum.** Built in 1839, the Lyceum has served as a library, a Civil War hospital, a residence, and an office building. It now houses two galleries with exhibits on the history of Alexandria, a third gallery with changing exhibits, and a gift shop. Some travel information for the entire state is also available here. ✉*201 S. Washington St., Old Town* ☎*703/838–4994* ⊕*oha.alexandriava.gov/lyceum* ⬛*Free* ⊙*Mon.–Sat. 10–5, Sun. 1–5.*

③ **Old Presbyterian Meeting House.** Built in 1774, the Old Presbyterian Meeting House was Presbyterian Alexandria's gathering place, not a "church," because the only "church" was the Church of England. Scottish patriots met there during the Revolution. Eulogies for George Washington were delivered here on December 29, 1799. In a corner of the churchyard is the tomb of an unknown soldier of the American Revolution. ⊠*321 S. Fairfax St., Old Town* ☎*703/549–6670* ⊕*www.opmh.org* ☎*Free* ⊙*Sanctuary weekdays 8:30–4; key available at church office at 316 S. Royal St.; Sun. services 8:30 and 11, Sept. –June; 10, July–Aug.*

❷ Stabler-Leadbeater Apothecary. Once patronized by George Washington and the Lee family, Alexandria's Stabler-Leadbeater Apothecary is the third-oldest apothecary in the country (the oldest is reputedly in Bethlehem, Pennsylvania). Some believe that it was here, on October 17, 1859, that Lt. Col. Robert E. Lee received orders to lead Marines from the Washington Barracks to suppress John Brown's insurrection at Harper's Ferry (then part of Virginia). The shop now houses a small museum of 18th-, 19th-, and 20th-century apothecary artifacts, including one of the finest collections of apothecary bottles in the country (more than 800 bottles in all). The apothecary remained in business until 1932. ⊠*105–107 S. Fairfax St., Old Town* ☎*703/838–3852* ☎*$4* ⊙*Apr.–Oct., Tues.–Sat. 10–5, Sun. and Mon. 1–5; Nov.–Mar., Wed.–Sat. 11–4, Sun. 1–4, by guided tour only, tour 15 min before and after the hr.*

ALEXANDRIA ESSENTIALS

TRANSPORTATION

BY CAR
Take either the George Washington Memorial Parkway or Jefferson Davis Highway (Route 1) south from Arlington to reach Alexandria. Stop first at the Alexandria Convention & Visitors Association in Ramsay House (221 King Street); they can give you a 24-hour permit for free parking at any two-hour metered spot, even if you're visiting from elsewhere in Virginia.

BY METRO
The King Street Metro stop (about 25 minutes from Metro Center) is right next to the Masonic memorial and a 10-block walk on King Street from the center of Old Town. On Saturday from 10 AM to midnight and on Sunday from 11 to 7 (even later in spring and summer), there's a free Dash About shuttle between the King Street station and Market Square near Ramsay House.

CONTACTS & RESOURCES
VISITOR INFORMATION **Contacts Alexandria Convention & Visitors Association** (☎*703/838–4200, 800/388–9119* ⊕ *www.funside.com*).

C&O CANAL & GREAT FALLS PARKS

12

In the 18th and early 19th centuries, the Potomac River was the main transportation route between Cumberland, Maryland, one of the most important ports on the nation's frontier, and the seaports of the Chesapeake Bay. Coal, tobacco, grain, whiskey, furs, iron ore, and timber were sent down the Potomac to Georgetown and Alexandria, which served as major distribution points for both domestic and international markets.

Although it was a vital link with the country's western territories, the Potomac had some drawbacks as a commercial waterway: rapids and waterfalls along the 185 mi between Cumberland and Washington originally made it impossible for traders to travel the entire distance by boat. Just a few miles upstream from Washington, the Potomac cascades through two such barriers: the breathtakingly beautiful Great Falls and the less dramatic but equally impassable Little Falls.

To help traders move goods between the eastern markets and the western frontier more efficiently, 18th-century engineers proposed that a canal with a series of elevator locks be constructed parallel to the river. George Washington founded a company to build the canal, and in 1802 (after his death) the firm opened the Patowmack Canal on the Virginia side of the river.

In 1828 construction of the Chesapeake & Ohio Canal began on the opposite side of the Potomac River. It eventually stretched from downtown Washington to Cumberland, Maryland. However, by the time it had opened, newer technology was starting to make canals obsolete. The Baltimore & Ohio Railroad, whose construction began the same day as the C&O, finally put the canal out of business in 1924.

C&O CANAL NATIONAL HISTORIC PARK

Extends 13 mi west from Georgetown, including Great Falls Tavern.

C&O Canal National Historic Park originates in Georgetown and encloses a 184.5-mi towpath that ends in Cumberland, Maryland. This relic of America's canal-building era and a few structures are still there. Construction along the Maryland bank began in 1828, using the principles of the Erie Canal in New York. When construction ended in 1850, canals stretched from downtown Washington to Cumberland through 74 locks. The original plan to extend a canal to the Ohio River was superseded by the success of the Baltimore & Ohio (B&O) Railroad, which eventually put the canal out of business.

> **DID YOU KNOW?**
>
> The public restroom at the intersection of 17th Street and Constitution Avenue was originally a lock house of an earlier canal through Washington.

Construction of the C&O Canal and the B&O Railroad began on the same day, July 4, 1828. Initially, the C&O provided an economi-

C&O Canal &
Great Falls Parks

cal and practical way for traders to move goods through the Washington area to the lower Chesapeake. During the mid-19th century, boats carried as much as a million tons of merchandise a year. But the C&O Canal suffered a flood in late spring 1889 and couldn't recover from the financial disaster that ensued. Ownership then shifted to the B&O Railroad, the canal's largest stockholder, and operation continued until 1924, when another flood ended traffic. The railroad transferred ownership of the canal to the federal government in 1938 to settle a $2 million debt.

In the 1950s a proposal to build a highway over the canal near Washington was thwarted by residents

CANAL BOAT RIDES

There are two visitor centers in the sections of the C&O Canal National Historic Park closest to Washington: one in Georgetown and the other at Great Falls Tavern. Both the Georgetown and the Great Falls Tavern visitor centers offer mule-drawn canal-boat rides. The trips are the same distance and price. Georgetown is your starting point if you are Metro-dependent or if you'd like to pair a ride with lunch and shopping. Pick Great Falls for a more rural experience that you can pair with hiking and a picnic.

12

of the Palisades (between Georgetown and Glen Echo) and others concerned with the canal's history and legacy. Since 1971 the canal has been a national park, providing a window into the past and a marvelous place to enjoy the outdoors.

BIKING, BOATING & FISHING

The C&O Canal National Historic Park and its towpath are favorites of walkers, joggers, bikers, and canoeists. The path has a slight grade, which makes for a leisurely ride or hike. Most recreational bikers consider the 13 mi from Georgetown to Great Falls Tavern an easy ride; you need to carry your bike for only one short stretch of rocky ground near Great Falls. You can also take a bike path that parallels MacArthur Boulevard and runs from Georgetown to Great Falls Tavern. Storm damage has left parts of the canal dry, but many segments remain intact and navigable by canoe.

The Boat House at Fletcher's Cove, on the D.C. side of the Potomac, rents rowboats, canoes, and bicycles and sells tackle, snack foods, and D.C. fishing licenses. Here you can catch shad, perch, catfish, striped bass, and other freshwater species. Canoeing is allowed on the canal and, weather permitting, on the Potomac. There's a large picnic area along the riverbank. ✉4940 Canal Rd., at Reservoir Rd., Georgetown ☎202/244–0461 ⊕www.fletchersboathouse.com ☯Late Mar.–May, daily 7:30–7; June–Aug., daily 9–7; Sept.–Nov., daily 9–6.

The towpath along the canal in **Georgetown** passes remnants of that area's industrial past, such as the Godey Lime Kilns near the mouth of Rock Creek, as well as the fronts of numerous houses that date from 1810. At the Foundry Mall you can start a tour of the area on foot, by bike, or by mule-drawn boat.

At the **Georgetown Visitor Center,** National Park Service rangers and volunteers provide maps, information, and canal history. From about mid-April through late October, mule-drawn canal-boat rides depart from the center. Tickets for the hour-long ride cost $7 and are available across the canal, next to the Foundry Building. The schedule varies by season, with limited rides in the spring and fall. In summer the boats run at least twice a day from Wednesday through Sunday. On summer weekends park rangers also lead walking tours of historic Georgetown. Call the visitor center for the exact schedule of canal-boat rides and/or walking tours the day before you plan to visit. ⊠ *1057 Thomas Jefferson St. NW, Georgetown* ☎ *202/653–5190* ⊕ *www.nps.gov/choh/ Visitor/Centers/Georgetown.html* ⊙ *Apr.–Oct., Wed.–Sun. 9–4:30; Nov.–Mar., weekends 10–4, staffing permitting.*

Great Falls Tavern Visitor Center, headquarters for the Palisades area of C&O Canal National Historic Park, has displays of canal history and photographs that show how high the river can rise. A platform on Olmsted Island, accessible from near the tavern, provides a spectacular view of the falls. On the canal walls are grooves worn by decades of friction from boat towlines. The Park Service offers hour-long, mule-drawn canal-boat rides from about mid-April through late October; tickets cost $7. The schedule varies by season, with limited rides in the spring and fall. In summer the boats run at least twice a day from Wednesday through Sunday. Call the visitor center for the exact schedule on the day of your visit. The tavern ceased food service long ago, so if you're hungry, head for the snack bar a few paces north. ⊠ *11710 MacArthur Blvd., Potomac* ☎ *301/299–3613 or 301/767– 3714* ⊕ *www.nps.gov/choh* 🎫 *$5 per vehicle, $3 per person without vehicle; good for 3 days at both Great Falls Park and C&O Canal National Historic Park* ⊙ *Daily 9–4:45.*

MAIN ATTRACTIONS

Chain Bridge, named for the chains that held up the original structure, links D.C. and Virginia. The bridge was built to enable cattlemen to bring Virginia herds to the slaughterhouses along the Maryland side of the Potomac. During the Civil War the bridge was guarded by Union troops stationed at earthen fortifications along what's now Potomac Avenue NW. The Virginia side of the river in the area around Chain Bridge is known for its good fishing and narrow rapids. ⊠ *Glebe Rd., Rte. 120, Arlington.*

Glen Echo Park preserves the site of Washington's oldest amusement park (1911–68) and a stone tower from the town's earlier days. The village of Glen Echo was founded in 1891 by Edwin and Edward Baltzley, brothers who made their fortune from the invention of the eggbeater. The brothers were enthusiastic supporters of the Chautauqua movement, a group begun in 1874 in New York as a way to promote liberal education among the working and middle classes. The brothers sold land and houses to further their dream, but the Glen Echo Chautauqua lasted only one season. The National Park Service administers this 10-acre property and offers year-round dances Friday through Sunday in the 1933 Spanish Ballroom, classes in the arts, two children's theaters, two art galleries with ongoing exhibits, artist demonstrations, and a children's museum with environmental education workshops. You can ride on a 1921 Dentzel carousel May through September. ✉7300 *MacArthur Blvd. NW, Glen Echo* ☎301/492–6229, 301/634–2222 *events hotline* ⊕*www.nps.gov/glec* 🖃*Park free, carousel ride $1, cost varies for dances.*

12

GREAT FALLS PARK, VIRGINIA

23 mi northwest from Georgetown.

Part of the National Park System, Great Falls Park is on the Virginia side of the Potomac, across the river from C&O Canal National Historic Park. Great Falls Park's 800 acres are a favorite place for outings. The steep, jagged falls roar into the narrow Mather Gorge—a spectacular scene. There are stunning views of the Potomac here, and a marker shows the river's high-water marks. The site, overlooking the falls, had an amusement park built by the railroad that operated from Georgetown, Rosslyn, and stations between during the early 1900s. Fifteen miles of trails lead past the old Patowmack Canal and among the boulders along the edge of the falls.

You can fish (a Virginia, Maryland, or D.C. license is required for anglers 16 and older), climb rocks (climbers must register at the visitor center beforehand), or—if you're an experienced boater with your own equipment—go white-water kayaking (*below* the falls only). However, you can't camp overnight, drink alcoholic beverages, or wade or swim in the park. As is true all along this stretch of the river, the currents are deadly. Despite frequent signs and warnings, there are occasionally those who dare the water and drown.

A tour of the **Great Falls Park Visitor Center and Museum** takes 30 minutes. ■TIP➔ Staff members also conduct park walks year-round; the visitor center tour and guided park walks are included in the price of admission. You're encouraged to take self-guided tours along well-marked trails, including one that follows the route of the old Patowmack Canal; the visitor center provides maps for the various trails. ✉9200 *Old Dominion Dr., McLean, VA* ☎703/285–2966 or 703/285–2965 ⊕*www.nps.gov/grfa* 🖃*$5 per vehicle, $3 per person without vehicle; good for 3 days at both Great Falls Park and C&O Canal National Historic Park; annual park pass $20* ⊘*7* AM*–dark; visitor center mid-Oct.–mid-Mar., daily 10–4; mid-Mar.–mid-Oct., weekdays 10–5; weekends 10–6; hrs subject to change.*

C&O CANAL & GREAT FALLS PARKS ESSENTIALS

TRANSPORTATION

BY CAR

To reach Great Falls Park, take the scenic and winding Route 193 (Exit 13 off Route 495, the Beltway) to Route 738 (Old Dominion Drive), and follow the signs. It takes about 25 minutes to drive to the park from the Beltway. C&O Canal National Historic Park is along the Maryland side of the Potomac and is accessible by taking Canal Road or MacArthur Boulevard from Georgetown or by taking Exit 41 off the Beltway and then following the signs to Carderock. There are several roadside stops accessible from the southbound lanes of Canal Road where you can park and visit restored canal locks and lock houses.

CONTACTS & RESOURCES

Contacts **National Park Service** (✉ *Georgetown Visitor Center, 1057 Thomas Jefferson St. NW, Georgetown* ☎ *202/653–5190* ⊕ *www.nps.gov/choh*).

MOUNT VERNON, WOODLAWN & GUNSTON HALL

Long before Washington, D.C., was planned, the shores of the Potomac had been divided into plantations by wealthy traders and gentleman farmers. Most traces of the colonial era were obliterated as the capital grew in the 19th century, but several splendid examples of plantation architecture remain on the Virginia side of the Potomac, 15 mi or so south of D.C. In one day you can easily visit three such mansions: Mount Vernon, the home of George Washington and one of the most popular sites in the area; Woodlawn, the estate of Washington's stepgranddaughter; and Gunston Hall, the home of George Mason, author of the document that inspired the Bill of Rights. On hillsides overlooking the river, these estates offer magnificent vistas and make a bygone era vivid.

MOUNT VERNON

Fodor's Choice
★
☾

16 mi southeast of Washington, D.C., 8 mi south of Alexandria, VA.

Mount Vernon and the surrounding lands had been in the Washington family for nearly 90 years by the time George inherited it all in 1761. Before taking command of the Continental Army, Washington was a yeoman farmer managing the 8,000-acre plantation, of which more than 3,000 acres were under cultivation. He also oversaw the transformation of the main house from an ordinary farm dwelling into what was, for the time, a grand mansion.

> ### WORD OF MOUTH
>
> "Anyone going to Mount Vernon should not miss the education center. There is a multimedia show in there that will knock your socks off. It is the best multimedia show in the Washington area bar none."
>
> –FauxSteMarie

In 2006 Mount Vernon opened the state-of-the-art Orientation Center and Museum and Education Center, which is not to be missed. George Washington comes to life through interactive displays, life-sized models, action-adventure movies, short educational videos, and more than 500 artifacts on display for the first time.

The red-roof house is elegant though understated, with a yellow pine exterior that's been painted and coated with layers of sand to resemble white-stone blocks. The first-floor rooms are quite ornate, especially the large formal dining room, with a molded ceiling decorated with agricultural motifs. Throughout the house are other smaller symbols of the owner's eminence, such as a key to the main portal of the Bastille—presented to Washington by the Marquis de Lafayette—and Washington's presidential chair. As you tour the mansion, guides are stationed throughout the house to describe the furnishings and answer questions.

You can stroll around the estate's 500 acres and three gardens, visiting the workshops, the kitchen, the carriage house, the greenhouse, the slave quarters, and, down the hill toward the boat landing, the tomb of George and Martha Washington. There's also a pioneer farmer site: a 4-acre hands-on exhibit with a reconstruction of George Washington's 16-sided treading barn as its centerpiece. ■TIP→**Among the souvenirs sold at the plantation are stripling boxwoods that began life as clippings from bushes planted in 1798, the year before Washington died.** A tour of the house and grounds takes about four hours. Private evening candlelight tours of the mansion with staff dressed in 18th-century costumes can be arranged.

George Washington's Distillery & Gristmill, located 3 mi from Mount Vernon on Route 235, is open daily April–October. During the guided tours, led by historic interpreters, you can meet an 18th-century miller, watch the water-powered wheel grind grain into flour just as it did 220 years ago, and learn techniques of distilling using five of the original copper stills. Tickets can be purchased either at the distillery and gristmill itself or at Mount Vernon's Main Gate. ⊠*Southern end of George Washington Pkwy., Mount Vernon, VA* ☎*703/780-2000* ⊕*www.mountvernon.org* ⊠*$13, gristmill $4, combination ticket $15* ⊙*Mar., Sept., and Oct., daily 9–5; Apr.–Aug., daily 8–5; Nov.–Feb., daily 9–4.*

THE VIEW OUT BACK

Beneath a 90-foot portico is George Washington's contribution to architecture and the real treasure of Mount Vernon: the home's dramatic riverside porch. The porch overlooks an expanse of lawn that slopes down to the Potomac. In springtime the view of the river (a mile wide where it passes the plantation) is framed by redbud and dogwood blossoms. United States Navy and Coast Guard ships salute ("render honors") when passing the house during daylight hours. Foreign naval vessels often salute, too.

BIKING

An asphalt bicycle path leads from the Virginia side of Key Bridge (across from Georgetown), past Ronald Reagan National Airport, and through Alexandria all the way to Mount Vernon. Bikers in moderately good condition can make the 16-mi trip in less than two hours. You can rent bicycles at several locations in Washington.

A great place to rent a bike is the Washington Sailing Marina (☎*703/548-9027,* ⊕*www.washingtonsailingmarina.com*), which is beside the Mount Vernon Bike Trail just past the airport. A 12-mi ride south will take you right up to the front doors of Mount Vernon. All-terrain bikes rent for $6 per hour or $22 per day; cruisers cost $4 per hour or $16.50 per day. The marina is open 9–5 daily.

WOODLAWN

3 mi west of Mount Vernon, 15 mi south of Washington, D.C.

Woodlawn was once part of the Mount Vernon estate. From here you can still see traces of the bowling green that fronted Washington's home. The house was built for Washington's step-granddaughter, Nelly Custis, who married his favorite nephew, Lawrence Lewis. (Lewis had come to Mount Vernon from Fredericksburg to help Uncle George manage his five farms.)

The Lewises' home, completed in 1805, was designed by Dr. William Thornton, a physician and amateur architect from the West Indies who drew up the original plans for the U.S. Capitol. Like Mount Vernon, the Woodlawn house is constructed of native materials, including the clay for its bricks and the yellow pine used throughout its interior. ■TIP➡Built on a site selected by George Washington, the house has commanding views of the surrounding countryside and the Potomac River beyond. In the tradition of Southern riverfront mansions, Wood-lawn has a central hallway that provides a cool refuge in summer. At one corner of the passage is a bust of George Washington set on a pedestal so the crown of the head is at 6 feet, 2 inches—Washington's actual height.

12

Woodlawn was once a plantation where more than 100 people, most of them slaves, lived and worked. As plantation owners, the Lewises lived in luxury. Docents talk about how the family entertained and how the slaves grew produce and prepared these lavish meals as well as their own. As intimates of the Washingtons' household, the Lewises displayed a collection of objects in honor of their illustrious benefactor. Many Washington family items are on display today. In 1957 the property was acquired by the National Trust for Historic Preservation, which had been operating it as a museum since 1951.

Also on the grounds of Woodlawn is the **Pope-Leighey House** (⊕ *www. popeleighey1940.org*). Frank Lloyd Wright designed his Usonian houses like this one as a means of providing affordable housing for people of modest means. It was built in 1940 and moved here from Falls Church, Virginia, in 1964. ✉ *9000 Richmond Hwy., Mount Vernon, VA* ☎ *703/780–4000* ⊕ *www.woodlawn1805.org* 💲 *$7.50 for either Woodlawn or Pope-Leighey House, combination ticket $13* 🕑 *Mar.– Dec., Tues.–Sun. 10–5; limited guided tours in Mar. because of annual needlework show; tours leave every ½ hr; last tour at 4:30.*

GUNSTON HALL

12 mi south of Woodlawn, 25 mi south of Washington, D.C.

Gunston Hall Plantation, down the Potomac from Mount Vernon, was the home of another important George. Gentleman farmer George Mason was a colonel of the Fairfax militia and author of the Virginia Declaration of Rights, the model for the U.S. Bill of Rights, which called for freedom of the press, tolerance of religion, and other fundamental democratic principles. Mason was a framer of the Constitution but refused to sign the final document because it didn't stop the importation of slaves, adequately restrain the powers of the federal government, or include a bill of rights. Mason's objections spurred the movement for the inclusion of the Bill of Rights into the Constitution.

Mason's home was built circa 1755. ■TIP➡The Georgian-style mansion has some of the finest hand-carved ornamented interiors in the country. It's the handiwork of the 18th-century's foremost architect, William Buckland, who also designed the Hammond-Harwood and Chase-Lloyd houses in Annapolis. Gunston Hall is built of brick, black walnut, and yellow pine. The style of the time demanded symmetry in all structures, which explains the false door set into one side of the center hallway. The house's interior, which has carved woodwork in styles from Chinese to Gothic, has been meticulously restored, with paints made from the original formulas and carefully carved replacements for the intricate mahogany medallions in the moldings. Restored outbuildings include a kitchen, dairy, laundry, and smokehouse. A schoolhouse has also been reconstructed.

The formal gardens, under excavation by a team of archaeologists, are famous for their boxwoods—some now 12 feet high—thought to have been planted during George Mason's time, making them among the oldest in the country. The Potomac is visible past the expansive deer park. Also on the grounds is an active farmyard with livestock and crop species; special programs, such as history lectures and hearth-cooking demonstrations, are offered throughout the year. ■ TIP→A tour of Gunston Hall takes at least 45 minutes; tours begin at the visitor center, which includes a museum and gift shop. ⊠ *10709 Gunston Rd., Mason Neck, VA* ☎ *703/550–9220* ⊕ *www.gunstonhall.org* ⊕ *$8* ⊗ *Daily 9:30–5; first tour at 10, last tour at 4:30.*

MOUNT VERNON, WOODLAWN & GUNSTON HALL ESSENTIALS

TRANSPORTATION

BY CAR

To reach Mount Vernon from the Capital Beltway (Route 495), take Exit 1 and follow the signs to George Washington Memorial Parkway southbound. Mount Vernon is about 8½ mi south. From downtown Washington, cross into Arlington on Key Bridge, Memorial Bridge, or the 14th Street Bridge and drive south on the George Washington Memorial Parkway past Ronald Reagan National Airport through Alexandria straight to Mount Vernon. The trip from D.C. takes about a half hour.

For Woodlawn, travel southwest on Route 1 to the second Route 235 intersection (the first leads to Mount Vernon). The entrance to Woodlawn is on the right at the traffic light. From Mount Vernon, travel northwest on Route 235 to the Route 1 intersection; Woodlawn is straight ahead through the intersection.

To visit Gunston Hall, travel south on Route 1, 9 mi past Woodlawn to Route 242; turn left there and go 3½ mi to the plantation entrance.

BY PUBLIC TRANSIT

Getting to Mount Vernon and the neighboring plantations by public transportation requires that you take both the Metro and a bus. For all three destinations, begin by taking the Yellow Line train to the Huntington Metro station.

For Mount Vernon, you can take Fairfax County Connector Bus 101, 151, or 152 ($1) from Huntington Metro station. Buses of each line leave about once an hour—more often during rush hour—and operate weekdays from about 4:30 AM to 9:15 PM, weekends from about 6:30 AM to 7 PM.

For Woodlawn, take Bus 151, 152, or 171 ($1) from Huntington Metro station. Route 171 begins earlier and runs later than the other two buses and well beyond Woodlawn operating hours. Buses returning to the station have the same numbers but are marked HUNTINGTON.

Bus Information **Fairfax County Connector** (☎ *703/339–7200* ⊕ *www.fairfax-connector.com*).

CONTACTS & RESOURCES

12

BOAT TOURS

The *Spirit of Mount Vernon* makes a pleasant trip from Washington down the Potomac to Mount Vernon from mid-March through mid-October. Tickets include discounted admission to the estate. You can also take lunch, dinner, and moonlight cruises on the *Spirit of Washington,* which departs from Washington as well but doesn't go quite as far as Mount Vernon. Tickets include your meal and, on the dinner and brunch cruises, live entertainment. Prices range from $39 (to Mount Vernon, round-trip without a meal) to $82, depending on the meal served (if any) and the day of the week.

Boat Information **Spirit of Mount Vernon** and **Spirit of Washington** (✉ *Pier 4, 6th and Water Sts. SW, Southeast, Washington, DC* ☎ *866/302-2469 boat reservations* ⊕ *www.spiritcruises.com*).

BUS TOURS

Gray Line runs 6-hour trips to Mount Vernon (with a stop in Alexandria), departing daily at 8 AM from Union Station. A ticket is $45 and includes admission to the mansion and grounds.

Tourmobile offers five-hour trips to Mount Vernon June 15 through Labor Day, departing from Arlington National Cemetery daily at 11 AM. You purchase tickets the same day of your tour, beginning at 8 AM at Arlington, and the $30 ticket includes admission to the mansion. Advance reservations are not accepted and there is limited seating.

FEES & SCHEDULES **Gray Line** (☎ *800/862 1400* ⊕ *www.grayline.com*). **Tourmobile** (☎ *202/554–5100* ⊕ *www.tourmobile.com*).

ANNAPOLIS, MARYLAND

Although it has long since been overtaken by Baltimore as the major Maryland port, Annapolis is still a popular destination for pleasure boating. On warm, sunny days, the waters off City Dock become center stage for an amateur show of power boaters maneuvering through the heavy traffic. Annapolis's enduring nautical reputation derives largely from the presence of the U.S. Naval Academy: its midshipmen throng the city streets in white uniforms in summer and in navy blue in winter.

Annapolis also has a wealth of 18th-century architecture, including more surviving colonial buildings than any other place in the country. Maryland is the only state in which the homes of all its signers of the Declaration of Independence still stand. The houses are all in Annapolis, and you can tour two of the four—the homes of Samuel Chase and William Paca. Although chain stores and eateries are encroaching upon the old parts of town, the legacy of the historic buildings endures.

This history began in 1649, when a group of Puritan settlers moved from Virginia to a spot at the mouth of the Severn River, where they established a community called Providence. Lord Baltimore, who held the royal charter to settle Maryland, named the area around this town Anne Arundel County, after his wife. In 1684 Anne Arundel Town was established across from Providence on the Severn's south side. Ten years later, Anne Arundel Town became the capital of Maryland and was renamed Annapolis, for Princess Anne, who later became queen. It received its city charter in 1708 and became a major port, particularly for the export of tobacco. In 1774 patriots here matched their Boston counterparts (who had thrown their famous tea party the year before) by burning the *Peggy Stewart,* a ship loaded with taxed tea. Annapolis later served as the nation's first peacetime capital (1783–84).

MAIN ATTRACTIONS

1 **Annapolis & Anne Arundel County Conference & Visitors Bureau.** Start your visit at Annapolis's main visitor center. Here you can pick up maps and brochures or begin a guided tour. ⊠*26 West St., Historic Area* ☎*410/280–0445 or 888/302-2852* ⊕*www.visitannapolis.org* ☉*Daily 9–5.*

12

9 ★ **Hammond-Harwood House.** Ninety percent of this 1774 home is original. A fine example of colonial five-part Georgian architecture (a single block with two connecting rooms and wings on each side), the Hammond-Harwood House is the only verifiable full-scale example of William Buckland's work. It was also his final project, as he died the year the house was completed. Exquisite moldings, cornices, and other carvings appear throughout (note especially the garlands of roses above the front doorway). The house was meant to be a wedding present from Matthias Hammond, a planter and revolutionary, to his fiancée, who jilted him before the house was finished. Hammond died a bachelor in 1784. The Harwoods took over the house toward the turn of the 19th century. Today it's furnished with 18th-century pieces, and the garden's plants also are reflective of the period. ■**TIP→Tours leave at the top of the hour and are approximately 40 minutes; the last tour begins at 4.** ✉ *19 Maryland Ave., Historic Area* ☎ *410/263–4683* ⊕ *www.hammondharwoodhouse.org* ✍ *$6* ⊙ *Apr.–Oct., Tues.–Sun. noon–5; Nov.–Mar. open for group tours, special events, and select weekends only; check ahead for opening times.*

5 **Historic Annapolis Foundation Museum Store.** The Historic Annapolis Foundation operates its museum store in a warehouse that held supplies for the Continental Army during the Revolutionary War. Here you can shop, check out a diorama of the city's 18th-century waterfront, and rent taped narrations for walking tours. ✉ *77 Main St., Historic Area* ☎ *410/268–5576* w *www.annapolis.org* ✍ *Free* ⊙ *Mon.–Sat. 10–6, Sun. 11–5. Variable extended hrs in summer.*

15 **Historic London Town and Gardens.** This National Historic Landmark on the South River is a short car ride from Annapolis. The 17th-century tobacco port of London was made up of 40 dwellings, shops, and taverns; one of its landmarks was a magnificent three-story waterfront brick house built by William Brown circa 1760 as an upscale tavern. London disappeared in the late 18th century; its buildings were abandoned and left to decay. It's now the site of an ongoing archaeological excavation. In May, July, and September you can join in on an occasional dig day (call for schedule). Docents conduct 45 to 60-minute Historic Area tours; allow more time to wander the grounds, which include 8 acres of beautiful ornamental and woodland gardens. From April to December, house tours leave on the hour (the last is at 3). Garden tours are self-guided. ✉ *839 Londontown Rd., Edgewater* ☎ *410/222–1919* ⊕ *www.historiclondontown.com* ✍ *$12* ⊙ *April–Dec., Tues.–Sat. 10–4, Sun. noon–4.*

4 **History Quest.** Historic Annapolis Foundation also operates this site, a three-story warehouse built in 1791 following a fire the preceding year that destroyed an entire block near City Dock. It's now an orientation center, with displays of Annapolis history, including photos of archaeological finds from the site that date back to the 17th century. Guided tours leave from here, and you can rent taped narrations for self-guided walking tours. ✉ *99 Main St., Historic Area* ☎ *410/268–5576* ⊕ *www.annapolis.org* ✍ *Free* ⊙ *Mon.–Sat. 10–6, Sun. 11–5. Variable extended hrs in summer.*

⑦ Information Booth. From April to October the information booth on City Dock, adjacent to the harbormaster's office, is open and stocked with maps and brochures. ✉ *Dock St. parking lot, Historic Area* ☎ *410/280–0445.*

⑥ Kunta Kinte–Alex Haley Memorial. A series of plaques along the waterfront recounting the story of African-Americans in Maryland

leads to a sculpture group depicting the famed author reading to a group of children. Beside the statue, a stone with three plaques commemorates the 1767 arrival of the African slave immortalized in Alex Haley's *Roots.* ✉ *Market Sq.* ⊕ *www.kintehaley.org.*

⑬ Maryland State House. Completed in 1780, the State House has the nation's largest wooden dome and is the oldest state capitol in continuous legislative use; it's also the only one in which the U.S. Congress has sat (1783–84). It was here that General George Washington resigned as Commander-in-Chief of the Continental Army and where the Treaty of Paris was ratified, ending the Revolutionary War. Both events took place in the Old Senate Chamber, which is filled with intricate woodwork (attributed to colonial architect William Buckland) featuring the ubiquitous tobacco motif. Also decorating this room is Charles Willson Peale's painting *Washington at the Battle of Yorktown,* a masterpiece by the Revolutionary War period's finest portrait artist. The Maryland Senate and House now hold their sessions in two other chambers in the building. Also on the grounds is the oldest public building in Maryland, the tiny redbrick Treasury, built in 1735. ■TIP→**Note that you must have a photo ID to enter the State House.** ✉ *State Circle, Historic Area* ☎ *410/974–3400* ⊕ *www.msa.md.gov/msa/homepage/ html/statehse. html* 🎫 *Free* ⊙ *Public areas weekdays 9–5, weekends 10–4; ½-hr tour usually at 11 and 3.*

⑧ U.S. Naval Academy. Probably the most interesting and important site in
Fodor'sChoice Annapolis, the Naval Academy runs along the Severn River and abuts
★ downtown Annapolis. Men and women enter from every part of the United States and many foreign countries to undergo rigorous study in subjects that range from literature to navigation to nuclear engineering. The academy, established in 1845 on the site of a U.S. Army fort, occupies 329 waterfront acres. The centerpiece of the campus is the bright copper-clad dome of the interdenominational **U.S. Naval Academy Chapel** (⊙ *Mon.–Sat. 9–4, Sun. 1-4*).

On the grounds, midshipmen (the term used for women as well as men) go to classes, conduct military drills, and practice for or compete in intercollegiate and intramural sports. **Bancroft Hall,** closed to the public, is one of the largest dormitories in the world—it houses the entire 4,200-member Brigade of Midshipmen. The **Statue of Tecumseh,** in front of Bancroft Hall, is a bronze replica of the USS *Delaware*'s

12

wooden figurehead, "Tamanend." It's decorated by midshipmen for athletic events; during exams, students pitch pennies into his quiver of arrows for luck. If you're there weekdays at noon in fair weather, you might see midshipmen muster outside Bancroft Hall for inspection and then march to lunch to the music of the Drum and Bugle Corps.

Adjoining Halsey Field House is the **USNA Armel-Leftwich Visitor Center** (⊠*52 King George St., Historic Area* ☎*410/293-8687*), which has exhibits of midshipman life, including a mockup of a midshipman's room, and the *Freedom 7* space capsule flown by astronaut Alan Shepard, an academy graduate. Walking tours of the Naval Academy led by licensed guides leave from here. You must have a photo ID to be admitted through the academy's gates, and only cars with Department of Defense registration may enter the grounds. ⊕*www.navyonline.com* 🎟*Grounds tour $8* ⊙*USNA Armel-Leftwich Visitor Center: Mar.–Dec., daily 9–5; Jan. and Feb., daily 9–4. Guided walking tours generally leave Mon.–Sat. 10–3 and Sun. 12:30–3; call ahead to confirm tour times.*

⑪ **William Paca House and Garden.** Paca (pronounced *Pay*-cuh) was a signer
★ of the Declaration of Independence and a Maryland governor from 1782 to 1785. His house was completed in 1765, and its original garden was finished in 1772. Inside, the collection of American, English, and continental European artifacts and paintings is displayed in the same manner it might have been while the Paca family was in residence. The paint schemes and architectural details of the period between 1765 and 1780 have also been re-created. The adjacent 2-acre garden provides a longer perspective on the back of the house, plus worthwhile sights of its own: upper terraces, a Chinese-style bridge, a pond, a wilderness area, and formal arrangements of 18th-century heirloom plants. An inn, Carvel Hall, once stood in the gardens. After the inn was demolished in 1965, it took eight years to rebuild the gardens. ■TIP➔**You can take a self-guided tour of the garden, but to see the house you must go on the 45-min. docent-led tour, which leaves every hour at half past. The last tour leaves 1½ hours before closing.** ⊠*186 Prince George St., Historic Area* ☎*800/603–4020 or 410/267–7619* ⊕*www.annapolis. org* 🎟*House and garden $8* ⊙*April–Dec., Mon.–Sat. 10–5, Sun. noon–5; Feb.–Mar., Sat. 10–5, Sun. noon–5.*

ALSO WORTH SEEING

③ **Banneker-Douglass Museum.** This former church has changing exhibits, lectures, films, and literature about the African-American experience in Maryland. The church plays host to performances, lectures, and educational programs, and the addition houses both permanent and changing exhibits. Audio and visual presentations and hands-on exhibits make the museum engaging for kids, while also bringing home the hardships of slave life. It's named for Frederick Douglass, the 19th-century abolitionist, and Benjamin Banneker, a Maryland astronomer, surveyor, and mathematician who helped Pierre-Charles L'Enfant survey what would become Washington, D.C. ⊠*84 Franklin St., Historic Area* ☎*410/216– 6180* ⊕*www.bdmuseum.com* 🎟*Free* ⊙*Tues.–Sat. 10–4.*

NEED A
BREAK?
The reconstructed Market House Pavilion (⊠ *City Dock, Historic Area*) is a collection of about 13 food stalls in the center of Market Square. Most are national chains that sell baked goods, fast food, and seafood. There's no seating, but you can stand and eat at a few counters. Another option is to picnic anywhere on the dock.

⑩ Chase-Lloyd House. Built by the prominent colonial architect William Buckland, the Chase-Lloyd House was begun in 1769 by Samuel Chase, a signer of the Declaration of Independence and future Supreme Court justice. Five years later the tobacco planter and revolutionary Edward Lloyd IV completed the work. The first floor is open to the public, and contains some impressive sections of Buckland's handiwork, including a parlor mantelpiece with tobacco leaves carved into the marble. (Buckland was famous for his interior woodwork; you can see more of it in the Hammond-Harwood House across the street and in George Mason's Gunston Hall in Lorton, Virginia.) The house, furnished with a mixture of 18th-, 19th-, and 20th-century pieces, has a staircase that parts dramatically around an arched triple window. For more than 100 years the house has served as a home for older women, who live upstairs. ⊠ *22 Maryland Ave., Historic Area* ☎ *410/263–2723* ⊡ *$2* ☉ *Mar.–Dec., Tues.–Sat. 2–4.*

② St. Anne's Church. St. Anne's Episcopal parish was founded in 1692; King William III donated the Communion silver. The first St. Anne's Church, built in 1704, was torn down in 1775. The second, consecrated in 1792, burned down in 1858. Parts of the walls survived and were incorporated into the present structure, finished the following year. The churchyard contains the grave of the last colonial governor, Sir Robert Eden. ⊠ *Church Circle, Historic Area* ☎ *410/267–9333* ⊕ *www. stannes-annapolis.org* ⊡ *Free* ☉ *Weekdays 6–6, Sat. 6–2; services on Sun., call for times.*

⑫ St. John's College. Since 1937, St. John's has been best known as the birthplace of the Great Books curriculum, which includes reading the works of great authors from Homer to Faulkner and beyond (it's also the alma mater of Francis Scott Key, lyricist of "The Star Spangled Banner"). All students at the college follow the same curriculum for four years, and classes are conducted as discussions rather than lectures. Climb the gradual slope of the long, brick-paved path to the impressive golden cupola of **McDowell Hall,** the third-oldest academic building in the country, just as St. John's is the third-oldest college in the country (after Harvard and William and Mary). St. John's grounds once held the last living Liberty Tree, under which the Sons of Liberty convened to hear patriots plan the revolution against England. Damaged in a 1999 hurricane, the 400-year-old tree was removed; its progeny stands to the left of McDowell Hall. The **Elizabeth Myers Mitchell Art Gallery** (☎ *410/626–2556*), on the east side of Mellon Hall, presents exhibits and special programs that relate to the fine arts. On King George Street is the **Carroll-Barrister House,** now the college admissions office. The house was built in 1722 at Main and Conduit streets and was moved onto campus in 1955. Charles Carroll (not the signer of the Declaration of Independence but his cousin), who helped draft Maryland's Declaration of Rights, was born here. ⊠*60 College Ave., at St. John's St., Historic Area* ☎*410/263-2371* ⊕*www.sjca.edu.*

14 **Thurgood Marshall Memorial.** Born in Baltimore, Thurgood Marshall (1908–93) was the first African-American Supreme Court justice and was one of the 20th century's foremost leaders in the struggle for equal rights under the law. Marshall won the decision in 1954's *Brown v. Board of Education,* in which the Supreme Court overturned the doctrine of "separate but equal." Marshall was appointed United States Solicitor General in 1965 and to the Supreme Court in 1967 by President Lyndon B. Johnson. The 8-foot statue depicts Marshall as a young lawyer. ⊠*Lawyer's Mall, Rowe Blvd. and College Ave., Historic Area.*

12

WHERE TO EAT

In the beginning, there was crab: crab cakes, crab soup, whole crabs to crack. This Chesapeake Bay specialty is still found in abundance, but Annapolis has broadened its horizons to include eateries—many in the Historic District—that offer many sorts of cuisines. Ask for a restaurant guide at the visitor center.

$$$–$$$$ ✗**Treaty of Paris Restaurant.** This is where Benjamin Franklin, John Adams, and John Jay celebrated the end of the American Revolution, and 225 years later you can celebrate as they did at this handsome restaurant decorated with period reproduction furniture and fabrics. For dinner you can select from a variety of continental dishes, fine steaks, or seafood. Sunday brunch is legendary, with buffet and carving stations laden with fresh fruit, omelets, crepes, pastries, and seafood filling the entire dining room. ⊠*Maryland Inn, 58 State Circle, Historic Area* ☎*410/263-2641* ▭*AE, D, DC, MC, V.*

$$$ ✗**Café Normandie.** Wood beams, skylights, and a four-sided fireplace make this petite French restaurant homey. Out of the open kitchen comes an astonishingly good French onion soup ($8), made daily from scratch. Bouillabaisse ($28), puffy omelets, crepes, and seafood dishes are other specialties. The restaurant's breakfast, served only on weekends, includes poached eggs in ratatouille, eggs Benedict, seafood omelets, and crepes, waffles, and croissants. ⊠*185 Main St., Historic Area* ☎*410/263-3382* ▭*AE, D, DC, MC, V.*

$$$ ✗**Carrol's Creek.** Walk, catch a water taxi from City Dock, or drive over the Spa Creek drawbridge to this local favorite in Eastport. Whether you dine indoors or out, the view of historic Annapolis and its harbor is spectacular. The all-you-can-eat Sunday brunch ($22) is worth checking out, as are the seafood specialties. Any of the entrées, including the herb-encrusted rockfish fillet ($28) or pan-seared sea scallops with spicy coconut red curry sauce ($25), can be turned into a four-course meal, with the addition of soup, salad, and dessert for $14 more. ⊠*410 Severn Ave., Eastport* ☎*410/263-8102* ⊕*www.carrolscreek. com* ▭*AE, D, DC, MC, V.*

$$$ ✗**Middleton Tavern.** Horatio Middleton began operating this "inn for seafaring men" in 1750; Washington, Jefferson, and Franklin were among its patrons. Today two fireplaces, wood floors, paneled walls,

and a nautical theme make it cozy. Seafood tops the menu; the Maryland crab soup and broiled Chesapeake Bay rockfish are standouts. Try the tavern's own Middleton Ale, perhaps during happy hour or during a weekend blues session in the upstairs piano bar. Brunch is served on weekends, and you can dine outdoors in good weather. At times this place can get very crowded. ⊠ *City Dock at Randall St., Historic Area* ☎410/263-3323 ⊕*www.middletontavern.com* ⊟*AE, D, DC, MC, V.*

$$$ ✕**The Wild Orchid Café.** You can't help but feel at ease when you step inside this charming bungalow-style restaurant, complete with a fireplace, hardwood floors, and baskets of flowers. Seasonal menus highlight ingredients from the Chesapeake Bay area with southern and French touches. The popular five-course meal ($39) offers selections like pan-seared grouper with Low Country grits, crab and corn chowder, and micro greens. Sunday brunch, served from 9 to 3, includes "Sunrisers," specialties like crab and spinach strudel and a poached egg frittata topped with lump crabmeat; there is also an à la carte lunch menu. ⊠*909 Bay Ridge Ave., Eastport* ☎410/268-8009 ⊕*www. thewildorchidcafe.com* ⊟*AE, D, DC, MC, V.*

$$–$$$ ✕**49 West Coffeehouse and Gallery.** This is the kind of spot you might wish was in your neighborhood—a cozy place for hanging out with friends while listening to talented musicians. In what was once a hardware store, one interior wall is exposed brick and another is exposed plaster on which hangs art for sale by local artists. This tiny, eclectic, casual eatery serves wines, micro-brewed beer, and mixed drinks as well as meals. Cover charges begin at $6. ⊠*49 West St., West Side* ☎410/626-9796 ⊕*www.49westcoffeehouse.com* ⊟*AE, DC, MC, V.*

$$–$$$ ✕**Cantler's Riverside Inn.** Boat owners tie up at the dock of this local institution, which opened in 1974. Inside, there are wooden blinds and floors, and nautical artifacts laminated beneath tabletops. Food is served on disposable dinnerware atop butcher paper, which makes it that much easier to get down and dirty cracking open and diving into just-steamed Chesapeake blue crabs. Outdoor dining is available seasonally. Cantler's serves other seafood dishes, but the crabs are the best. ⊠*458 Forest Beach Rd.* ☎410/757-1311 ⊕*www.cantlers.com* ⊟*AE, D, DC, MC, V.*

$$ ✕**Joss Café & Sushi Bar.** It's small, noisy, and crowded, and you'll probably have to wait in line for a table at this sushi joint, but as Joss's fans will tell you, it's worth it. Aside from the incredibly fresh sushi, the tempuras are light and crisp, and the chicken katsu and beef teriyaki are tender and delicious. There's a good wine list, but a cold Kirin beer often hits the spot. ⊠*195 Main St., Historic Area* ☎410/263-4688 ⚑*Reservations not accepted* ⊟*AE, MC, V.*

$$ ✕**Rams Head Tavern.** Tour the tiny Fordham Brewing Company, housed inside this English-style pub. Then settle in for better-than-usual tavern

fare (locals swear by the burgers), including spicy shrimp salad, crab cakes, and beer-battered shrimp, as well as more than 100 beers—30 on tap—from around the world. Brunch is served on Sunday. Nationally known folk, rock, jazz, country, and bluegrass artists perform at the Rams Head Tavern on Stage, a separate theater serving drinks and meals. ⊠ *33 West St., Historic Area* ☎ *410/268–4545* ⊕ *www.ramshead tavern.com* ▤ *AE, D, DC, MC, V.*

12

$–$$ ✕ **Chick and Ruth's Delly.** Deli sandwiches (named for local politicos), burgers, subs, milk shakes, and other ice-cream concoctions are the bill of fare at this very busy counter-and-booth institution. Built in 1899, the edifice was a sandwich shop when Baltimoreans Chick and Ruth Levitt purchased it in 1965. They also ran a little boardinghouse with 12 rooms and only two bathrooms above the deli. It was renovated after a fire and became the Scotlaur Inn. ⊠ *165 Main St. Historic Area* ☎ *410/269–6737* ⊕ *www.chickandruths.com* ▤ *No credit cards.*

WHERE TO STAY

There are many places to stay near the heart of the city, as well as area bed-and-breakfasts and chain motels a few miles outside town. Prices vary considerably. They rise astronomically when the Maryland legislature is in session and for "Commissioning Week" at the Naval Academy (late May). A unique "Crabtown" option is Boat & Breakfasts, in which you sleep, eat, and cruise on a yacht or schooner. Be sure to book ahead, and be aware that this is not for the faint of purse. Contact the visitor center for information.

Two reservation services operate in Annapolis. **Annapolis Accommodations** (⊠ *41 Maryland Ave.* ☎ *410/263–3262* ⊕ *www.stayannapolis.com*) specializes in medium- to long-term rentals. Their office is open 9–5 weekdays. **Annapolis Bed & Breakfast Association** (⊕ *www.annapolisbandb. com*) books lodging in 14 B&Bs in the old section of town, which has many restaurants and shops, and in Eastport.

$$$$ ⊡ **Annapolis Marriott Waterfront.** You can practically fish from your room at the city's only waterfront hotel. Rooms are designed in warm earth-tone colors and have balconies over the water or large windows with views of the harbor or the historic district. A handful of rooms even have two-person whirlpool tubs in the bedroom. Pusser's, the outdoor bar by the harbor's edge, is popular in nice weather. Prices vary considerably depending upon the time of year and day of the week. **Pros:** Views; waterfront location; rooms with whirlpool tubs; free bike rentals; free newspaper delivery; 74-ft. schooners docked on property offer harbor cruises. **Cons:** Pricey during the summer months; rooms overlooking entrance are noisy. ⊠ *80 Compromise St., West Side* ☎ *410/268–7555 or 800/336–0072* ⊕ *www.annapolismarriott.com* ➥ *150 rooms* �slIn-room: wireless. In-hotel: restaurant, bars, gym, concierge, laundry service, parking (fee), no-smoking rooms* ▤ *AE, D, DC, MC, V.*

$$$ ⊡ **Governor Calvert House.** This home facing the State House was built in 1727 and lived in by two former Maryland governors. During its 1984 expansion workers discovered a hypocaust (central heating system) in the basement: you can view it through a section of the floor.

Rooms in the historic section are furnished with period antiques; newer rooms have period reproductions. This is a no-smoking property. **Pros:** Historic charm; great location; wonderful views of State House or Colonial Gardens from rooms. **Con:** Some of the rooms, especially in the historic section, are small. ⊠ *58 State Circle, Historic Area* ☎ *410/263–2641 or 800/847–8882* ⊕ *www.annapolisinns.com* ⤴ *54 rooms* ⚘ *In-room: Wi-Fi. In-hotel: laundry service, parking (fee)* ⊟ *AE, D, DC, MC, V.*

$$$ 🖭 **Maryland Inn.** If walls could talk, imagine what you'd hear as you walk through the halls at this elegant inn. Eleven delegates of the 1786 U.S. Congress stayed here, and legend has it that Benjamin Franklin and John Adams enjoyed a libation or two every so often at the Inn's Tavern. Many of the guest rooms date back to the Revolutionary War era (the wooden porches and marble-tile lobby are Victorian). Mahogany furniture and a velvet wing chair rest on aqua carpeting in the guest rooms, which also have floral wallpaper and draperies and many antique furnishings. Radiators heat the rooms. Some rooms have sitting suites. This is one of the three Historic Inns of Annapolis; register at the Governor Calvert House. This is a no-smoking property. **Pros:** Historic charm; great location; celebrated Treaty of Paris Restaurant located here. **Cons:** Check-in is at the Governor Calvert House; some rooms are small. ⊠ *16 Church Circle, entrance on Main St., Historic Area* ☎ *410/263–2641 or 800/847–8882* ⊕ *www.annapolisinns.com* ⤴ *39 rooms, 5 suites* ⚘ *In-room: kitchen (some), Wi-Fi. In-hotel: restaurant, bar, laundry service, parking (fee)* ⊟ *AE, D, DC, MC, V.*

$$$ 🖭 **Robert Johnson House.** One of the three Historic Inns of Annapolis, this hotel is actually three cleverly integrated 18th-century houses that overlook the State House and Governor's Mansion. Some guest rooms are furnished with 19th-century antiques and four-poster beds; others are furnished with reproductions. Register at the Governor Calvert House. This is a no-smoking property. **Pro:** Historic charm. **Cons:** Check-in is at the Governor Calvert House; some rooms are small. ⊠ *23 State Circle, Historic Area* ☎ *410/263–2641 or 800/847–8882* ⊕ *www.annapolisinns.com* ⤴ *26 rooms* ⚘ *In-room: Wi-Fi. In-hotel: laundry service, parking (fee)* ⊟ *AE, D, DC, MC, V.*

$$ 🖭 **Hampton Inn and Suites.** There's a fireplace, coffee bar, and pool table (upstairs) in the two-floor lobby of this hotel, which is minutes from historic Annapolis. Rooms are traditional, and the apartment-style suites have fully equipped kitchens. A free hot breakfast is served daily in the lobby. **Pros:** Suites are ideal for families; nice breakfasts. **Con:** No shuttle service provided to historic area. ⊠ *124 Womack Dr.,* ☎ *410/571–0200* ⊕ *www.hamptoninn.com* ⤴ *86 rooms, 31 suites* ⚘ *In-room: kitchen (some), microwaves, refrigerators, Ethernet. In-hotel: pool, gym, laundry facilities, laundry service, public Wi-Fi,* ⊟ *AE, D, DC, MC, V* ⏝|CP.*

$ 🖭 **Scotlaur Inn.** You'll feel like a member of the family when you walk into this friendly B&B in the heart of the historic district. On the two floors above Chick and Ruth's Delly (named after the parents of the owner, Ted Levitt), you'll find 10 rooms papered in pastel colonial prints with simple, but very comfortable furnishings. The beds are topped with fluffy comforters, teddy bears, and lots of pillows. Chandeliers in each room and marble floors in the private bathrooms bring this place a long way from its first days as a boardinghouse. Check-in and breakfast are in the deli downstairs. On Friday and Saturday there's a two-night minimum stay. **Pros:** Old-fashioned charm at a great price; within walking distance of all major sites; breakfast included. **Cons:** Rooms are small. ✉ *165 Main St., Historic Area* ☎ *410/268–5665* ⊕ *www.scotlaurinn.com* ⇋ *10 rooms* ♿ *In-hotel: Wireless, restaurant, no elevator* ▭ *MC, V* ❏ *BP.*

ANNAPOLIS, MARYLAND, ESSENTIALS

TRANSPORTATION

BY CAR

The drive (east on U.S. 50 to the Rowe Boulevard exit) normally takes 35–45 minutes from Washington. During rush hour (weekdays 3:30–6:30 PM), however, it takes about twice as long. Also beware of Navy football Saturdays. Only cars with Department of Defense stickers driven by those with military IDs are allowed on the Naval Academy grounds.

Parking: Parking spots on Annapolis's historic downtown streets are scarce, but there are some parking meters for $1 an hour (maximum two hours). You can park on residential streets free where allowable; the maximum parking time is two hours. You can pay $5 ($10 for recreational vehicles) to park at the Navy–Marine Corps Stadium (to the right of Rowe Boulevard as you enter town from Route 50), and ride a free Annapolis Transit shuttle bus downtown. Annapolis Transit also offers free shuttle transportation within the Historic Area. There are three parking garages in the downtown area: Gott's Court (adjacent to the Visitor Center) off of Calvert or Northwest Street, Hillman Garage (close to City Dock, but spaces fill quickly) off of Main Street, which both charge $1.25 per hour, and Knighton Garage (a five-minute walk from the Visitor Center) off of West Street at Colonial Drive, which charges $1 an hour. All three have a $10 per day maximum, and on Sunday mornings from 6 AM to 1 PM parking is free.

CONTACTS & RESOURCES

BOAT TOURS

When the weather's good, Watermark Cruises runs boat tours that last from 40 minutes to 7½ hours and go as far as St. Michaels on the Eastern Shore, where there are a maritime museum, yachts, dining, and boutiques. Prices range from $10 to $65. If it's wind in the sails that holds your fancy, Schooner Woodwind has two-hour sailing cruises aboard a 74-foot wooden staysail schooner up to four times daily (depending on season), except Monday, when, May 14–Labor Day, there's a sunset sailing only. Trips begin at $34.

Fees & Schedules Schooner Woodwind (✉ *80 Compromise St., departs from Annapolis Marriott Hotel, Historic Area,* ☎ *410/263–7837* ⊕ *www.schooner woodwind.com*). **Watermark Cruises** (✉ *City Dock, Historic Area, Box 3350,* ☎ *410/268–7601 or 800/569-9622* ⊕ *www.watermarkcruises.com*).

BUS TOURS

Discover Annapolis Tours leads one-hour or 40-minute narrated minibus tours ($16 or $12.50) that introduce the history and architecture of Annapolis. Tours leave from the Visitor Center or History Quest daily April through November and most weekends December through March.

Fees & Schedules Discover Annapolis Tours (☎ *410/626–6000* ⊕ *www. discover-annapolis.com*).

WALKING TOURS

The Historic Annapolis Foundation rents four self-guided walking tours that use audiotapes and maps: "Annapolis Highlights," "African-American Annapolis," "Rebels to Statesmen: Revolution in Annapolis," and "A City Divided–Annapolis During the Civil War." The cost for each is $10, and tickets can be purchased online or in person at HistoryQuest, 99 Main Street.

Several tours leave from the visitor center at 26 West Street, from the City Dock information booth (when open), and from 99 Main Street. On Annapolis Walkabout tours ($11), experts on historic buildings take you around the historic district and the U.S. Naval Academy. Tours are held weekends from April to October. Guides from Watermark (formerly Three Centuries Tours) wear colonial-style dress and walk you to the State House, St. John's College, and the Naval Academy. The cost is $15. The two-hour tours depart daily April to October at 10:30 from the Visitor Center, 26 West Street. From late October through March, tours depart Saturdays only from the Information Booth at Annapolis City Dock at 1:30. The company also offers a 90-minute "Colonial Stroll" ($12) daily from April to November at 10:30; tours depart from 44 Calvert Street.

Fees & Schedules Annapolis Walkabout (☎ *410/263–8253* ⊙ *Apr.–Oct., weekends*). **Historic Annapolis Foundation Walking Tours** (✉ *99 Main St., Historic Area* ☎ *410/267-6656* ⊕ *www.annapolis.org*). **Watermark** (☎ *410/268-7601 or 800/569-9622* ⊕ *www.annapolis-tours.com*).

Travel Smart Washington, D.C.

WORD OF MOUTH

"Please stay near a Metro line and don't bring the car at all. Parking is expensive and can be difficult to find; traffic is bad and the routes are confusing. Just wear sneakers and enjoy the fact you're burning off pounds.

— Thank you, the Commuters"
—kgh8m

GETTING STARTED

■ RESOURCES

ONLINE TRAVEL TOOLS

ALL ABOUT WASHINGTON, D.C.
The **Smithsonian Web site** (⊕*www.si.edu*) is a good place to start planning a trip to the Mall and its museums. You can check out the exhibitions and events that will be held during your visit.

Cultural Tourism D.C. (⊕*www.culturaltourismdc.org*) is a nonproft coalition whose mission is to highlight the city's arts and heritage. Their Web site is loaded with great information about sights, special events, and neighborhoods, including self-guided walking tours.

Billing itself as D.C.'s online community for the Web, **dcregistry.com** (⊕*www.dcregistry.com*) lists more than 4,000 home pages with everything from arts and entertainment to real estate. There are discussion forums and a chat room, too.

Gay & Lesbian *The Washington Blade* (⊕www.washblade.com) is the city's weekly gay newspaper. In addition to news and features, *Metro Weekly* (⊕www.metroweekly.com) has a guide to bars and clubs, including a calendar of events..

Kids & Families **washingtonfamily.com** (⊕www.washingtonfamily.com) features a "Best for Families" as voted on by area families. Families may also want to check out **washingtonparent.com** (⊕www.washingtonparent.com) and **washingtondckids.com** (⊕www.washingtondckids.com) for kid-friendly activities and special events.

News & Happenings The Web site of the *Washington Post* (⊕www.washingtonpost.com) has a fairly comprehensive listing of what's going on around town. Also check out the site of *Washington CityPaper* (⊕www.washingtoncitypaper.com), a free weekly newspaper. The *Washingtonian* (⊕www.washingtonian.com) is a monthly magazine.

Safety Transportation Security Administration ([TSA] ⊕www.tsa.gov)

Time Zones Timeanddate.com (⊕www.timeanddate.com/worldclock) can help you figure out the correct time anywhere.

Weather Accuweather.com (⊕www.accuweather.com) is an independent weather-forecasting service with good coverage of hurricanes, tornadoes and storms.

Weather.com (⊕www.weather.com) is the Web site for the Weather Channel.

VISITOR INFORMATION

You can gather information about the city before your trip and stop in at the D.C. Visitor Information Center when you arrive. The center is located in the Ronald Reagan Building and International Trade Center, two blocks from the National Mall and one block from the White House Visitor Center.

The Washington, D.C., Convention and Tourism Corporation's free, 104-page publication titled *The Official Visitors' Guide* is full of sightseeing tips, maps, and contacts. You can order a copy online or by phone, or pick one up in their office.

The most popular sights in D.C. are run by the National Park Service (NPS) or the Smithsonian, both of which have recorded information about locations and hours of operation.

Events & Attractions National Park Service (☎202/619–7275 "Dial-a-Park" ⊕www.nps.gov). **Smithsonian** (☎202/633-1000, 202/633-5285 TTY ⊕www.si.edu). **White**

House Visitor Center (☎202/208–1631 ⊕www.nps.gov/whho).

Information Center D.C. Visitor Information Center (✉1300 Pennsylvania Ave. NW, Washington, DC ☎866/324-7386, 202/289-8317 ⊕www.dcchamber.org).

State Information State of Maryland (☎866/639-3526 ⊕www.mdisfun.com). **Virginia Tourism Corporation** (☎804/786–2051 or 800/847–4882 ⊕www.virginia.org).

Tourist Information Washington, D.C., Convention and Tourism Corporation (✉901 7th St., NW, 4th floor, Washington, DC ☎202/789–7000 or 800/422–8644 ⊕www. washington.org).

▮ THINGS TO CONSIDER

GEAR

Walk along the National Mall or in Downtown and you can encounter people wearing everything from three-piece suits to shorts and T-shirts. Business attire in D.C. tends to be fairly conservative; it's around the campuses of Georgetown and American University where you can find more eclectic dressing. But D.C. is also understood to be a major year-round tourism destination, so the key is to dress comfortably and for the weather.

In fall, temperatures hover around the 50s and 60s, but it can get cooler, so pants, long-sleeve shirts, and a coat are appropriate. Winter is relatively mild in the D.C. area, with temperatures ranging from the 20s at night to the 40s and 50s and lately even the 60s during the day. There are usually one or two major snowstorms and an occasional ice storm. Pack clothes that can be layered and bring a warm coat.

D.C. in spring is gorgeous, with lots of sun, an occasional rainstorm, and temperatures ranging from the 40s to 60s. Pack light sweaters, pants, and a lightweight coat. Summer is muggy and hot, with temperatures in the 80s and 90s and high humidity. Expect an evening thundershower or two. Plan on wearing cool, breathable fabrics like cotton, and bring a sweater for overly air-conditioned buildings.

Most important, D.C. is a walking town. Distances, especially on the Mall, are long. Whatever the reason for your visit, wear comfortable shoes.

▮ RENTAL CARS

If you're staying in D.C., there really is no need to rent a car. Public transportation in the city is convenient and affordable, to say nothing of the fact that driving in Washington, D.C., is not for the faint of heart.

Many families visiting D.C. find it much more affordable to stay in a hotel in Virginia or Maryland. If you choose to stay outside of the District, check whether the hotel is within walking distance of a Metro station or offers shuttle transportation to D.C. when you're making your reservations. If neither is the case, then you'll need to rent a car.

Daily rental rates in Washington, D.C., begin at about $40 during the week and about $22 on weekends for an economy car with air-conditioning, automatic transmission, and unlimited mileage. This does not include airport facility fees or the tax on car rentals.

In Washington, D.C., many agencies require you to be at least 25 to rent a car. However, employees of major corporations and military or government personnel on official business may be able to rent a car even if they're under age 25.

▮ GUIDED TOURS

Collette Vacations, in partnership with Smithsonian Journeys Travel Adventures, has a five-day "Spirit of Washington, D.C." tour that includes guided tours of the Freer Gallery, National Gallery of Art, and National Museum of the

American Indian led by Smithsonian historians; a tour of the Library of Congress; and a narrated coach tour of the city's monuments and memorials, including a visit to Arlington National Cemetary. Globus has two itineraries that include two nights in D.C.: "America's Historic East," an eight-day tour of Washington, D.C. and Philadelphia; and "Eastern U.S. and Canada Discovery." Both trips include a half-day guided city tour and free time, followed by an illumination tour of the monuments. Mayflower Tours offers a seven-day "Washington, D.C. and Williamsburg" tour that includes four nights in D.C. with visits to the U.S. Capitol, Library of Congress, Arlington Cemetery, and monuments, as well as stops at Mount Vernon and Jamestown. Tauck Travel also has a "Williamsburg and Washington, D.C." itinerary, which includes two nights in D.C. WorldStrides, which specializes in educational student travel, has 10 "Discover D.C." programs that are designed to enrich the study of U.S. history and government.

Recommended Companies Collette Vacations (☎800/340–5158 ⊕www.collettevacations.com). **Globus** (☎866/755–8581 ⊕www.globusjourneys.com). **Mayflower Tours** (☎800/323–7604 ⊕www.mayflowertours.com). **Tauck** (☎800/788–7885 ⊕www.tauck.com). **WorldStrides** (☎800/468–5899 ⊕www.worldstrides.com).

SPECIAL-INTEREST TOURS

Elderhostel offers several guided tours for older adults that provide fascinating in-depth looks into the history and beauty of D.C. The non-profit educational travel organization has been leading all-inclusive learning adventures around the world for more than 20 years. In addition to the programs listed here, Elderhostel also has several other world studies and history programs in D.C. All Elderhostel programs include accommodations, meals, and in-town transportation.

Presented in conjunction with the Close Up Foundation, the nation's largest non-profit citizenship education organization, "Monumental D.C." is a four-night program that includes seminars on many of the figures memorialized on and near the National Mall. Prices start at $973 per person.

"Washington, D.C., A Capital Intergenerational Adventure" is designed for grandparents and their grandchildren ages 11 to 14. The five-night trip starts at $1,133 per person. Highlights include workshops and activities at Mount Vernon, the International Spy Museum, and several Smithsonian museums; as well as a tour of the broadcast studio and control room of "Close-Up on C-Span." You'll even have an opportunity to be a part of the audience.

"Discover Washington, D.C.: Our Nation's Capital" enables participants to learn more about our nation's cultural and political foundations through presentations at memorials and museums, visits to historical neighborhoods, meetings and seminars with Washington policy makers, and an evening at the theater. This five-night program starts at $1,073 per person.

Contact Elderhostel (☎800/454–5768 ⊕www.elderhostel.org).

TRANSPORTATION

Although it may not appear so at first glance, there's a system to addresses in D.C., albeit one that's a bit confusing for newcomers. The city is divided into the four quadrants of a compass (NW, NE, SE, SW), with the U.S. Capitol at the center. Because the Capitol doesn't sit in the exact center of the city, Northwest is the largest quadrant. Northwest also has most of the important landmarks, although Northeast and Southwest have their fair share. The boundaries are North Capitol Street, East Capitol Street, South Capitol Street, and the National Mall.

▌BY AIR

A flight to D.C. from New York takes a little less than an hour. It's about 1½ hours from Chicago, 3 hours from Denver or Dallas, and 5 hours from San Francisco. Those flying from London should expect a trip of about 6 hours. From Sydney it's an 18-hour flight.

▌TIP➡If you travel frequently, look into the TSA's Registered Traveler program. The program, which is still being tested in several U.S. airports, is designed to cut down on gridlock at security checkpoints by allowing prescreened travelers to pass quickly through kiosks that scan an iris and/or a fingerprint. How sci-fi is that?

Airlines & Airports Airline and Airport Links.com (⊕www.airlineandairportlinks.com) has links to many of the world's airlines and airports.

Airline Security Issues Transportation Security Administration (⊕www.tsa.gov) has answers for almost every question that might come up.

Air Travel Resources in Washington, D.C. U.S. Department of Transportation Aviation Consumer Protection Division (☎202/366–2220 ⊕www.airconsumer.ost.dot.gov).

AIRPORTS

The major gateways to D.C. are **Ronald Reagan Washington National Airport (DCA)** in Virginia, 4 mi south of downtown Washington; **Dulles International Airport (IAD)**, 26 mi west of Washington, D.C.; and **Baltimore/Washington International–Thurgood Marshall Airport (BWI)** in Maryland, about 30 mi to the northeast.

Reagan National Airport is closest to downtown D.C., and has a Metro stop in the terminal. East Coast shuttles and shorter flights tend to fly in and out of this airport. However, the Mid-Atlantic region is prone to quirky weather that can snarl air traffic, especially at Reagan National. Dulles is configured primarily for long-haul flights. BWI offers blended service, with its many gates for no-frills Southwest Air, as well as international flights. Although the Metro doesn't serve Dulles and BWI, there is affordable and convenient public transportation to and from each airport. Prices vary between each of the three area airports, so be sure to compare fares before booking your flights.

▌TIP➡Long layovers don't have to be only about sitting around or shopping. These days they can be about burning off vacation calories. Check out ⊕www.airportgyms. com for lists of health clubs that are in or near many U.S. and Canadian airports.

Airport Information Baltimore/Washington International-Thurgood Marshall Airport (☎410/859–7100 ⊕www.bwiairport. com). **Dulles International Airport** (☎703/572–2700 ⊕www.metwashairports. com/Dulles). **Ronald Reagan Washington National Airport** (☎703/417–8000 ⊕www. metwashairports.com/National).

GROUND TRANSPORTATION: REAGAN NATIONAL

By Car: Take the George Washington Memorial Parkway, north, for approximately 1 mi. Exit on I–395 North; bear left onto US-1 North toward downtown. For the city center, turn left on Madison Drive NW and turn right on 15th Street NW. The drive takes 20–30 minutes, depending on traffic and your destination.

By Metro: The Metro station is within easy walking distance of terminals B and C, and a free airport bus shuttles between the station and Terminal A. The Metro ride downtown takes about 20 minutes and costs about $1.85, depending on the time of day and your final destination.

By Shuttle: SuperShuttle, a fleet of bright blue vans, will take you to any hotel or residence in the city. The length of the ride varies, depending on traffic and the number of stops. The approximately 20-minute ride from Reagan National to downtown averages $13.

By Taxi: Expect to pay $10–$15 to get from National to downtown.

Contacts SuperShuttle (☎800/258–3826 or 202/296–6662 ⊕www.supershuttle.com). **Washington Metropolitan Area Transit Authority** (☎202/637–7000, 202/638–3780 TTY ⊕www.wmata.com).

GROUND TRANSPORTATION: BWI

By Car: Exit BWI and follow I–95 West. Take Exit 2B to MD-295 South for 24 mi; exit on US-50 West toward Washington. Continue on New York Avenue for about 3 mi; continue on Mount Vernon Place NW for 2 mi. Continue on Massachusetts Avenue NW; turn left on Vermont Avenue NW at Thomas Circle. Turn right on K Street NW; take a left on 17th Street NW and you're now basically in the city center. Distance is about 34 mi and should take 50–60 minutes.

By Public Transit: Amtrak and Maryland Rail Commuter Service (MARC) trains run between BWI and Washington, D.C.'s Union Station from around 6 AM to 10 PM. The cost of the 30-minute ride is $17–$41 on Amtrak and $7 on MARC, which runs only on weekdays. A free shuttle bus transports passengers between airline terminals and the train station (which is in a distant parking lot).

Washington Metropolitan Area Transit Authority (WMATA) operates express bus service (Bus B30) between BWI and the Greenbelt Metro station. Buses run between 6 AM and 10 PM. The fare is $3.10.

By Shuttle: SuperShuttle will take you to any hotel or residence in the city. The ride from BWI, which takes approximately 60 minutes, averages $35.

By Taxi: The fare from BWI is about $60–$70.

Contacts Amtrak (☎800/872–7245 ⊕www. amtrak.com). **Maryland Rail Commuter Service** (☎410/539-5000, 410/539-3497 TTY, 866/743-3682 ⊕www.mtamaryland.com). **SuperShuttle** (☎800/258–3826 or 202/296–6662 ⊕www.supershuttle.com). **Washington Metropolitan Area Transit Authority** (☎202/637–7000, 202/638–3780 TTY ⊕www. wmata.com).

GROUND TRANSPORTATION: DULLES

By Car: From Dulles Airport, exit onto Dulles Airport Access Road and follow this for 14 mi; merge onto VA-267 East. Merge onto I–66 East; follow this for approximately 6 mi and exit to the left on E Street Expressway. Take the ramp to E Street NW. Total distance from the airport to downtown is about 27 mi and should take about 45 minutes.

By Public Transit: Washington Flyer links Dulles International Airport and the West Falls Church Metro station. The 20-minute ride is $9 one-way and $16 round-trip for adults, free for children under six. Buses run every half hour from 5:45 AM to 10:15 PM. All coaches are accessible to those in wheelchairs. Fares may be paid with cash or credit card at the ticket counter near Door 4 at the Arrivals/Baggage Claim Level. Board the bus just outside the door.

The Washington Metropolitan Area Transit Authority (WMATA) operates express bus service between Dulles and several stops in downtown D.C., including the L'Enfant Plaza Metro station. Bus 5A, which costs $3.10, runs every hour between 5:30 AM and 11:30 PM. Make sure to have the exact fare, as drivers cannot make change.

By Shuttle: The roughly 45-minute ride from Dulles on the SuperShuttle runs $32.

By Taxi: The fare from Dulles is about $50–$60.

Contacts SuperShuttle (☎800/258-3826 or 202/296-6662 ⊕www.supershuttle.com). Washington Flyer (☎888/927-4359 ⊕www.washfly.com). Washington Metropolitan Area Transit Authority (☎202/637-7000, 202/638-3780 TTY ⊕www.wmata.com).

▌BY BUS

ARRIVING & DEPARTING

Washington's Greyhound bus terminal is approximately four blocks north of Union Station.

Affectionately known as the Chinatown Bus, several bus lines run between Chinatown in New York City and Chinatown in Washington, D.C. The most reliable is called Today's Bus. The buses are clean, the service is satisfactory, and the price—$20 one-way and $35 round-trip—can't be beat, except, perhaps by recent competitor BOLTBUS. The buses at BOLTBUS have the advantage of leaving from two locations in Manhattan—one in Midtown, the other in Chinatown and arriving at 11th and G St. NW in front of the Metro Center station. They offer more legroom, Wi-Fi hotspots, power outlets, and a loyalty ride-free program. Nonrefundable tickets can be purchased on the Web site or, if unreserved seats remain,

before boarding. Prices are as low as $1 if purchased far enough in advance.

Information BOLTBUS (✉11th and G St. NW ⊕www.boltbus.com). Greyhound (✉1005 1st St. NE ☎800/231-2222 for fares and schedules, 202/289-5160 for D.C. terminal ⊕www.greyhound.com). Today's Bus (✉610 I St. NW ☎202/408-8200 ⊕www.todaysbus.com).

▌GETTING AROUND D.C.

Most of the sightseeing neighborhoods (the Mall, Capitol Hill, Downtown, Dupont Circle) are near Metro rail stations, but a few (Georgetown, Adams-Morgan) are more easily reached by the red, white, and blue buses operated by the Washington Metropolitan Area Transit Authority. The No. 42 bus travels from the Dupont Circle Metro stop to and through Adams-Morgan. Georgetown is a hike from the closest Metro rail station, but you can take a Georgetown Metro Connection shuttle to any Metrobus stop from the Foggy Bottom or Dupont Circle Metro stations in D.C. or the Rosslyn Metro station in Virginia. The D.C. Circulator is another option for getting to Georgetown.

Complete bus and Metro maps for the metropolitan D.C. area, which note museums, monuments, theaters, and parks, can be picked up free of charge at the Metro Center sales office.

Fares & Transfers: All regular buses within the District are $1.35; express buses, which make fewer stops, are $3.10. For every adult ticket purchased, two children under the age of four travel free. Children five and older pay the regular fare.

Free bus-to-bus transfers, good for three hours, are available from the driver when you board. To transfer Metro-to-bus, take a pass from the rail-to-bus-transfer machine in the Metro station after you go through the turnstile and before you board your train. When you board the bus, you'll pay a transfer charge (45¢

on regular metrobus routes and $2.20 on express routes). There are no bus-to-Metro transfers.

Payment & Passes: Buses require exact change in bills, coins, or both. You can eliminate the exact-change hassle by purchasing bus fare in advance at the Metro Center sales office, open weekdays from 7:30 AM to 6:30 PM. You can purchase seven-day bus passes for $11. For some bus routes you can get the SmarTrip card, a plastic card that holds any fare amount. The cost of each ride is deducted as you board the bus. You can also order Metrobus passes online with a credit card. There's no charge for shipping and handling, and passes are mailed within two days of your order via first class mail.

D.C. Circulator: The D.C. Circulator has three routes and charges $1. The Circulator, a joint project of the WMATA and the District of Columbia government, is designed to serve only the core of the city and its major attractions.

The Convention Center–Southwest Waterfront Route cuts a path from north to south, running from the D.C. Convention Center at 6th and Massachusetts NW, to the Southwest Waterfront, at 6th Street and Maine Avenue. The Georgetown–Union Station route goes east to west, journeying from Union Station to Georgetown (intersection of M Street and Wisconsin Avenue NW). Both of these routes are operated daily from 7 AM to 9 PM.

The third loop, operating on weekends only from 10 AM to 6 PM, is the Smithsonian–National Gallery Loop. It circles the National Mall.

Passengers can pay cash when boarding (exact change only) or use Metro Farecards, SmarTrip cards, all-day passes, and Metro bus transfers. Tickets also may be purchased at fare meters or multispace parking meters on the sidewalk near Circulator stops. Machines accept change or credit cards and make change. You only

have to wait about 5–10 minutes at any of the stops for the next bus.

Information D.C. Circulator (☎202/962–1423 ⊕www.dccirculator.com). **Metro Center sales office** (✉12th and F Sts. NW ☏No phone). **Washington Metropolitan Area Transit Authority** (☎202/637–7000, 202/638–3780 TTY⊕www.wmata.com).

BY CAR
A car is often a drawback in Washington, D.C. Traffic is horrendous, especially at rush hour, and driving is often confusing, with many lanes and some entire streets changing direction suddenly during rush hour. Even longtime residents carry maps in their cars to help navigate confusing traffic circles and randomly arranged one-way streets. Most traffic lights stand at the side of intersections (instead of hanging suspended over them), and the streets are dotted with giant potholes. The city's most popular sights are within a short walk of a Metro station anyway, so it's best to leave your car at the hotel. Touring by car is a good idea only for visiting sights in Maryland or Virginia.

GASOLINE
Gas tends to be slightly higher in the District than it is in Maryland or Virginia. As a rule, gas stations are hard to find in the District, especially around Pennsylvania Avenue and the National Mall. Your best bets are a BP station at the corner of 18th and S streets NW, the Mobil station at the corner of 15th and U streets NW, the Exxon station at 2150 M Street NW, and the Mobil station at the corner of 22nd and P streets NW.

LAY OF THE LAND
Interstate 95 skirts D.C. as part of the Beltway, the six- to eight-lane highway that encircles the city. The eastern half of the Beltway is labeled both I–95 and I–495; the western half is just I–495. If you're coming from the south, take I–95 to I–395 and cross the 14th Street Bridge to 14th Street in the District. From the north, stay on I–95 South. Take the exit

to Washington, which will place you onto the Baltimore–Washington (B-W) Parkway heading south. The B-W Parkway will turn into New York Avenue, taking you into downtown Washington, D.C.

Interstate 66 approaches the city from the southwest. You can get downtown by taking I–66 across the Theodore Roosevelt Bridge to Constitution Avenue.

Interstate 270 approaches Washington, D.C., from the northwest before hitting I–495. To reach downtown, take I–495 East to Connecticut Avenue South, toward Chevy Chase.

PARKING
Parking in Washington, D.C., is an adventure; the police are quick to tow away or immobilize with a boot any vehicle parked illegally. If you find you've been towed from a city street, call ☎202/727–5000 or log on to ⊕www.dmv.washingtondc.gov. Be sure you know the license-plate number, make, model, and color of the car before you call.

Private parking lots downtown often charge around $5 an hour and $25 a day. There's free, three-hour parking around the Mall on Jefferson and Madison drives, though these spots are almost always filled. There is no parking near the Lincoln or Roosevelt memorials. The closest free parking is in three lots in East Potomac Park, south of the 14th Street Bridge.

ROADSIDE EMERGENCIES
Dial 911 to report accidents on the road and to reach police, the highway patrol, or the fire department. For police nonemergencies, dial 311.

Emergency Services U.S. Park Police (☎202/619–7300).

RULES OF THE ROAD
In D.C. you may turn right at a red light after stopping if there's no oncoming traffic. When in doubt, wait for the green. Be alert for one-way streets,

"no left turn" intersections, and blocks closed to car traffic. The use of handheld mobile phones while operating a vehicle is illegal in Washington, D.C. Drivers can also be cited for "failure to pay full time and attention while operating a motor vehicle."

Radar detectors are illegal in Washington, D.C., and Virginia.

During rush hour (6–9 AM and 4–7 PM), HOV (high-occupancy vehicle) lanes on I–395 and I–95 are reserved for cars with three or more people. All the lanes of I–66 inside the Beltway are reserved for cars carrying two or more during rush hour, as are some of the lanes on the Dulles Toll Road and on I–270.

BY METRO
The Metro, which opened in 1976, is one of the country's cleanest, most efficient, and safest subway systems. It begins operation at 5 AM on weekdays and 7 AM on weekends. The Metro closes on weekdays at midnight and weekends at 3 AM. Don't get to the station at the last minute, as trains from the ends of the lines depart before the official closing time. During the weekday peak periods (5–9:30 AM and 3–7 PM), trains come along every three to six minutes. At other times and on weekends and holidays, trains run about every 12–15 minutes.

The Metro's base fare is $1.65; the actual price you pay depends on the time of day and the distance traveled, which means you might end up paying $4.50 if you're traveling to a distant station at rush hour. Up to two children under age five ride free when accompanied by a paying passenger.

Buy your ticket at the Farecard machines; they accept coins and crisp $1, $5, $10, or $20 bills. If the machine spits your bill back out at you, try folding and unfolding it lengthwise before asking someone for help. Some newer machines will also accept credit cards. You can buy one-day passes for $7.80 and seven-day passes for

$39. Locals use the SmarTrip card, a plastic card that can hold any fare amount and can be used throughout the Metro, bus, and parking system. The cost of each ride is deducted as you enter the subway. Buy passes or SmarTrip cards at the Metro Center sales office or online.

Insert your Farecard into the turnstile to enter the platform. Make sure you hang on to the card—you need it to exit at your destination.

Eating, drinking, smoking, and littering in stations and on the trains are strictly prohibited.

Metro Information Washington Metropolitan Area Transit Authority ([WMATA] ✉12th and F Sts. NW, sales center ☎202/637-7000, 202/638-3780 TTY, 202/962-1195 lost and found ⊕www.wmata.com).

BY TAXI

You can hail a taxi on the street just about anywhere in the city, and they tend to congregate around major hotels. If you find yourself on a quiet street in a residential area, either walk to a busier street or phone for a taxi. Although it depends on your location and the time of day, a taxi ought to arrive in 10 to 15 minutes. There are a number of different cab companies in the city, and as a result, D.C. cabs do not have a uniform appearance (unlike New York's yellow cabs, for example). And you may find yourself in a taxi that's older and a bit run-down.

After 70 years of a zone system, taxis in the District are now on time and distance meters. The base rate for the first 1/6-mile is $3. Each additional 1/6-mile and each minute stopped or traveling at less than 10 mph. is 0.25¢. There is a $2 surcharge per piece of large luggage in the trunk and a 0.50¢ per bag handling charge. There is a $2 surcharge for radio dispatch. During D.C.-declared snow emergencies, there is an additional 25% surcharge. The maximum fare for trips starting and ending in the District is $18.90 plus applicable surcharges.

Maryland and Virginia taxis also have meters. These taxis can take you into or out of D.C., but are not allowed to take you between points in D.C.

Taxi Companies Diamond (☎202/387-6200). **Mayflower** (☎202/783-1111). **Yellow** (☎202/544-1212).

BY TRAIN

More than 80 trains a day arrive at Washington, D.C.'s, Union Station. Amtrak's regular service runs from D.C. to New York in 3¼–3¾ hours and from D.C. to Boston in 7¾–8 hours. Acela, Amtrak's high-speed service, travels from D.C. to New York in 2¾–3 hours and from D.C. to Boston in 6½ hours.

Two commuter lines—Maryland Rail Commuter Service (MARC) and Virginia Railway Express (VRE)—run to the nearby suburbs. They're cheaper than Amtrak, but they don't run on weekends.

Amtrak tickets and reservations are available at Amtrak stations, by telephone, through travel agents, or online. Amtrak schedule and fare information can be found at Union Station as well as online.

Amtrak has both reserved and unreserved trains available. If you plan to travel during peak times, such as a Friday night or near a holiday, you'll need to get a reservation and a ticket in advance. Some trains at nonpeak times are unreserved, with seats assigned on a first-come, first-served basis.

Information Amtrak (☎800/872-7245 ⊕www.amtrak.com). **Maryland Rail Commuter Service** ([MARC] ☎800/325-7245 ⊕www.mtamaryland.com). **Union Station** (✉50 Massachusetts Ave. NE ☎202/371-9441 ⊕www.unionstationdc.com). **Virginia Railway Express** ([VRE] ☎703/684-1001 ⊕www.vre.org).

ON THE GROUND

▮ BUSINESS SERVICES & FACILITIES

Imagine two Washington Monuments laid end-to-end, and you will have an idea about the size of the Washington Convention Center, the District's largest building. Recognized nationally for its architectural design, the Center also has a $4 million art collection featuring 120 sculptures, oil paintings, and photos from artists around the world.

Should you find yourself in need of business services while in D.C., Capital Business Center at the Convention Center, and FedEx Kinko's, across the street from the Convention Center, provide everything from photocopying and digital printing to shipping–receiving packages. In addition, several companies offer translation and interpretation services, including Capital Communications Group, Comprehensive Language Center, and MFM Conference Interpretation. Capital Communications Group also offers multilingual city tours.

Convention Center Washington Convention Center (✉801 Mt. Vernon Place NW ☎202/249-3000 or 800/368-9000 ⊕www. dcconvention.com).

Business Services Capital Business Center (✉801 Mt. Vernon Place NW ☎202/249-3969 ⊕www.capitalbusinesscenter.com). FedEx Kinko's (✉800 K St. NW ☎202/487-6150 or 888/231-9867 ⊕www.fedex.com).

Translation Services Capital Communications Group (☎202/349-1444 ⊕www. capcomgroup.com) Comprehensive Language Center (☎703/247-0714 or 800/634-5764 ⊕www.comprehensivelc.com). MFM Conference Interpretation (☎202/347-2725 or 800/814-6548 wwww.mfmgroup.com).

▮ COMMUNICATIONS

INTERNET

If you're planning on bringing your laptop with you to D.C., you will have no problem checking e-mail or connecting to the Internet. Most of the major hotels offer high-speed access in rooms and/or lobbies and business centers.

In addition, dozens of D.C. area restaurants and coffee shops provide free wireless broadband Internet service, including branches of Così all over town. The Martin Luther King Jr. Memorial Public Library and 21 other branches of the D.C. Library System offer Wi-Fi access free of charge to all library visitors. At Kramerbooks & Afterwords Café you can check your e-mail for free on the computer located at the full-service bar.

Contacts Così (⊕www.getcosi.com). **Cybercafes** (⊕www.cybercafes.com) lists more than 4,000 Internet cafés worldwide. **Kramerbooks & Afterwords Café** (✉1517 Connecticut Ave. NW ☎202/387-1400 ⊕www.kramers.com). **Martin Luther King Jr. Memorial Library** (✉900 G St. NW ☎202/727-1111 ⊕www. dclibrary.org).

▮ DAY TOURS & GUIDES

We recommend any of the tours offered by the Smithsonian Associates Program, A Tour de Force, and Anecdotal History Tours of D.C. For price and convenience, you can't beat the Old Town Trolley Tours or Tourmobile buses, which take you to all the major historical and cultural landmarks in the city. What's great about those tours is that you can get on and off as you please and stay as long as you like at any spot; you can re-board for free all day long.

From April through October, Washington Walks has two-hour guided tours that are interesting and, at $10 per person, affordable. From February to November, join a free tour of the monuments and memorials with DC by Foot. If it's too hot to walk, hop on board Capitol River Cruises for a look at the city from the water.

For families we recommend the bike or Segway tours, the D.C. Duck tour (younger kids will get a kick out of the quackers that are given to all riders), a mule-drawn barge ride on the C&O Canal, the Bureau of Engraving and Printing tour, and any of Natalie Zanin's historic strolls, especially the Ghost Story Tour of Washington. Traveling on your own? Check out the six-hour D.C. Party Shuttle Tour.

BICYCLE TOURS

Bike the Sites Tours has knowledgeable guides leading daily excursions past dozens of Washington, D.C., landmarks. All tours start at the Old Post Office Pavilion. Bicycles, helmets, snacks, and water bottles are included in the rates, which start at $40. The Adventure Cycling Association, a national organization promoting bicycle travel, recommends tours around the region.

Contacts Adventure Cycling Association (☎ 800/755-2453 ⊕ www.adventurecycling. org). **Bike the Sites Tours** (☎ 202/842-2453 ⊕ www.bikethesites.com).

BOAT TOURS

During one-hour rides on mule-drawn barges on the C&O Canal, costumed guides and volunteers explain the waterway's history. The barge rides, which cost $7 and are run by the National Park Service, depart from its visitor center Wednesday through Sunday from April through November.

Capitol River Cruises offers 45-minute sightseeing tours aboard the *Nightingale* and *Nightingale II,* Great Lakes boats from the 1950s. Beverages and light snacks are available. Hourly cruises depart from Washington Harbor noon to 9 PM April to October. Prices are $12 for adults and $6 for children 3 to 12.

Several swanky cruises depart from the waterfront in Southwest D.C. The *Odyssey III,* specially built to fit under the Potomac's bridges, departs from the Gangplank Marina at 6th and Water streets SW. Tickets are approximately $43 for the weekday lunch cruise, $58 for the weekend brunch cruise, and $87-103 for the daily dinner cruise. As the prices suggest, this is an elegant affair; jackets are requested for men at dinner. The sleek *Spirit of Washington* offers lunch and dinner cruises that range from $32 to $105. Sightseeing tours to Mount Vernon on the *Spirit of Mount Vernon* cost $42.95, which includes the cruise and Mount Vernon entrance fee. As of this writing, Spirit Cruises also plans to offer cruises from the new National Harbor on the banks of the Potomac River in Maryland. Located just minutes from D.C., National Harbor is scheduled to open in stages with a hotel and convention center, shops, restaurants, and condominiums.

Departing from Alexandria, the glass-enclosed *Dandy* and *Nina's Dandy* cruise up the Potomac year-round to Georgetown, taking you past many of D.C.'s monuments. Lunch cruises board weekdays starting at 11 AM. Depending on the day, dinner cruises board at 5:45 or 6:30 PM. Prices are $43–$51 for lunch and $83–$92 for dinner. The *Dandy* and *Nina's Dandy* also offer special holiday cruises.

From April through October, D.C. Ducks offers 90-minute tours in funky converted World War II amphibious vehicles. After an hour-long road tour of landlocked sights, the tour moves to the water, where for 30 minutes you get a boat's-eye view of the city. Tours depart from Union Station and cost $26.10 for adults and $12.60 for children ages 4–12; seating is on a first-come, first-served basis.

Contacts C&O Canal Barges (⊠ Canal Visitor Center, 1057 Thomas Jefferson St. NW, Georgetown ☎ 202/653-5190 ⊕ www.nps. gov/choh). **Capitol River Cruises** (⊠ 31st and K Sts. NW, Georgetown ☎301/460–7447 or 800/405–5511 ⊕www.capitolrivercruises. com). **Dandy Cruises** (✉Prince St. between Duke and King Sts., Alexandria, VA ☎703/683–6076 ⊕www.dandydinnerboat.com). **DC Ducks** (✉50 Massachusetts Ave. NE, Union Station ☎202/832–9800 ⊕www.dcducks. com). *Odyssey III* (✉600 Water St. SW, D.C. Waterfront ☎202/488–6010 or 800/946–7245 ⊕www.odysseycruises.com). *Spirit of Washington* (✉Pier 4, 6th and Water Sts. SW, D.C. Waterfront ☎202/554–8013 or 866/211–3811 ⊕www.spiritcruises.com).

BUS TOURS

All About Town has half-day, all-day, two-day, and twilight bus tours to get acquainted with the city. Tours leave from various downtown locations. An all-day tour costs $44–$56, half-day and twilight tours cost $32.

Capital Entertainment Services offers guided half-day "Monument and Memorial," and "African American Heritage" bus tours priced at $25 for adults and $15 for children ages 5–11. One popular tour is "Duke Ellington's Neighborhood Tour," which includes stops at his childhood neighborhood, the African American Civil War Memorial, and the National Museum of American History.

D.C. Party Shuttle Tours offers a daily six-hour "D.C. It All" tour, where you hop on and off with the guide at 12 locations. The cost is $60 for adults and $55 for children under 12. Their three-hour "D.C. The Lights" nightlife tour costs $35 per person.

Gray Line's four-hour tour of Capitol Hill, Embassy Row, and Arlington National Cemetery leaves Union Station at 8 AM (late June–late October) and 2 PM (year-round) and costs $38; tours of Mount Vernon and Old Town Alexandria depart at 8 AM (year-round) and 2 PM (late June–late October) and cost $40. An all-day trip combining both tours leaves at 8 AM (year-round) and costs $60. There's also a two-and-a-half hour tour on Saturday mornings presented in conjunction with the International Spy Museum that showcases more than 25 sites used by infamous spies. Included in the cost of $79 per person is same-day admission to the Museum.

Gross National Product's Scandal Tours, led by members of the GNP comedy troupe, last 1½ hours and cover scandals from George Washington to George Bush. The tours, held on Saturdays at 1 PM, cost $30 per person; reservations are required.

On Location Tours has a three-hour tour that visits more than 30 locations used in the filming of movies and TV shows, including *No Way Out, The Exorcist, Wedding Crashers, All the President's Men, West Wing,* and *24*, among others. Tours run Friday through Sunday beginning at 2 PM and cost $32 per person.

Contacts All About Town (☎301/856–5556 ⊕www.allaboutown.com). **Capital Entertainment Services** (✉3629 18th St. NE, Washington, DC ☎202/636–9203 ⊕www. washington-dc-tours.com). **Gray Line** (☎301/386–8300 or 800/862–1400 ⊕www. graylinedc.com). **Gross National Product** (☎202/783–7212 ⊕www.gnpcomedy.com). **On Location Tours** (☎212/209–3370 ⊕www. screentours.com). **Washington D.C. Party Shuttle** (☎202/756–1983 ⊕www.washingtondcpartyshuttle.com).

ORIENTATION TOURS

Old Town Trolley Tours, orange-and-green motorized trolleys, take in the main downtown sights and also head into Georgetown and the upper Northwest in a speedy two hours if you ride straight through. However, you can hop on and off as many times as you like, taking your time at the stops you choose. Tickets are $32 ($28.80 on the Web site) for adults. Tourmobile buses, authorized by the National Park Service, operate in a similar fashion, making 25 stops at historical sites between the Capitol and Arlington National Cemetery. Tickets, available at kiosks at Arlington National Cemetary, Union Station, and the Washington Monument, are $25 for adults. Tourmobile also offers three seasonal tours including a "Twilight City Tour," "Mt. Vernon Tour," and "Frederick Douglass Tour."

Contacts Old Town Trolley Tours (☎202/832–9800 ⊕ www.historictours.com). **Tourmobile** (☎202/554–5100 or 888/868–7707 ⊕ www.tourmobile.com).

PRIVATE GUIDES

In business since 1964, the Guide Service of Washington puts together half-day and full-day tours of D.C. sights, including those off the beaten path. A Tour de Force has limo tours of historic homes, diplomatic buildings, and "the best little museums in Washington." Tours are led by Jeanne Fogle, a local historian. Nationally known photographer Sonny Odom offers custom tours for shutterbugs at $50/hour, with a four-hour minimum.

Contacts Guide Service of Washington (✉734 15th St. NW, Suite 701, Washington, DC ☎202/628–2842 ⊕www.dctourguides. com). **Sonny Odom** (✉2420F S. Walter Reed Dr., Arlington, VA ☎703/379–1633 ⊕www. sonnyodom.com). **A Tour de Force** (✎Box 2782, Washington, DC20013 ☎703/525–2948 ⊕www.atourdeforce.com).

SEGWAY & SCOOTER TOURS

Rest your feet and glide by the monuments, museums, and major attractions aboard a Segway. Guided tours usually last from two to four hours. D.C. city ordinance requires that riders be at least 16 years old; some tour companies have weight restrictions and only offer tours from April through November. Tours cost around $65-70 per person and are limited to 6 to 10 people.

City Scooter Tours offers three-hour tours on mobility scooters on Wednesday afternoons and Sunday mornings from early spring through early fall. Guides take riders along the National Mall and Tidal Basin and share historical facts and fascinating stories about the nation's capitol.

The cost is $75 per person and includes an electronic headset.

Contacts Capital Segway (☎202/682–1980 ⊕www.capitalsegway.com). **City Segway Tours** (☎877/734–8687 ⊕www.citysegway-tours.com). **City Scooter Tours** (☎888/441–7575 ⊕www.cityscootertours.com). **Segs in the City** (☎800/734–7393 ⊕www.segsinthecity.net).

GOVERNMENT BUILDING TOURS

Special tours of government buildings with heavy security, including the White House and the Capitol, can be arranged through your representative or senator's office. Limited numbers of these so-called VIP tickets are available, so plan up to six months in advance of your trip. Governmental buildings close to visitors when the Department of Homeland Security issues a high alert, so call ahead.

You can also see the famous domed building with the United States Capitol Guide Service, which leads free tours Monday through Saturday from 9 AM to 4:30 PM. Tickets are distributed on a first-come, first-served basis from the Capitol Guide Service kiosk along the curving sidewalk southwest of the Capitol, near the intersection of First St. SW and Independence Avenue, beginning at 9 AM.

The Bureau of Engraving and Printing has fascinating tours that begin every 15 minutes from 9 to 10:45 and 12:30–2 on weekdays (as well as 2 to 3:45 and 5 to 7 in summer). The free tours are popular. During the peak season from March through August, tickets are given out on a first-come, first-served basis at the ticket booth on Raoul Wallenberg Place (formerly 15th Street). The booth opens at 8 AM and closes as soon as all tickets have been handed out; lines form early and tickets go quickly, usually by 9 AM. From September through February, tickets are not required; you line up at the Visitor's Entrance on 14th Street.

Foreign dignitaries are received at the Department of State's lavish Diplomatic Reception Rooms, but everyone else can get a peek on weekdays on 45-minute tours that begin at 9:30, 10:30, and 2:45. This is a fine-arts tour and not recommended for children under 12. Reservations are required and should be made at least three months in advance, either online or by phone.

Contacts Bureau of Engraving and Printing (⊠14th and C Sts. SW ☎202/874–2330 or 866/874–2330 ⊕www.moneyfactory.com/ locations). **Department of State** (⊠2201 C St. NW ☎202/647–3241, 202/736–4474 TDD ⊕http://www.state.gov/www/about_state/ diprooms/tour.html). **United States Capitol Guide Service** (☎202/225-6827 ⊕www.aoc. gov/cc/visit/index.cfm).

MEDIA TOURS

A much-used tool for spreading the word about democracy in foreign lands is the Voice of America. You can tour its headquarters on weekdays at noon and 3 PM. Reservations are recommended and can be made either online or by phone.

National Public Radio leads tours of its broadcast facilities on Thursday at 11 AM. Call four weeks ahead to reserve a spot. Want to know what goes on in the newsroom of the *Washington Post*? You can arrange a tour by calling in advance. Guided tours for groups of 10 to 25 are also offered at the Post's printing plants in Maryland and Virginia. Reservations are required and must be made in writing up to four weeks in advance.

Contacts National Public Radio (⊠635 Massachusetts Ave. NW, Washington, DC ☎202/513–3232 ⊕www.npr.org). **Voice of America** (⊠330 Independence Ave. SW ☎202/203–4990 ⊕www.voa.gov). **The** Washington Post (⊠1150 15th St. NW, Downtown ☎202/334–7969 ⊕www.washpost.com/ community/you/index.shtml).

WALKING TOURS

Guided walks around Washington, D.C., and nearby communities are routinely offered by the Smithsonian Associates Program; advance tickets are required. For a free walking tour of D.C.'s monuments and memorials, try DC by Foot. Tour D.C. specializes in walking tours of Georgetown and Dupont Circle, covering topics such as the Civil War, the Underground Railroad, and Kennedy's Georgetown. Anecdotal History Tours leads tours in Georgetown, Adams-Morgan, and Capitol Hill, as well as tours of the theater where Lincoln was shot and the homes of former presidents.

DC by Foot offers free tours (the guides work for tips, which makes them lively and entertaining) to the major memorials and monuments. Tours are at 2 and 6 every day, February 15 through November 15, rain or shine. Look out for the guides in blue T-shirts and orange caps at the start of the tour on the north corner of 15th Street and Constitution Ave. NW; the tours end at the Lincoln Memorial.

Washington Walks has a wide range of tours, including "I've Got a Secret" featuring Washington, D.C. lore, "Moveable Feast: A Taste of D.C.," a walking snack-a-thon through downtown, "Goodnight Mr. Lincoln," a kid's-eye-view of Abraham Lincoln for children ages 4-9, "In Fala's Footsteps," the life of Franklin Roosevelt from the perspective of his dog Fala, and "Before Harlem There Was U St," a walk along Washington's

"Black Broadway." Each tour costs just $10 per person.

The nonprofit group Cultural Tourism DC leads guided walking tours that cover the history and architecture of neighborhoods from the southwest waterfront to points much farther north: Or, if you'd prefer to explore neighborhoods on your own, their Web site features seven self-guided walking tours, all of which are highlighted with historic markers. You also can check out other cultural events, many free, happening around the city on the Cultural Tourism DC Web site. Spies of Washington Walking Tour, led by a retired Air Force officer and former president of the National Military Intelligence Association, visits sites in Washington associated with espionage over the past 200 years. The approximately two-hour tours cost $12 per person.

Step back in time on one of Natalie Zanin's interactive theatrical tours to learn about Washington, D.C. during the Civil War, WW II, or the 60s. Or you can sign up for a Ghost Story Tour, on which Zanin dresses as Dolly Madison's ghost and shares stories of hauntings around the city, including Lafayette Square Park, where Edgar Allan Poe's spirit is said to wander. Tours cost $10 for adults and $5 for children.

One of the more popular tours in the city is the U.S. National Arboretum's Full Moon Hike offered about twice a month, excluding July and August. It's a brisk five-mile walk through the grounds and hills by the Anacostia River, which afford beautiful views of the city at night.

Contacts Anecdotal History Tours (301/294-9514 ⊕www.dcsightseeing. com). **Cultural Tourism DC** (202/661-7581 ⊕www.culturaltourismdc.org). **DC by Foot** (571/431-7543 ⊕www. dcbyfoot.com).**Natalie Zanin's Historic Strolls**(301/588-9255 ⊕www.historicstrolls. com). **Smithsonian Associates Program** (202/357-3030 ⊕www.smithsonianas-

sociates.org). **Spies of Washington Walking Tours** (703/569-1875 ⊕www.spiesof-washingtontour.com). **Tour D.C.** (301/588-8999 ⊕www.tourdc.com). **U.S. National Arboretum Full Moon Hike** (202/245-4521 ⊕www.usna.usda.gov/education/events. html). **Washington Walks** (202/484-1865 ⊕www.washingtonwalks.com).

▌HOURS OF OPERATION

If you're getting around on the Metro, remember that from Sunday through Thursday the Metro closes at midnight, and on Friday and Saturday nights it stops running at 3 AM. Give yourself enough time to get to the station, because at many stations the last trains leave earlier than the closing times. If it's a holiday, be sure to check the schedule before you leave the station, as trains may be running on a different timetable. Bars and nightclubs close at 2 AM on weekdays and 3 AM on weekends.

Stores are generally open Monday–Saturday 10–6. Those near Metro stops or along busy streets stay open until 8 or 9. Most open on Sunday sometime between 10 and noon and close at 5 or 6. Museums are usually open daily 10–5:30; some have later hours on Thursday. Many private museums are closed Monday or Tuesday, and some museums in government buildings are closed weekends. The Smithsonian often sets extended spring and summer hours for some of its museums.

▌MONEY

Washington is an expensive city, comparable to New York. On the other hand, many attractions, including most of the museums, are free.

ITEM	AVERAGE COST
Cup of Coffee	$1 at a diner, $4 at an upscale café
Glass of Wine	$7–$10 and up
Pint of Beer	$5–$7
Sandwich	$5–$7
One-Mile Taxi Ride in Capital City	$5–$10
Museum Admission	Usually free

Prices throughout this guide are given for adults. Substantially reduced fees are almost always available for children, students, and senior citizens.

CREDIT CARDS

Throughout this guide, the following abbreviations are used: **AE**, American Express; **D**, Discover; **DC**, Diners Club; **MC**, MasterCard; and **V**, Visa.

Record all your credit-card numbers—as well as the phone numbers to call if your cards are lost or stolen—in a safe place, so you're prepared should something go wrong.

Reporting Lost Cards American Express (☎800/992–3404 in U.S., 336/393–1111 collect from abroad ⊕www.americanexpress. com). **Diners Club** (☎800/234–6377 in U.S., 303/799–1504 collect from abroad ⊕www. dinersclub.com). **Discover** (☎800/347–2683 in U.S., 801/902–3100 collect from abroad ⊕www.discovercard.com). **MasterCard** (☎800/622–7747 in the U.S., 636/722–7111 collect from abroad ⊕www.mastercard.com). **Visa** (☎800/847–2911 in U.S., 410/581–9994 collect from abroad ⊕www.visa.com).

▌ RESTROOMS

Restrooms are found in all the city's museums and galleries. Most are accessible to people in wheelchairs, and many are equipped with changing tables for babies. Locating a restroom is often dif-

ficult when you're strolling along the Mall. There are facilities at the Washington Monument, the Lincoln Memorial, the Jefferson Memorial, and Constitution Gardens, near the Vietnam Veterans Memorial, but these are not always as clean as they should be. A better option is to step inside one of the museums along the Mall.

Restrooms are available in restaurants, hotels, and department stores. Unlike in many other cities, these businesses are usually happy to help out those in need. There's one state-of-the-art public restroom in the Huntington Station on the Metro. All other stations have restrooms available in cases of emergency. You should ask one of the uniformed attendants in the kiosks.

Find a Loo The Bathroom Diaries (⊕www. thebathroomdiaries.com) is flush with un-sanitized info on restrooms the world over—each one located, reviewed, and rated.

▌ SAFETY

Washington, D.C., is a fairly safe city, but as with any major metropolitan area it's best to be alert and aware. Be aware of your surroundings before you use an ATM, especially one that is outdoors. Move on to a different machine if you notice people loitering nearby. Pickpocketing and other petty crimes are rare in D.C., but they do occur, especially in markets and other crowded areas. Keep an eye on purses and backpacks.

Panhandlers can be aggressive, and may respond with verbal insults, but otherwise are usually harmless. If someone threatens you with violence, it's best to hand over your money and seek help from police later.

The Metro is quite safe, with few incidents reported each year. Buses are also safe, but be aware that a few petty crimes have occurred at bus stops. Stick to those along busy streets.

The only scam you'll encounter in D.C. is an elaborate story from a panhandler. To evoke sympathy, a well-dressed panhandler may pretend to have lost his wallet and need money to get home, or a woman may say she needs cab fare to take a sick child to the hospital. A simple "I'm sorry" is usually enough to send them on their way.

■TIP➜Distribute your cash, credit cards, IDs, and other valuables between a deep front pocket, an inside jacket or vest pocket, and a hidden money pouch. Don't reach for the money pouch once you're in public.

▌TAXES

Washington has the region's highest hotel tax, a whopping 14.5%. Maryland and Virginia have no state hotel tax, but charge sales tax. Individual counties add their own hotel taxes, which range from 5% to 10%.

Sales tax is 5.75% in D.C., 6% in Maryland, and 4% plus local amounts in Virginia.

▌TIME

Washington, D.C., is in the Eastern time zone. It's 3 hours ahead of Los Angeles, 1 hour ahead of Chicago, 5 hours behind London, and 15 hours behind Sydney.

▌TIPPING

TIPPING GUIDES FOR WASHINGTON D.C.	
Bartender	$1 to $5 per round of drinks, depending on the number of drinks
Bellhop	$1 to $5 per bag, depending on the level of the hotel
Hotel Concierge	$5 or more, depending on the service
Hotel Doorman	$1–$5 for help with bags or hailing a cab
Hotel Maid	$2–$5 a day (either daily or at the end of your stay, in cash)
Hotel Room Service Waiter	$1 to $2 per delivery, even if a service charge has been added
Porter at Airport or Train Station	$1 per bag
Skycap at Airport	$1 to $3 per bag checked
Taxi Driver	15%, but round up the fare to the next dollar amount
Tour Guide	10% of the cost of the tour
Valet Parking Attendant	$2–$5, each time your car is brought to you
Waiter	15%–20%, with 20% being the norm at high-end restaurants; nothing additional if a service charge is added to the bill
Spa Personnel	15%–20% of the cost of your service
Restroom Attendants	$1 or small change
Coat Check	If there is a fee, then nothing

INDEX

Photo Credits: 4, Ken Hackett/Alamy. **Chapter 1: Experience Washington, D.C.:** 7, San Rostro/age fotostock. 8, Rough Guides/Alamy. 9 (left & right), William S. Kuta/Alamy. 10, William S. Kuta/ Alamy. 11 (top), Vittorio Sciosia/age fotostock. 11 (bottom), Michael Dwyer/Alamy. 12, Andre Jenny/ Alamy. 13 (left), Jeff Greenberg/age fotostock. 13 (right), Stock Connection Blue/Alamy. 14 (left), iofoto/Shutterstock. 14 (top center), Michael Dwyer/Alamy. 14 (bottom center), Rolf Richardson/Alamy. 14 (top right), Kevin D. Oliver/Shutterstock. 14 (bottom right), Dennis MacDonald/age fotostock. 15 (top left), Kropotov Andrey/Shutterstock. 15 (bottom left), David R. Frazier Photolibrary, Inc./ Alamy. 15 (top center), Stock Connection Distribution/Alamy. 15 (bottom center), Jeremy R. Smith Sr./Shutterstock. 15 (right), SuperStock./age fotostock. 18, Kokyat Choong/Alamy. 19, Rafael Macia/ age fotostock. 20, Kokyat Choong/Alamy. 21, JTB Photo Communications, Inc./Alamy. 22, National Cherry Blossom Festival. **Chapter 2: Neighborhoods:** 23, Stuart Pearce/age fotostock. 27, Dennis Brack/Aurora Photos. 28 (left), POPPERFOTO/Alamy. 28 (right), Dennis Brack/Aurora Photos. 29, Tramonto/age fotostock. 30 (top), Dennis MacDonald/age fotostock. 30 (center), Douglas Litchfield/ Shutterstock. 30 (bottom), Chuck Pefley/Alamy. 31 (top left), Dennis MacDonald/age fotostock. 31 (top upper center), Smithsonian Institution. 31 (top bottom center), Visions of America, LLC/Alamy. 31 (top right), Visions of America, LLC/Alamy. 31 (center left), Stock Connection Distribution/Alamy. 31 (center right), Franko Khoury National Museum of African Art Smithsonian Institution. 31 (bottom left), Gordon Logue/Shutterstock. 31 (bottom center), David R. Frazier Photolibrary, Inc./Alamy. 31 (bottom right), Vario Images GmbH & Co.KG/Alamy. 32, Frank Vetere/Alamy. 34 (top), DC St. Patrick's DayParade Photographers. 34 (2nd from top), National Cherry Blossom Festival. 34 (3rd from top), William S. Kuta/Alamy. 34 (4th from top), San Rostro/age fotostock. 34 (bottom), Visions of America, LLC/Alamy. 35, Lee Foster/Alamy. 36, Richard T. Nowitz. 39, Corcoran Gallery of Art. 42, SuperStock/age fotostock. 45, Hemis/Alamy. 48, Ilene MacDonald/Alamy. 51, TImothy Hursley/ National Portrait Gallery and Smithsonian American Art Museum, Smithsonian Institution. 54, Stuart Pearce/age fotostock. 57, Chuck Pefley/Alamy. 60, Carrie Webb/Alamy. 63, Kokyat Choong/Alamy. 65, Carrie Devorah/WENN/Newscom. 67, Rough Guides/Alamy. 69, Thomas M. Corcoran/age fotostock. 71, Bruno Perousse/age fotostock. 74, SUNNYphotography.com/Alamy. 77, Stuart Pearce/age fotostock. **Chapter 3: Museums:** 79, Directphoto.org/Alamy. 81, Chuck Pefley/Alamy. 82, Corcoran Gallery of Art. 83, Richard T. Nowitz/age fotostock. 84, Alex Segre/Alamy. 85, Prakash Patel. 86, Richard T. Nowitz/age fotostock. 87, LISA NIPP. 88, Dennis MacDonald/age fotostock. 89, Vittorio Sciosia/age fotostock. 90, Dennis MacDonald/age fotostock. 91, Lee Foster/Alamy. 92, Alvaro Leiva/age fotostock. 93, Chris Greenberg/Getty Images/Newscom. 94, Andre Jenny/Alamy. 95, Robert C Lautman. 96, William S. Kuta/Alamy. 97, Robin Weiner/U.S. Newswire. 98, United States Holocaust Memorial Museum. **Chapter 4: Monuments & Memorials:** 111, Oote Boe Photography/Alamy. 114, Hisham Ibrahim/age fotostock. 115, SuperStock/age fotostock. 116, pmphoto/Shutterstock. 117 (top left), Scott S Warren/Aurora Photos. 117 (bottom left), Dennis Brack/age fotostock. 117 (right), vario images GmbH & Co.KG/Alamy. 118 (left), William S. Kuta/Alamy. 118 (right), Jeremy R. Smith Sr/Shutterstock. 120 (top left), Ken Hackett/Alamy. 120 (top right), Rough Guides/Alamy. 120 (bottom), National Archives and Records Administration. 121 (top left), William S. Kuta/Alamy. 121 (top right), Chris A Crumley/Alamy. 121 (bottom), Jeremy R. Smith/Shutterstock. 122, Robert J. Bennett/age fotostock. 123, Vittorio Sciosia/age fotostock. 124, Bruno Perousse/age fotostock. 126, Dennis MacDonald/age fotostock. 127, Stuart Pearce/age fotostock. 128, Vittorio Sciosia/age fotostock. 129, Stuart Pearce/age fotostock. **Chapter 5: Official Washington:** 131, SuperStock/age fotostock. 134, Alvaro Leiva/age fotostock. 135 (left), Bartomeu Amengual/age fotostock. 135 (top right), Walter Calahan/FOLIO Inc. 135 (bottom right), SuperStock/age fotostock. 136 (top left, bottom left and bottom right), Prints and Photographs Division Library of Congress. 136 (top right), Classic Vision/age fotostock. 137 (left and top right), Architect of the Capitol. 137 (center right), José Fuste Raga/age fotostock. 137 (bottom), Walter Calahan/FOLIO Inc. 138 (center), Everett Johnson/FOLIO Inc. 138 (bottom), John Sayers/Public Affairs Office/Library of Congress. 140 (left), Dennis Brack/FOLIO Inc. 140 (top right), DCstockphoto.com/Alamy. 140 (center right), SCPhotos/Alamy. 140 (bottom right), Dennis Brack/age fotostock. 141 (left), José Fuste Raga/age fotostock. 142, SuperStock/age fotostock. 144, Dennis MacDonald/age fotostock. 147, Glenn Foden/cartoonstock.com. 148 (top left), Library of Congress Prints and Photographs Division. 148 (top right), Bettmann/CORBIS. 148 (bottom), Library of Congress Prints and Photographs Division. 149 (top left), Bettmann/CORBIS. 149 (top right), Carrie Devorah/WENN/Newscom. 149 (bottom), The Herb Block Foundation. 150 (left), The Washington Post. **Chapter 6: Where to Eat:** 155, dk/Alamy. 156, James Quine/Alamy. 160, Rasika. 161, Michael J. Colella. 162, Lounge 201. 163 (top), Rough Guides/Alamy. 163 (bottom), Belga Café. 164, Ceiba. 165, Lourdes Delgado/ Cafe Atlantico Restaurant. 166, 1789 Restaurant. 167 (top), Wolfgang Rueckl/Shutterstock. 167 (bottom), Leonidas. 168, Michael Matsil. 169 (top), Roddy Paine. 169

ABOUT OUR WRITERS

Mary Beth Bohman worked for five years as an in-house editor for Fodor's in New York before becoming a freelancer and moving to D.C. She is exploring her new home by way of its bike trails and is slowly learning to say "metro" instead of "subway." She worked on the Experience Washington, D.C. and Shopping chapters.

Growing up as the daughter of a U.S. diplomat, **Coral Davenport** got a first-hand look into the world of Washington—and yet still came back for more! After working in Greece as a foreign correspondent (and Fodor's writer), she returned to D.C. to report on Capitol Hill. Her writing has appeared in *USA Today*, *The Christian Science Monitor*, *Conde Nast Traveler*, *Congressional Quarterly*, and *The Times of London*. She updated the Museums chapter.

Writer and journalist **Valerie Hamilton** moved to Washington from Rome in 2005, dedicating herself to all-American life, liberty, and the pursuit of happiness. But when she contemplates Washington's self-importance, hot swampy summers, low skyline, noisy traffic, and bountiful museums, not to mention its big white neoclassical monuments, sometimes she thinks she never left Rome. Valerie pounded the pavement for this edition's Neighborhoods section, and has now made her peace with traffic circles. In addition to her day job in television news, she's been writing for Fodor's since 1996.

With a constant supply of soy milk and Matchbox cars on hand, **Beth Kanter** most often explores her adopted hometown of D.C. on foot running after her two children. Until they are old enough to read and tell her otherwise, her little ones often serve as the subject of her writing which has appeared in *Wondertime*, *Parents*, *American Baby* and the *Chicago Tribune*. Beth updated the Where to Stay chapter.

A fourth generation Washingtonian, freelance writer **Kathryn McKay** is the author of *Fodor's Around Washington, D.C. with Kids* and the updater of the Monuments & Memorials and Official Washington chapters. She has written for many local publications, including *Bethesda* magazine, *Northern Virginia* magazine, the *Washington Times*, and the *Washington Post*.

Cathy Sharpe, a freelance writer with more than 20 years of experience in travel, has lived in the Maryland suburbs of Washington since 1998. She loves seeing the metro area's wonders through the eyes of her four children. She updated the Side Trips and Travel Smart Washington, D.C. chapters.

Elana Schor was bit by the Washington bug at age eight, when she first applied to become a Capitol tour guide. She still delights in showing D.C. newbies the ropes as a correspondent for *The Guardian* and restaurant reviewer for *The Hill* newspaper. She updated the Where to Eat chapter. She has also covered the capital for Dow Jones and the *Sun Herald* of Biloxi, Mississippi.

Native Washingtonian and former reporter **Mitchell Tropin** teaches journalism and writing at Washington-area colleges. He spends lunch hours running the streets and parks of D.C. He updated the Nightlife, Performing Arts, and Sports & the Outdoors chapters.